Tokyo
Yokohama
Yokosuka

PACIFIC OCEAN

35°
140°
135°
130°

50 Miles
25
0

A MATTER OF ACCOUNTABILITY

This is a matter of accountability. The Navy is an institution that demands accountability. When a sophisticated piece of equipment is lost, someone must give an accounting for this loss. People must be held accountable or we'd have no way of control. It's not as if we were operating as a separate entity.
> —Court's Counsel Captain William R. Newsome,
> USS *Pueblo* Court of Inquiry

. . . in the half-light of the big courtroom . . . the audience seemed composed of staring shadows. They wanted facts. Facts! They demanded facts from him as if facts could explain anything!
> —Joseph Conrad, *Lord Jim*

A Matter of Accountability

THE TRUE STORY
OF THE PUEBLO AFFAIR

by Trevor Armbrister

Coward-McCann, Inc.

NEW YORK

For Mary Kemble Armbrister

PREFACE

An ill-prepared nation sends an unfit ship with an inexperienced crew on an unsuccessful, perhaps unnecessary mission off the coast of an unfriendly nation. The unexpected happens. The North Koreans attack. A startled Commander Lloyd M. Bucher decides he lacks the power to resist. He surrenders the ship.

Washington reacts with shock and anger. No one has ever imagined that such a thing could happen. And this is the most disturbing aspect of the entire affair. The United States has been caught by surprise before. Officials assumed that the Japanese would not attack Pearl Harbor in 1941. They assumed the Soviet Union would not install nuclear missiles in Cuba in 1962. They assumed that 161 years of U.S. naval tradition would protect USS *Pueblo* on the high seas when she could not really protect herself, when the Air Force and Navy could not speed to her assistance.

So in a sense *Pueblo* was a doomed ship, her fate sealed in advance, not so much by the North Koreans as by Americans themselves. How can so many decent and dedicated officials—civilian as well as military—commit so many blunders? Proceed upon such faulty premises?

The answer lies in the nature of the "system." By focusing on that system as it functioned—and malfunctioned—before, during, and after the seizure of USS *Pueblo*, I hope to enable readers to understand more fully the illness which afflicts the military today. For without public understanding, no cure is possible.

The great temptation in discussing the *Pueblo* affair is to ask, simply, "Who was to blame?" Commander Bucher? His immediate superiors in Japan and Hawaii? Former Secretary of Defense Robert S. McNamara? One morning in May, 1969, I posed that question to Representative Otis G. Pike, chairman of a House committee investigating the incident. Pike's reply was quick—and accurate. "There's blame enough for everybody here," he said.

This book could not have been written without the assistance and encouragement of the more than 300 men and women whose names appear later in the acknowledgments section. I am grateful to them all. I am particularly indebted to Captain Vincent C. Thomas and Lieutenant Commander Robert C. Vail, who helped me at the *Pueblo* court of inquiry in California and, later, at CINCPACFLT headquarters in Hawaii; Lieutenant Commander Jay Coupe at the Bureau of Naval Personnel, who patiently tracked down scores of participants in the *Pueblo* affair; Lieutenant Colonel Gerald M. Holland, Commander Joseph W. Marshall, Lieutenant Commander Kenneth W. Allison, and Miss Anna C. Urband of the Magazine and Book Branch, Department of Defense, who answered innumerable queries. Commander Jerry L. Cleveland and his wife were extremely helpful during my visit to Japan; the same can be said for Colonel Walter N. Moore, Jr., and his staff at Eighth Army headquarters in South Korea. Richard N. Kilpatrick arranged dozens of interviews for me at the Department of State and kindly took time out to guide me through the labyrinths of the *Pueblo* negotiations; he ranks as one of the most able government public affairs officials I've ever encountered. Colonel Rodger Bankson and Assistant Secretary of Defense Daniel Z. Henkin struggled to extract answers to my queries from the Joint Chiefs of Staff. James D. Atwater, Gerald Warren, and Herbert G. Klein paved the way for talks with members of the White House staff.

No sooner had I begun research on *Pueblo* than the *Saturday Evening Post*—with which I had been associated since 1962—ceased publication. So I am especially grateful to Edwin Kiester, Jr., the former executive editor of *True* magazine, who commissioned an article on one aspect of the incident and encouraged me to push on with the book. A kind lady in Minneapolis named Jeanette Noble helped arrange my trip to the Orient. Mary Beth Lawler handled numerous research chores in libraries. Betty Furey and Denise St. Germaine provided similar assistance.

Writers are notorious for missing deadlines. This writer is no exception. So a special word of thanks is due my publisher, Jack Geoghegan, my editors, Ellis Amburn and David S. Hull, and my agent, Theron Raines, for their unflagging enthusiasm even after I'd lollygaggled my way past the first—and second—deadline. James D. P. Bishop, Jr., Stephen L. Thomas, Harry I. Clarkson, Richard Oestreich, and Glen Wilkinson never wavered in their support. My wife, DuBos, put up with my travels away from home during much of 1969, then gamely provided lunch every day for the next eight months while I labored in the attic. She was my first reader, critic, and chaplain. Her assistance and encouragement were enormously helpful. Our two sons, Robbie and Alec, ferried their father's coffee cups from kitchen to attic and emptied the wastepaper baskets.

Finally, an extra note of appreciation to those who have read all or portions of the manuscript: Lieutenant Commander Steven R. Harris, Commander Lloyd M. Bucher, Skip Schumacher, Chief Warrant Officer Gene H. Lacy, Dunny R. Tuck, Harry Iredale III, and Photographer's Mate First Class Lawrence W. Mack of the *Pueblo* crew; Clark M. Clifford, Cyrus R. Vance, Rear Admiral Ralph E. Cook, Paul C. Warnke, Ambassador James F. Leonard, Peter Jessup, Harry K. Cook, Alfred LeS. Jenkins, Vice Admiral Harold G. Bowen, Jr., Major General Gilbert H. Woodward, Captains Vincent C. Thomas and Thomas L. Dwyer, Lieutenants Edward A. Brookes and John P. Arnold in Washington. Their suggestions and corrections improved the book enormously. I, of course, am solely responsible for any errors of fact or interpretation which still remain.

TREVOR ARMBRISTER

Chevy Chase, Maryland
April 1, 1970

★ ★ ★ PART ONE

1

Out of Japan on the fifth of Jan., the *Pueblo* came a steamin';
Round Kyushu's toe, past Sasebo, the Cap'n was heard a screamin';
"XO," he said, "full speed ahead; we've got us some spyin' to do;
Timmy be sharp," and with Charlie Law's charts, away like a turtle we flew. . . .
    —from a poem written by Communications Technician Third Class Earl M. Kisler during his detention in North Korea

★   ★   ★

Shortly before nine o'clock on the cold, gray morning of January 5, 1968, a slender, bespectacled Radioman Second Class named Lee Roy Hayes trudged down the tiny gangway and stepped aboard USS *Pueblo*. Dumping his gear in a storage locker, he climbed to the pilot house and entered the small radio shack. The ship was ready to sail. He was the last man to come on board, and he was very unhappy.

He had a date tonight with a lovely girl named Emiko Tanaka who worked at the New Fuji Bar in Yokosuka. Now he'd have to miss that date; he wouldn't even be able to call and explain why. Less than an hour before, at quarters on USS *Mars*, he had received word of his transfer to *Pueblo*. He had protested, of course, and asked to see the skipper. He liked his duty on *Mars*; he was a "plank-owner," and he thought it was very unfair to transfer him away on such short notice. But the skipper hadn't been available, and the executive officer had said there wasn't time to file a formal complaint. Orders were orders; Hayes would have to leave.

So now he examined the vessel that would be his home for the next thirty days. It had to be the smallest ship in the Navy. Imagine walking *down* a gangway. *Pueblo* was obviously overcrowded, as well. The bunks were tiered four high in the forward berthing compartment. The galley was tiny, and there didn't seem to be many toilets, shower stalls, or wash basins below. Hayes had said good-bye to his friends on *Mars,* and one of them had asked where *Pueblo* was sailing. He didn't know but said he thought "somewhere near North Korea." Then he added, "Those nuts may try to capture us." He didn't believe that, of course; it was merely a joke. Still, he had an eerie feeling that this was an unlucky ship, that *something* was going to happen to him. He decided to see his new skipper, Commander Lloyd M. Bucher, as soon as possible and request a transfer back to *Mars.*

At that moment Bucher was sitting in the wardroom below, sipping eggnog and swapping stories with friends from the staffs of Submarine Flotilla Seven and Commander, Naval Forces, Japan. Some of these officers had brought their wives and children aboard, which irritated *Pueblo*'s executive officer, Lieutenant Edward R. Murphy, Jr. This, Murphy thought, was not the time for a *party.* But he knew better than to complain to Bucher directly. He had learned months before that Bucher insisted on running the ship *his way* and that any suggestions which he, as executive officer, might make would only aggravate the already tense relationship which existed between them. Murphy entered the wardroom. "We're ready to go," he said.

Pueblo was scheduled to steam out of the Yokosuka Naval Base—just south of Tokyo—at nine o'clock sharp. But now the harbor master decided that she should wait until some larger, more *representative* symbols of United States naval power had left their berths. USS *Seadragon* would depart first, he said, followed by the guided missile cruiser USS *Providence.* His sense of priorities could hardly be faulted, since *Pueblo* didn't seem suited for an ocean voyage. At 176 feet 6 inches, she was shorter than some fleet tugs; her beam was less than 33 feet, her displacement only 935 tons. She was a converted Army FS, a coastal freighter built in Wisconsin nearly twenty-five years before, and nothing about her suggested that she would soon become the most talked-about ship in the Navy.

There were, to be sure, some indications that she was equipped to do more than carry cargo. The large white beads on her bow—GER-2—identified her as the second in a series of General Environmental Research vessels. Signal antennae of all sorts, shapes, and sizes bristled from her decks and superstructure. Domelike direction finders and triangulators hung from her forward mast. Finally, there was the fact that among her eighty-three-man crew were two civilian ocean-ographers, two Marine Corps linguists, and twenty-eight communications technicians who worked inside the secret "research spaces."

Communications Technician First Class Michael W. Alexander glanced at his watch—9:15. The day before, he'd given one set of dun-garees and six pairs of undershorts to the driver from George's Laundry. Bucher had sent his dress blues to be cleaned, as well; so had Murphy. George's was twice as expensive as the Navy Exchange laundry, but it promised faster, more reliable service. That driver had sworn to deliver the laundry before the ship's departure. "Damn," Alexander said to himself. It was too late for that.

The last of the visitors stepped ashore; the gangway was secured. In the pilot house Boatswain's Mate Second Class Ronald L. Berens stood at the helm. In the radio shack Lee Hayes checked to make sure that *Pueblo* was up on the harbor frequency. On the flying bridge Signalman Second Class Wendell G. Leach started breaking out his flags.

"Answer all bells," shouted the officer of the deck, Chief Warrant Officer (W-3) Gene H. Lacy. And then, "Single up." Sailors sprang to cast off the lines. *Pueblo* backed away from berth nine on the Forrestal Causeway. From the flying bridge Bucher issued an order. Someone switched on a tape recorder, and over the 1MC speaker blared the ship's theme song: "The Lonely Bull" by Herb Alpert and the Tijuana Brass.

Standing on the fantail, Communications Technician Second Class John A. Shilling had watched both *Seadragon* and *Providence* leave the harbor. Now he glanced up at the deck of the communication relay ship USS *Arlington* 100 feet above and behind him. Her sailors were leaning over the rail. "What's a *Pueblo?*" one of them called. "What's a GER?" His companions laughed. "I guess they got a kick out of 'The Lonely Bull,'" Shilling says. "They'd never heard a Navy ship playing a song before."

With her two General Motors six-cylinder engines throbbing noisily, *Pueblo* steamed into the wrinkled channel. Azuma Island lay on her port side, the signal tower on her starboard. She cleared the breakwater and turned to starboard. Her course would take her down past Kannon Zaki, through the Van Diemen Strait and around the island of Kyushu to the port of Sasebo. She was scheduled to arrive on January 7.

On this mission—her first—*Pueblo* would be sailing under several sets of instructions. Her operations order (CTF-96 OPORD 301-68) set forth general operations and communications procedures. Her sailing order was more specific. She was to leave Sasebo on January 8, steam through the Tsushima Strait (which separates Japan and South Korea) and then sail north toward the Tuman River, which marks the boundary between North Korea and the Soviet Union. Pausing there briefly, she was to cruise south again through three separate operating areas, code-named MARS, VENUS, and PLUTO. She was to determine the extent of North Korean naval activity; pinpoint the number, type, and location of North Korean radar facilities; and finally, shadow Soviet ships in the Tsushima Strait.

At no time during her mission was she to approach any closer than 13 miles from the North Korean coast; the sailing order was very specific about that. Nor was she to break radio silence—or EMCON—until she had been detected, and then only to send back situation reports. Furthermore, she was to stow or otherwise cover her two .50 caliber machine guns in such a manner as to insure that they elicited no interest from Soviet and North Korean vessels. She was to use these guns "only in cases where threat to survival is obvious." If everything proceeded according to plan, she would complete her mission and return to port by February 4.

By midafternoon on that first day, the sun had disappeared behind a thick bank of clouds. The temperature dropped sharply. The icy spray stung the faces of the men swabbing the well deck. A storm was building. The swells grew heavier. The ship began to pitch and roll. Bucher had hoped to test his machine guns. That was clearly impossible now.

Throughout the afternoon and evening he remained on the flying bridge, stepping down to the radio shack from time to time to ask Lee Hayes for new weather reports. All the forecasts were gloomy. In the pilot house Murphy, the navigator, was plotting course changes in an effort to counter the storm's fury. The waves were rising between 15 and 20 feet. *Pueblo's* bow wavered from side to side, responsive as a sullen child to the helmsman's directions. The ship's inclinometer measured one pitch at 44 degrees, one roll at 47.

"That ship would roll and you'd swear she'd never come up again," remembers Fireman Lawrence E. Strickland. "I was putting footsteps halfway up the bulkhead." The men below decks worried about the pounding, the shuddering, the awesome roar of the gales topside. They wondered how much more of this the little ship could take.

Trays and plates and cups were flying all over the galley. Commissaryman Second Class Harry Lewis, the black cook from Long Island, couldn't prepare any hot meals. He and his assistant, Commissaryman Third Class Ralph E. Reed, passed out cold cuts and crackers. They had few customers; the little pills that Hospital Corpsman First Class Herman P. (Doc) Baldridge kept passing out didn't solve the problem. In the radio shack Lee Hayes was trying to tie down his gear and copy weather messages at the same time. The ship rolled again—45 degrees. He left his desk and vomited over the side. The wind blew the vomit back in his face.

Inside the research spaces Communications Technician Third Class John W. Grant felt his chair slipping out from under him. He reached up to grab a piece of electronic gear but couldn't hold on; the back of his head smacked against a patch panel and almost knocked out the jacks. The boatswain's mate of the watch kept shouting "Prepare for heavy roll" into the 1MC; the men below decks steeled themselves for the lurch that followed. There was no 1MC speaker in the research spaces; Grant and his colleagues couldn't hear the warnings.

During *Pueblo*'s stay in Yokosuka Lieutenant Steven R. Harris, the officer in charge of the research detachment, had complained about the volume of classified publications the ship was supposed to carry. Many of these documents, he thought, were unnecessary. Finally, forty-five minutes before departure, *Pueblo* had been granted a "hazardous duty allowance." He and his men could offload some of this material in Sasebo. Now he tried to stack his publications in some kind of order. The pitches and rolls made it impossible.

In the forward berthing compartment Communications Technician Second Class Ralph McClintock was reading John O'Hara's novel *From the Terrace*. The lights flickered; the rolls tossed him about so much that he kept losing his place. All around him other men were gripping towel racks and even light bulbs to steady themselves. "It was impossible," says Marine Corps Sergeant Robert J. Chicca. "The bow would hit a trough and it would bounce you six inches off your bunk."

Six or seven inches of water sloshed through the compartment. Fireman Norman W. Spear watched his shoes float away; he never found them again. Hours earlier, he had mashed his hand closing a hatch cover. He wanted to see a doctor. Now all that he and his shipmates could do was pump out the water, swab the deck of that compartment, and curse the ill fortune which had placed them aboard this luckless ship.

The storm had been raging for more than twenty-four hours. The roar was so great that the men in the engine room couldn't hear each other speak. They communicated by reading lips and flashing hand

signals. On the flying bridge Bucher was trying desperately to keep
the ship from turning into a trough, bellowing new commands into
the voice tube: All ahead full on one engine, ahead one-third on the
other. He decided to steam toward the lee side of a nearby island. It
would be calmer there, and he could wait out the night.

The ship was experiencing problems with her steering apparatus
—not as severe as in the past, but worrisome nonetheless. The signal
generator for a piece of precision high-frequency equipment was malfunctioning. Then, too, the storm had sheared away part of a direction-
finding antenna. Bucher told Hayes to contact COMNAVFORJAPAN
headquarters in Yokosuka so he could explain the delay.

By the afternoon of January 7 the storm had abated considerably.
Pueblo butted her way south through the settling swells at a speed of
12.5 knots. She entered the Van Diemen Strait, rounded the tip of Kyushu, and turned north toward Nagasaki and Sasebo. Late that evening
the officer of the deck, a twenty-year-old ensign named Timothy L.
Harris, spotted a light directly ahead. If the ship followed the course
that the navigation team had plotted, she'd reach that light in no time
at all. Harris disliked the navigator, Murphy, and didn't want to summon him to the bridge. He called for Bucher instead.

"All stop," Bucher ordered. Then he rang up a backing bell. The
twin screws reversed their pitch. Another 500 yards and *Pueblo* would
have struck a reef.

2

At eleven o'clock on the morning of January 8—while *Pueblo* steamed toward Sasebo—a lean, taciturn, forty-nine-year-old Air Force Brigadier General named John W. Harrell, Jr., was listening to an intelligence briefing in the converted hospital building which served as headquarters for the 314th Air Division at Osan, South Korea. A few days earlier Harrell had received a copy of *Pueblo*'s sailing order and noted that the Navy considered her mission to be routine. There was no need, the Navy said, for the Air Force to prepare a strip alert or take any other precautionary measures on the ship's behalf.

Harrell was becoming concerned about the belligerency of the North Koreans in the Demilitarized Zone. The number of incidents there had skyrocketed over the past twelve months. He was bothered as well by reports of increased air activity off the North Korean coast, near the port of Wonsan. This, he thought, was damned unusual for the dead of winter.

Although he had few aircraft available at Osan, Harrell could always requisition planes from U.S. bases in Japan to provide a strip alert—if the Navy requested one and if he gave Japan ample notice. He didn't want to interfere with a Navy operation. Still, it occurred to him that the Navy was adopting a fairly cavalier attitude about the North Koreans. Now he told his acting assistant chief of staff for intelligence, Lieutenant Colonel Robert R. Orcutt, to check with Japan and make sure that *Pueblo* needed no Air Force assistance.

Orcutt telephoned Fifth Air Force headquarters at Fuchu Air Station, 45 miles west of Tokyo. The officer there said he would relay the query to COMNAVFORJAPAN headquarters in Yokosuka. Six hours later, Orcutt received his reply. The Navy still considered *Pueblo*'s mission to be routine. There was no need for a strip alert.

At eight o'clock on the gray, chilly morning of January 9, *Pueblo* entered Sasebo harbor and tied up at India Basin. Steve Harris and Communications Technician First Class Donald R. Peppard began to sort out the publications they could offload as a result of the hazardous duty allowance. The job would take them all day. To Harris it seemed clear that *Pueblo* would have to remain in port longer than scheduled. The storm had caused a slight crack in the hull; a Japanese scuba diver had to assess the damage. The ship's fathometer and radar had to be checked. The steering gear needed repairs. That signal generator had to be replaced. Without it *Pueblo* couldn't begin her mission. And Quartermaster First Class Charles B. Law wanted to test the loran (long-range electronic navigation receiver); he wasn't convinced that it was accurate.

Bucher stepped aboard the heavy repair ship USS *Ajax* to report to Rear Admiral Norvell G. (Bud) Ward, a sandy-haired former submariner who, as Commander, Service Group Three, was *Pueblo*'s "administrative commander." He was responsible for seeing to it that the ship was ready in a material sense to begin her mission, that all her equipment was functioning and she had an adequate number of spare parts. He was charged as well with ensuring that *Pueblo* was properly "organized" and that her organization followed what he refers to as "tried and true principles."

In carrying out these duties, however, Ward was severely handicapped. He knew when and where the ship was sailing but was cognizant "only in general terms" of her intelligence mission. He realized that the ship's purpose was "to carry the detachment which collected the information." Still, neither he nor any member of his staff possessed a high enough clearance to know what went on inside the research spaces. He had to *assume* that any deficiencies in that area had already been taken care of by someone else.

Nonetheless, Ward had received copies of the ship's underway training reports. He had been advised as well of the difficulties she'd encountered during her voyage from San Diego to Japan. "Commander Bucher made known his concern about stability," the admiral recalls. "This was investigated by the Ship Repair Facility at Yokosuka and they said, in effect, that the ship wouldn't turn over. They warned, however, if anything else was added topside, that there was this danger."

Now aboard *Ajax,* Ward and Bucher spent ninety minutes reviewing *Pueblo*'s problems. For Bucher this was a final opportunity to inform his superiors of any deficiencies he had in either matériel or crew. But Ward doesn't recall any conversation about the ship's faulty steering apparatus or her lack of explosive destruct devices. He does remember discussing the two .50 caliber machine guns: "We agreed quickly that you couldn't do very much with them."

Next afternoon Ward inspected *Pueblo* personally. "I was impressed by Bucher," he remembers. "And I was favorably impressed by the appearance and attitude of his crew, the enthusiasm they displayed." He did, however, harbor qualms about the ship's seaworthiness "If you want to know whether or not I would have liked being aboard her on the ocean, I would have said, 'No, thank you.' Some of the things I'd glory in as a young officer are no longer appealing. The spirit may be willing, but the flesh is quite weak."

Bucher watched the admiral leave, then assembled his crew on the mess decks. "There's been a lot of speculation about where we're going and what we're going to be doing," he began. "Well, I don't want any more of that. You're not supposed to try and guess. Nobody here's a dummy. You speculate too much, and you'll figure it out. What we're doing is highly classified. It's also completely legal. We're operating under international law. And that's about all I can tell you—except for one more thing. Don't make any firm personal plans. We'll sail out of here, and we may not be back for a year."

For many of the enlisted men Sasebo was a cleaner, quieter, far more appealing liberty port than Yokosuka. They drank at the Acey-Ducey Club on the naval base, then explored the Hell Bar, the Arizona Bar, and the Club Alaska over in Saki Town. Scotch whiskey cost 25 cents a shot; a quart of Asahi Beer cost only 60 cents. "The girls weren't bugging you to buy them drinks so much as up in Yokosuka," says Communications Technician First Class Francis J. Ginther. They were pretty and friendly enough, only not quite so pushy. How was it, Ginther wondered, that—despite all the secrecy—these bar girls all seemed to know what *Pueblo*'s mission was, when and where she was sailing and the date she was due back in port? Even among the crew, only the CT's and the men on the navigation detail were supposed to know that. Ginther suddenly had "a weird feeling" about his forthcoming voyage. "Something," he sensed, "was going to go wrong."

In his cabin aboard ship, Bucher was finishing some personal letters. One was addressed to Maurice H. (Skip) Palrang, his old football coach at Boys Town in Nebraska. "The day I began to fight," he wrote, "was the day you put us skinny kids on opposite sides of those posts and said, 'Now, let's separate the men from the boys.' . . . There was not more than one or two really talented football players but you made us think we were the greatest. The reaction was to win from teams that we should never have [played]. We won with desire and because we were the best-coached and drilled team. That is the way I try to run my ship and the way I have tried to instruct my people. . . ."

A second letter, this one to Boys Town public relations director Henry Straka, was more prophetic. "I personally do not think I have much of a chance for making captain for many reasons," Bucher noted. "My next assignment will pretty well determine what is in store for the future. . . ." Although he wasn't the sort to show it, Bucher had doubts about the ship's mission. "We could be pretty lucky," he told the associate oceanographer, Harry Iredale III, "or we could run into trouble."

After dinner on this final night in port Bucher joined Murphy, Tim Harris, Lacy, and the ship's operations officer, Lieutenant j.g. F. Carl (Skip) Schumacher, at the Florida Bar. They swapped stories for awhile, then Bucher started playing blackjack with the mama-san. He remembers looking up and noticing that Murphy was talking to one of the hostesses. That Murphy would even enter a bar with his fellow officers was surprising enough; that he would talk to a bar girl was astonishing. The tall, bespectacled, thirty-year-old navigator was a Christian Scientist who neither smoked nor drank and seemed to frown upon anyone who did. So exasperated had Bucher become with Murphy's performance as executive officer over these past few weeks that he planned to request his relief. But, "in fairness to Ed," he had decided to "let him have one patrol." He hadn't sent the letter, nor had he submitted Murphy's fitness report. Now he wondered whether or not Murphy was the "goody two-shoes" that everyone assumed he was.

Several miles from the Florida Bar, Steve Harris and an officer from the Naval Security Group detachment were finishing a spaghetti dinner. Harris wanted to return to the ship as soon as possible. He and Don Peppard had already offloaded most of the classified documents specified in their hazardous duty allowance, but he had just discovered that he was due to receive a new shipment. One which, in bulk at least, would more than compensate for everything he'd removed. The news was enormously discouraging. Every agency of the U.S. government seemed to be trying to pile paper on *Pueblo*. Any more of this, he thought, and the little ship might sink.

The shipment arrived at five o'clock next morning. And just as Harris had feared, many of these documents were clearly superfluous. Take, for example, NWP (Naval Warfare Publication) 33. *Pueblo* was only supposed to receive one copy. But here were *ten* copies. The giant computer in Washington had made another mistake. Harris discussed it with Bucher, but there was really nothing either man could do. They would simply have to carry these excess documents on their first mission and then try to get permission to offload them upon their return. It occurred to Harris now that he had more paper than he could ever hope to fit inside his limited supply of weighted bags. In an emergency he might have trouble jettisoning them. He thought about mentioning this to Bucher but decided against it. What possible emergency would *Pueblo* ever encounter?

At six o'clock on the cold, blustery morning of January 11 *Pueblo* eased away from her berth and pulled into the Sasebo channel. Her sailing order had said to avoid detection while steaming north; Bucher had thought that by leaving at dawn he could sneak past the Soviet destroyer escort in the Tsushima Strait. *Pueblo*'s departure was routine in all but one respect. The 1MC speaker on the bridge began malfunctioning. Bucher couldn't play "The Lonely Bull."

★　　★　　★

Lieutenant Colonel Robert Orcutt left South Korea and flew back to his regular post at Fifth Air Force Headquarters in Fuchu, Japan. Something about *Pueblo*'s mission still bothered him, so once again he checked with the Navy to make sure that no strip alert would be required. Don't worry, the Navy replied, *Pueblo*'s voyage is routine.

★　　★　　★

By noon the ship was entering the Tsushima Strait, plowing through moderate swells and heading north by northwest toward the South Korean coast. Bucher's plan was to follow the curve of the Korean peninsula to the forty-second parallel—remaining between 30 and 40 miles from land to avoid detection—and then reverse his course, swing south again, and survey the North Korean ports of Songjin, Chongjin, Mayang-do, and Wonsan. He could finish by January 27 and still have a week to mingle with the Soviets in the Tsushima Strait. With luck, he'd have enough fuel to bypass Sasebo on the way home. He'd steam through the Shimonoseki Strait—which separates the islands of Kyushu and Honshu—proceed through the Inland Sea, and then veer out into the ocean and sail directly to Yokosuka.

That afternoon Bucher was able to hold abandon ship and general quarters drills on deck. Then the temperature dropped. The swells grew heavier. The ship began to pitch and roll. Up forward in the fo'c'sle Ralph McClintock and Seaman Steven J. Robin were trying to operate the ancient side-loading laundry machine. Its rusty steam pipes hissed and belched, and it took them more than five hours to wash one bag of clothes. McClintock aimed a kick at the side of the machine. The bow hit another trough. He lost his balance and missed.

Next day the winds intensified. The seas grew black. Waves broke over the deck. "The rolls were constant at thirty to forty degrees," remembers Communications Technician Second Class Peter M. Langenberg. "It was just like riding a bronco. I didn't have any confidence in that ship." In the research spaces Communications Technician Second Class Bradley R. Crowe was turning the knobs on his electronic gear. Suddenly his chair flew out from under him. He slid on his back out the door of the spaces—just like a soda bottle disgorged from a vending machine.

"The ship was rolling so badly, being beaten so badly, that I couldn't make my way into the operating area," Bucher recalls. He changed course and sailed east for 110 miles, putting the sea on his quarter until the storm subsided. Then he turned north again. At eleven thirty on the evening of January 13 *Pueblo* lay 35 miles east of Wonsan. Charles Law made an entry in the quartermaster log: "Arrived southern border, MARS op area."

A few days prior to leaving Yokosuka *Pueblo* had received her two .50 caliber machine guns. Rear Admiral Frank L. Johnson, COMNAVFORJAPAN, had stressed that Bucher should not uncover them unless it was absolutely necessary. *Pueblo*'s sister ship, USS *Banner*, carried her guns in the laundry and for a while there had been a debate as to where—if at all—*Pueblo* should mount hers. Murphy wanted them on the bridge. Bucher disagreed. The clatter they'd make up there, he said, might disrupt the ship's communications or affect her sensitive electronic gear. Furthermore, there was no place on the bridge to stow ammunition. Far better, he decided, to place one gun amidships, the second forward of the fo'c'sle near the anchor windlass.

The trouble was that from these locations the guns had limited arcs of fire. They could not provide anything even approaching 360-degree coverage. In some situations a sailor might have to lift the weapon from its mount and carry it to the other side of the ship before he could fire a shot. Even worse, the guns boasted no splinterplates or protective armor, and the only way a man could reach them was to cross the open deck.

Now, as *Pueblo* steamed north, Bucher began holding drills. How long would it take to remove the tarps, load the guns, and open fire? His most successful effort required almost ten minutes, his worst over an hour. Crew members threw barrels and oil drums over the side, then tried to sink them. Even at a range of less than 50 yards they seldom succeeded.

The guns were old, temperamental, difficult to aim. They jammed often. Their firing pins were hard to set and required constant adjustments. As weapons officer, Schumacher wondered what would happen if *Pueblo* ever had to fight. "But I was reassured by almost everyone that it would never happen," he says. "I honestly believed the worst we might suffer would be a dent or some scraped paint."

Several months earlier, while the ship was undergoing conversion at Bremerton, Washington, Bucher had told Murphy to request security clearances for Quartermaster Third Class Alvin H. Plucker and several other men on the navigation team. Charles Law had a clearance already, but he couldn't remain on the bridge all the time. He'd need relief. And until these men received their clearances they wouldn't be able to enter the chart room off the pilot house. Murphy relayed the order to a stocky, crew-cut, soft-spoken yeoman first class named Armando M. Canales and assumed that he would take care of the necessary paperwork.

Although Canales had earned fine efficiency ratings during a recent Pentagon tour, he was basically a specialist, not the jack-of-all-trades that a ship as small as *Pueblo* needed. He paid too much attention to detail and, in his willingness to help others, tended to leave his own work undone. Often a three- or four-inch stack of papers covered his desk. Don Peppard offered to assist him, but Canales always refused. He said he wanted to straighten things out by himself.

As executive officer, Murphy was responsible for the ship's administration. Ideally, he might have set up a system which called for periodic reports on the status of this or that project. Murphy had no system. He, too, paid far too much attention to detail. "You'd hit Ed's in-basket with something," Schumacher says, "and he might never get it out." Murphy didn't always know what Canales was doing. Nonetheless, he assured Bucher that all the men on the navigation team had received their proper clearances.

Bucher asked to see them. Murphy didn't have them. Surprised and angry, Bucher rushed to the ship's office just aft of the forward berthing compartment. And there, in a stack of papers, he found the clearance requests. They had been typed but never mailed. "He chewed the XO's ass something awful for this," recalls Photographer's Mate First Class Lawrence W. Mack. "He said, 'These men are key personnel;

they have to be cleared for secret, and this is one helluva time to find out that you screwed up.' "

Murphy had reminded Canales on several occasions to send the letters. Canales had forgotten. Now it was too late.

Canales tried to catch up on his correspondence. How could he type a letter while *Pueblo* pitched and rolled? His tiny office was freezing. He wore a sweater, a foul-weather jacket, and two or three pairs of heavy wool socks. He still couldn't remain at his desk for more than an hour or two at a time. He asked Lacy for a heater. Then he asked Murphy. Still no heater.

This didn't really surprise him. "Murphy didn't get involved," Canales recalls. "He tried to get away from things. One time I had to show him a document and he was supposed to explain it to the old man. Only he wouldn't do it. He had *me* explain it." Canales sensed that Murphy's communications with Bucher were practically nonexistent. He thought of it as a "conflict of silence." In his opinion Murphy was tired and totally dispirited; he seemed to take each of Bucher's criticisms as a personal affront. On several occasions he mentioned the fitness reports he'd received from previous commanders. He said they didn't augur well for his future in the Navy. Then, too, he seemed to have a number of personal problems—most related to his family's clothing and hardware store in northern California. One evening, soon after leaving Sasebo, he told Canales to look up the regulation that covered resigning a commission.

In March Gene Lacy would come up for promotion to the grade of chief warrant officer (W-4). Bucher had written a glowing fitness report. Nothing had happened. Bucher worried about that. He fretted also about the fact that *Pueblo* hadn't received the routine reports that every ship was supposed to get in the mail. Once again, he went to see Canales.

"I said, 'I'm gonna inspect this office, so open up all your drawers and let me check what you got down there,' " he recalls. "I found mail from back in June that hadn't been distributed yet. And this was January. There had never been an officer control data report (OCDR) submitted, and this was something that had to be done every month. Well, none had ever left that ship." He found Lacy's fitness report in the pages of a book. "I was so goddamn mad. This was a guy's career. I spent a whole night sleeping on it, then had Canales in for a Captain's Mast [a nonjudicial disciplinary proceeding] and busted him. Ed deserved to be busted, too. Well, I really had his ass."

So irritated was Murphy that he left the wardroom for several meals and ate with the crew. So small and informal was *Pueblo* that word of the rift spread quickly.

Breakfast went down aboard ship from 6 to 7:30 A.M.; lunch from 11 to 12:30, and dinner from 5 to 7:30. Bucher also instituted a "soup down" from 3 to 3:30 each afternoon, an extra snack which benefited the men on watch. The meals were solid, unspectacular. Harry Lewis was constantly serving roast beef, and although some of the CT's— especially those who'd spent their careers ashore—kept urging him to prepare exotic salads, the rest of the crew seemed content. They recognized the tiny galley's limitations, and if they faulted Lewis at all, they cited his habit of leaning too hard on the salt shaker or dipping too deep into the sugar bowl for his rich desserts.

When Ralph Reed was cooking, however, the gripes multiplied. The lantern-jawed, twenty-six-year-old Pennsylvanian was slow and contrary; he didn't seem to care about preparing the meals. Yet he had a saving grace. He knew how to bake sweet rolls and doughnuts. So did his assistant, a soft-spoken Mormon from Utah named Dale E. Rigby.

Twice a day, after "soup down" and again after dinner, movies were shown on the mess decks or in the officers' wardroom. Electrician's Mate First Class Gerald W. Hagenson had selected most of the thirty films on board, and some of the younger crewmen complained about his taste. He seemed to have a weakness, they said, for such dubious dramas as *Frankenstein and the Space Monster.* Still, they had to admit that he'd also picked some winners: *Cat Ballou, The Man in the Gray Flannel Suit,* and *The Second Best Secret Agent in the Whole Wide World.*

When he wasn't serving as projectionist, Seaman Edward S. (Stu) Russell wandered about selling cookies and candy. Everyone called him "the Carpetbagger." A slim, bespectacled, rather intense fellow, Russell held a degree in psychology from the University of Southern California, and although he had undergone only eleven days of boot training before joining the ship, he figured out *Pueblo's* mission immediately. Espionage, he thought, was a risky business, and one day he mentioned his qualms to his buddy Communications Technician Second Class Anthony A. LaMantia. "What happens," he asked, "if someone decides to come out and pick us up?"

"You're crazy," LaMantia replied. "The chances are one in a million."

Ensign Tim Harris was still seasick and had to spend most of the time in his bunk. He had just finished reading Leon Uris' *Armageddon.* Seaman Roy J. Maggard and Fireman Apprentice Richard E.

Arnold began to grow beards and urged their friend Seaman Earl R.
Phares to follow suit. Phares tried, felt uncomfortable, and resumed
shaving again. In the forward berthing compartment the men played
poker every night. The stakes were small: nickle, dime, quarter; three
raises and stop. Communications Technican Second Class Rodney H.
Duke, a soft-spoken minister's son from Mississippi, was a consistent
winner. So was his friend Brad Crowe.

During the night Crowe would poke Lee Hayes in the ribs and
ask him to join the game. The lateness of the hour didn't really matter,
for although there was reveille on *Pueblo,* it was seldom enforced. Unlike most of his shipmates. Hayes had no set watches. He did, however,
have to copy the area weather reports. All were in Morse code, some
in the more complicated "five-number groups" which enabled their
senders to convey more information in a shorter period of time. One
of these "schedules" arrived at three o'clock in the morning. He'd type
the report and send it to the officers and the quartermaster of the
watch.

Early one morning Ralph McClintock carried one of these messages into the wardroom. Bucher was sitting there alone wearing a
T-shirt, khaki trousers, sneakers, and sunglasses. "It seemed as if he
never slept," McClintock remembers. "You'd see him around at all
kinds of odd hours."

By January 16 the ship lay 35 miles east of the port of Chongjin.
Steve Harris reported that North Korean long-range coastal radar had
detected her presence. Bucher was not concerned. He felt sure that the
North Koreans were merely sweeping. They had no idea what they'd
found. *Pueblo* steamed north through chilly mists to a point opposite
the mouth of the Tuman River. Next morning she reversed course and
sailed closer to shore. From the flying bridge Bucher and Schumacher
spotted smoke rising from factories near Chongjin. Through their
binoculars they also detected torpedo boats—black gnats in the distance—patrolling the harbor's mouth. Occasionally they saw freighters
and fishing boats. Bucher changed course to open the track and avoid
detection.

The sky was gun-metal gray. The seas were choppy. A numbing
wind swept down from Siberia. Snow began to fall and ice crept over
the deck, accumulating rapidly—first on the fo'c'sle, the hawse pipes,
and the forward lifelines, then on the antennae themselves. The canvas
tarp on the forward .50 caliber gun resembled a glistening marsh-
mallow.

Icing on any ship is dangerous. On *Pueblo* it was critical. So top-
heavy was she already that a mere four inches would cause her to

capsize. Boatswain's Mate First Class Norbert J. Klepac unlimbered a high-pressure hose. The water froze before it rolled off the deck. Other men swarmed forward with wooden mallets, chipping hammers, shovels, and salt. From time to time Harry Lewis brought them soup and coffee. Larry Strickland thought the situation called for something stronger. He approached Bucher, who had joined his men in the chipping effort—and in the snowball fight that followed—and jokingly suggested that he deserved a cup of Navy grog. Later that evening, when the working party finally secured, each of its members received a tiny bottle of Coronet brandy.

3

Even at this point only a few men in the ship's company knew where *Pueblo* was or what she was doing. Earl Phares considered her "a legitimate oceanographic ship with a little hanky-panky on the side." One afternoon he and his friend Seaman Robert W. Hill, Jr., were trying to guess her mission. Hill pointed to the thicket of antennae amidships. "We're probably receiving messages," he said, "from Korean prisoners of war."

Pueblo's communications technicians knew the ship's mission, of course, but they were forbidden to mention it, and their insistence on secrecy puzzled and angered some of their shipmates. "If those guys ever saw someone approaching the research spaces," Phares remembers, "they'd shut the door. And if you asked them what they were up to, they'd change the subject real fast."

As "spies," however, the ship's CT's hardly fitted a James Bond mold. Most of them were simply intelligent young men who liked to fiddle with complex electronic gear. Inside the small (11 feet by 30 feet) research spaces they huddled over an array of operator consoles, tape decks, teleprinters, and whisper-sensitive radio receivers. Their primary objective was to update the United States' "data base" on North Korean coastal defenses. Where were the radar stations located? Were they designed for ordinary navigation, surface or air search, early air warning, or fire control? What frequencies did they use? What were the shapes and durations of their pulses on an oscilloscope—steep, shallow, square, or round? Did they linger for a 100,000th of a second or a 500,000th? Once the CT's determined these characteristics, the United States would be able—in the event of a war—to jam or trick that radar.

A second objective was to monitor and record North Korean coded transmissions. The more of this text the United States possessed, the easier it would be for National Security Agency specialists at Fort Meade, Maryland, to break that code. The CT's were to eavesdrop on "plaintext" messages as well: radio chatter, for example, between North Korean pilots. Analyzing this data, intelligence specialists could draw a more accurate picture of the North Korean Air Force, its order of battle, morale, and equipment. Finally, the CT's were to gather as much information as possible on the capabilities and limitations of the North Korean Navy.

Pueblo's twenty-eight-man detachment was separated into six distinct branches: an "I," or interpreter, branch with Russian and Korean linguists; a "T," or technical analyst, branch; an "M," or maintenance, branch; an "A," or administration, branch; an "R," or Morse code, branch; and an "O," or operator, branch. No physical barriers divided the men in these branches; each was supposed to know the fundamentals of the other's job.

Among the men in the "I" branch were the two Marine Corps sergeants, Robert J. Hammond and Robert J. Chicca. Both had taken a thirty-six-week course in Korean at the Defense Language Institute in Monterey, California. Both had served short tours of duty in South Korea. Yet both felt unqualified to serve as Korean interpreters. They'd mentioned this to their superiors in Japan, but it hadn't done them any good. Their service records said they spoke and understood the language. Therefore it was so.

On January 17, with the ship in position off Chongjin, Hammond began listening to Morse code and voice transmissions, especially those in the very high and ultrahigh frequency ranges. His job was to intercept them and hand them to Chicca, who in turn would compare the Korean words with words on secret code lists, then type and record them for later analysis. The two Marines had another responsibility: to inform Bucher the moment they intercepted something which might signal a threat to *Pueblo*. "There wasn't much traffic," Chicca recalls. "We weren't very busy. We considered the trip a waste of time."

For oceanographers Dunny R. Tuck, Jr., and Harry Iredale this type of mission was routine. Tuck, a balding, convivial bachelor from Richmond, Virginia, had joined USS *Banner* for her cruises along the Soviet and Chinese coasts the summer before. Iredale, a short, bespectacled Penn State graduate with a degree in mathematics, had served aboard *Banner*, as well. *Banner*'s skipper at the time, Lieutenant Robert P. Bishop, had viewed civilian oceanographers with suspicion and hadn't allowed them to take a station for the first several days of the voyage. Tuck and Iredale quickly agreed that Bucher seemed more sensitive to a scientist's needs.

And at this point those needs were fairly encompassing. The only information which the U.S. Naval Oceanographic Office had on the waters off North Korea dated from surveys which the Japanese had conducted in the 1930's. The surveys were incomplete. To obtain the data they were seeking—true water temperatures at various depths, water salinity and conductivity—Tuck and Iredale relied primarily on bathythermograph drops and Nansen casts. Although the bathythermograph itself—a rocketlike device positioned on the fantail—could be used while the ship was moving, it only provided data on water temperatures and thermal layer structures. It wasn't always accurate. Far better, then, to rely on a Nansen cast—despite the fact that it required the ship to lie dead in the water for nearly forty-five minutes.

So twice a day, usually after breakfast and lunch, they walked forward to the oceanographic winch on the well deck and lowered a dozen yellow, canister-shaped bottles over the side on a wire with a 100-pound weight. Five or ten minutes later they dropped a lead weight slide down the wire. The Nansen bottles flipped over, trapping their one-liter water samples inside. Recovering the bottles, the two oceanographers mounted them on a rack, drained the samples for analysis, then recorded their temperatures.

As soon as the ship returned to Yokosuka, Steve Harris would have to submit a summary of the electronic data which he and his CT's had collected to Captain Everett B. (Pete) Gladding, Director, Naval Security Group Activities, Pacific. He'd have to turn in his logs and signal recordings to the National Security Agency station in Japan. The more he thought about this, the more concerned he became, for the CT's had thus far succeeded only in taping some Morse code transmissions and recording emissions from the radar network at Chongjin. And these were hardly exciting. It was a shame, because this was likely to be his final cruise aboard *Pueblo*. He'd already received orders to report to San Francisco by March 1. He'd wanted to do so well out here. But what could anyone expect from a shakedown cruise in the dead of winter?

Bucher shared his research officer's pessimism. He'd wanted so much to go where the action was. And he'd been convinced that the last place he'd ever find that action was North Korea. The mission was bound to be unprofitable; the weather alone would guarantee that. He, too, was due for relief in a few months. With luck he could complete three missions and still return to the United States by May 13— the first anniversary of *Pueblo*'s commissioning. He hadn't received his orders yet; he hoped for an assignment to the Command and General Staff College at Fort Leavenworth, Kansas.

As soon as this mission was over, he'd have to handle two necessary but rather unpleasant chores. The first was to find a new executive officer. In his opinion Murphy was totally incompetent; he couldn't get anything done. And he was never around when Bucher tried to find him. Just the other day Chief Engineman Monroe O. Goldman had tried to quit as master at arms because of his constant hassles with Murphy. Bucher had talked him out of it, but the situation would probably get worse.

His second chore, a far more complicated one, would be to straighten out his relationship with his research officer. The present confusion, he had to admit, wasn't Steve Harris' fault. The culprit was the arrangement—insisted upon by the National Security Agency and the Naval Security Station—which made Harris directly responsible to Captain Gladding in Hawaii instead of to Bucher himself.

They argued about this constantly. Did Harris have authority to send messages without Bucher's knowledge or approval? Harris said he did. Bucher disagreed. Did Bucher have access to everything inside the research spaces? Harris shook his head. The captain didn't have a "need to know."

Whoever heard of a captain not having complete command and control over everyone and everything on his ship? Of a commander taking orders from a lieutenant? It was ridiculous—a clear violation of Naval regulations. Already he and Harris had begun a joint letter setting forth their opposing views. They'd mail it the moment they reached port. Not to the Naval Security Station in Washington; the officers there were under the thumb of the National Security Agency and would side with Harris automatically. No, this letter would go directly to the Pentagon—to the Chief of Naval Operations.

Given the state of the weather and the watches which had to be stood, all six officers seldom gathered for meals in the wardroom at the same time. But Bucher always showed up on schedule and so, usually, did Lacy. In Bucher's opinion Lacy was a fine officer: quiet and capable, the kind of man you could depend on to keep cool in a crisis. He thought highly of Schumacher, as well, but for different reasons. Schumacher was enormously competent, intellectually keen, a voracious reader. Equally important, he had a sense of humor; he was a good man to have at a party.

From Schumacher's point of view the entire wardroom was full of seeming contradictions. Consider: Murphy read the Bible often and piled back issues of the *Christian Science Monitor* on the deck of his cabin. Yet Steve Harris was the Protestant lay leader; he seemed even more religious. Harris kept a collection of flawed pipes in his stateroom and smoked them from time to time. He was a pedigreed intellectual, an English major at Harvard. Yet when it came to literature, Bucher could talk rings around him. In Bucher's library were a full set of Winston Churchill's *History of the English-Speaking Peoples,* Lawrence Durrell's *The Alexandria Quartet,* and several volumes of Shakespeare's plays. Now, he told Schumacher, he'd have some time on his hands. He'd already reread *Hamlet* and was about to start on *King Lear.* Then he'd get to *Othello* again. *Othello,* he often said, was his favorite character.

Bucher was a student of Civil War history, and he was always quoting from *Lee's Lieutenants,* especially those passages which described how strict Lee had been with his officers, how he'd had some of them shot for being out of uniform. Yet Bucher would let his men grow beards, would even let them wear psychedelic clothes aboard ship. Sometimes Schumacher wondered if Bucher wasn't *too* lenient.

At dusk on January 18 *Pueblo* began steaming south toward the port of Songjin. From the bridge the officers could spot the masts and cargo booms of occasional merchantmen, still hull down at a range of 5,000 yards. Larry Mack photographed them with a 400 mm telephoto lens and later, examining the negatives, Bucher tried to identify them in a naval publication. As *Pueblo* passed Orang-dan, Tuck thought he saw smoke rising from shore. Later that evening, near Musu-dan, one of the young CT's told Harris that he had just intercepted a powerful electronic signal.

By nine o'clock next morning *Pueblo* lay dead in the water 15 miles east of Songjin. The sky was overcast. The ice up forward had diminished to a point where Tuck was able to remove the tarp from his winch and lower a Nansen cast with no trouble. In the research spaces the CT's were beginning to log the first of thirty different radar signals they would intercept that day. From all indications one of them was a new "CROSS-SLOT," or early air warning radar. They couldn't be sure; the ship's direction-finding antennae hadn't locked onto it long enough to pinpoint its type or exact location.

During the day *Pueblo* operated between 14 and 18 miles from the coast, usually withdrawing at night to between 20 and 25 miles. Bucher's sailing order told him to approach no closer than 13 miles, and he had instructed Charles Law to draw a red line paralleling the coast and to crosshatch everything inside of it. Then he had told Law to draw a blue line at 14 miles. Anytime the ship even approached this line, the navigators had orders to call him to the bridge. He required his officers to read and initial those orders every day.

Because the ship was supposed to maintain radio silence, he could not rely on radar or his fathometer to determine positions. A shore installation would need only fifteen seconds or so to pick up an electromagnetic or sonic emission and detect the ship's presence. He had to depend on other, less precise techniques.

The navigation team obtained morning and afternoon sunlines as well as "local apparent noon." If the sky was clear, they tried to get celestial fixes on morning and evening stars. They took visual fixes, as well, matching the specific shore lights and topographic features they saw with the information on their charts. And they used their loran receiver.

In most cases loran is accurate to within plus or minus 2 miles. But it is susceptible to atmospheric disturbances—particularly at night —and propagation resulting from the storms of the past few days was playing havoc with its results. Here in the Songjin area it often required forty-five minutes to get a fix. And the fixes which emerged were placing *Pueblo* 5 nautical miles from the spot where both celestial navigation and the dead-reckoning track showed her to be.

An experienced navigation team might have been able to handle such discrepancies with ease. *Pueblo*'s team was relatively green. To be sure, Bucher was an excellent navigator. Years in the submarine force had honed his skill at this exacting task, and he often said that it was the most challenging work aboard ship. Murphy was capable, and Charles Law considered himself, perhaps justifiably, as one of the better navigators in the Pacific Fleet. But Bucher and Murphy had other concerns beside navigation, and Law—who was averaging eighteen hours a day on the bridge—desperately needed relief.

If Murphy and "Army" Canales had obtained those security clearances for the junior enlisted men, the problem might never have arisen. Without them Alvin Plucker and his colleagues couldn't enter the chart room. So other men with clearances issued for other reasons— Photographer Larry Mack, Signalman Wendell Leach, and Electronics Technician Second Class Clifford C. Nolte—had to become instant navigators.

To Mack loran was as inscrutable as a Chinese puzzle. "Frankly, I had difficulty operating it," he recalls. "The signals were jumping all over on the screen, and it was hard to match them up. I couldn't do it. If I got two good fixes in a four-hour watch, I was doing pretty good. I shouldn't have been up there. I didn't function the way a navigator should."

What puzzled Mack even more was that he was supposed to enter all his fixes—the bad as well as the good—in the quartermaster's log. He couldn't erase the obvious mistakes. He and Leach talked about this, and one night Leach mentioned it to Murphy. "Sir, are you sure you want us to log these erroneous fixes?"

Naval regulations were very specific about this. "Yes," Murphy said.

While the ship was on station, Bucher told his navigators to take a fix every twenty minutes. Because of their inexperience and the propagation problems, this was clearly impossible. From time to time, in order to determine their exact position, he and Murphy had to do what they hadn't wanted to do: authorize a quick sweep of the radar and a single- or double-ping reading on the fathometer.

Late on the afternoon of January 19 *Pueblo* left Songjin and set a southeasterly course toward Operation Area MARS. U.S. intelligence suspected that North Korea based her four W-class submarines at Mayang-do. With any luck *Pueblo* might photograph them and supply new data on their habits. Even further to the south was the deep-draft port of Wonsan. Soviet nuclear subs often operated from Wonsan, especially during the winter months when massive ice floes endangered their activities at Vladivostok. A chance to eavesdrop on them—this would make the mission worthwhile. As the ship steamed south, Murphy expressed his forebodings to Photographer Mack. "Most of the crew doesn't know this, so don't say anything," he warned, "but they've had fire control radar locked on us for days."

4

Rear Admiral John Victor Smith was a most unhappy man. A tall, slender Annapolis graduate, son of the famed Marine Corps General "Howling Mad" Smith, he thought of himself as an operational commander, a seagoing, *action*-oriented officer. So he had been surprised and disappointed when, in the fall of 1967, the orders arrived naming him senior negotiator for the United Nations Command at the Military Armistice Commission meetings in Panmunjom, Korea. Fortunately, it was only a six-month tour, and at the end, if he was lucky, awaited a third star.

And he would deserve it. For he could think of nothing more insulting to a patriotic American than having to sit at the narrow table in Panmunjom and listen while North Korea's Major General Pak Chung Kuk vilified his country. Lately, Pak had been ranting about some alleged violations of his country's territorial waters.

Radio Pyongyang echoed his diatribes. On January 6 it announced: "The U.S. imperialist aggressor army, which has been incessantly committing provocative acts lately on the sea off the eastern coast, from 0600 hours this morning again dispatched many armed boats, mingled with fishing boats, under the escort of armed warships into the coastal waters of our side . . . to perpetrate provocative acts. . . ."

And again on January 11: "The U.S. imperialist aggressor troops dispatched from early this morning hundreds of fishing boats and spy boats disguised as fishing boats into the coastal waters of our side off the eastern coast. . . . As long as the U.S. imperialist aggressor troops conduct reconnaissance by sending spy boats, our naval ships will continue to take determined countermeasures."

Because he occupied such a sensitive post—and because he thought the North Koreans just might be crazy enough to try to capture him someday at Panmunjom—Smith had deliberately excluded himself from access to classified information. He knew nothing about the operations of U.S. ships in the area. Still, he knew enough to brand these charges as lies. Asked about them, he replied, "The usual Communist garbage."

At the U.S. Embassy in Seoul, South Korea, copies of the Pyongyang broadcasts were placed on the desk of the political counselor, forty-three-year-old Richard A. Erickson. Erickson, a plump, cigar-chomping diplomat whose Tammany Hall manner belied a shrewd, incisive mind, thumbed through them quickly. He saw nothing new. Seventy-five hundred miles away, in Room 4206 at the State Department in Washington, the "country director" for South Korea, a balding, soft-spoken man named Benjamin A. Fleck, reached the same conclusion. Inside Room 300, the "spook locker" at COMNAVFORJAPAN headquarters in Yokosuka, intelligence officers received copies of the January 6 "warning." Because they considered it "sheer propaganda," they tacked it on the "no interest board." They never saw the January 11 report.

On January 19 the captain of the Japanese freighter *Shingashi Maru* returned home after a voyage to North Korea. Although he had made the trip many times, he had never seen so much naval activity in Wonsan. It was odd, especially for this time of year, and he decided to report this to a friend at the Japanese Maritime Self-Defense Force office in Kobe. The friend was interested indeed and sent a report to MSDF headquarters in Tokyo. Days would elapse before this information was relayed to U.S. Navy intelligence in Yokosuka.

By ten o'clock on the evening of January 19 a group of thirty-one North Korean Army lieutenants had slipped through the DMZ and were racing south across the mountains toward Seoul.

Their assignment: Attack the Blue House and assassinate South Korea's President Park Chung Hee.

For the past several weeks, they'd undergone rigorous training, memorizing floor plans of the Blue House, cutting paths through clumps of tiny trees with their bare hands, running barefoot over rocky terrain with 60-pound packs on their backs. At last they were ready to strike the blow that would plunge South Korea into chaos.

Dressed in ROK Army fatigues and armed with grenades, subma-chine guns, and nine-inch daggers, they slithered around U.S. and South Korean patrols and still managed to cover more than 6 miles an hour. Then, in a forest near the U.S. Second Division headquarters at Camp Howze, they came upon four woodcutters who, sensing their identity immediately, begged for their lives. Some of the North Koreans wanted to kill the woodcutters. Their leader said no; they had bigger game to think about. They warned the woodcutters, released them, and continued.

At least once every forty-eight hours Schumacher inspected the two .50 caliber machine guns to see if ice had formed inside their can-vas tarps. He didn't have to remove the tarps; a glance would suffice, for now that the ship had reached its southernmost operating area, ice was less of a hazard. Thus far on the patrol the .50's had only been fired twice—most recently off Chongjin—and they had performed er-ratically, as he had expected they would. As the gunnery officer, Schu-macher also had custody of the ten Thompson submachine guns on board. They were supposed to be used in conjunction with repel boarders or anti-floating mine drills. Because of the weather—and the nature of this mission—the ship hadn't conducted such drills since leaving Sasebo. The submachine guns remained in their locker.

After breakfast every morning Schumacher returned to his state-room and prepared the patrol report, describing by name, characteris-tics, and time of reception all the visual, radar, and electronic contacts *Pueblo* had made during the past twenty-four hours. To these he added a list of the ship's positions and course changes. Between noon and two o'clock he gave the report to Bucher, who checked his work, made corrections, and added comments of his own.

Bucher's comments were laced with pessimism. The direction-finding equipment on the foremast had been malfunctioning. While Cliff Nolte scrambled aloft to repair it, the ship had drifted uncom-fortably close to the 13-mile limit set forth in his orders. The sub-marines he'd hoped to find near Mayang-do had not materialized. And what was worse, the CT's hadn't collected anything new.

He spoke to Steve Harris about this frequently, either in his state-room or in the research spaces. Often he would stand there watching intently while the CT's twisted the knobs on their equipment, not really understanding what they were doing but wishing them success anyway. It was no use. The trip was a complete waste of time, he wrote in his report. Any benefits which might have accrued from watch-standing and time at sea were overshadowed by the weather, which kept almost everyone in bed and permitted no training at all. Still, there was one consolation. Even if he and his crew picked up no significant intelligence, they would at least have contributed to a thorough oceanographic survey. Tuck and Iredale had been conducting their Nansen casts and BT drops at evenly spaced locations between the forty-second and thirty-ninth parallels. They seemed happy with the results.

For the past few days Murphy had been feeling despondent. He didn't stand set watches, but he did have to be up on the bridge to take morning and evening stars. Then, too, he was on call any time the navigators doubted the ship's position. With Mack, Leach, and Nolte up there, these doubts occurred frequently. He wasn't getting enough sleep.

Bucher was riding him constantly; unfairly, he thought, and the worst of that was still to come, for as soon as the ship returned to port, Bucher would submit that delayed fitness report. He knew what the captain would probably say about his performance. It wasn't fair. One or two bad fitness reports, however unjustified, could ruin a man's career. He'd already given eight years of his life to the Navy—and this at a time when his family had been desperately trying to put that clothing and hardware business back on its feet. Resigning from the Navy was the only sensible solution.

At 5:20 on the afternoon of January 21 Lacy summoned Bucher to the bridge. In the gathering dusk, about 1,000 yards away, he could make out a North Korean subchaser, a modified S01, churning southward at better than 25 knots. *Pueblo* was laying to; her ensign was down, as it had been throughout the patrol, and the only hint of her nationality was the "GER-2" on the bow. The subchaser slowed as she approached: 500 yards, 400. Bucher ordered Larry Mack to photograph her. Mack saw only one man on her bridge. The subchaser passed 300 yards off *Pueblo*'s port bow, then turned toward Wonsan. Lacy read the beads on her hull—number 26—and felt it was "impossible for us not to have been detected." Mack agreed. On the flying bridge Bucher, Murphy, Steve Harris, and Schumacher talked about this. The subchaser had evidenced no *real* interest. Bucher decided the North Korean was probably asleep at the switch. *Pueblo* had not been detected. "It was a call on our part," Schumacher remembers. "In hindsight, a bad call." Hours later, Bucher set a course for Wonsan. If he still had no success by the night of the twenty-third, he'd leave Wonsan, steam north toward Songjin, and cruise back down again.

★   ★   ★

As soon as they heard the news about the guerrillas from the terrified woodcutters, ROK Army commanders organized search parties to sweep the area north of Seoul. The National Police tripled its guard around the Blue House. But the thirty-one assassins were moving faster than anyone expected them to; they slipped around and behind the Army screen and, by ten o'clock that Sunday night, January 21, were marching in formation less than a mile from the Blue House.

Just ahead was a small checkpoint. "Stop and identify yourselves," the policeman said.

The North Koreans didn't even break their stride. Their leader, twenty-eight-year-old Lieutenant Kim Shin-jo, shouted back that he and his men belonged to a ROK counterintelligence unit attached to the 26th Division. They were returning home from a mission in the mountains.

The policeman let them pass, then picked up a telephone.

At ten fifteen Erickson was catching up on some reading at his home in the embassy compound. When he first heard the racket, he assumed it was fireworks. But this was an odd hour for a celebration. He listened again. *That* was machine-gun fire. And it was close. He rushed to his office.

Reports came in throughout the night. The National Police had killed most of the guerrillas and forced the survivors to flee toward the mountains. Still, the North Koreans had managed to penetrate within 1,000 yards of the Blue House. The implications of that achievement wouldn't be lost on President Park Chung Hee. Heads would probably roll. And that wouldn't be all. For in the days to come, Erickson realized, as Park and his Cabinet ministers grasped the enormity of this outrage, they would insist upon retaliation against North Korea. And this would spell trouble for the United States.

5

The intelligence officer on watch in the spook locker at Yokosuka that Sunday night was a crew-cut, barrel-chested, twenty-nine-year-old lieutenant named Edward A. Brookes, a 1960 graduate—with a degree in biology—of Pennsylvania's tiny Ursinus College. A few months later he was a classmate and friend of Lieutenant Ed Murphy at Officers' Candidate School in Newport, Rhode Island. Brookes then had served an uneventful first tour and left the Navy in March of 1965. Within eight months he regretted that decision; civilian life wasn't for him, so he called the detailer at the Bureau of Naval Personnel in Washington. "I asked what was available if I decided to come back in," he recalls. "One month later they said they had this billet with COMNAVFORJAPAN, and I accepted it."

For the next six months at Yokosuka he served as the "collection-reporting officer" on the intelligence staff and, from all accounts, performed commendably. In May, 1966, he took over the job of fleet support—providing intelligence to all ships in the area. For such a young and relatively inexperienced officer it was a tremendous responsibility. Ed Brookes was no intellectual—everyone recognized that —but he was dedicated and willing to work long hours. And he was always happy to fill in whenever the other officers wanted to play golf or go to a cocktail party. Captain Thomas L. Dwyer, the tall, urbane assistant chief of staff for intelligence, grew to depend on him. Even Rear Admiral Frank L. Johnson, Commander, Naval Forces, Japan, himself, respected the bull-necked lieutenant's judgment.

For the past few hours Brookes had been standing by the intelligence ticker in Room 300, ripping off all the "intsums" on the Blue House raid and stacking them neatly on his desk. In the morning he'd show them to Captain Dwyer. "I thought the news was quite significant," he remembers, "and there was also some air activity in North Korea that didn't seem right to me."

By eight fifteen on the morning of January 22 Dwyer had reached his office inside the spook locker and was leafing through the traffic from Seoul. Did the Blue House raid signal a threat to *Pueblo*? Should they tell Bucher to abort his mission? The raid had occurred less than twelve hours before, and the reports were still too fragmentary. The best thing to do was solicit the admiral's advice. They could present the facts and offer recommendations; they could even order Bucher to come home immediately, but it would be wiser to let the admiral make that decision himself.

And now Admiral Johnson was shaking his head. "The things these North Koreans do; they're unpredictable," he sighed. Dwyer and Brookes should keep him informed of any late-breaking developments. Meanwhile, *Pueblo* would stay on patrol. She only had a few days to go on this mission, anyway, and as yet, there simply wasn't enough information to justify bringing her home.

Dwyer and Brookes kept watch on the ticker. By early afternoon it was clear that with this bold stroke, North Korean Premier Kim Il Sung had precipitated a major international crisis—one which could very well lead to a resumption of the Korean War.

"Do you think the situation is hot enough now to bring Bucher home?" Dwyer asked.

Brookes hesitated. For all the commotion, he hadn't seen any evidence that the North Koreans even knew where *Pueblo* was. "No, sir," he replied.

Still, he should say something to Bucher. He thought of sending a message directly to *Pueblo* on the special support intelligence channel. Then he discarded the idea. It wouldn't be wise to clog that channel with superfluous information. The fleet intelligence broadcast, which every ship received, was sure to include "umpteen intsums" on the Blue House raid. *Pueblo* would get the news that way; for all Brookes knew, she'd probably received it already.

Inside the research spaces a few CT's were listening to a pop station. They weren't supposed to be doing this—Steve Harris had warned them to concentrate fully on their jobs—so when they heard about the Blue House raid, they decided not to mention it. Harris would want to know their source, and this would ultimately mean trouble.

Although the fleet intelligence broadcast continued for twenty-four hours a day, Harris had no time to read it. The only messages he saw were those addressed directly to him—as 467Y—or to *Pueblo* herself.

And these were coming in frequently now. One, relayed from COMNAVFORJAPAN in Yokosuka, said that the CNO had just decided to substitute two 20 mm mounts for the .50 caliber machine guns on all AGER's. About time, Harris thought. Most of the other messages dealt with technical matters. None mentioned the Blue House raid.

At noon on January 22 *Pueblo* lay dead in the water 20 miles north and east of Wonsan. The sea was calm. The international day shapes for conducting hydrographic operations fluttered from the main mast. Up forward, Tuck and Iredale were taking a Nansen cast.

Twenty-five minutes later the starboard lookout reported that two North Korean fishing trawlers were approaching the ship from about 6 miles away. Bucher called for Photographer Mack and hurried to the bridge. The trawlers continued closing: 8,000 yards, then 5,000; now 3,000. They flew no flags—just pennant numbers, 1065 and 1062. Still, there could be no doubt as to their nationality. A red star nestled in a white circle on each of their stacks; the names on their sterns translated into English as "Rice Paddy" and "Rice Paddy One."

Both were heavily laden, with lines and fishing nets stowed forward. They did not appear to be armed, nor did they seem to have very much in the way of communications gear—just a triple long-wire antenna between their masts.

Suddenly, at 1,500 yards, one of the trawlers altered her course and steamed directly toward *Pueblo*, passing 100 yards off the starboard bow. From the bridge Bucher counted nineteen men, some in thick coats. The trawler circled *Pueblo*, then steamed north about 9,000 yards and lay to near her companion for fifteen or twenty minutes. At two o'clock they began a second approach, closing this time to within thirty yards, churning aft along the ship's port side, cutting close across her stern, then swinging hard to pass along her starboard side. Bucher watched them intently but didn't hoist any new signals. By three o'clock both trawlers had retired to the northeast, tiny specks now on the gray horizon. Bucher left the bridge. "Develop those pictures right away," he said to Larry Mack. "Put your negatives in slide mounts. I want to study them later in detail."

The moment those trawlers reached port, he knew, their captains would report *Pueblo's* presence. Now was the time to break radio silence; he prepared a situation report: ". . . these are the first craft to display any interest of 19 sighted since we departed the Tsushima Straits . . . at 220325 Zulu Jan/68 two North Korean ships . . . have made 26 BT drops and 10 Nansen casts at present posit. . . . Intentions: remain in present area. . . ." He gave the message to Radioman Hayes and told him to send it out immediately.

At dusk *Pueblo* withdrew from the coast and lay to at a point 25 miles southeast of Wonsan. Her running lights were dimmed, and she was bobbing gently now, a gray cork on the billowy sea. In the wardroom Bucher was examining Mack's negatives. "You know, Captain," Schumacher said, "I'll bet those guys are sitting in Wonsan right now looking at pictures of us."

Up forward in the fo'c'sle, John (Tiny) Higgins, Jr., a 6-foot, 5-inch fireman from St. Joseph, Missouri, was trying to figure out how to run the laundry machine. By mistake he poured powder bleach into the vat and whitened Engineman First Class Rushel J. Blansett's dungarees. Blansett, he knew, would be furious when he found out. On the mess decks Stu Russell was adjusting the movie projector. Tonight's feature was *The Flight of the Phoenix,* starring Jimmy Stewart. In the forward berthing compartment the poker game continued. Brad Crowe had been playing for hours. Or was it days? He hadn't slept in a very long time. At one point he'd been four dollars ahead. Now he was twenty behind. He decided to skip the movie and keep on with the game.

Inside the radio shack Lee Hayes was still attempting to reach Japan. He used Morse code to establish initial contact and asked the Naval Communcations Station at Yokosuka to activate the 100-words-per-minute Orestes circuit to Kamiseya. If he could "terminate" with Yokosuka on circuit 32, technicians there could patch him into Kamiseya on circuit 21. Now he could hear Japan, but Japan couldn't hear him. "Change frequencies, change frequencies," Japan advised.

In the tiny crypto room adjacent to the research spaces, a lean, mournful-eyed communications technician first class named Donald E. Bailey had already cut and scanned the tape that he would send through a machine called the KW-7. It would emerge as a random stream of marks and spaces. This encoded stream would then modulate the ship's transmitter. Bailey was ready to send Bucher's situation report. But he couldn't begin to transmit until Lee Hayes established a link. And Hayes was having no luck.

One problem was propagation—always tricky in the Sea of Japan. It wasn't too hard to get a message out during the daylight hours, but ionospheric disturbances at night played crazy games with communications. Sunspot activity resulted in garbling; high-frequency signals tended to slip right over receiving stations. And the fact that the station at Kamiseya lay behind a mountain range didn't help matters at all.

Another problem was sheer congestion on the frequencies *Pueblo* used. Every ship in the Navy, it seemed to Lee Hayes, waited until this time of night to start communicating. Most of them had high antennae, powerful transmitters. *Pueblo* had low power, a low antenna profile. And then, in order for a coded message to get through, both operators—Bailey in the spaces below and the CT at the other end—had to synchronize perfectly. If *Pueblo*'s signal faltered for even half a second, that synchronization would collapse. Hayes would have to start the process all over again.

At eight o'clock Hayes walked down to the research spaces and asked Steve Harris if he could send out the situation report in Morse code; that way he knew he could get it through. Harris said no. The message was classified; it had to reach Japan on a secure circuit. Anyone could intercept Morse code. To be sure, the sandy-haired radioman could use an old code, transfer it to Morse, and send it out in that manner. Harris thought that would be too tedious. "Keep trying," he said. Hayes walked back to the radio shack.

Later that evening Bucher knocked at the door to the research space. A CT opened it. Bucher entered and asked Bailey if he was having any luck. Bailey shook his head.

Bucher was angry now, not only because of the communications delay but also because he had just discovered that those two Marine Corps sergeants, Chicca and Hammond, weren't fully qualified as Korean interpreters. They hadn't been able to tell him anything during the incident with those fishing trawlers. If Harris had mentioned this before, he might have considered aborting the mission. But it really wasn't Harris' fault. The officers back at the Naval Security Group in Kamiseya never should have assigned these men to the ship.

Hours passed. On the flying bridge Gene Lacy felt uneasy. He saw occasional lights flicking on and off and sensed the ship was "being followed." Or was it only his imagination? The watch changed at midnight. In the pilot house Larry Mack was trying to ascertain the ship's position. The dead-reckoning track placed her 20-odd miles from shore. But loran indicated that she was inside the 13-mile line. Damn that loran anyway; always malfunctioning. He mentioned his problem to Ensign Tim Harris, the officer of the deck. Reluctantly, Harris called Murphy to the bridge.

The navigator was exhausted and in a grouchy mood. "Some people think I'm made of iron," he grumbled.

"Well, sir," Mack replied, "I'm not sure of our position, and it would be most unfortunate if we got into that red area and they came out and threw us a line and said, 'You're our prisoners.' "

"I wouldn't worry about that," Murphy said. "We'll pull off and tell them to go suck egg."

Murphy lit off the radar. No reason to worry anymore. The ship was well outside the red line.

Off to the left Murphy could see the lights of Wonsan. Directly ahead about 2 miles some fishing boats were laying nets. At 1:45 that morning a bright orange flare shot up over the fishing boats. It hung in the stillness for ten or fifteen seconds.

Lee Hayes had been working without a break for nearly twenty hours now; he needed something to keep him alert, and as the night wore on he made several trips to the coffee urn in the mess decks below. Back in the radio shack once more, he raised, then lowered, then raised again the power on his transmitter. Cliff Nolte had already checked the transmitter for him and said it was functioning perfectly.

Hayes couldn't understand why Japan didn't answer. He had tried a dozen frequencies; none of them worked, and now it was five o'clock in the morning. "I was getting kinda nervous," he recalls. "I was afraid the captain and the other officers—they might think it was all my fault."

During the night *Pueblo* drifted 5 miles to the southeast, and as the blackness slowly gave way to a dull gray dawn, she lay about 16 miles from the island of Nan-do. At eight o'clock Bucher ordered full speed ahead, north by northwest, on a course of 300 degrees. As the engines responded, he reminded himself to tell Murphy to air out that bedding in the forward berthing compartment. The stench down there was awful.

Don Bailey didn't even notice the smell. He had been up all night waiting for Hayes to establish communications with Japan. He had missed dinner the night before and was so tired now that he couldn't even think about breakfast. The moment this mission was over, his lot would improve. Orders had already been cut, and soon he would start flying on those EC-121 patrols near the North Korean and Soviet coasts. He told Communications Technician Second Class Donald R. McClarren to wake him if anything happened. Then he left the crypto room, climbed into his bunk, and within two minutes was sound asleep.

Larry Strickland felt positively naked without that little St. Christopher's medal on the chain around his neck. The chain had broken while he was fixing a valve in the auxiliary engine room some weeks ago, and he had been carrying the medal around in his pocket. As he dressed for duty this morning, he had a sudden urge to repair that chain, an inexplicable feeling that he might need the medal soon. Then he thought his shipmates would consider this peculiar. He abandoned the idea.

The sea was calm; there was almost no wind, and from where he was standing on the bridge Gene Lacy could see that most of the ice on the deck had melted to a thin glaze. There were just a few thick pockets now, particularly around the masts and up forward near the winch and the machine-gun mount. The weather forecast from Japan had mentioned the possibility of snow flurries sometime today. Lacy was ready for them. Several pairs of socks covered his feet, and he was wearing a regular flight jacket underneath his Mark II foul-weather jacket. And best of all, those two hand-warmers he'd bought in Japan were nestled against his tummy.

Too many years in diesel engine rooms had impaired his hearing somewhat, but otherwise, Lacy reflected, the Navy had been good to him. If it hadn't been for Canales' screwup on that fitness report, he would have made W-4 in a few more weeks. It didn't bother him that much; he knew he'd make it before he retired. And if he was really lucky, he'd be able to serve out his last year or two in the Seattle area. A friend of his, a retired police chief, owned a fishing boat, and he could spend those crisp fall weekends tracking the salmon down around Westport.

Lee Hayes was beginning to worry about his number two transmitter. It had always been temperamental, and now, at 9 A.M., it was overheating—its output varying between 300 and 500 watts. He decided to switch over to transmitter number one and telephoned Steve Harris in the research spaces to tell him about it. The lieutenant was unhappy. "Number one isn't that good," he said. But half an hour later Harris called back. "We have them five–bye," he cried. "Don't touch that transmitter. Don't breathe on it."

At 10:45 on the morning of January 23 *Pueblo* lay dead in the water 16 miles east of Ung-do island. A light haze obscured his view of the coast; still, Bucher felt sure that this was the best possible place from which to survey and photograph any ships leaving or entering Wonsan.

In the crypto room below, Don Bailey stepped back to his teletype machine. He had slept less than three hours. He finished transmitting Bucher's initial situation report, then turned to the captain's second report. The circuit to Kamiseya was solid at last; he wouldn't need fourteen hours to send this one.

". . . 68% fuel," the message began; "weather: wind, 280; four knots, sea state 0; barometer 30.24, falling . . . had 18 different contacts during the night. No identification made due to darkness. Closest was 3,000 yds. At 221645 Zulu one contact ignited a large orange flare which glowed for about 30 secs. Meaning purpose unclear. No escorts during the night or early morning. No attempt made at surveillance/ harassment. No significant ELINT; water depth 36 fathoms; intentions: remain in area. No longer under surveillance. This is last sitrep this incident. UNODIR reverting to EMCON."

Harry Lewis was finishing preparations for the noon meal. Turkey roll with cranberry sauce, peas, mashed potatoes with gravy, and apple pie for dessert. In all his years in the Navy, Lewis had never seen such a tiny galley. He disliked *Pueblo* intensely, and often, on this patrol, he told his friend Boatswain's Mate Third Class Willie Columbus Bussell how close he'd come to getting a transfer several months ago.

The trouble had really begun back at the shipyard in Bremerton. He'd fallen far behind on his payments for a 1966 Ford; the dealer had repossessed the car and sent a nasty letter to Bucher. The captain was mad; he didn't want his sailors running out on their debts. So Lewis had received orders to an LST in San Diego.

But then Harry Lewis made a mistake. His replacement was already aboard; he had only sixteen days to go before he left *Pueblo* forever. And he baked a cake. Bucher tasted the cake, and the cookies and pastries that followed. And Bucher decided that Harry Lewis would never leave that ship.

So Lewis had persevered, and over the past few months he'd come to learn a great deal about the appetites of his shipmates. Next to cakes and cookies, Bucher loved ice cream. So did Schumacher. Rushel Blansett, the burly, balding engineman, never ate potatoes. He said he wanted to lose weight. Yet whenever *Pueblo* was in port, Blansett would drink bottle after bottle of Coors' Beer. Lewis wondered if Blansett understood anything at all about calories. Peter Langenberg always came back for second and third helpings. Yet he remained as thin as a needle—a Norman Rockwell, *Saturday Evening Post* cover sailor with apple cheeks, saucer-blue eyes, and curly brown hair. Lewis thought he would blow away in a stiff breeze. Somehow, he decided, he would have to fatten him up.

The chow line extended from the mess decks into the starboard passageway. On the bulkhead by Murphy's stateroom hung a bulletin board, filled now with schedules, notices, and month-old Christmas cards. Langenberg looked at the menu for tonight's meal: chop suey. Then he looked for the movie: *We Join the Navy*. That was one he could miss.

At 11:45 Charles Law stepped up to the bridge to replace Lacy as officer of the deck. A husky, fun-loving, twenty-seven-year-old bachelor from Chehalis, Washington, Law was the only enlisted man to qualify as an OOD. Bucher depended upon him to such a degree that some crew members thought of Law as "the ghost XO." The captain liked him, too, one reason being that he had once been a quartermaster himself, and often, during the long, monotonous voyage across the Pacific, he and Law had made bets to see who could spot the evening's first star. And Law, who was blessed with 20–13 vision in one eye and 20–14 in the other, had usually prevailed.

There was a danger, of course, in letting any enlisted man become *too* familiar. Back at Bremerton, Bucher had reduced Law one rate (and then suspended the sentence) because of his feisty attitude, and now, on patrol, he kept pressing Law—do this, do that, do the other thing, and show me some results. Law complained about this constantly. "Bucher's just like a Sears and Roebuck catalogue," he said. "Big, fat, and fulla cheap shit." And everyone understood the nature of their relationship.

Just before noon Law sighted another ship 7 or 8 miles away approaching from the south at better than 20 knots. He telephoned the wardroom.

"Let me know when it comes within three miles," Bucher replied. "And light off the radar."

One minute passed; two minutes; five minutes; the telephone rang again. "Three miles, Captain," Law said, "and closing fast. The radar puts us around sixteen miles from Ung-do."

Tuck looked up from his plate. He was going to lower a Nansen cast sometime this afternoon as part of a time-series test. "If we take a station now," he suggested, "it'll give them some idea what we're doing here." Bucher nodded approval.

The Sony portable tape recorder lay in the captain's stateroom. Bucher slung it over his shoulder, pulled a white ski cap—with a little fur ball on top—down over his ears, and hurried to the flying bridge. Murphy followed him. Several months ago Murphy had tried to obtain a copy of *Jane's Fighting Ships* to have on hand in case *Pueblo* ever needed it. But this request, like so many others, had been rejected. *Pueblo*, the Navy decided, was too small to merit this publication.

Peering through the "big eyes"—the 22-inch binoculars on the flying bridge—Bucher identified the contact now as a North Korean subchaser, a modified S01. And she was at general quarters already; men in battle helmets were standing by her 3-inch cannon and the two 37 mm gun mounts. From her bridge North Korean officers were staring back at him.

Bucher sent for Steve Harris. The research officer appeared a minute or so later and began leafing through a thin set of pictures of Soviet-built ships. This was an S01 all right: 130 feet long, a displacement of 207 tons, a top speed of 25 knots, two rocket launchers forward of her bridge. Bucher turned to Leach, the sallow-faced signalman, and told him to raise the international signal for conducting hydrographic operations.

Harry Iredale had stepped into the chief petty officers' quarters to get his foul-weather jacket, cap, and gloves, and now he was waiting for Tuck to come by. Tuck didn't appear. That was odd—they always went forward together. Iredale glanced at his watch. Maybe Tuck had gone forward by himself. He decided to look.

Tuck was having trouble removing the tarp over the ocean-ographic winch. It was covered with ice; the ropes around the bottom were stiff, and it took him about five minutes to pull it clear. Then Iredale arrived. They lowered the cable slowly, attaching the heavy brass bottles at standard intervals.

The S01 approached on the port quarter. Then she began to cir-cle *Pueblo,* passing within 500 yards on her second swing.

In the wardroom Schumacher was writing his narrative report covering the previous day—a longer, more complicated assignment than usual because of the confrontation with those two fishing trawlers. Now he heard Law's voice over the 1MC. "Mr. Schumacher, lay up to the bridge. Mack, PM1, lay up to the bridge." Schumacher grabbed his Nikon 35 mm camera. Let Mack worry about the black-and-whites. He might be able to get some nice color slides this afternoon.

Bucher was holding a microphone and speaking into his tape recorder. Mack was setting up a tripod on the 0-1 level. Ensign Tim Harris arrived; Bucher told him to sit in the captain's chair and keep a running narrative.

The S01 hoisted a signal. Leach broke it down. "What nation-ality?"

Larry Mack was squinting through his viewfinder. He couldn't blame the North Koreans for their confusion. There was the captain in his wash khakis, leather flight jacket, and that crazy ski cap. The other men were running around in equally colorful garb; he was wear-ing a black watch cap and red and white gloves himself. Then he no-ticed something else. The barrel of that 3-inch gun was pointed di-rectly at him.

"Raise the ensign," Bucher ordered. It was 12:14.

The number one engine had been down for the past few min-utes. A fuel injector had burned out, and Engineman Third Class Dar-rell D. Wright was trying to change it. Norman Spear was there to help him. They slipped the new injector into place, and Wright decided to test it. He called the pilot house and asked Murphy for permission to light off the engines. Murphy said no. There was some activity up on the surface. It wouldn't be wise to create any unnecessary disturbance.

Almost immediately, Bucher countermanded that order. To be sure, the captain thought, this would turn out to be nothing more than routine harassment. The SO1 might keep him company for the next day or two, in much the same way that Soviet ships had shadowed USS *Banner*. Still, he might have to engage in some tricky maneuvers. Better to light off both engines now. Wright received his instructions and reported back within seconds: "Ready to answer all bells."

The SO1 was beginning her third pass around the ship. Suddenly she hoisted a new set of flags, the red and yellow Oscar and the black and yellow Lima: "Heave to or I will open fire."

Bucher was dumbfounded. What were those guys talking about? *Pueblo* was dead in the water already. He contacted Murphy over the voice tube and told him to check the meaning of "heave to" in the dictionary. And, he added, confirm the ship's location once more.

A radar sweep validated the noon position: 15.8 miles from the island of Ung-do; the picture on the scope was clearly identifiable on the charts. Despite the haze, Murphy could see the Hodo-Pando peninsula. He telephoned Harris and asked him about "heave to."

"It means stop and head into the wind," Harris replied. Murphy climbed up to the flying bridge.

There was no porthole in the research spaces, and Harris—who had just returned there—wondered what was happening outside. Initially, there hadn't been any reason for concern. The presence of an enemy ship—this was what he and his men had been hoping for. He knew that *Pueblo* still lay dead in the water, and, surprisingly, he felt a "sudden urge to get out of there." He couldn't telephone Bucher directly; there was no link between the research spaces and the flying bridge. All he could do was call the pilot house and ask whoever answered to relay his message. Or, perhaps even better, enlist one of the CT's as a messenger.

Bucher was thinking now about the same problem; it was ridiculous not to have direct communications between the flying bridge and the research spaces. He stepped down into the pilot house to confirm the ship's position himself, then turned to one of the sailors. "Get Mr. Harris on the phone. Tell him we'll have some more message traffic, so leave the circuit open. Don't secure the net."

The captain still wasn't concerned. The fix he'd just taken agreed almost exactly with those earlier fixes. The circuit to Japan was still 5–bye. Back on the flying bridge again, he told Leach to hoist a reply: "I am in international waters." And then, "I intend to remain in present location until tomorrow. . . ."

Now Lacy spotted three tiny white slashes, the feathery wakes of torpedo boats approaching in a line from the west. Bucher reached for the "big eyes." They were P-4's, closing at better than 40 knots. The tubes on their port and starboard beams were covered, but sailors were manning their deck-mounted machine guns. Bucher ordered the word passed over the 1MC: "All hands remain below decks."

Larry Strickland was walking along the forward passageway. He peeked out a porthole and saw the S01. "Those guys are at general quarters already," he thought to himself, "and we're not doing anything about it." He felt for the St. Christopher's medal in his right hip pocket.

In the radio shack was a cabinet which contained message blanks for reporting harassment. The addressees had been listed on the tops of these forms already—all *Pueblo*'s officers had to do was provide the details. Schumacher began drafting a message:

AGER-2/JOPREP/PINNACLE 3/100: USS *Pueblo* encountered one S01 North Korean patrol craft at 0300Z posit 39.25.2N/ 127-55.OE; dead in the water. . . . S01 pennant number 35 approached from 180, speed 15 and circled the ship once, on second trip around hoisted code Juliet Oscar Bravo translated as nationality. *Pueblo* hoisted US ensign, then ran up Hotel Juliet Delta, code translated hydrographer. On third swing no. 35 code Oscar Lima translated, "heave to or I will fire on you." . . . Ship continued to circle *Pueblo;* intentions: to remain in area if considered feasible otherwise to withdraw slowly to the northeast. . . .

Bucher scanned and approved the message. It would go out to the high-level officers in Address Indicating Group (AIG) 7623 as a Joint Operational Report (JOPREP), an umbrella the Navy uses to cover anything from harassment at sea to a measles epidemic. The "Pinnacle" designator would merit special attention and the precedence— "flash"—would hurry it along. Schumacher turned, descended the ladder, and ran toward the research spaces.

Don Bailey was sitting by the teletype inside the crypto room "talking" to a chief communications technician at Kamiseya named Richard A. Haizlip. "Got company outside," he tapped at 12:44, "and more coming so will have to keep this up for awhile. . . . It not too bad out here but lonely. . . . When we are under way it gets so rough that you can't do anything, so I will be glad to get back, and I sure could use some liberty now. I didn't think I'd miss the old lady so much. Over to you."

Harris was saying something now which Bailey didn't understand. "I am trying to find out what the OIC wants (garble), but now everyone is topside worrying (garble). . . ."

At 12:49 Bailey began transmitting JOPREP PINNACLE-1, the message which Schumacher had drafted and brought into the spaces.

"Roger your last," Haizlip replied. "Do you have any more traffic? How's it feel to be threatened?"

"Got some more company and not doing so good with them. So will have to keep this circuit up. Please stay with me on this circuit."

"Roger, Roger, know what you mean about that company and will stay down so you can come to me. Put a test on your next start. Until you get traffic we can keep frequency fairly clear. Over to you."

Bailey hunched over the machine. "The quick brown fox," he tapped, "jumped over the lazy dog's back." It was 1:16.

The lead P-4 approached on *Pueblo*'s port quarter, veered sharply under the fantail, and churned down the starboard side. Then she wheeled out to join the S01. The second torpedo boat positioned herself off the port bow, the third off the starboard bow. A fourth P-4 was ripping toward them across the gentle swells, and now, at an altitude of 1,500 feet, two snub-nosed MIG-21's whooshed over the ship, circled, and shrieked past again.

Bucher turned to his engineering officer. "How long would you need to scuttle the ship?"

Lacy had thought about this back at Bremerton, but at the time his major concern had been to keep the ship afloat. *Pueblo* had no sea cocks. Scuttling would be a complicated procedure requiring at least two and one half hours. Too long.

The water depth was 30 fathoms—only 180 feet. Scuttling here wouldn't deny *Pueblo*'s documents or gear to a salvage team. Furthermore, if they scuttled the ship, they'd flood the engine room. The ship would wallow helplessly, unable to maneuver once help arrived. Without power she wouldn't be able to maintain radio contact with Japan. *Pueblo* carried a Mark 10 26-foot whaleboat and enough life rafts for ninety men. But what if some of those men tumbled into the water? Its temperature was 35 degrees. They wouldn't survive more than five minutes.

"Do you want to go to general quarters?"

Bucher hesitated. This would mean calling men with helmets and life jackets to their battle stations on deck and manning the .50 caliber machine guns, perhaps convincing the North Koreans that *Pueblo* was provocative when she was not, perhaps giving them an excuse to turn this into some kind of international incident. No. GQ would not be necessary. The North Koreans were simply trying to intimidate him. And he had every right to be where he was. He would stay there indefinitely.

In the galley Earl Phares and Seaman Apprentice Richard J. Rogala were tidying up after the noon meal. They kept the milk out and had just finished cleaning the traps and silverware. From a porthole in the mess decks "Army" Canales was watching the P-4's, trying to remember the name of that movie he'd seen not long ago in which this U.S. ship was surrounded by gunboats full of "gooks" and . . . *The Sand Pebbles.* He turned to Monroe Goldman. "I know these Orientals," he said. "This isn't the end of it." Goldman nodded and stepped to his quarters to get some cigars. In the forward berthing compartment, John Shilling wondered what would happen if he had to abandon ship. He didn't know how to swim.

Schumacher returned to the flying bridge and started taking pictures. Bucher told him to draft a second JOPREP PINNACLE immediately. He entered the radio shack and reached for another message blank.

In the pilot house Murphy assembled a plotting team and told its members to trace the movements of every North Korean ship. The plot would be of great assistance in preparing the narrative report. All the senior officers back in Japan would want to study it closely. He checked the diagrams and times, then peered out at the S01. Eight or ten soldiers in full battle dress were stepping now from the subchaser to the deck of the lead P-4. And the P-4 was backing down toward *Pueblo.* He shouted for Bucher. It was 1:17.

Darrell Wright was standing by the throttle controls trying to hide his nervousness. Ever since the captain had ordered him to light off both engines and prepare to answer all bells, he had known that something really hairy was happening topside. He didn't dare leave the engine room to try to find out what. He looked over at Norman Spear. He was nervous, too. Spear always said he was going to get a job digging graves for a cemetery in Portland, Maine, when he finished this hitch, and Wright used to kid him about it. Wright couldn't think of anything funny to say right now.

The P-4 continued backing down on *Pueblo*'s starboard quarter: 100 yards, 50, 30. Mike Alexander heard the soldiers cocking their rifles. He glanced at his friend, Communications Technician First Class Charles R. (Joe) Sterling. Sterling had heard them, too. For a moment neither man spoke.

Bucher stared at the troops in the boarding party, stunned by their sheer gall. Those guys were *serious.* Well, he'd be damned if he'd let

them get away with a stunt like that. He would withdraw. But slowly—
in a dignified manner befitting an American ship.

The special instruction attached to his operations order was very
specific about this: right there in the first paragraph, the sentence
beginning "Retirement under any circumstances. . . ." He was to
stand firm in his right to sail international waters but not be so insistent
on asserting those rights as to endanger the ship. He was to move only
when subjected to pressure, and then very slowly and only far enough
away to ease the situation. So if he pushed the throttle to the wall, he
would, in a literal sense, be violating his orders. Bucher was not a man
to violate orders—or even interpret them loosely.

He ordered Leach to hoist a new signal—one which might confuse
the North Koreans long enough for him to slip away: "Thank you for
your consideration. I am departing the area." Then he spoke to the
pilot house, told Law to ask the navigator to suggest a new course—one
which would enable him to open the coast, gain room for maneuvering,
and reach the 100-fathom curve as soon as possible.

Law called back, "Zero-eight-zero."

Where was Murphy? Why wouldn't Murphy ever speak to him
directly?

"Is the navigator there?"

"Yes, sir," Law replied. Murphy stepped to the voice tube.

"Ed, is this a good course?"

"Yes, sir," Murphy said.

"Right to zero-eight-zero," Bucher told the helmsman, Ron Berens.
"All ahead one-third."

The twin screws surged and grabbed at the water. *Pueblo* swung
around in a wide circle and aimed for the open sea. But Bucher had
forgotten something.

"Slow down, slow down," Tuck was yelling, waving from the forward winch.

"Friar," Bucher bellowed back, "get that damn gear up here because I'm leavin'. Now."

Tuck was concerned. This was as spooky as anything he'd ever
experienced on USS *Banner*. Retrieving the Nansen cast, he hurried
to the bridge, then to his stateroom. There, in a cabinet, was a file of
the ship's positions for each of his oceanographic stations. He could
always copy them later from another log. He began to destroy the file.

Schumacher finished drafting the second JOPREP PINNACLE:

. . . S01 joined by 3 P-4 patrol craft number 601, 604 and 606.
S01 has sent international code translated "Follow in my wake; I
have a pilot aboard." S01 and P-4 604 lying to discussing situation

300 yards on starboard bow. 606 is just forward on starboard beam and 601 is on the starboard quarter. Two MIG's sighted on starboard bow circling; 604 is backing toward bow with fenders rigged with an armed landing party. . . . *Pueblo* all ahead one-third. . . . Intentions to depart the area."

Bucher approved the message. Schumacher started toward the research spaces.

Now Lacy suggested setting "Condition Zebra"—dogging down all the hatches and portholes. Bucher nodded. The boarding attempt was serious, but not, by itself, sufficient cause to start destroying the ship's equipment and classified documents. That should wait until there was a more positive indication that the North Koreans intended to attack. Still, it would be a good idea to alert people to this possibility. Bucher stepped to the voice tube and relayed an order for broadcast over the 1MC: "Prepare to execute emergency destruction."

Don Bailey sat at the teletype in the crypto room, his back to the men in the research area. An old leg injury was bothering him; he couldn't see what was going on, and nobody was telling him anything definite. Steve Harris had said he wanted to check every transmission— to make sure that every word that left the ship was accurate. But where was Harris now? Bailey knew Schumacher had come into the spaces, and he thought he heard John Grant mention a boarding party. Someone else was asking about emergency destruction. Mistakenly, Bailey assumed the worst; he leaned forward over the machine.

and they L
plan to opv fire on us now
They plan to open five fie fire of us now
jxy pplan to open fire on us now
    North Korean war vessels pa puplan tv openffire JZ-Ship posit 39/3
    Ship posit W/39/25.5N 127/54.9E. . . .
We are being boarded . . .
Ship position 3925, 12754.3
Ship position 2 EEEEEE 3824,1 + 754N
We are being boarde
                    d
SOS, SOS, SOS, SOS, SOS . . . .

It was 1:30.

On the starboard bulkhead in the pilot house stood the Hi-Comm, a clear-channel, high-frequency voice link to Japan and Hawaii designed for use in emergencies. Throughout the patrol *Pueblo* had monitored the Hi-Comm but had never used it to transmit. Now Murphy got word over the circuit: QSY, QSY—stand by to shift frequencies. He stepped into the radio shack and told Lee Hayes that a shift was imminent.

Hayes switched to the new frequency, and Murphy tried to transmit. But the circuit control in Hawaii kept repeating the new frequency code over and over again. Hayes switched back to the old frequency. Murphy still couldn't get through. The channel was clogged; the operator wouldn't stop long enough for him to break in.

The S01 was lying back about 3,000 yards, and she had lowered her "heave to" flags. But now a second S01, number 26—the same one that had passed *Pueblo* two days before—had joined the chase. The P-4's were keeping pace with *Pueblo,* two of them porpoising across her bow at ranges of 10 to 20 yards, their guns aimed at the flying bridge. Bucher ordered his speed increased: two-thirds, on up to full. The P-4 on his starboard quarter uncovered her port torpedo tube and trained it out 30 degrees. Bucher told Leach to hoist a new signal: "You are interfering with my free passage in international waters." But Leach couldn't encode it, couldn't find the right words in his manual.

Suddenly the first S01 got under way again, closing rapidly on *Pueblo*'s port quarter, an obvious attempt to force Bucher back toward land. He couldn't outrun the S01; the only thing to do was present as small a target angle as possible in case those North Koreans had any wild ideas. Bucher shouted course changes to Ron Berens at the helm: "Right to zero-eight-five, right to zero-nine-zero." The two MIG's made another pass, swooshing low over the ship.

The S01 was closing fast on the port quarter: 2,000 yards, 1,900. Flags fluttered from her mast: "Heave to or I will open fire on you."

Bucher ignored the order.

Schumacher had returned from his second trip to the crypto room. One glance told him the situation was critical. Assuming the North Koreans didn't open fire, he could have the .50 calibers manned and ready to operate in about ten minutes. He turned to the captain. "Do you want the guns manned?"

Bucher shook his head. "I knew that to send a man up to that forward gun mount," he recalls, "would have mean certain death for him. He would have had to remove the cover, which was frozen. . . . I saw no point in senselessly sending people to their death. I was still hopeful that it was nothing more than intimidation and that I could perhaps get away."

The S01 churned forward, 1,800 yards. The P-4's opened out 200 yards in every direction.

Seaman Larry Joe Marshall and Fireman Peter M. Bandera were washing clothes in the laundry. Marshall was sucking on an orange. He peered out a porthole, saw the P-4's, and promptly stuck out his hand with the middle finger extended. Then he noticed something odd: The P-4's were veering sharply away from *Pueblo,* weren't paying any attention to him at all.

Ralph McClintock suddenly felt cold. He went to the forward berthing compartment to pick up his turtleneck sweater. Roy Maggard's duty station at general quarters was the forward machine gun. General quarters had not yet been called, and Maggard was asleep in his rack. Peter Langenberg decided to wake him up and started kicking the soles of his feet. Larry Strickland stepped to his locker to get some extra packs of cigarettes; he put one of them in his sleeve. In the radio shack Lee Hayes turned to Schumacher and asked permission to destroy his secret message folder.

"Not yet," Schumacher replied. "I'll have to ask the captain."

Bob Chicca rushed through the galley, past the research spaces, to the forward berthing compartment. "Everybody get down," he yelled. "Hit the deck. They're going to open fire."

Tony LaMantia looked up from his rack just long enough to tell Chicca he was crazy, then rolled over and went back to sleep. Stu Russell stared at Chicca in disbelief. "I was sort of smart ass," he remembers. "I said, 'What do you want me to do—make myself small?' And everybody kinda laughed it off."

Fireman Michael A. O'Bannon didn't believe it either. "They can't do that," he said. "They wouldn't dare. We're in open waters. And we're an American ship."

6

In each ship there is one man who, in the hour of emergency or peril at sea, can turn to no other man. There is one alone who is ultimately responsible for the safe navigation, engineering performance, accurate gunfire and morale of his ship. He is the Commanding Officer. He is the ship!—Joseph Conrad (inscribed on a bronze plaque in the Office of the Chief of Naval Operations)

★   ★   ★

Ba-roooom, Ba-roooom, Ba-roooom. . . . The first salvo of cannon fire from the S01 whistled over the flying bridge. One or two rounds smashed into the radar and signal masts. Bucher fell backward to the deck, jagged pieces of shrapnel stabbing at his right ankle and calf and, incredibly, very painfully, at his rectum. Almost simultaneously, the P-4's on both sides of the ship began raking *Pueblo*'s hull with machine-gun fire. In the pilot house "Doc" Baldridge was keeping the quartermaster's notebook. His hand trembled as he wrote, "1330—NK warships open fire. . . ."

"Everybody all right?" Schumacher was looking up from the wing of the signal bridge.

"I'm okay," Bucher yelled. "Just got some glass in my ass."

Bucher staggered to his feet. *Pueblo* was steaming at full speed: 12.5 knots. He thought of ordering flank speed—an extra .6 knots—but didn't want to take the risk of overloading the engines. Then, too, that little push wouldn't really make any difference. The P-4's were capable of at least 50 knots, the S01 of 25 or more. He couldn't outrun them. And the S01 was closing quickly on his port quarter now: 1,700 yards, 1,600.

Pueblo was already maintaining a course of 110 degrees. He couldn't order the ship any farther to the right without jeopardizing his chances of reaching the 100-fathom curve. Too much of a turn, in fact, and he'd be heading toward the North Korean coast. Still, he had to do *something*. He leaned over the brass voice tube. "Right to one-two-zero."

Below, in the pilot house, Ron Berens was lying on his side, his eyes focused on the compass above him. He turned the wheel. *Pueblo* swung slowly to the right.

"FRIGIDAIRE, FRIGIDAIRE [COMNAVFORJAPAN's voice-call sign], this is ALMOND UNIFORM, ALMOND UNIFORM. Are under attack by North Korean SIERRA OSCAR ONE, I say again, SIERRA OSCAR ONE and PAPA FOUR, I say again, PAPA FOUR torpedo boats, my posit one five decimal six miles from Ung-do. I spell, UNIFORM NOVEMBER GOLF, break DELTA OSCAR, break, over. . . ." A few feet away, Murphy was still trying to contact Japan on the Hi-Comm circuit. He wasn't getting anywhere. Circuit control in Hawaii cut him off in midsentence and told him to shift frequencies. Murphy asked Lee Hayes to see what he could do.

Hayes could hear the machine-gun bullets smacking against the side of the ship. Coming closer to him. He hadn't slept for thirty hours, but he wasn't tired. He tried the Hi-Comm; Hawaii kept droning on. "The frequency was repeated over and over fifty or sixty times," he says. "I tried to break in, but they couldn't hear me." Then he found the problem. There was no output on the output meter. He called over to Schumacher. "The transmitter won't load up. It won't work."

"Forget it," Schumacher said. "Set up your other transmitter on the same frequency."

Hayes did. "FRIGIDAIRE, FRIGIDAIRE. . . ." Still no answer. He didn't know that the first salvo had knocked out the WRC-1 antenna coupler on the mast, that now there could never be an answer.

When the SO1 first signaled "Heave to," Communications Technician First Class James A. Sheppard had been standing on the bridge. He ran to the research spaces and asked Steve Harris if he could begin emergency destruction.

"I said we couldn't do it because we didn't have permission yet," Harris remembers. "I thought, 'Well, we'll just barrel on out of here. Let's hurry up and do it,' you know. I mean, we couldn't just go ahead and start destructing by ourselves. Suppose we got away and all the stuff was smashed up and the skipper had never said, 'Yes, do it'? Where would I be? I knew it was getting tight, though, and I was hoping that somebody up there would remember to give the order."

Sheppard stepped into the aft berthing compartment. He said a prayer. When he returned to the spaces, the firing had already started. Everyone had hit the deck. Surely this was the time to start emergency destruction. He looked for Harris.

Chief Communications Technician James F. Kell was one step ahead of him. He and Sheppard urged Harris to give the order immediately.

Harris telephoned the pilot house and spoke to Murphy. Then he turned to the two CT's. "We don't have permission yet," he said.

Kell didn't even stop to think that he was disobeying an officer's command. "At that point," he remembers, "I took it upon myself to give the order to destruct."

The pain in Bucher's ankle was bearable. The pain in his rectum was excruciating. He looked up as the two MIG's screeched over the ship and wheeled to make another pass. The P-4's were firing at point-blank range. The S01 was churning closer. Bucher expected another salvo in a few seconds. And now it occurred to him that there were too many people on the flying bridge. They had no protection at all. He would stay there with Leach, his signalman, and Robin—what the hell was Robin doing there anyway?—and Law, his quartermaster; he could depend on Law and Tim Harris, who was keeping the narrative; he told Harris to go below to the pilot house. Up to this point he had refrained from ordering emergency destruction. "I didn't know what their intentions were, whether they would follow me out to sea." But now "I realized that these people intended to make a full-scale incident out of this." Unaware that Kell had already passed the word, he yelled into the voice tube, "Commence emergency destruction."

Navy regulations forbid jettisoning classified documents and equipment over the side in less than 100 fathoms (600 feet). Harris telephoned the pilot house and asked Murphy to check the water's depth.

"35 fathoms," Murphy said.

Harris decided to destroy and burn the equipment and publications instead of dumping them into the sea. With the tools at his disposal the job would take several hours. "In retrospect, it wasn't the wisest decision," he says. "But those were the rules."

Just an hour or two before, Don Peppard had posted the emergency destruction bill on the first bay bulletin board. It assigned CT's by name to specific tasks. The trouble was that the bill was predicated on a general quarters situation. It didn't consider the possibility that destruction might begin before the sounding of general quarters. And Bucher had not yet issued that order. So there were too many men inside the research spaces, and they were the wrong men.

Although he had served in the Navy since 1953, Senior Chief

Communications Technician Ralph D. Bouden had never participated in a destruction drill. He lifted a sledgehammer and swung it against a piece of machinery. The sledgehammer's handle broke off. Bob Hammond was having trouble, too. His sledgehammer kept bouncing back in his face; it didn't even seem to chip paint. John Grant was trying to loosen the screws which held his equipment in the bay. He didn't have a screwdriver. He used his nails instead.

Some of the CT's started fires in the passageway. The smoke billowed back into the spaces. There were no portholes in the spaces; no one had thought to provide any ventilation. The smoke stung the men's eyes and made them choke. Joe Sterling was shouting above the din, "Everyone who's not on watch, get out of here."

Seconds passed. Harris "assumed" that Bucher "had his reasons" for not ordering general quarters. This delay, he feels, "got us off to a slow and somewhat disorganized start."

In the tiny crypto room Don Bailey was kneeling in front of the teletype. "I figured it was time to get scared," he says. "There was so much smoke I couldn't see a foot and a half away. Layton told me [mistakenly, at that moment] that the ship was being boarded. Other guys were giving me stuff, sticking their heads in and hollering. I wouldn't even look up. In a situation like that, you don't wait to see who's telling you."

Bailey bent over his machine:

SOS SOS SOS SOS SOS SOS SOS SOS SOS SOS SOS SOS SOS. SHIP POSITION 39-34N, 127-54E; SHIP POSITION 39-34N, 127-54E. SOS SOS SOS SOS SOS SOS SOS SOS SOS SOS SOS SOS SOS SOS SOS SOS SOS SOS
OUR POSITION 39-34N, 127-54 E. WE ARE HOLDING EMERGENCY DESTRUCTION. WE NEED HELP. WE ARE HOLDING EMERGENCY DESTRUCTION. WE NEED SUPPORT.
SOS SOS SOS. PLEASE SEND ASSISTANCE PLEASE SEND ASSISTANCE PLEASE SEND ASSISTANCE PLEASE SEND ASSISTANCE SOS SOS SOS WE ARE BEING BOARDED. HOLDING EMERGENCY DESTRUCTION. . . .

Roy Maggard tumbled out of his rack. He hadn't heard the call for general quarters, but he assumed it would come at any second. He was supposed to man the forward machine gun. He would have to cross the exposed well deck and climb a ladder on the port side of the ship. He would need "three or four minutes" to remove the canvas tarp. Then he would have to unlock the ammunition box. "I thought we were all going to be dead," he says. "I just wanted to be home."

Earl Phares was assigned to help Maggard on the forward gun. "I knew I had to go," he remembers. "I kept saying to myself, 'I don't want to get shot; I don't want to get shot.' " Then it occurred to him that Gunner's Mate Second Class Kenneth R. Wadley had the key to the ammunition box. He didn't know where Wadley was. He kept moving anyway.

At that moment Wadley was racing in the opposite direction, toward the aft end of the ship. He was surprised that no one had ordered general quarters or given him any definite instructions.

From the port side of the pilot house, Communications Technition First Class Michael T. Barrett was watching the S01. Suddenly he shouted, "They're swinging their guns; they're swinging their guns. Everybody down."

Ba-roooom, Ba-roooom, Ba-roooom. . . . The second salvo ripped into the ship. A cannon shell burst through the window behind the captain's chair, missing Tim Harris' head by inches, streaking out of the window just in front of him. Incredibly, it didn't explode. But flying glass was everywhere. Harris felt a sharp pain at the back of his neck. He reached up to touch it. He drew his hand back and saw blood. He picked up the narrative and stepped into the chart room.

Steve Robin had come to the flying bridge to deliver a message and had remained there out of curiosity. Now he was hugging the deck. He felt something like a hot poker jab at his left elbow. A few feet away Wendell Leach was lying behind the flag box. He realized dumbly that pieces of shrapnel had entered his thigh and right calf. He remembers feeling very cold.

Bucher got to his feet. He'd scraped his knee but hadn't been hit again. He tossed his Sony tape recorder into the water. Then he looked below and noticed Larry Mack's Leica on its tripod on the 0-1 level. "Throw that goddamn thing over the side and take cover," he shouted.

Seconds before, Lacy had suggested sounding general quarters. Bucher had hesitated. "I did not want to give these people cause for attacking us," he remembers. "I really felt strongly about my orders in connection with not provoking an international incident." But that incident had already begun. He leaned over the voice tube. "Sound general quarters."

He felt his first responsibility was to keep his superiors informed of what was happening. Bailey was taking care of that on the teletype. His second task was to complete emergency destruction. "Yet I did not want to come under such severe attack," he says, "that it would have been impossible to destroy the classified material. I did not feel there was any point in attempting to go to war with the group of ships. I was completely and hopelessly outgunned. Those guys were between thirty-five and fifty yards away. There was just no way to get to our guns or even to get the ammo lockers open."

At that point—just ten or fifteen seconds after ordering GQ— Bucher made the decision which was to render inevitable every other decision he made that afternoon. He yelled into the voice tube, "Set modified GQ. Pass the word to all hands to stay clear of the weather decks. Repeat, no personnel are to come topside."

The men who had been rushing toward the machine guns stopped in their tracks. Maggard waited for someone to form a repair party. Phares remained in the galley. Wadley began passing out helmets in the passageway below. In his pocket he carried the key to the small-arms chest near the captain's stateroom on the starboard side of the ship. "I thought about issuing small arms," he says. "I didn't open the locker because the orders didn't come."

William D. Scarborough was sleeping in the aft berthing compartment when a shell ricocheted off the deck just above him. Insulation and paint chips dropped in his hair. He shook his head to get rid of the ringing noise in his ears and, at that moment, heard Murphy relay the call for modified general quarters over the 1MC. "I didn't know what was coming off," he remembers. "I jumped out of my rack. Larry Marshall was trying to dog this hatch, and I was trying to undog it at the same time."

Then Scarborough realized that this was a real attack. He started breaking out gear for the eleven men in repair party five at the aft end of the ship. "I had to tell the men twice to set Condition Zebra," he says, "get the ship buttoned up. Everybody froze, so the second time I said it, I really hollered it out. Then they turned to. They knew their jobs."

Because there was no 1MC outlet in the research spaces, the CT's didn't hear the order for modified GQ, and it wasn't until several seconds later—when someone called down from the pilot house on the secure telephone—that they grasped what was happening. The CT's whose names were on the emergency destruction bill reported for duty. In setting Condition Zebra, their shipmates had switched off *Pueblo*'s air supply. The CT's opened portholes in Lieutenant Harris' office and the CPO quarters, but smoke from the trash-can fires outside the door to the spaces continued to surge through the passageway. Even with his turtleneck sweater pulled over his head, Ralph McClintock was having trouble breathing. He ran to the mess decks, popped an ice cube into his mouth, and ran back again. He didn't see Steve Harris and wondered what had happened to him.

As operations officer, Schumacher should have been custodian of

Pueblo's registered publications. But as Schumacher hadn't received his Special Intelligence (SI) security clearance until the end of December, Harris had volunteered for the chore. He had to make sure these publications were being destroyed. He raced to the RPS safe at the aft end of the ship.

"Steve had some keylists," Gene Lacy recalls. "I grabbed some and took them to where people were burning in the forward passageway. I told [Fireman Apprentice Steven E.] Woelk and [Fireman Duane D.] Hodges to give them a hand."

The first salvo had shattered some of the windows in the pilot house; the second had blown them all out. Lee Hayes was sprawled on the deck, Radioman Third Class Charles H. Crandell, Jr., Murphy, and Schumacher on top of him. Hayes got to his feet. The acrid smell of cordite filled his nostrils. He tried the Hi-Comm again: "FRIGIDAIRE. . . . FRIGIDAIRE. . . . This is ALMOND UNIFORM. . . ." He heard no reply.

The ship's incinerator stood alongside the stack on the 0-1 level. Four feet high and two feet wide, it could only handle three or four pounds of paper at a time. Because it wasn't fuel fed, it couldn't burn bulky material. A man had to remove the heavy binders from his publications and then rip out the pages. Schumacher opened the two storage lockers under the captain's chair, then reached into the Officer of the Deck's safe. He grabbed an armload of ID and Recognition publications and raced to start the incinerator.

Bucher bellowed new course changes into the voice tube: "Right to one-three-zero; right to one-four-zero. . . ." *Pueblo* was steaming almost parallel to the coast. The S01 was still trying to force her back toward shore. Bucher looked around and saw smoke rising from the incinerator. He assumed the publications that his men were burning came from the research spaces as well as the ship's allotment.

The two MIG's whooshed past. At 1,500 feet one of them fired four rockets. Bucher saw them splash into the sea about 5 miles away.

Ba-roooom, Ba-roooom, Ba-roooom. . . .

"The S01 had closed to a range of 900 yards on my port quarter," Bucher says. "He continued to fire salvos at approximately thirty-second to one-minute intervals, six to fourteen shots in a continuing sequence. After about the third salvo it occurred to me that most of the firing was being directed toward my flying bridge. All of the windows in the canopy had been shot out or were holed in two or three places. One shell had also struck the captain's chair three feet to the left of the voice tube. I was standing at the tube. I decided it would be prudent to clear the flying bridge."

The repel boarders bill called for issuing the Thompson submachine guns to members of the crew. The general quarters bill did not. Bucher didn't consider using his small arms. "I knew the Thompson was effective only to fifty yards," he says. "Sure, you could hit something with it, but it's of no value. We didn't have any more than two or three hundred rounds of ammunition, about two clips for each gun. We didn't have an allowance for any more than that."

Pueblo carried fifty grenades. But they were concussion grenades designed for use against swimmers. Bucher didn't consider using them, either. He saw a coffee mug near the captain's chair. "I just took that fuckin' cup and whoosh—I threw it at this P-4 that was firing from about fifty yards away. I was so goddamn mad, I missed him. I guess it was a futile thing to do."

Bucher raced for the ladder to the 0-1 level and shouted for Law, Leach, and Robin to follow him. The P-4 on the starboard quarter 40 yards away promptly opened fire and "raked across the stack and directly across the ladder I was climbing down, the bullets striking just to my left side and then the next bullet striking just to my right side. I don't know how I didn't get hit."

Charles Law jumped 10 feet to the starboard side of the 0-1 level. "Robin and Leach landed on top of me," he remembers. "We were all too scared to get hurt."

Bucher entered the pilot house. Several enlisted men were hugging the deck. So was Murphy. Bucher kicked him and told him to get to his feet.

Inside the chart room was the secure telephone to the research spaces. Bucher cranked the growler and lifted the receiver. There was no answer. He waited about a minute, then realized he was holding the ship's service phone. Someone was probably trying to answer him on the secure phone.

Harris came on the line. The CT's, he said, had already destroyed most of the electronic equipment with sledgehammers and fire axes. Most of the registered publications in the ship's allotment had been destroyed as well. A few of the men were loading the research detachment's publications into weighted bags. Harris said he couldn't jettison those bags until the ship arrived at the 100-fathom curve. When would that be?

Bucher couldn't say. "I hung up and stepped outside," he recalls. "Salvos were continuing to come in. We were still running at full speed, still opening the coast."

Robin joined Schumacher at the incinerator. He was having trouble keeping the fire alive and was running out of matches. Schumacher gave him his cigarette lighter and stepped back to the pilot house. Then he remembered the pile of classified publications in the safe in his stateroom. He told the captain that he was going below.

Murphy was watching the radar console. Bucher asked him if "Army" Canales was destroying the material in the ship's office. Murphy nodded. Bucher prayed "that we could get the material destroyed before the ship was sunk or we were all killed."

Hayes had given up on the Hi-Comm circuit. He gathered the cryptographic materials in the radio shack and peered outside. One of the P-4's was drumming a steady tattoo of bullets against the port side of the ship. The captain had told him not to burn anything on the bridge itself; the smoke might attract the North Korean gunners. "I knew I had to go back to the incinerator," he recalls. "I was really scared, but I thought, 'Well, if I don't go now, I'll never forgive myself.'

"I started out the starboard side and got down real low until I reached the burner. The winch for the whaleboat gave me some cover. I put my stuff in and watched it burn. I didn't want to stick around, but I figured I had to. If we ever got out alive, I'd have to say what I actually did destroy."

In the next few minutes Hayes made three more trips to the incinerator. He still had a pile of documents marked "confidential." He tied them to Nolte's electronics tool box and dragged the box from the shack. "Nolte came back and said, 'What the hell are you doing with my tool box?' " Hayes recalls. "I said, 'You don't need it where you're going.' He had a funny look on his face. Then he grinned and helped me throw it over the side."

Harry Iredale noticed that the door to the helmet locker was open. He slapped a helmet on his head and raced to the CPO quarters. He found the bathythermograph sheets with notations of ship positions and began tearing them into quarter-inch squares, "just in case we'd come across the line." Then he exchanged his Navy workboots for a pair of Hush Puppy loafers "in case I had to do any running or swimming."

"Doc" Baldridge was sure that someone was going to be killed or wounded in the next few seconds. He asked Murphy for permission to break out his first aid kit. Murphy nodded. Baldridge scampered below to the battle dressing station on the mess decks.

The island of Nan-do, visible only an hour or so before, had faded into the afternoon haze. *Pueblo* had cleared the coast by at least 20 miles. The water was deeper now—almost 50 fathoms. Already the SO1 and the P-4's had blasted the ship with ten to fifteen salvos of cannon fire and more than a thousand rounds of machine-gun fire. No one had been killed. *Pueblo* had suffered no serious matériel casualties.

But the flying bridge was a shambles. The antennae were shot away. The guy wires to the masts were gone. Bucher had the distinct impression that the firing was "controlled." The S01 was pausing after each salvo. The P-4's were strafing sporadically; they hadn't fired their torpedoes. The second S01 hadn't even joined the battle. He knew the North Koreans could blow him out of the water whenever they chose.

He couldn't complete the destruction unless he won some respite from the cannon fire. He ordered Leach to raise the international signal for protest. The North Koreans ignored the flags. Then Lacy suggested stopping the ship. Bucher nodded. Lacy ordered, "All stop." It was 1:37.

"I considered that any further efforts to gain the open sea would only be futile," Bucher says, "and would result in severe damage to the ship or, more importantly, the men on the ship. I felt that any further, or any, resistance on our part would only end up in a complete slaughter of the crew. I decided that if the destruction was progressing satisfactorily and, depending on what their next action would be, that I would surrender the ship."

Lacy was still officer of the deck. Bucher gave him the "conn" and rushed below to his stateroom. He searched through the file cabinet and the locker above his desk but couldn't find any message folders pertaining to *Pueblo*'s mission. He did spot copies of official correspondence, which he gave to a sailor in the passageway outside. Then he remembered his personal sidearms, a .22 Ruger Black Hawk pistol and a .38 Smith & Wesson revolver. He passed them to the sailor and told him to throw them over the side.

He left his cabin. Small fires were burning on the mess decks, in the yeoman's office, in the passageway between the research spaces and the CPO quarters. There seemed to be a lot of smoke, but no one complained to him that it was hindering destruction. He noticed that both of the crypto safes were open and empty. This had to mean that the report he'd received from Steve Harris about the progress of the destruction was accurate. He reached the pilot house and took over the conn again.

A few feet away, Law and Crandell were ripping pages from publications and destroying chart catalogues. Nolte was swinging a sledgehammer. Bucher told him to spare the transmitter.

Below, in the crypto room, Don Bailey pecked at the teletype: "WE ARE LAYING TO AT PRESENT POSITION. . . . PLEASE SEND ASSISTANCE. . . ."

The firing stopped. The S01 closed to 800 yards and hoisted a signal: "Follow me, I have a pilot on board."

Bucher remained convinced that his only recourse was surrender. He did not request advice from his other officers or from Japan. "I felt the decision was my own," he says. "I felt that the situation had been adequately reported and that I had given all the information that I needed to give or was necessary for command decision to be made by higher authority."

"All ahead one-third," he told Berens. The ship moved forward at 5 knots. If he was going to capitulate, he might as well do so in as slow and dignified a manner as possible. *Pueblo* swung around in a wide arc and followed the S01.

Bailey sent: "WE ARE NOW BEING ESCORTED INTO PROB WONSAN RE-PEAT WONSAN. WE ARE NOW BEING ESCORTED INTO PROB WONSAN REPEAT WONSAN. ARE YOU SENDING ASSISTANCE? ARE YOU SENDING ASSISTANCE? ARE YOU SENDING ASSISTANCE? ARE YOU SENDING ASSISTANCE?"

The answer from Kamiseya clattered over the machine. Bailey leaned forward and read: "WORD HAS GONE TO ALL AUTHORITIES. WORD HAS GONE TO ALL AUTHORITIES."

It was 1:45.

7

At COMNAVFORJAPAN headquarters the morning had passed
uneventfully. Rear Admiral Frank L. Johnson drove up to Tokyo to
give the welcoming address at the annual Pacific Command Tropical
Cyclone conference in the Sanno Hotel. In his absence the chief of
staff, Captain Forrest A. (Buster) Pease, was in charge. Inside the
spook locker Captain Thomas L. Dwyer, the assistant chief of staff for
intelligence, was leafing through a copy of *Stars and Stripes*. The paper
carried an account from Seoul of the Blue House raid of two nights
before. The story said this was an attempt to assassinate South Korea's
president. Funny. The intelligence reports Dwyer had seen had merely
mentioned the presence of infiltrators near the Blue House. They
hadn't attributed such significance to the event, and for a moment
Dwyer wondered if he and Lieutenant Ed Brookes should have sent
that warning message to *Pueblo* after all. But there was really no
cause for alarm. A watch officer had just tacked the first situation report from the ship on the "interest board." The North Koreans, it said,
had finally detected *Pueblo*. Dwyer and Brookes had expected this.
Everything seemed routine.

Shortly before noon Dwyer stepped out of the spook locker and
headed for the officers' club to meet his wife for lunch. Normally he
stayed at his desk until twelve thirty or one, but today he and his wife
were going shopping. Dwyer had always enjoyed antiques and over the
years had become quite knowledgeable about them. So when his maid
had said that her landlady might be willing to sell some fine pieces at
reasonable prices, he had promised to stop by.

What he and his wife were really seeking was an antique hibachi,
a brazier they could use in their home. They didn't want a standard
ceramic hibachi, nor did they particularly favor the Kansai model

with an overlapping top, the kind that was so popular down around Kyoto. But if they could find a rectangular Kanto, that would be nifty indeed. And that was just what the landlady was offering, a beautiful Kanto for only a few thousand yen. Dwyer paid her and started to leave. It was past one o'clock already; he wanted to drop the hibachi at his home on Upper Halsey Road and get back to the office. But the landlady, all bows and smiles and polite chuckles, wouldn't let him go. She showed him a sandalwood statue of Kannon, the Goddess of Mercy; she pressed him to accept as a gift two exquisite sandalwood devils. Dwyer knew he couldn't accept them. Still, he was tempted. He decided to stay a while longer.

Inside the "command cave" beneath Edwina's Hill, Lieutenant Commander Alger L. Wilson was finishing a pork chop sandwich that his wife, Maxine, had prepared that morning. He always tried to eat lunch at his desk on Tuesdays so he could read the latest issue of *Time* magazine. The Penn Central's Stuart Saunders was on the cover this week; the lead story concerned "Railroads of the Future." He turned to the "letters" page.

Several hundred yards away, inside the spook locker, Lieutenant Commander Carl L. Hokenson, Jr., was preparing to go home for lunch. Actually, he had the watch and wasn't supposed to leave. But Ed Brookes had volunteered to sit in for him. Hokenson grabbed his cap and started toward the door, lingering there for a few seconds to talk to a secretary. Brookes moved into the communications shack.

The Naval Security Group station at Kamiseya was just beginning to relay another message from *Pueblo*: ". . . on third swing no. 35 code Oscar Lima translated 'Heave to or I will open fire on you.' . . ." It was 1:12.

Brookes ripped the message from the teleprinter, turned, and saw that Hokenson still hadn't left the room. "Hey, Carl, c'mere. This looks like maybe it's hot."

Hokenson read it slowly. He decided to show it to the chief of staff, whose office was only 25 feet away.

At that moment Captain Pease was sitting at his walnut desk, peering out from behind a sign which proclaimed in Japanese, "Nuclear submarines are not dangerous,' exchanging idle conversation with two Japanese admirals who were paying a courtesy call. Pease found it difficult to concentrate on what they were saying. His eyes flickered from their faces to the blue carpet, to the beige sofas, even—despite himself—to the clock on the wall. Then he noticed something odd. Hokenson was standing behind the swinging door, waving his arms back and forth. Excusing himself, he got up and walked to the door. Hokenson handed him the message. He reached for his glasses.

"I said to Carl, 'This looks like we might have some trouble,' " he remembers, " 'so keep alert and let me know. Make sure you notify N-3, Captain [William H.] Everett.' "

Hokenson stepped back to the spook locker and told Brookes to contact Everett in the command cave. Everett was out to lunch. Al Wilson came on the line. Because there was no teletype or secure telephone link between the spook locker and the cave, Brookes had to speak guardedly. "Our friend is having a few problems," he began. "I'll send the message over."

Brookes looked for someone who possessed a high enough security clearance to hand-carry the message. Neither he nor Hokenson could afford to leave. Lieutenant Commander Duane L. Heisinger was busy with something else. But Lieutenant Anthony J. Celebrezze, the chubby, dark-haired son of a former Secretary of Health, Education and Welfare, certainly fit the bill. Celebrezze took the paper, raced down the steps, and began jogging toward the cave, arriving three minutes later.

Al Wilson put down his copy of *Time*. His immediate boss, Commander Charles G. Schoenherr, had just returned from lunch. "I gave him the message," Wilson says. "He looked at it and said, 'Okay,' real slow-like. Captain Everett had come back, too, so we went in to brief him." It was 1:21.

Inside the spook locker another message, Pinnacle Two, chattered across the teleprinter: "SO1 joined by three P-4 patrol craft number 601, 604 and 606. SO1 has sent international code translated 'Follow in my wake. . . .' Two MIG's sighted on starboard bow circling; 604 is backing toward bow with fenders rigged with an armed landing party on board. . . ."

Hokenson raced to find Pease. The Japanese admirals were still sitting there, oblivious to the crisis. Pease came to the door, read the message, and scowled. "Tell Captain Everett to notify Fifth Air Force immediately," he said. "Push the contingency button."

Hokenson told Brookes to get ready to send a "critic," a message that takes precedence over anything else on the circuit.

". . . and they plan to open fire on us now. . . . North Korean war vessels plan to open fire. . . ." From Bailey's informal "chatter" Brookes could see that the situation was deteriorating quickly. He quoted Bailey's remarks in the critic and sent it on its way. There were no "general service" circuits in the spook locker. Brookes realized that the operators in the cave needed to know what he was sending and receiving. He handed a copy of the critic to Celebrezze and asked him to hurry. It was 1:29.

Wilson read Pinnacle Two and passed it to Schoenherr. "This was a little exciting," he recalls. "MIG's overhead. That was *unusual.*" Schoenherr told him to call Fifth Air Force. Wilson asked an enlisted man to contact Fuchu on the secure telephone. Then he stepped into the soundproof booth outside Everett's office and asked for "drop number three hundred." He did not tag his call with a "precedence" (routine, priority, immediate, or flash). "The phone was secure, so I thought there was no need for that," he remembers. "We here at COMNAVFORJAPAN treat all secure calls as priority." Fifth Air Force, however, did not. Wilson didn't know that yet, because neither he nor anyone else had ever rehearsed emergency procedures. He waited for his "contact man" on the operations staff, Lieutenant Colonel James F. Dugan, to come on the line. It was 1:35.

Captain Dwyer returned to the spook locker. Hokenson told him about the crisis and outlined what he'd done. Later, Dwyer would say that "Carl was the best possible person to have on watch in an emergency."

Twenty-nine miles away, at the Naval Security Group station in Kamiseya, Dick Haizlip was sitting at the teletype "talking" to *Pueblo.* If he had followed standard procedures, he would have placed Bailey's informal remarks in the "operator's chatter box" where no one would have seen them. But Haizlip saw their importance immediately and alerted his boss, Captain James W. (Bill) Pearson. Now Pearson told his CT's to readdress Pinnacle Two as a "critic" and shoot it to Washington. Two minutes later he asked them to handle Pinnacle One in the same manner. It was 1:38.

For the past few minutes Captain Pease had been trying to locate Admiral Johnson in Tokyo. "We were very security conscious," he remembers. "We had to talk in riddles. I didn't want to say too much because the operator might be listening."

At 1:45 Johnson picked up a telephone in the lobby of the Sanno Hotel.

"Looks like *Pueblo*'s had the course," Pease began. "She may be gone."

Johnson didn't understand what Pease was talking about. He asked if *Pueblo* was experiencing mechanical difficulties.

"I tried to imply the trouble was a lot more serious," Pease recalls. "I said, 'She may even be beyond our ability to get her back.'

"He asked if I had alerted SAR [Sea-Air Rescue] units. He was still thinking in terms of operational hazards at sea, like engine failures."

Pease replied that SAR would not be useful in this situation, that

Fifth Air Force had been alerted, that Johnson ought to return to Yokosuka as soon as possible.

Johnson asked Pease to have a Navy helicopter meet him at Hardy Barracks.

The Navy said no choppers were available. The Army at Camp Zama said it might be able to provide one in about an hour.

Captain Everett and Commander Schoenherr had rolled back the curtains on the front wall of the command cave and were trying to pinpoint *Pueblo*'s position on a huge map of the Sea of Japan. Al Wilson was watching them from the door of the soundproof booth on the second deck. He had been standing there with the secure phone in his hand for the past twenty minutes. Lieutenant Colonel Dugan was not in the office. His assistant, Major Raymond A. Priest, Jr., was on the line. And Wilson was not getting through to Priest.

In order to speak over a secure phone both parties must "synchronize" at the same time, must read from a sequence of numbers on authentication cards. The process should require no more than five or ten minutes. But if one party is using the wrong codes, reading the wrong numbers, it can take forever. And this was what was happening now. Over and over Wilson said, "Count ten and go secure on my count. . . ." It didn't work.

Finally, at about 1:53—because this wasn't a "precedence" call, it wasn't entered in the log; no one is sure of the exact moment—both officers "synchronized" simultaneously.

"*Pueblo*," Wilson began, "Ichthyic One. . . ."

But Priest had never heard of *Pueblo*. He wasn't cleared to know. And "Ichthyic" meant nothing to him. "Please repeat," he said.

"Formerly Clickbeetle," Wilson said.

Priest thought he had heard Lieutenant Colonel Dugan use that term referring to USS *Banner, Pueblo*'s sister ship.

"Go ahead," he said.

Wilson explained that he'd received a call from *Pueblo*. She was under attack. He gave the time and the ship's position and said he was requesting assistance.

Priest asked Wilson to repeat the time and the coordinates. Wilson did. "That's all," he said.

"That sounds great," Priest said. "I'll take care of it."

As a former exercise director for the Air Force in South Korea, Priest was thoroughly familiar with this sort of mock crisis. The Air Force ran such tests continually. Still, he thought the Navy was overdoing it this time. He set out down the hall from the command center to find someone who could tell him what this was all about.

Commander Thomas E. McDonald was the Navy's chief liaison officer at Fuchu. An affable, sandy-haired Annapolis graduate with an MA in aerospace operations management, he was responsible for keeping Fifth Air Force officials informed of Navy operations as well as for alerting COMSEVENTHFLT and COMNAVFORJAPAN to Air Force intentions. At 1:55 that afternoon he was winding up a routine meeting in Room 217 of the headquarters building. He decided to contact COMNAVFORJAPAN about something which had come up during the meeting and placed a call to the spook locker on an insecure phone.

"Gee, Commander," Duane Heisinger said, "I've got a real flap going on. Could you call me back in about an hour?"

"There was tension in his voice," McDonald remembers. "I hung up obsessed with the idea that this was the most unusual reply I'd ever gotten on the phone. I rushed out of the office and across the hall to Room 218, our intelligence center, to find out if some big disaster was going on. I didn't know what it could be."

"Hey, Tom."

McDonald turned and saw Ray Priest coming down the hall, stepping quickly despite his injured leg. "He'd scribbled some notes from his phone call with Wilson on a piece of paper," McDonald recalls. "He handed them to me and said, 'Hey, does this mean anything to you? Boy, you guys really play for keeps in an exercise.'

"I saw the words 'Pueblo,' 'North Koreans,' 'boarding,' and 'request assistance.' I knew immediately what the problem was at COMNAVFORJAPAN, what the problem was, period." McDonald rushed to find the director of operations. It was 1:58.

8

Monday, January 22, had not been a very good day for Pentagon public relations. The Air Force—oops!—had lost four H-bombs off the coast of Greenland. The U.S. Command in Saigon said that a recent patrol action inside Cambodia was "inadvertent." At beleaguered Khe Sanh the Marines were pulling back, and on the Senate floor Arkansas Senator John McClellan delivered a scorching attack on the Navy's controversial TFX fighter plane.

Shortly before midnight EST the first of the *Pueblo* critics arrived at the Defense Intelligence Agency Signal Office (DIASO) in Room 1D884 at the Pentagon. A clerk relayed it to the National Military Command Center (NMCC) in Room 2D901A. A watch officer there contacted Brigadier General Ralph D. Steakley, chief of the Joint Reconnaissance Center. Steakley called the director of the Joint Staff, Vice Admiral Nels C. Johnson. At 12:03 he telephoned General Earle G. Wheeler, the chairman of the Joint Chiefs of Staff. Twenty minutes later he notified Robert S. McNamara, the Secretary of Defense. McNamara remembers that the message was "confused."

Almost simultaneously, the critic arrived at the communications center on the fifth floor of the State Department. There a computer decrypted it and flashed it on a TV screen. An analyst pressed a button, sending it up by the SCAT system to the Operations Center in Room 7516. The officer in charge of the evening watch, a husky, bushy-browed man named Richard W. Finch, had been on duty during the flap over the Blue House raid thirty-six hours before; he remembers feeling thankful that "things had calmed down somewhat." This watch, in fact, had been "fairly ordinary," and in another hour or so he would hop into his white Saab and drive home to Reston, Virginia.

"Hey, we got something hot here." Finch looked up as a military liaison officer, Commander Richard Thomas, began tearing something from the teleprinter. Finch noted the words "critic" and "*Pueblo*," but everything else seemed confused. He needed the time and location. "When you get these things in messages," he says, "they don't always make sense. All you may know is that it's east of Eden and north of Shangri-La." Finch asked Thomas to get more details from the NMCC. Then he picked up a scrambler phone. The Under Secretary of State, Nicholas deB. Katzenbach, should know about this immediately. So should the Secretary, Dean Rusk. In the next hour he'd have to place nearly fifty calls.

Inside the Situation Room in the White House basement, a stocky, twenty-four-year-old watch officer from Hackensack, New Jersey, named Andrew J. (Bud) Denner was sitting at his austere desk, his back to the three small TV sets which perched on a shelf against the far wall. In the days to come Denner would hand-carry so many messages to the Cabinet Room and the Mansion that President Johnson would tell him, only half jokingly, to "get yourself a pair of roller skates." But at this moment, just before midnight, he had no inkling of what lay ahead.

Then he heard a metallic "thunk"; he reached to his right and pulled a message from the pneumatic tube. "CRITIC CRITIC CRITIC" danced across its top; the message itself contained only one line. The time and location were garbled. "All we got out of it was the name of the ship, *Pueblo*," Denner remembers. "Normally, if there's a garble on a critic, you'll get a follow-up in one or two minutes. It didn't happen in this case."

The chief of the watch, thirty-three-year-old Jim Brown, began placing telephone calls—to Arthur J. McCafferty, the director of the Situation Room; to George E. Christian, the President's press secretary; to Walt W. Rostow, the President's adviser for national security affairs. Denner tried to "check out what type of ship this was." At first he didn't have much luck. "I couldn't find any people in the Pentagon," he says, "who'd ever heard of *Pueblo*."

9

For the past several minutes *Pueblo* had been following the North Koreans toward the port of Wonsan. The S01 was traveling at 15 knots and soon moved out ahead about 3,000 yards. The P-4's, however, were staying close, veering to within 20 yards in their porpoiselike maneuvers. Now the P-4 on *Pueblo*'s port bow drew back on her beam. Its officers signaled Bucher to increase his speed.

Bucher decided to stay at one-third. "I continued to ignore their requests," he says, "and indicated by waving my hands and shrugging my shoulders that it was not possible. [I was] yelling something unintelligible which I knew they couldn't understand, and I continued to yell that sort of gibberish."

Inside the crypto room Don Bailey was kneeling by the teletype reading the traffic from Kamiseya: "COMNAVFORJAPAN IS REQUESTING ASSIT. WHAT KEY LIST DO YOU HAVE LEFT?" And then a few seconds later: "LAST WE GOT FROM YOU WAS, 'ARE YOU SENDING ASSIT?' PLEASE ADVISE WHAT KEY LIST YOU HAVE LEFT AND IF IT APPEARS THAT YOUR COMM SPACES WILL BE ENTERED?"

Bailey couldn't reply immediately. The smoke was swirling around him, stinging his eyes and making him choke.

Tuck was erasing the ship's positions off the "A" sheets he'd maintained for his Nansen casts. He stopped by the CPO quarters and saw that Iredale was tearing the bathythermograph records into little pieces. He mentioned this to Bucher. Schumacher had sent Crandell to the forward electronics space, told him to open the file cabinet and burn all the classified paper in a wastepaper basket. Now Schumacher said that all the radio publications had been destroyed; he was going below. Lacy reported that repair parties two and five had broken out their gear and were awaiting further instructions. The ship still hadn't suffered any flooding or serious matériel damage; the only fires on board had been started by the men themselves.

In the ship's office on the hold deck "Army" Canales was having an impossible time. Although he retained a few "secret" papers, most of his files were marked "confidential." Among them were the crew's service records. They were low priority; he would worry about them later. He started fires in three trash cans and tried to get rid of his bulkier publications first. Smoke enveloped him in seconds. "I burned my hands stoking that stuff around," he says. "I had to go topside to get some air."

In the research spaces Frank Ginther was demolishing equipment with a sledgehammer. He swung the hammer so many times that his arms felt numb; he passed the hammer to Brad Crowe. Crowe used it for a while and gave it to someone else. Then he ripped pages from publications and handed them to Peter Langenberg.

The trash-can fires in the passageway outside weren't consuming these pages fast enough. Steve Harris realized he might have to jettison some of his material over the side after all. He didn't have a sufficient number of weighted bags. He told Langenberg to go forward and bring back some laundry bags. They were filled with dirty clothes. Langenberg emptied ten of them and left them outside the door to the spaces.

Peppard and McClintock began stuffing their publications into one of the bags. Then they had a better idea. Why not dump all this material in one big pile on the deck and set fire to it? They could use an extinguisher to keep the blaze from racing out of control. It seemed a lot safer to do this than toss the bag overboard and risk getting shot by the P-4's. But Harris vetoed the plan. He wasn't sure he could control the fire; he felt it might create unnecessary confusion, endanger the ship's electrical system, and pose an additional hazard to the crew. He didn't report this to Bucher. He wasn't sure where Bucher was and didn't have time to search for him.

Bucher at that moment was standing in the pilot house. The lack of communications with the research spaces was beginning to worry him. Did silence mean that the CT's were succeeding in their destruction efforts? Or did it mean that they were encountering serious problems? He had to make sure that Harris and his men completed the process before the North Koreans boarded the ship. He would inspect the spaces himself. He'd need more time. Perhaps he could feign some sort of mechanical difficulty. He picked up the microphone for the 1MC. "All stop," he ordered. It was almost two o'clock.

The S01 spun around in a swirl of foam and raced back toward the ship. The P-4's opened out to 100 yards.

In the research spaces Kell gave Hammond a pile of encoding plates and told him to throw them over the side from the CPO quarters. Hammond opened the porthole and tossed out six of the plates. Bullets smacked into the side of the ship only inches away. The North Koreans were firing at *him*. He picked up the rest of the plates and carried them back to the spaces.

Schumacher was trying to burn some publications in the starboard passageway. Just a few feet behind him Hodges was feeding another fire. Woelk, Crandell, and Chicca were passing him papers. The passageway was crowded and filled with smoke. Schumacher lifted his trash can and moved around the corner.

Ba-rooom, Ba-rooom, Ba-roooom. . . .

Pueblo shuddered under the impact of the S01's fire. One shell struck forward by the laundry. A second hit the mainmast and showered debris on the deck. A third exploded inside the starboard passageway, splattering blood and pieces of flesh on the bulkheads and deck.

"Corpsman! Corpsman!" someone yelled for Baldridge.

Duane Hodges' right leg and abdomen were a tangle of red pulp. Woelk stumbled, then fell to his knees and crawled toward the wardroom. Shrapnel had entered his chest and groin. Chicca staggered back to the galley, bleeding profusely from the thigh. Crandell sprawled across the passageway. Shards of hot metal had knifed into his legs; he couldn't walk. In falling he'd smashed his hand against the bulkhead; the slim gold band that his wife had given him for a Christmas present flew off his finger. Almost delirious with pain, he started screaming, "I've lost my wedding ring, I've lost my wedding ring."

Ba-roooom, Ba-roooom, Ba-roooom. . . .

Schumacher got to his feet, picked up some publications, and tossed them into the trash-can fire. They were soaked with blood and would not burn.

In the pilot house Bucher received word that one man had been injured critically. "All ahead one-third," he said. *Pueblo* turned and began to follow the North Koreans again.

The firing stopped. Bucher started below. The registered publications locker was open. So was the door to the electronics space. Don Peppard was burning publications in a wastepaper basket. Smoke was billowing out through a porthole. Bucher continued.

In the galley Ralph Reed and several other men had been burning classified material. Now they placed a pressure bandage on Chicca's wound, wrapped it in handkerchiefs and torn skivvy shorts, and treated him for shock. Reed went forward to get some stretchers. Wright, Schumacher, and Law carried Chicca into Murphy's stateroom. They dropped a blanket over him and elevated his legs.

Reed returned with the stretchers. He and Baldridge lifted Woelk to a table in the wardroom, applied a battle dressing, and gave him a morphine surrette.

"For God's sake, help this man. He's dying."

Baldridge heard the captain shout. He turned and saw two sailors carrying Hodges down the passageway. He and Reed placed Hodges on a stretcher. His right femur was gone; intestines protruded from his lower abdomen. Baldridge shot a unit of Dextran into a vein in his left arm. Then he used Eperneperan. Hodges' pulse was weak. His respiration was shallow and gasping.

"Can you amputate that leg?"

"No, sir," Baldridge said. That would only increase the bleeding and hasten Hodges' death. "But I'll need some more morphine."

Bucher told him to ask Murphy to open the narcotics locker. Then he stepped toward the research spaces.

A cannon shell had smashed a hole in the small arms locker near his stateroom. Smoking trash cans and blood-soaked publications clogged the passageway. Crandell was propped up against a bulkhead, moaning softly now. "There's wounded here," Bucher screamed. "Someone get a corpsman."

Lewis and Bussell carried Crandell into the forward berthing compartment. Maggard was standing there bandaging Langenberg, who had been wounded in the neck.

Scarborough passed by Murphy's stateroom and saw the executive officer reach in his safe for morphine surrettes. "There was a look of complete bewilderment on his face," Scarborough recalls.

Murphy gave the surrettes to Baldridge and tried to comfort Hodges. The sailor's bleeding had stopped; he was in no apparent pain. Murphy realized he would die soon. There was nothing anyone could do about that. He climbed to the 0-1 level and spotted some pages from secret publications lying on the deck. He threw them over the side. Then he crept toward the pilot house. One of the P-4's opened fire again. He hugged the deck.

The trash-can fires had warped the bulkhead separating the passageway outside the research spaces from the CPO quarters. The paint was peeling and blistering; the fires were spreading from the cans onto the deck itself. The CT's couldn't see what they were doing. The smoke hindered their breathing.

Kell thought he heard an order to stop the burning. He couldn't "pin down where it came from" but felt sure it stemmed "from competent authority." He relayed the word to his men. They stomped on some of the fires and let others die out. Then they went inside the spaces and continued to rip pages from publications. Machine-gun fire rattled against the side of the ship. They dropped to the deck.

The door to the spaces was closed. Bucher stared at the five little buttons. He couldn't remember the combination for the locking system. He shouted and pounded on the door. Someone opened it. He stepped inside. No one was moving.

"Get the hell off that deck," Bucher screamed. "Let's get going. Destroy that gear."

Then Bucher noticed "at least three large naval mattresses six feet by three feet" full of classified documents.

Harris was standing by the entrance to the crypto room.

"Let's get this stuff outta here," Bucher said.

Harris replied that most of the crypto material had already been destroyed. Stacks of papers had been burned. The rest would be stuffed in bags and thrown over the side.

Bucher told him to hurry.

The CT's were back on their feet, swinging sledgehammers and fire axes. A piece of equipment in the corner had been thoroughly demolished. One crypto machine to the left of the door had been bashed apart, its contents reduced to powder. In another twenty minutes the destruction would be complete. "I felt we had plenty of time," Bucher says, "as we were still some distance from land and I did not know when or if they were even going to board us."

Now he stepped into the crypto room and looked over Don Bailey's shoulder. Kamiseya was requesting more information. He dictated slowly:

HAVE O KEYLIST AND THIS ONLY ONE HAVE, HAVE BEEN REQUESTED TO FOLLOW INTO WONSAN, HAVE THREE WOUNDED AND ONE MAN WITH LEG BLOWN OFF, HAVE NOT USED ANY WEAPONS NOR UNCOVERED 50 CAL. MAC. DESTROYING ALL KEY LISTS AND AS MUCH ELEC EQUIPT. AS POSSIBLE. HOW ABOUT SOME HELP, THESE GUYS MEAN BUSINESS. HAVE SUSTAINED SMALL WOUND IN RECTUM, DO NOT INTEND TO OFFER ANY RESISTANCE. INTERROGATIVE QSL, INTERROGATIVE QSL. DO NOT KNOW HOW LONG WILL BE ABLE TO HOLD UP CIRCUIT AND DO NOT KNOW IF COMM SPACES WILL BE ENTERED.

Two minutes later, at 2:07, Kamiseya replied:

ROGER, ROGER. WE DOING ALL WE CAN. CAPT HERE AND CNFJ ON HOT LINE. LAST I GOT WAS AIR FORCE GOING HELP YOU WITH SOME AIR-

CRAFT BUT CAN'T REALLY SAY AS CNFJ COORDINATING WITH I PRESUME KOREA FOR SOME F-105. THIS UNOFFICIAL BUT I THINK THAT WHAT WILL HAPPEN.

"ROGER YOUR LAST, ROGER YOUR LAST," Bailey tapped.

Bucher returned to the spaces and reminded Harris to jettison those bags. Harris said he would. Bucher climbed the ladder. "I was thinking about the destruction," he says, "plus I was somewhat angry at my inability to offer effective resistance or do anything about what was going on." He clenched his teeth and swung his foot at a pipe fitting on the deck. He raised his voice and cursed his fate, screaming out every four-letter word he knew. He kicked a fitting again. Then he entered the pilot house.

Pueblo was steaming at two-thirds.

"Goddammit," Bucher said. He took the conn from Lacy and ordered the speed reduced to one-third.

A P-4 churned alongside; its officers signaled Bucher to go faster. Bucher grabbed a megaphone. "I continued to play dumb," he says, "calling back some unintelligible words to them, shrugging my shoulders and raising my hands in the air."

Bucher told Leach to raise the international code signal for "Request medical assistance." Then he asked Murphy to go below and check on Hodges' condition.

As navigator, Murphy was responsible for the loran record book, the chronometer log, the position and contact logs, the observation sheets, the quartermaster's notebook—for every piece of paper, in fact, which detailed the ship's positions. He could have burned them or thrown them over the side. He decided not to. "I considered [them] to be part of the evidence the U.S. would have [for] any action that was being taken against this harassing incident," he says. "To me, this was an incident; it was my responsibility to keep the record intact."

In the starboard passageway the fires were smoldering and dying. Murphy ordered the men to continue burning. Then he went to his cabin to make sure that all of the classified material there had been removed. Reed was caring for Chicca. Murphy tried to comfort him, then went to find Hodges in the wardroom. Baldridge said he could no longer detect any pulse. Murphy gave him oxygen. It was no use.

The message from Kamiseya clattered over the teletype: "STILL READ YOU QRK FIVER FIVER. GO AHEAD KEEP KW-7 ON THE AIR LONG AS YOU CAN. WE STAYING RIGHT WITH YOU."

Bailey replied: "ROGER, ROGER WILL KEEP THIS UP UNTIL LAST MIN-

UTE WILL STAY UP UNTIL THE LAST MINUTE AND SURE COULD USE SOME HELP NOW."

Kamiseya: "ROGER, ROGER, WE STILL WITH YOU AND DOING ALL WE CAN. EVERYBODY REALLY TURNING TO AND FIGURE BY NOW AIR FORCE GOT SOME BIRDS WINGING YOUR WAY."

Bailey: "ROGER, ROGER, SURE HOPE SO. WE PRETTY BUSY WITH DE-STRUCTION RIGHT NOW. CAN'T SEE FOR THE SMOKE."

Kamiseya: "ROGER, ROGER WISH I COULD HELP MORE. ALL INFO YOU PASS BEING SENT TO AREA COMMANDER AND THEY IN TURN COORDINATING FOR WHATEVER ACTION GOT TO BE TAKEN. SURE PROCESS ALREADY BEING INITIATED FOR SOME IMMEDIATE RELIEF. COMSEVENTHFLT, CNFJ AND NSA GROUP PAC ALL GOT INFO RIGHT AWAY."

Bailey: "ROGER YOUR LAST AND SURE HOPE SOMEBODY DOES SOME-THING. WE ARE HELPLESS AT THIS TIME. CANNOT DO ANYTHING BUT WAIT."

Bucher stepped out on the wing of the signal bridge and saw Schumacher and Hayes at the incinerator. He descended the ladder by the stack, grabbed a publication himself, and tore out its pages. He stuffed them into the fire. Then he returned to the pilot house.

In the research spaces the CT's kept wielding their fire axes and sledgehammers. Harris couldn't believe his eyes. "I saw those guys mashing up this great equipment, and I said, 'Why, why?'" he recalls. "Axes going into the guts of that precision equipment—it was hide-ous."

Despite his wound, Langenberg had tossed some electronic gear out of a porthole in the CPO quarters, then heaved a bag of classified documents over the rail on the 0-1 level. But this was the only bag that had left the spaces thus far. The others remained inside. Harris realized that jettisoning all of them would be difficult. Anyone who stepped out onto the weather deck ran the risk of attracting fire. Now he telephoned Bucher in the pilot house. He said he had disposed of most of his material, but he might not be able to get rid of everything. He wanted Bucher's permission to notify Japan.

Bucher felt sure that all the bags he'd seen below had already gone over the side. "I didn't go into any detail," he says, "but I asked him if this included crypto material. He said no. This was material of his own of a technical nature—the pubs and manuals the CT's needed in their work. I said send the message."

Kamiseya: "WHO I GOT THAT END OF CIRCUIT? WHAT STATUS OF CLASSIFIED MATERIAL LEFT TO DESTROY?"

Bailey replied: "WE HAVE THE KW-7 AND SOME CARDS IN THE 37 AND 14 TO SMASH. I THINK THAT'S JUST ABOUT IT."

Kamiseya: "CNFJ ADVISED 5TH AIR FORCE ALERTED REPEAT CNFJ AD-
VISED 5TH AIR FORCE ALERTED."

Bailey was sure American jets would arrive at any moment. He
shouted for Steve Harris. It was 2:20.

Lacy told Bucher that the repair parties still reported no damage
below the water line, no fires except for those the men had started
themselves.

Bucher asked him again if the ship could be scuttled.

Lacy shook his head. "Not quickly," he said. To be sure, he could
remove the gaskets from the cooling pipes that led to the engines. But
it would take time to flood the engine room, and there was just no
way to funnel that water into other compartments. He could disable
the engines easily enough. Cut the lube oil lines, and the bearings
would burn out in 20 minutes. But what would that accomplish?
Pueblo would need her mobility once help arrived.

Bucher agreed with him. "The information I received was that
there would be aircraft very shortly," he says. "I didn't want to disable my ship. I didn't want to disable my engines."

One of the P-4's pulled alongside. Its signalman hoisted a familiar
command: "Oscar, Lima. . . . " Bucher recognized the flags: "Heave
to. . . ."

"All stop," he ordered.

In the engine room Scarborough said, "Well, I think we all better
have a cigarette. It may be the last one we'll get." No one had any
cigarettes left. Strickland remembered the pack he'd placed in his
sleeve hours before and passed it around. Then he remembered something else. He reached into his right hip pocket and pulled out his
St. Christopher medal.

On the mess deck Fireman John A. Mitchell began pouring water
into the frying pan that he'd been using to burn Larry Mack's negatives. Visions of Communist prison camps raced through his mind.
Still, he was convinced that "someone would come to help us in
time—just like in the movies." Michael Barrett didn't agree. He tore the
rate from his uniform. The North Koreans would shoot him, he
thought, the moment they learned he was a CT.

Charles Law stepped below to put on his wool socks and thermal
underwear. He realized the North Koreans were about to board the
ship; he tried to joke about it. "These people better let me go by
the seventh of February," he said, "or my girl's gonna get mad back in
Yokosuka." Then Law saw Murphy on the john. "He was just sittin'
there staring blankly." Steve Harris saw him, too, and remembers that
his pants were pulled up. Murphy had torn some classified papers into

little pieces and tried to flush them down the toilet. He had pressed
the handle. Nothing had happened. He had forgotten that the pump
cut off at general quarters.

Kamiseya: ". . . CAN YOU PROVIDE CURRENT SITREP INCLUDING IN-
TENTIONS KORCOMS IF POSSIBLE, DAMAGE AND INJURIES SUSTAINED?"

Bailey: "ROGER AND DESTRUCTION OF PUBS HAVE BEEN INEFFECTIVE.
SUSPECT SEVERAL WILL BE COMPROMISED."

Bucher watched the P-4 approach on his port bow. A boarding
party—two officers and ten enlisted men—crouched on its deck. Bucher
didn't consider using his small arms. His men might shoot "four or
five" North Koreans, but the P-4 would veer away and the S01 would
move in for the kill. Resistance now wouldn't have "any real effect
on the outcome of the engagement." Besides, "I did think that once
they found out we were an American ship, not a South Korean ship,
they just might leave the ship, go."

He shouted over the 1MC, "BM1 Klepac, lay forward to assist the
boarders."

Norbert Klepac asked Willie Bussell to help him. "I'll go with
you," Harry Lewis said. They moved toward the well deck.

Lacy asked Bucher if he wanted to remind the crew about the
Code of Conduct, instruct them to give only their names, rates, and
service numbers. Bucher nodded and told him to do it.

Kamiseya: "CAN YOU GIVE ME A LIST OF WHAT YOU HAVEN'T DE-
STROYED? CAN YOU GIVE ME A LIST OF WHAT YOU HAVEN'T DESTROYED?"

Bailey: "HAVE BEEN DIRECTED TO COME TO ALL STOP AND BEING
BOARDED AT THIS TIME. BEING BOARDED AT THIS TIME."

Suddenly Bucher remembered he was wearing a ski cap. He ran
to his cabin to find his Navy hat with the gold braid on its visor. He
put on some long-handled drawers and boots and wrapped a pair of
black socks around his bleeding ankle. Then he saw Murphy and
asked, "How's Hodges?"

"He's resting," Murphy said.

"How did the rest of the destruction go?"

"Real good, I think."

Murphy left. Schumacher came down to get his hat and foul-
weather jacket. Bucher started back toward the bridge.

Stu Russell and Richard Arnold were standing in the auxiliary
engine room on the hold deck. The generator engines were running,
and for a long time they didn't know that the ship had stopped. Russell
had a sudden urge to get out of there. He climbed the ladder. "Down
below, it had been all nice and clean and white and metal polished,"
he says. "The difference in the air pressure pushed all the smoke and

burning paper down the hatch as we came out. And it was real dark up there. I thought that was the end of the ball game. They were going to zap us."

Harris ordered everyone out of the research spaces. The men filed out slowly. McClintock finished stuffing maps and publications into a large, tubular bag and left it by the door. He noticed five little fires still burning along the passageway. He stopped at the mess decks long enough to plop a piece of hard candy into his mouth. Then he followed the others.

Kamiseya: "ROGER YOUR LAST. IT ON WAY TO CNFJ."

Bailey: "4 MEN INJURED AND 1 CRITICALLY, AND AM GOING OFF THE AIR NOW AND DESTROYING THIS GEAR."

Kamiseya: "ROGER, GO AHEAD. CAN YOU TRANSMIT IN THE CLEAR? CAN YOU TRANSMIT IN THE CLEAR?"

But Bailey was already out the door.

One man, Ralph Bouden, still remained in the crypto room. He demolished a piece of equipment, then stepped through the research spaces and into the passageway. Publications still clogged the deck. They were so deep in places, he says, that "you almost had to wade through" them.

Bucher expected the North Koreans to come alongside the well deck forward. But the P-4 was drifting back to the port quarter. He wondered what would happen if the Air Force appeared. Or was it already too late for that?

The P-4 swung too far out and missed on its first approach. Now it made a second try. Klepac didn't want to receive the line. He knew he had no choice. The P-4 bobbed closer. The men on its deck were aiming their AK-47's at him. He caught the line. He and Bussell and Lewis pulled. He ran the line through a chock and slipped it over a metal bit. It was 2:32.

On the wing of the signal bridge Lee Hayes reached in his wallet and threw everything over the side except his ID card. Then he looked at Bucher. "Oh, God," he heard the captain say. "Oh, God, what do we do now?"

★ ★ ★ PART TWO

10

In the spring of 1965 the Assistant Secretary of Defense (Deputy Director of Defense Research and Engineering) was a wiry, bespectacled, bushy-haired physicist named Dr. Eugene G. Fubini. Then fifty-one, Fubini had taken his doctorate in Rome, come to the United States in 1939, and spent the postwar years working for CBS and Airborne Instruments, Inc. By 1961, when President John F. Kennedy asked him to come to the Pentagon, he was acknowledged to be one of the nation's leading authorities on electronics espionage.

For a man of Fubini's caliber a government job almost always necessitates a financial sacrifice, and in his case—with a wife and six children to support—the income slash was meaningful. Nonetheless, he accepted the post and moved into Room 3E 1014. He had enormous power. The director of the National Security Agency, Lieutenant General Marshall S. Carter, reported directly to him, and he in turn reported directly to the Secretary of Defense, Robert S. McNamara. He used that power judiciously, and after a while it was clear to everyone that his unconventional dress and excitable manner belied both a capacity for hard work and a mind like a vacuum cleaner. Throughout the Pentagon he became known as "Fub-Scrub—the czar of intelligence collection." Hardly anyone on USS *Pueblo* had ever heard of Gene Fubini. Yet he, more than anyone else, was responsible for sending that ship toward her fateful rendezvous.

Ever since 1961, Fubini had become increasingly concerned about the capabilities and intentions of the Soviet fleet. Clearly, the Soviets had decided to challenge U.S. supremacy, not only in the Mediterranean but in the Pacific, as well. Their shipbuilding program, already far more ambitious than the U.S. Navy's, was accelerating rapidly. And even more worrisome—the Soviets were dispatching dozens of "fishing trawlers" (AGI's) complete with radomes, direction-finding antennae, and communications whips to positions off Norfolk, San Diego, Cape Kennedy, Guam, and the nuclear submarine base at Holy Loch, Scotland.

"Their trawlers were following our fleet," Fubini recalls, "bothering us, listening to us, copying everything we said. They knew our tactics and the technical parameters of our equipment. They probably knew more about our equipment than we did. So I began to wonder: Why can't we take a leaf from their book? Why can't we do the same thing? If we could mingle with them, we'd know what they were up to."

To be sure, the United States had long been utilizing combat ships to gather intelligence off foreign shores. Destroyers and destroyer escorts often carried mobile vans bristling with antennae, as well as special detachments to operate the equipment. (The destroyers *Maddox* and *Turner Joy* were cruising on one of these "DeSoto patrols" in the Gulf of Tonkin in 1964 when they were allegedly attacked by "enemy" torpedo boats, thus precipitating the first U.S. bombing of North Vietnam.) And the program had achieved results.

But as technology advanced, the amount of equipment these ships were asked to carry increased significantly. So did the number of personnel needed to operate it. Naval intelligence kept pressing for more special units to embark in more and more ships.

The Navy hierarchy decided this had to stop. The intelligence people would just have to find some other platform. These "spook" activities plainly degraded a fighting ship's capabilities. Furthermore, withdrawing a destroyer from its normal rounds and sending it to eavesdrop off a foreign coast was provocative. It provided limited coverage at a very high price. It was hardly cost-effective. And in Robert McNamara's Pentagon, cost-effectiveness was the password.

One possible alternative was to use the Auxiliary General Technical Research ships—the AGTR's: *Oxford, Jamestown, Georgetown, Belmont, Liberty, Muller,* and *Valdez*—converted Victory and Liberty class vessels of Second World War vintage. They were noncombatants, they were large enough to carry ample equipment and personnel, and they were efficient; signals detected by one of these ships in 1962 prompted the aerial surveillance of Cuba which disclosed the presence of Soviet missiles.

But AGTR's were also frightfully expensive to build and maintain. Even more significant, they were—in the argot of the Pentagon— "responsive to national tasking"; they performed their chores primarily for the National Security Agency and seldom collected intelligence against the Navy's "targets."

The Chief of Naval Operations in the spring of 1965 was a soft-spoken, Georgia-born aviator named Admiral David L. McDonald. McDonald didn't particularly like Washington, and he hadn't wanted the job. Yet he was ideally suited for it. He was a diplomat in a blue suit, the kind of man who could navigate the Navy's needs through Congressional rocks and shoals; friends marveled that he could charm a rattlesnake even while cutting off its head. Eighteen months before, as commander of the U.S. Sixth Fleet in the Mediterranean, McDonald had become concerned about the Soviet AGI's mingling so freely among his ships; and now, as he listened to Gene Fubini, he agreed that something had to be done about it.

On April 20, at a Pentagon luncheon, he and Fubini broached the problem to several senior colleagues. Among them were Rear Admiral Frederick J. Harlfinger II, a stocky, balding submariner, a former Naval Academy boxer who was then Assistant Director for Collection at the Defense Intelligence Agency; and Vice Admiral Rufus L. Taylor, a tight-lipped South Carolinian who was then Director of Naval Intelligence.

The prospects they faced were depressing. They could no longer afford to degrade combatant ships. Nor could they use the AGTR's. The flood of Specific Intelligence Collection Requirements—SICR's— was increasing so rapidly that the existing AGTR's were having trouble keeping pace with their national tasking assignments. They couldn't be sidetracked to handle Navy requests. And building a flock of additional AGTR's would cost too much money.

One obvious answer was to build a trawler fleet and equip it the same way the Soviets did. But the Navy didn't have funds to build the *combat* ships it needed; how could McDonald ever justify spending money on trawlers? The best solution was to drag a few ships out of mothballs and convert them especially for this operation. This way, and at a very small cost indeed, they could at least test the concept: Assign these ships to tactical missions, begin collecting intelligence against purely Naval targets, and monitor the activities of the Soviet fleet without having to rely anymore on handouts from the NSA.

A few days after the luncheon McDonald asked Taylor and Harlfinger to join three other men—Vice Admiral J. B. Colwell, the Deputy Chief of Naval Operations for Fleet Operations and Readiness; Rear Admiral Bernard F. Roeder, the Director of Naval Communications; and Captain Ralph Cook, director of the hush-hush Naval Security Group—to study the feasibility of launching a new intelligence collection program. Within six weeks he had their recommendations. The Navy should proceed with a three-phase effort.

Phase one called for a single, unarmed ship to operate in the Western Pacific, phase two for two additional ships to steam around in the same area. Once these vessels proved themselves, the Navy could expand the program, building a flock of new ships and deploying them around the world to provide continuous coverage in areas where American ships seldom operate. Fubini endorsed the concept. So did his immediate boss, Dr. Harold Brown, the Director of Defense Research and Engineering. So did Cyrus R. Vance, the Deputy Secretary of Defense.

Some aspects of this proposal, however, bothered Admiral McDonald. "We all said, 'Now wait a minute, fellas,'" he recalls. " 'Good God, are we gonna have a Navy ship that doesn't carry any guns?' I'd wake up in the middle of the night and see a Red Chinese or Russian sub letting them have it. So I thought as long as we weren't going to arm them, wouldn't it be better not to commission them as *Navy* ships? But there was a question of how and under whose orders these ships would operate. If you let the CIA have them, they'd run them into Wonsan at night. What we were talking about were Navy ships that *really weren't* Navy ships. Maybe we should have said we don't agree. But if I'd done that, they would have laughed me out of the Pentagon.

"Really, this was sort of a minor ship, you know—the nearest thing you could get to a fishing boat. It was just supposed to pick up radar intercepts and stay in international waters. That way, it wouldn't have a chance to run aground. Maybe I was short-sighted, but with all the other things we had to worry about in 1964 and 1965, this was pretty low on the totem pole. I remember feeling, 'Well, okay, let's get two or three of these damn spitkits, then wait and see how they're paying out before we go for the whole program.' "

Even though he agreed with the basic concept, Admiral Roeder shared McDonald's misgivings. "I thought it was sort of a crummy way to do the job," he recalls. "Earlier, we'd built the AGTR's, and in my opinion, that was the way to do it—not with these little buckets. It didn't look like a good idea to me. I told them so, but I didn't seem to carry the day."

Roeder didn't press the point. He was due to leave the Pentagon soon, anyway, and he could see that the main thrust for the program was coming from the Office of the Secretary of Defense—more specifically, from Gene Fubini's shop. It wouldn't be wise to argue with Gene Fubini.

Fubini at the time had problems of his own. He had wanted the first two phases to consist of thirty ships. The budget people had slashed that request to three. He had wanted forty *new* ships in phase three; he would receive only a dozen, fifteen at most. He had urged the Navy to use converted tuna boats. They cost only $1,000,000 each, and they had fine power plants. Officials at the Naval Ships Systems Command disagreed. Tuna boats, they insisted, were too light and too small. They couldn't carry enough electronic equipment, and it would cost too much to reconfigure them. The Navy seemed to be leaning toward AKL's, old cargo ships of the type made famous in *Mr. Roberts*. And it was true—they *were* economical. Fubini thought of them as garbage scows. But there was little he could or should do. His business was to define the concept, then supply the options to the individual services. They had to manage the program themselves.

For the past several months technicians from the Naval Security Station at 3801 Nebraska Avenue, N.W., in Washington, D.C., had been coordinating with other specialists at NSA and in the REWSON (Reconnaissance, Electronics Warfare, Special Operations, Naval intelligence processing system) section at the Naval Ships Systems Command, and they had pretty well determined the types and amounts of equipment these new ships would carry. Now all that remained was the job of selecting an appropriate hull.

Admiral Horacio (Rivets) Rivero, Jr., the aggressive 5-foot, 2-inch Vice Chief of Naval Operations, kept pressing the DCNO for Fleet Operations and Readiness, Vice Admiral John B. Colwell, to make a decision. So Colwell turned to a senior captain on his staff, John M. Oseth, gave him a pile of documents, and said, in effect, "Take over the sparking of this thing."

Oseth had several strikes against him already. So highly classified was the project that he wasn't told what type of mission these ships would undertake. He knew they were to receive "special equipment"— and that was all he knew. He wasn't privy to details about the equipment's size or weight or means of operation. And even worse, he had almost no money to spend.

He looked at tuna boats. He thought about fleet tugs. He even considered some old destroyer escorts from the reserve fleet. All of them had liabilities. Eventually, reluctantly, he settled on AKL's—but only as "the least unsuitable hulls that could be made immediately available."

Then Oseth heard about USS *Banner*. For as long as anyone could remember, *Banner* had been steaming about in the Marianas— ferrying coconuts, pigs, and pregnant women from Boredom to

Tedium and then back again. Now she was sailing toward the United States and retirement in the mothball fleet. Her skipper, a lean, olive-complexioned lieutenant from South Carolina named Robert P. Bishop, longed for a more challenging assignment. Oseth decided to oblige him. A team of cost estimators intercepted *Banner* at Midway Island. By the time the ship reached Pearl Harbor, they'd concluded that *Banner* would serve very nicely as the first of the new intelligence collectors. A few weeks of fitting out at the Puget Sound Naval Shipyard in Bremerton, Washington, and she'd be ready to sail again. Bishop was delighted. And so was John Oseth.

There wasn't any time to lose. Unless *Banner* left the yard before October, 1965, she wouldn't be able to operate effectively in the Sea of Japan. Winter storms would restrict her movements until the following spring. The Naval Ships Systems Command, NSA, and the Naval Security Group kept the pressure on John Oseth, and he in turn applied that pressure to the shipyard. "The financial people at NSSC somehow came up with the dough," he recalls, "and being a proper supervisor, I didn't ask any questions. I considered Admiral Rivero's stripes to be my own on this project, and I made it clear to the shipyard that this was a matter of the highest national priority."

Banner's conversion cost $1,500,000—excluding the research spaces —and required less than seven weeks. Security precautions were extensive; much of the work was accomplished at night. Technicians from Ling-Temco-Vought's ElectroSystems Division installed the complex electronic gear. Originally, the code name for their effort was Project Field Mouse. Then someone in the Pentagon remembered that "Field Mouse" also denoted an earlier Air Force endeavor which had turned out to be a fiasco. He changed the code name to Project Sod Hut.

Banner's living conditions were abysmal. No ventilation was provided, no air-conditioning. The forward berthing compartment had been a refrigeration space. One sailor found that he couldn't turn over in his bunk without hitting the pipe directly above him. "That ship was literally put together like a plate of hash," Captain Oseth remembers. "There wasn't time for anything else."

Nor was there any time for normal shakedown training. On October 1 *Banner* chugged out of Bremerton and steamed directly toward Yokosuka. She carried a flock of communications technicians and boasted a new motto: "Readiness Through Research." As she pitched and rolled her way across the Pacific, one of the CT's set down his frustrations in iambic pentameter:

We are the men of the *Banner,* and this must be the spot;
Where we were doomed to serve on the ship that God forgot;

We sweat and toil and strain; it's more than a man can stand;
We're not supposed to be convicts; just defenders of our land.

Banner tied up at Yokosuka on October 17. But she couldn't tarry there; she had to leave on her first patrol almost immediately. Its code name was Clickbeetle.

The Soviet Union had long claimed that her territorial waters extended 12 miles from the mouth of Siberia's Cape Povorotny Bay. The United States disputed this claim, holding that it violated the "baseline" concept recognized by international law. What would happen, the Navy wondered, if the United States tested this—if *Banner* sailed to within 4 miles of the mouth of this bay? How would the Russians react?

Banner steamed north to find out. Ice began to accumulate forward and on her superstructure. Soviet destroyers and patrol boats pressed close around her, slashing and veering to within 25 yards, warning her of dangers ahead. Her skipper, Lieutenant Bishop, took this harassment in stride. His foremost concern was the ice. He had no steam hoses, and he knew that if he gathered more ice, *Banner* would capsize. And now a fresh storm was beginning to kick up whitecaps. He radioed COMNAVFORJAPAN headquarters in Yokosuka and said he was planning to withdraw. Hours later he received a reply. "Get your fanny back up there," the message said, in effect. "Don't be intimidated."

The storm had intensified. *Banner* swung around and steamed directly into it. In the next twenty hours she progressed *minus 2 miles*.

As his retirement drew closer, John Oseth handed responsibility for the project to Captain Willard Y. (Dixie) Howell, the burly, graying chief of the Plans and Programs Section of the Operations and Readiness Division. Deputy Secretary of Defense Cyrus Vance had already given a go-ahead on phase two; now it was Howell's job to find and arrange for the conversion of two more AKL's. Hopefully, their hulls would be identical.

"We went through the entire roster of Navy ships," he recalls, "and there were only five of these ships still in existence, mostly in the backwaters somewhere. The Army said it still had some old coastal freighters lying around in mothballs, so we sent a survey team to go on board each one of these ships. It turned out that the ones we owned were absolute wrecks; it would have been cheaper to start over than try to save them. The ones the Army had were in much better shape. It was kind of embarrassing."

The two most seaworthy of these coastal freighters were moored at Charleston, South Carolina, and Rio Vista, California. Howell arranged for their transfer to the Navy, then tried to find out how much money would be available for their conversion. No one would tell him. Howell asked what kinds of missions they would be undertaking. The answers he got were noncommittal. Still, it was obvious to him that these ships were an important new breed; they deserved a new designation. He proposed Auxiliary General Environmental Research—AGER. The Navy deferred a decision.

Thoroughly frustrated, Howell approached his boss, Vice Admiral J. B. Colwell, the DCNO for Fleet Operations and Readiness. "I said I want to get all the way in or all the way out," he recalls, "and the admiral said, 'Dixie, I'll let you know.' That afternoon, he called me up. 'Dixie,' he said, 'you're out.' "

Responsibility for the day-by-day handling of the program shifted again—this time to a young lieutenant commander named Carroll S. (Deke) Jones in the "beachjumpers" (communications deception, psychological warfare, escape and evasion) branch of the Plans and Programs Section. He began drafting requests for funds. Austerity was the name of the game. There would be no extra money to improve living conditions or provide other frills. Fifteen million dollars, he thought, should cover the conversion of both ships very nicely.

Navy comptrollers slashed that request to $11,500,000. Then, in December, 1965, McNamara's budget experts—known in the Pentagon as the "bean counters"—reduced it even further, to $8,600,000.

While Jones worried about his shrinking bank account, the program inched forward inexorably. Across the Potomac from the Pentagon, in a shabby little office at the Munitions Building on Constitution Avenue, a tiny, gray-haired lady named Mrs. Emily Fish picked up a sheaf of documents and read about the Navy's acquisition of these two Army ships. As a senior assistant to the Naval Historian, it was her job to recommend names for all new Navy ships. And the Army had named these vessels so *unimaginatively*: FS-389, FS-344. She wanted names with a more pleasant ring; the names of small cities, perhaps. *Palm Beach*—that sounded appealing enough. So did *Pueblo*. The Secretary of the Navy would have to approve her choices, of course, but after all these years that was just a formality. No one in Washington knew more about these matters than Mrs. Emily Fish.

Lieutenant Rudolph R. Black had been skipper of USS *Tatnuck*, an 850-ton fleet tug, for just three months when, in April, 1966, he received orders to tow *Pueblo* from Rio Vista to Bremerton. This, at least, would give him a change of pace; his normal assignment was to tow ancient hulks loaded with surplus ammunition far out to sea so demolition experts could blow them up properly. As soon as he saw *Pueblo*, however, he wondered if there had been some mistake. Gobs of rust mottled her hull, and it was obvious that she hadn't received any maintenance in years. Furthermore, she had been cannibalized. But Black had served in the Navy since 1947, and he knew better than to question his superiors' wisdom. He placed some running lights on board, attached a towing bridle to the end of a 900-foot anchor chain, and steamed back toward Bremerton. For awhile he had worried about leaks, but *Pueblo* turned out to be an easy tow, and the voyage was uneventful. At noon on April 22 he pulled the ship to within half a mile of the yard and retrieved his cable. Pusher boats took over from there and eased *Pueblo* to Pier 6.

One of the first men to visit *Pueblo* that afternoon was a lean, wrinkled, sixty-three-year-old master quarterman named Jack O. Young. He remembers that "she just didn't seem to be a Navy ship." As he strolled about, he noticed a dead flying fish lying on the deck. He had never seen one before, so he stopped and picked it up by its tail. Just a baby, he thought; only 14 inches long. He wondered how it had gotten there; he wanted to ask someone about it. But the ship was deserted; he was the only man on board.

The ship's conversion began on the morning of July 5. Machinists, riggers, painters, welders, pipefitters, sheet-metal workers, and electricians—members of every trade—swarmed all over *Pueblo,* sandblasting her hull, removing her cargo winches and boom, testing her engines and machinery, examining every inch of cable.

To Rear Admiral Floyd B. Schultz, commandant of the Puget Sound Naval Shipyard, *Pueblo* seemed hardly seaworthy. Her lines were square rather than curved, and he couldn't understand why Washington was making such a fuss about her. His orders were very specific: He was not to make any announcement of *Pueblo*'s arrival or say anything which might attract attention to her. His job was to convert the ship and not ask any questions. Yet he still hadn't received any specific sets of plans. If only those people in Washington would pay as much attention to plans and policy as they did to secrecy.

11

For a somewhat different reason, this seeming lack of plans and policy was also worrying thirty-nine-year-old Lloyd M. (Pete) Bucher. For the past two years Bucher had been serving as assistant operations officer on the staff of Submarine Flotilla Seven (SUBFLOTSEVEN) in Yokosuka. His job, a responsible one indeed, entailed writing specific operating instructions for each of the twelve to fifteen U.S. submarines patrolling the western Pacific. In order to do this effectively he had to know what plans, if any, the United States had for conducting aerial or surface reconnaissance in the areas where he was dispatching these subs.

What bothered him most was the fact that there didn't seem to be any coordination between the SUBFLOTSEVEN staff and the operations people at COMNAVFORJAPAN who were plotting USS *Banner*'s patrols. One of these new intelligence ships was enough to worry about. But now he heard that two more would soon be steaming his way. He mentioned the problem to his boss, Captain Maury A. Horn, and they decided to hash it out with the assistant chief of staff for intelligence at COMNAVFORJAPAN, Captain Thomas L. Dwyer.

In every other respect during this summer of 1966, Bucher was a contented man. He loved Japan and the Japanese, and even if his wife, Rose, didn't share this enthusiasm completely, at least she had, like a good scout, pitched in to help with church and civic activities on the base—serving, for example, as secretary-treasurer of the Yokosuka Little League. Over the years Bucher had made hundreds of friends in the Navy, and hardly a week passed now that one or more of them didn't arrive in Japan to fill this or that billet on this or that submarine. He wanted to meet each one of them at Haneda Airport, of course, and although the drive from "Little America" up to Tokyo was both nerve-wracking and time-consuming, Rose seldom complained about it.

Even better, she seemed to understand his schedule, which was brutal enough. The staff was so small and his responsibilities were so pressing that he was going back to the office after dinner more and more frequently, sometimes remaining at his desk until two or three o'clock in the morning. He couldn't go to a friend's house for dinner without receiving a telephone call sometime during the evening which usually sent him scurrying back to work. He had to miss poker games at the submarine sanctuary; he even had to abandon his membership in the Royal and Disreputable Order of YOCAMS, a group of officers that met on the third Friday of every month for an uninhibited evening of singing and carousing—and this after he'd gone through the YOCAMS' rigmarole of obtaining on a little pink card written promises from his wife and the maid that they would never ask questions about what went on at these gatherings.

But all these sacrifices of time and pleasure would pay off soon enough, for Bucher was due to receive command of a diesel submarine. Hadn't that letter from his detailer at the Bureau of Naval Personnel in Washington indicated as much? Most submarine skipper billets, he knew, were filled by Annapolis men, so this assignment would be an honor indeed. Who would have thought years ago that a boy with such humble origins could ever rise so far so fast?

Bucher was born in Pocatello, Idaho, on September 1, 1927. Within a few weeks he was adopted by William and Mary Bucher. William Bucher had served in World War I and come back to Idaho to open a restaurant. He was a fine chef, but he had a weakness for gambling and—considering the fact that Prohibition was then in full force —a rather injudicious habit of serving mixed drinks to his customers. State officials frowned upon this. William Bucher lost his restaurant.

In 1929 Mary Bucher died of cancer; two-year-old Pete was sent to live with his grandparents on their farm outside Pocatello. The Depression cut through Idaho like a scythe. His grandparents couldn't continue payments on the farm; their mortgage was foreclosed. They piled into a car, their only asset, and drove to Long Beach, California.

His grandmother managed apartments and his grandfather sold Hoover vacuum cleaners, but they still couldn't struggle out of debt. Pete moved into his aunt's home in Glendale and attended first grade there. His aunt sent him back to live with his grandparents. Then his grandfather died. His uncle Howard was seriously ill, and his aunt didn't feel she could help him at all. His grandmother said she could no longer afford to take care of him, either, and sent him back alone by train to Idaho. He was seven years old.

He lived for a year in Idaho Falls, down by the powerhouse, with the other itinerants. "I was the only kid around there," he remembers, "and I learned a lot from those guys. They were expert whittlers and card sharks, nice guys, but sometimes they got drunk and mean. Sometimes they made me sleep outside by the coal bin."

He didn't know what had happened to his father. He didn't go to school. He had no money, no clothes. The Idaho Falls police nabbed him for shoplifting. State welfare officials placed him in an orphanage in Boise. Most of the other boys were Mormons; he was the only "Catlicker," and they teased him about this unmercifully. He tried to run away on several occasions, but he never got very far before the authorities found him and dragged him back.

On Saturdays he worked at the home of a lady named Mrs. Clark, mowing the lawn and trimming the shrubs for the sum of 25 cents. Mrs. Clark served on the orphanage's board of directors; she was a Catholic herself, and the ribbing Pete was receiving because of his religion absolutely infuriated her. She spoke to Father Edward Kelly, the Bishop of Boise, and, on June 28, 1938, Bishop Kelly addressed a letter to St. Joseph's Orphanage in the little town of Culdesac, near the Slickpoo Indian Reservation.

"Dear Mother Cyril," he began, "there is a Catholic boy 10 years old at the Children's Home Finding-Aid Society at Boise who is legally adopted by this institution. The boy has just made his first communion and seems to be very pious. Some of the Catholic leaders of Boise have interested themselves in him. No one can be found to adopt him. Would you accept him and what would be the technicalities for you to adopt him?"

Mother Cyril replied that she would, and on July 18 Miss Nelle Grete, assistant to the superintendent of the Boise orphanage, dispatched another letter to Culdesac: "We are sending Lloyd on the stage leaving here tonight at 3:14. He will arrive in Jacques Spur at 3:54 tomorrow afternoon. . . . We are sending a box of clothing and his personal effects which will be checked through on the stage with him. . . . I hope Lloyd will fit into your institution and that later you may be able to find a good home for him. . . ."

For the first time in his life, Pete Bucher felt safe. There was no one at St. Joseph's to hit him or taunt him. The sisters gave him their love, and he blossomed under their care. Not that he didn't have to work anymore; there were eleven cows to milk twice a day and ears of corn to shuck and traps to bait for the coyotes at night. But there was also time for singing and swimming and playing basketball. He sent away for his Tom Mix ring; he followed the exploits of Buck Rogers and Flash Gordon. He loved to read, and the other children, most of whom were Indians, kept asking him to read aloud to them. He started with the Big Little Books and then progressed to the novels of Robert Louis Stevenson, Willa Cather, Rafael Sabatini, and Rudyard Kipling. In the seventh grade he studied physiology; he even studied Latin.

One evening in 1940 the movie *Boys Town,* with Spencer Tracy and Mickey Rooney, came to the theater in Lewiston. He begged the sisters to let him see it. Lewiston, they replied, was too far away. It didn't really matter; he knew the outline of the story, anyway—how the famous Father Flanagan had started the "City of Little Men" in Omaha, Nebraska. And this was enough. Nothing he'd ever seen or heard had impressed him quite so much. With the directness and the naïve optimism which were already becoming apparent in his character, he wrote to Boys Town immediately and applied for admission.

When the sisters found out about this, they were chagrined. But if this was what he really wanted, they would help as best they could. On February 11, 1941, Sister Mary Genevieve sent a personal appeal to Father Flanagan.

"We are receiving more applications daily than we can really take care of," he replied on April 1. "We would like to know if we must consider this a charity case. Judging from your letter, we presume that we must." And again on April 28: "We regret exceedingly that there is so little information available regarding this boy's parentage. . . ."

Sister Mary Genevieve persisted. The tuberculin test given young Pete in May had indeed been positive, but an X ray had later indicated there was no tuberculosis. Surely Father Flanagan realized that the test result was a mistake. Surely Father Flanagan valued the contribution that this fine boy would make to his splendid institution. . . .

Whatever doubts Father Flanagan may have held about Bucher crumbled under this barrage. "I shall plan to admit this lad on Monday, September 15," he wrote. "I shall appreciate your timing his arrival here between the hours of 8 A.M. and 4 P.M. since those are the office hours of the welfare department. . . . I am sorry, dear Sister, that I have no . . . means of paying for a lad's transportation. . . ."

Once again, Sister Mary Genevieve was equal to the challenge. She helped Pete pack—one sweater, one pair of oxfords, one pair of high-top shoes, two pairs of overalls, one bathrobe, one hockey cap, eighteen handkerchiefs—and then she gave him a special pass, No. C-241022, which she'd somehow managed to cumshaw from the Union Pacific Railroad Company. "Ordinarily, we limit travel concessions," President W. M. Jeffers had explained, "but in view of [your letter] and the circumstances that make this trip necessary. . . ."

Not yet twenty-five years old in 1941, Boys Town was already the most famous school of its kind in the world, a place where homeless, abandoned, neglected young men could develop their potential. The regimen was Spartan. Boys woke up at 6 A.M.; classes began an hour later and continued until 4 P.M. On Saturdays boys could sleep until 7 A.M. Boys received an allowance of 30 cents each week, but they had to save at least half of that. Boys cleaned their own rooms and worked in the Victory Garden. Their clothes were flawed and came from J. C. Penney's. Their meals were predictably dull: "Georgie Porgie" cereal for breakfast, ring bologna and spinach for lunch, pork chops and mashed potatoes for dinner. "Boys correspond with girls if they wish," a brochure from that era advised. "Boys do not have dates as do the boys from the [Omaha] city schools, but they do have the opportunity of contact with girls at athletic contests."

Almost everyone went out for the football team. The schedule each year was studded with public and parochial school powerhouses— Chelsea High School in Massachusetts, Hollywood High School in California, Gonzaga in Washington, D.C., Trinity High School in Sioux City, Iowa—institutions with enrollments as large as colleges'. Coach Maurice H. (Skip) Palrang, the Vince Lombardi of his day, a 6-foot, 5-inch 240-pound disciplinarian, scoffed at the odds. The size of a school didn't matter; neither did the size of its players. Speed, conditioning, desire, an unflinching will to win—these were the qualities he stressed.

In 1942 Bucher arranged a play-off between the eighth and ninth grade teams for the junior high school championship. Ever since coming to Boys Town he had been known by his given name of Lloyd. But "Lloyd" was too stuffy. He wanted to be called Pete, after his special hero, All-America end Pete Pihos from Indiana University. His classmates equivocated. Then Bucher scored the touchdown that won the game and the championship for the ninth grade. No one at Boys Town ever called him Lloyd again.

Next fall he started at left tackle for the varsity squad. He was only a sophomore; he weighed less than 160 pounds, but for the next three seasons he was a regular in that position. An old photo album shows him crouching in a four-point stance, number 39 in a blue and white uniform, a forced scowl on his face, the ribbed helmet atop his head resembling a sawed-off walnut shell. His teammates remember that he was the one who organized pep rallies and bonfires, introducing the coaches and captains before every game and leading the applause. They remember, too, how he used to write other teams on his own, challenging them to come to Boys Town and "take a lickin'." Most of all they remember his dedication to the fundamentals of blocking and tackling, his habit of charging the dummy down by the goalpost again and again long after everyone else had trooped in for supper.

"He was eager and smart," Coach Palrang recalls. "He hit fast; he had a fine follow-through, and he was a terrific downfield blocker. I was using the Chicago Bears' T-formation, and he was the first kid to understand it. He could call changes in the line. One of our best plays was a sweep around end. Pete's job was to nail the halfback while the end took care of the deep safety. I remember one game; I think it was during his senior year. We ran that play four times, and four times Pete knocked that halfback flat on his fanny and we went for long touchdowns. I could always depend on him to do his job."

He ran the 100-yard dash and the 440 and 880 for the Boys Town track team. He threw the discus and scored five points in an intramural game of "commando basketball." "Well, first you put on a large pair of boxing gloves," he explained in a 1943 letter to a friend. "Next go out on the floor and warm up. Then the game starts. You may hit anybody just as long as you do not hit below the belt or above the neck. . . .

"I sure am glad that Clarence joined the Navy because that's what I want to join," the letter continues. "We sure have been seeing some swell shows here lately, namely *My Gal, Sal* and *Pride of the Yankees.* Boy, was it swell. Gosh! Well, school is out now and I got to go. Your pal, Lloyd Bucher—Pete the tramp."

His classmates elected him president his sophomore and junior years and vice-president his senior year. He wasn't a hell-raiser; he didn't smoke or drink or have to go to "court" for rules infractions nearly as often as some of the other boys. But he did skip more than his share of classes, hiding in the "apartment" until, inevitably, Clarence M. (Mit) Stoeffel, Jr., the end coach, mechanical drawing instructor, and truant officer, came to get him. His teachers awarded him A's in religion and aerodynamics and F's in Latin and algebra. In the spring of 1944 he ran away from Boys Town, returning late in July for football practice. His teachers chastised him for taking "French leave" and flunked him in all his courses. He attended summer school, and as Boys Town shifted to a numerical grading system that fall, his marks improved: a 72 in Latin, a 98 in military studies. On several occasions he made the honor role. The last line of his biography in the school yearbook read, "Pete would like to be an officer in the Navy."

On October 2, 1945—eight months before he was scheduled to graduate—Bucher stuffed $7 into his pocket, hitchhiked to San Diego, and enlisted in the Navy. "I can remember thinking, 'Isn't that screwy?'" says class president Frank W. Roe, today a successful trucking company executive in Seattle, Washington. "Here's a guy who has so much on the ball, and he just ups and leaves."

"I thought I wanted to go to college; I thought I wanted to play football," Bucher remembers, "but I was just generally mixed up about what the hell I really was going to do. And I wanted to see the world." The Navy paid him $50 a month, sent him to quartermaster school in Gulfport, Mississippi, then assigned him to a stores ship, USS *Zelima*. It wasn't long before he regretted leaving Boys Town.

"The Navy isn't hard although it's strict as heck about everything," he wrote to a teacher, Harold Crawford, early in 1947. "Right now I'm laid up in the hospital with a broken ear drum which I received while boxing. I can see now that I kicked most of my chances that I had at Boys Town in the seat of the pants, as I usually do. I probably caused more hair to fall or get gray than anyone out there. . . .

"If I said I was sorry for the school I skipped it would be a lie, I think. But I *am* sorry for the lies I told when I was caught. I have put a stop to that habit. I've made it a point to tell the truth no matter what. I owe everything I am or ever will be to Boys Town and its activities. The one thing there that I never did slough off in was football. I certainly owe everything to Skip.

"Please let me know if it's okay if I finish my schoolwork in the Navy and get a diploma. I'm sure I could complete the work. Cause, well, gee, I just gotta get a diploma if I'm gonna go to college. . . ."

With that diploma finally in hand, Bucher left the Navy in October, 1947. He tended bar at the Elks Club in Lewiston, Idaho; he followed the harvest and worked on a farm in Newberry, Oregon. He enrolled at the University of Nebraska in Lincoln in the spring of 1948 but dropped out after one semester and returned to Omaha. He joined a construction gang bulldozing runways for the city's new airport; he loaded freshly slaughtered meat into freezers at a Swift & Company packing plant; he worked in a brickyard.

He tended bar again at the Surf Room of the Commodore Hotel, pouring free drinks for his friends and turning his back when they tried to pay. He did the same thing at the American Legion Club, Post No. One, downtown. "He was talking with his hands a lot; he couldn't stay still; he always had to be on the go," remembers Edward H. Case, a chunky, balding Omaha CPA. "We were rooming together that summer, 1948 it was, and we had this corner room at 2613 California Street, right across from the Dental College. I borrowed his car one time, a brown 1936 Plymouth, and I got a ticket. So I rushed down to the police station to take care of it, and Lord, there were fifteen other tickets written out against him there.

"It was hot that summer, and we used to lay awake at night and talk. He wasn't like a lot of them that came out of the service and condemned it, you know. If he couldn't say anything nice, he wouldn't mention it, period. He was always talking about Skip Palrang, who'd been sort of a father to him. He used to say what a thrill it had been to play for Skip against some of those big schools like North Catholic up in Detroit and how he'd look up and see forty-three thousand people in Briggs Stadium there and really feel scared. But only until the kickoff. Once the game began he never was scared."

In the fall of 1949 Bucher returned to the University of Nebraska. He won a letter in freshman football and pledged Sigma Nu fraternity. Soon he was forced to abandon both activities. The GI Bill gave him only $60 a month—not nearly enough; he borrowed $400 from a bank and earned extra money by tending bar at the Elks Club and waiting on table at a sorority house. On weekends he drove back to Omaha and worked in the brickyard.

And then, at a Creighton University spring football prom in Omaha, he met Rose Rohling. She had attended the University of Missouri for awhile, and now she was working as a telephone operator for Northwestern Bell: a quiet girl, unassuming and devout, pretty in a sturdy, rather wholesome way. She could be stubborn, too; she didn't put up with his guff, and he had to admire her spunk. She was quite unlike any girl he had ever dated before.

The owner of the apartment that Rose and her sister were sharing in 1950 was a prominent Omaha businessman named Fred W. Martin. He and his wife liked both girls enormously, and they placed their stamp of approval on Rose's new beau. "We'd sit out in the kitchen for hours and talk about science, philosophy, and business," Martin recalls. "He'd ask my advice about planning his career and what investments to make and even what kind of car to buy. I could see that the relationship between Pete and Rose was blossoming, and there was talk of marriage. But Pete was pretty discouraged. Rose's folks were sticklers on family background, and Pete didn't have any background at all. But he never asked my advice about this. He seemed to feel that this was something they'd have to work out themselves."

As a conscientious provider, a bright, hard-working young man who would someday achieve success no matter what he did, Bucher had possibilities. But as a romantic suitor, his sense of timing left much to be desired. He proposed to Rose in the front seat of his battered 1936

Plymouth; he slipped the engagement ring over her finger a few days later during a visit to his dentist's office.

The wedding took place in Rose's hometown of Jefferson City, Missouri, on June 10. "I drove Rose to the church," remembers Charles T. Mitchell, the supervisor of the Boys Town print shop, "and when I got there I could see that Pete was really nervous. It was hotter than hell that day; Pete was sweating, and he kept yelling at Jim Gunnell, his best man, to get him a handkerchief. He said it real quiet at first, then louder and louder until you could hear him halfway down the aisle. They had a nice reception after the ceremony, and that's when Dan Henry—he was six-foot-six and an end on the football team—grabbed Rose's bridal bouquet, and all the girls started screaming and chasing him. It was quite a scene."

No sooner had the Buchers returned from a honeymoon trip to the Lake of the Ozarks than the Korean War broke out. The Navy began recalling its inactive reservists first, and Bucher, L. M., QM2, received orders to report to a ship in Seattle. University officials interceded; the orders were canceled on one condition. Bucher had to agree to join the Naval Reserve Officers Training Corps (NROTC) unit and serve two more years on active duty after his graduation. At the time it seemed an excellent bargain.

He and Rose found a tiny basement apartment in Lincoln. She went to work for the telephone company. He worked part-time as a switchman for the Chicago, Burlington and Quincy Railroad and coached a midget football team. "I can remember him knocking on doors asking for money to buy helmets," Charley Mitchell says. "He'd yell at those kids, trying to get the best out of them. If they lost, okay. But if he thought they were sloughing off, he'd really tear into them."

The years at Boys Town, as frustrating as they had been academically, had given him a chance nonetheless to develop his own set of values, the attitudes and principles which most young men acquire automatically from parents and relatives at home. The years he'd spent in the Navy and afterward, working in Omaha, had let him hone those values. He was calmer now. He seemed to have a sense of direction. And he was applying himself to his studies.

He never made the Dean's List, but his grades were respectable enough. He "aced" a course in Scientific Latin and Greek. He did well in chemistry, zoology, geology, and physiology. He cut up cadavers, and for awhile he thought of becoming a veterinarian. In the summer of his sophomore year he spent three weeks at the University of Pennsylvania's School of Veterinary Medicine. Reluctantly, he decided against this as a career. He couldn't afford all those years of postgraduate study. He would become a geologist instead, land a job with an oil company, and travel to Latin America or the Middle East.

He left Nebraska in June, 1953, with a degree in secondary education, an associate degree in geology, and a number of credits toward a master's degree in micropaleontology. He had a commission as well as an ensign in the Naval Reserve, and after a tour at the Combat Information Command (CIC) School in Glenview, Illinois, he reported aboard USS *Mt. McKinley.*

The Navy hadn't really changed since he'd left it six years before, but an officer's stripes certainly heightened a man's appreciation of service life. He was still planning on a career as a geologist, of course —the Arabian-American Oil Company had already offered to send him to the University of Houston for a year, then out to the Middle East for two and a half more years—but meanwhile it wouldn't do any harm to see what other challenges the Navy could provide. Early in 1955 Bucher applied to submarine school at New London, Connecticut.

His next-door neighbor at New London was a mild-mannered Nebraska-born officer named Charles R. Clark. The son of an oil company geophysicist, Clark had lived in six different states before he was even six weeks old; he'd joined the Navy, he liked to say, "in order to settle down." His wife, an attractive, gregarious brunette named Jimmie, got along well with Rose, and Clark and Bucher soon became close friends—neither man ever suspecting that their paths would cross again so meaningfully twelve years later. "We were lieutenant j.g.'s at the time," Clark remembers, "and competing against each other. Jimmie and I used to go over to the Buchers' to play charades. That was our idea of a big social evening."

The schedule at submarine school was so demanding that they had time for little else. One of the tests entailed descending to the bottom of a 110-foot tank in an old Momsen lung. Although it wasn't mandatory—it was, in fact, quite dangerous; a few men had already died in the attempt—Bucher elected to make a "free ascent," rising to the surface without the aid of a breathing apparatus.

"They gave you a set of goggles and told you to leave the hatch and follow the 'bubble' on up," he recalls. "Well, I was at the fifty-foot lock and I stepped out of this damn thing and my glasses filled up with water. When you can't see and you're under water in a weightless condition, you don't know which way you're going. But I didn't know that. So rather than reach up and pull those glasses off and indicate to those people that I was in some kind of trouble, I thought I'd just try to keep on going.

"I overdid it. I let out too much air. Some guy was yelling through this UQC to 'get that guy out of the water.' I pulled my glasses off at that point and I was upside down and passing sixty feet going down. There wasn't anybody coming for me and I didn't know where in the hell to go and by this time I was starting to need air.

"Finally, I felt some guy's hand on my wrist and he pulled me back up to the lock. The doctor took a look at me. I had swallowed a little water, but otherwise I felt okay. He said, 'How about it? You want to do it again? If you don't do it now, you'll probably never do it.' And I said, 'Okay, let's go.' "

In December Bucher left New London and reported aboard his first submarine, USS *Besugo*, as the supply, communications, and weapons officer. Submarine duty was everything he had ever expected it would be. The work was hard, but the wardroom was very close; there was a feeling of camaraderie, and the caliber of the enlisted men serving on that boat—well, if you asked him to and if he really believed in you, any one of those men would gladly push a peanut with his nose all the way back to Washington. The pay wasn't bad, either. To be sure, he was sending money back to Boys Town regularly now, as well as ten or twelve dollars every month to a boy in Germany through the War Orphan's Relief Plan, but he and Rose could live comfortably on an officer's salary, and besides, there were all those fringe benefits that a man had to consider.

"There was some question right from the start about how he looked at the Navy, whether or not he was going to make it a career," recalls Commander John G. Tillson, a tall, ruddy-complexioned Annapolis graduate who was then engineering officer on *Besugo*. "He realized he didn't have the background that some of the rest of us had. I told him the Navy was a great place for him, that he could go further faster in the service than he probably could anyplace else. Most people advised him to stay in, and it was about this time that he submitted the necessary papers."

On *Besugo* Bucher was "George," the junior officer who took care of all the Dirty Little Details. His seniors thought of him as a gregarious, immensely likable fellow, a "diamond in the rough." Privately, some of them emphasized the word "rough."

"He was different than most other officers," Tillson says. "For one thing, he never wore a sharp, smart uniform. His was always a little baggy, a little ill-fitting. But he never worried about that, never concerned himself with all the folderol. He believed in doing things the way he wanted to; he didn't give a damn about doing them in the fundamental, traditional ways. He just didn't understand these ways. He hadn't evolved, like most of the rest of us had, from a structure."

Far more than the Army or the Air Force, the Navy has always paid close attention to "structure," to style, to the necessary—indeed, in its view, socially desirable—separation between officers, who are gentlemen, and sailors, who are something else. Its mythology is handed down from one generation to another. Its officer corps is perhaps this nation's last public aristocracy. An Annapolis ring almost always guarantees its owner first shot at the choice commands—nearly two-thirds of all U.S. submarines today are skippered by Naval Academy graduates—and while a degree from a solid Midwestern school isn't a black mark at all, few admirals have ever come out of the universities of Kansas or Nebraska.

The system demands obeisance, frowns upon flamboyance. And in the view of *Besugo*'s commanding officer, a mere lieutenant j.g.—even as competent a fellow as Bucher—was overstepping his bounds by trying to organize the wardroom's social functions. Bucher was a fine leader, his fitness report noted, but he hadn't paid enough attention to detail in performing his job as weapons officer. Attention to detail! At the time *Besugo* boasted a better record in her weapons tests than any other sub in the squadron.

Prior to 1955 a submarine officer didn't have to worry about receiving the training necessary to serve aboard a nuclear-powered boat. There weren't enough of these boats in the fleet; he could "float" above them in his slow and slippery climb to the top. But then Rear Admiral Hyman G. Rickover lent his considerable energies to accelerating the nuclear power program. He and his staff conducted countless interviews, screening junior officers' records, winnowing the exceptional from the mediocre and sending them to postgraduate school. In retrospect, the implications of this were clear: A man who wanted command either had to join the program or leave the submarine force altogether. Yet so slowly did this Hobson's choice evolve that many young officers failed to grasp what was happening.

Early in 1958 Rickover's talent scouts summoned Bucher for an interview. *Besugo* lay in the shipyard at San Francisco awaiting decommissioning. Bucher had just received orders to another diesel submarine, USS *Caiman,* and he didn't try to impress his interrogators. "I didn't particularly want to study theoretical nuclear physics," he remembers. "I was tired of school, and it seemed to me that this was a lot of misery that I didn't need. I'd known some guys who'd bilged out of the program and some guys who'd made it, and they were never home; they were miserable."

A few weeks later, Bucher was interviewed again—this time by Rickover himself. Their meeting was brief. "His first question was where had I stood in my class, and I said, 'In the upper third, I think.' Then he looked at me and said, 'What's the matter with you, Bucher? Are you lazy or stupid?' "

In May of that year Bucher returned to Nebraska to speak at Boys Town's annual athletic banquet. He was Regular Navy by then, a full lieutenant with two gold stripes on his sleeve. "Remember, when you leave Boys Town," he began, "you've got the ball. Run with it. The world does not owe you anything. But you owe everything to the world. What you achieve depends strictly upon you. When the going gets rough, there will be times when it will be easy to feel sorry for yourself. Don't do it."

The message was stirring enough, but in later years his audience would remember something else. "His voice was hardly above a whisper," says Mit Stoeffel, the mechanical drawing instructor who used to catch him skipping classes. "He was so overwhelmed that he had been invited to speak to fifteen hundred people that he was weeping bullets."

His tour on *Caiman* was brief, and in July, 1959, he reported to Long Beach, California, as assistant plans officer for logistics on the staff of the Commander, Mine Forces, Pacific. (MINEPAC). The officer he replaced, Kurt F. Dorenkamp, had gone on to a top billet, and Bucher, characteristically, assumed the same thing would happen to him in time if he tried hard enough.

What types and quantities of minesweeping and mine countermeasures equipment should the Navy stockpile for the first six months of a projected World War III? Where? And what logistics support would these stockpiles need? Bucher's job was to answer such questions, and he tackled it with customary verve.

"Pete was one of the most turned-on people on that staff," recalls a wiry, graying commander named Harry E. Padgett. "He was never the type to belly up to the bar and complain. And Rose was really helping him; she was solid and damned attractive—not the young, superficial wife you see with so many ensigns and j.g.'s."

The Buchers bought a place on Mesaba Drive in Palos Verdes Estates, and for the first time in his Navy career, he was home for dinner almost every night. He read a biography of Leonardo da Vinci, became fascinated by art, and promptly removed all the books on watercolors in the Palos Verdes public library. Soon he was turning out some fairly respectable paintings. He dabbled in the stock market, favoring speculative issues. He became interested in politics, supported Richard Nixon in 1960, and walked out of an election night party when it appeared that John F. Kennedy would win.

He read the works of John Locke, Russell Kirk, and Ayn Rand; he subscribed to *National Review* and passed the magazine among friends. There was no doubt in his mind that anyone in America—no matter what his race, creed, or religion—could succeed once he put his mind to it. Hadn't his own experience proven this to be true? Why couldn't those liberal politicians understand that giveaway programs only stifled individual initiative?

At the time the John Birch Society was enlisting recruits by the thousands throughout Southern California, especially in Orange County. The Naval community at Long Beach was hardly immune to its campaign. The admiral, himself a member, encouraged the showing of its films on patriotism at the base theater. Bucher stopped by the John Birch book store one day and perused back issues of *American Opinion*. "I enjoyed those articles; they made sense to me," he says. But when he was asked to join, he declined. He couldn't fault the Birchers on philosophical grounds; there was just something about the organization that didn't seem quite right.

In the summer of 1961 he received orders to another submarine, a diesel-powered "Guppie 2A" named USS *Ronquil,* and for the next three years he remained aboard, rising from third officer to navigator and executive officer. *Ronquil's* deployments to the West and North Pacific were long and sometimes hazardous. In one instance, which is still so highly classified that only a few top Washington officials know the details, *Ronquil* ran into the type of emergency situation that every submariner dreads. She couldn't surface, she couldn't turn away under normal power, and her oxygen supply was dwindling rapidly. Bucher recommended a plan which, if unsuccessful, might have resulted in catastrophe; a risky course, but at the moment the only possible means of escape. The skipper took his advice; *Ronquil* glided free. Years later, describing that experience, a former enlisted man on *Ronquil* would shake his head and say, "Bucher has more guts than the law allows."

A normal submarine tour extends from eighteen to twenty-four months, and in 1963 Bucher received orders to Fleet Ballistic Missile Submarine Navigators' School in Dam Neck, Virginia. From there he would move to a nuclear submarine, USS *Robert E. Lee.* Yet without the necessary training in nuclear propulsion, he knew he could never attain command of a boat like the *Lee.* Normal rotation had just stripped away most of *Ronquil's* experienced officers and crew, and now she was about to embark on another voyage across the Pacific. The man who was due to relieve Bucher had just returned from "West-Pac"; his wife had suffered a nervous breakdown when she had learned that he'd have to leave home again so soon. *Ronquil*'s new skipper, Commander Peter F. Block, hadn't served in WestPac before, and Bucher realized he'd probably need help on this first deployment. For all these reasons, he decided to pass up the school assignment. The squadron commander telephoned Washington; the orders were canceled. He remained aboard *Ronquil*.

His final months on the boat were among the most rewarding and challenging of his life. Once, a few days out of Pearl Harbor, *Ronquil*'s engines malfunctioned; she lay dead in the water. Someone suggested calling for a tug. Bucher scoffed at the thought. He and his engineering officer, Lieutenant Phillips C. Stryker, Jr., rolled up their sleeves and helped repair the engines themselves.

"Pete was working terribly hard and getting almost no sleep at all," recalls James N. Kaelin, now a Lynchburg, Virginia, engineer. "But he never griped. I never met anyone who had such loyalty to the boat, to the Navy, to America, and he could infuse this in the men who worked for him. He had a knack of making his subordinates feel that what they were doing was vitally important."

Ronquil's enlisted men admired him enormously, and he reciprocated their affection, seeing nothing wrong in hoisting a few beers on liberty with, for example, the chief of the boat. "He always treated you like a shipmate, not a grubby seadog," says a retired chief torpedoman named Albert E. Niess. By Annapolis standards, such fraternization was unacceptable, but Bucher had never been overly conscious of rank. On one occasion, at an officers' club party in San Diego, an admiral objected to the way the Buchers were dancing. Their "dip," he said, offended his sense of "decency." Bucher ignored the admiral, who only persisted in his intrusions. Rose began to cry. When the admiral came back again, Bucher exploded. Two of his friends had to restrain him physically.

In retrospect, in terms of his own career, the decision to stay aboard *Ronquil* was perhaps unwise. Yet at the time he was sure it was the only loyal, sensible thing to do. Besides, he'd still have ample opportunities to command a diesel boat in the future. There is a story, perhaps apocryphal, that when he left *Ronquil* and reported, in July 1964, to the staff of SUBFLOTSEVEN in Yokosuka, scores of officers and enlisted men volunteered to serve with him as soon as he received his first command.

And now, in the fall of 1966, it seemed that this command was finally within his grasp. His fitness reports at Yokosuka had been superior—as, he reflected, they should have been. He wasn't a boastful man, yet he was confident that he knew more about the nuts and bolts of submarine operations in WestPac than anyone else on the staff. Hadn't everyone turned to him for advice on the night that USS *Tiru* ran aground on Frederick Reef off Australia? And hadn't he been the one to make the quick, *correct* decisions? The letter from his detailer back in Washington hadn't been too specific, of course, saying only that he was under active consideration as a prospective skipper and that the odds appeared to be in his favor. Nonetheless, his spirits soared.

His colleagues remember how he used to "leadpipe" the younger officers on the staff, beguiling them into accepting wagers they couldn't possibly win; how he filled his pockets with parlor tricks—fake dice, ink blots, phony dog messes—and left them in appropriate locations; how he relished singing and telling his seemingly endless supply of raunchy stories and "camel" jokes and how, at a formal dinner party in the submarine sanctuary one evening, he showed up wearing glasses, a false nose, and—as Captain Fred T. Berry describes it—"the goddamndest-looking wig you ever saw."

Suddenly, that happy world began to disintegrate. A second letter from the Bureau of Naval Personnel informed him that he would *not* receive command of a submarine, after all. It was almost as if someone had told him he had cancer. "He didn't go off in a tantrum," Lieutenant Roderic C. Bazzel recalls, "but you could sense the hurt and disappointment. He didn't act like Pete for quite a while."

The submarine detailer in Washington at the time, the man who had made this decision, was an Annapolis graduate named Captain Lando W. Zech. For Zech the choice had been difficult. Bucher qualified for command—there was no question about that. But there were only seventeen billets for submarine skippers and thirty-five other men who were equally qualified. No matter how often he added up the points, Bucher still ranked about twentieth on his list.

Then Zech began to hear from some of Bucher's past and present commanding officers—Rear Admiral Charles D. Nace, Captain Enders P. Huey, Captain Henry B. Sweitzer—all of them outstanding men with fine reputations. And it was obvious that they felt he'd made a mistake. He could not reverse his ruling; it was too late for that. But on the weight of their recommendations, Zech decided to do the next best thing. He went to the surface ship detailer and strongly urged him to give Bucher the next available command.

A few weeks later Bucher received his orders: USS *Pueblo,* an AKL undergoing conversion at Bremerton, soon to be deployed to WestPac as one of those new intelligence collectors. Funny—not so long ago, he'd been complaining about the seeming lack of plans and policy governing these ships' operations. Now he was going to take command of one of them himself. And even more coincidental—USS *Banner* was in Yokosuka ready to welcome her new commanding officer: Charles Clark, his old friend from submarine school. Maybe two good Nebraska boys could pick up where they left off in New London twelve years ago and show the Russians a thing or two about charades.

Just before Christmas the SUBFLOTSEVEN staff threw a farewell party for the Buchers at the submarine sanctuary. There were songs and speeches, and someone presented him with a plaque, and someone else offered a toast, and a few of the wives began to cry, and soon he was crying himself, unashamedly—for this was sayonara, not just to the staff but to the submarine service, as well, and in a few days he would be gone for briefings on the new program in Hawaii and Washington, D.C.

12

The Naval Security Station in Washington, D.C., is a rambling, rather attractive assortment of two- and three-story Georgian brick buildings that nestle off verdant Nebraska Avenue, N.W., not far from WRC-TV. Until World War II the property belonged to the Mt. Vernon Seminary, an expensive and fashionable school for girls, but then, when the seminary moved to its present location on Foxhall Road, the Navy acquired the site as headquarters for its burgeoning cryptographic activities. Smartly tailored Marine guards check all visitors' credentials, and a green barbed-wire gate swings open to admit military traffic at the press of a buzzer; still, the setting and atmosphere are pleasantly pastoral, the only discordant notes sounding when rabbits grazing on the lawn accidentally trip the sensitive alarms.

As he waited inside Building 1 that morning in January, 1967, Lieutenant Steven R. Harris felt an occasional twinge of nervousness. Ever since last September, he'd known that his next assignment would be USS *Pueblo*. Now he was about to meet his new commanding officer. He wanted to make a good impression, but he hadn't had a haircut in weeks. Then Bucher entered the room, and one glance told Harris that he needn't have worried. Bucher's hair was even longer than his own.

With his pale complexion, pinched mouth, and narrow chin, Harris hardly matched the stereotype of the dashing young Naval officer. Acutely self-conscious, physically clumsy, and slightly overweight, he fit no image quite so perfectly perhaps as that of the harried academican—an associate professor, say, of biochemistry or nuclear physics.

And he was the first to recognize this. If he had chosen a career as an officer of the line, his Andy Gumpish appearance and shy, almost apologetic manner might conceivably have weighed against him on the promotion scale. The Navy, like other large institutions, could be awfully unfair about that. But he was a specialist now in a sensitive, demanding field where promotions depended not on personality but on performance. And his performance had been very good indeed.

Actually, he'd stumbled onto intelligence work almost by accident. "As an only child," he remembers, "I was kind of a loner. I didn't socialize too much. When it came to sports, I was pretty cold. But I did like anything that had to do with photography or electronics, especially from a nuts and bolts point of view."

At Melrose High School in Massachusetts he played the clarinet and was elected president of the band. He joined the dramatic society and was named "class actor" as well. His favorite composer was—and is—Rachmaninoff. Trolleys still clanged through Boston while he was growing up; he sensed the nostalgia in their impending disappearance from the urban scene and became a member of the Seashore Electric Railway Association, an organization which collects old street cars at a museum in Kennebunkport, Maine.

Both of his parents were teachers; they pressed him to excel academically, and although he wasn't a natural scholar, his marks were high enough to gain him admission to Harvard, which he entered in the fall of 1956. There he majored in English, specializing in English authors through the eighteenth century and receiving for his considerable pains a string of respectable C's. He rowed the single scull for Lowell House, and during his sophomore and junior years he filled in as a part-time announcer for the college radio station.

His ancestors on his father's side had arrived on the *Mayflower;* his mother's ancestors had passed along the family motto—*Amor Patriae Exitat*, "Love of Country Motivates Me"—and it was this tradition, coupled with a realization that he'd have to spend at least two years in the service anyway, which prompted him to join the Harvard NROTC.

No sooner had he left Cambridge than he received orders to report to a destroyer tender, USS *Grand Canyon*, as her communications officer. The work was enjoyable enough, but *Grand Canyon* spent most of her time in port. He wanted a taste of sea duty and in April, 1962, succeeded in transferring to a destroyer, USS *Forest Sherman*, in a similar billet. Within six months he realized he'd made a mistake. "This wasn't working out well for me," he remembers. "The pace was a little too fast. You almost need a fighter pilot's temperament, and I'm not quite of that cut."

Unhappy as a "ship-driver," his alternatives seemed clear: either leave the Navy altogether or find a specialty field receptive to his talents. He visited his detailer in the Bureau of Naval Personnel and asked what billets were available. The detailer, noting his interest in electronics and photography, suggested a thirty-six-week course in Russian at the Defense Language Institute. "I thought, 'Gee, that's great'," Harris says. He accepted immediately.

In October, 1964, Harris reported to the Naval Security Group Activity at Fort Meade, Maryland. "The work we were doing was extremely sensitive and difficult," remembers Lieutenant Commander John T. Hodgkinson, a round-faced Bates College graduate who was then Harris' immediate superior. "And we had the cream of the crop in our department. At the start I would have ranked Steve in the lower third. He led with the Ivy League background and had a certain aloofness. Later I ranked him fifth or sixth. He did see the big picture, and he had a noteworthy perseverance."

From time to time Harris left Fort Meade to command small detachments of communications technicians on one-shot assignments. Although details concerning these missions are still classified, it is perhaps important to note that several senior officers—among them Commander Peter Block—had occasion to measure his performance and found it almost flawless. And it is a matter of record that as a result of his work at Fort Meade, he won a Navy Commendation medal.

His prospects on the social front seemed to be improving, as well. Stepping out of church one evening early in 1965, he struck up a conversation with a dimpled blonde of Finnish descent, a lovely girl named Esther Uotinen. She needed a ride home; he volunteered, and they stopped for supper at a Howard Johnson's restaurant. For a budding romance, the setting was only slightly more appropriate than Bucher's dentist's office. Nonetheless, in October they were engaged; in December they were married. Harris' mother sang at the reception in the officers' club at Walter Reed Army Hospital.

They had no time for a honeymoon right away. The small apartment on 24th Street in Foggy Bottom needed refurbishing, Harris was busy preparing for his *Pueblo* assignment, and now, on this morning in January as he and Bucher sat in the Naval Security Station poring over the sets of blueprints and the schematics of the research spaces, he felt sure that this was going to be an enjoyable tour indeed. Bucher seemed so informal, so very down-to-earth.

At noon they drove to Maggie's on Wisconsin Avenue for a beer and pizza lunch. Bucher had already received his briefings at NSA and the Pentagon; he was due to fly to Bremerton almost immediately, but first he wanted to spend an afternoon sight-seeing. He hadn't been to Washington in more than twenty years, he said—not since the day that Boys Town had played Gonzaga in Griffith Stadium—and he particularly wanted to see the new exhibits at the Smithsonian Institution.

The weather was unseasonably warm—almost 90 degrees—so Harris rolled back the top of his Karmann-Ghia convertible and drove down Massachusetts Avenue, slowing as he approached the start of Embassy Row. Suddenly, for reasons he no longer remembers, he decided to stop at his own apartment. He was gone for less than ten minutes, but when he stepped into the lobby again, Bucher was asleep on a chair, a copy of *Time* magazine spread over his face. The night life was catching up with him, Harris suspected. No matter; there wouldn't be time for that where they were going. He drove along Pennsylvania Avenue, passed the White House, then turned toward the Washington Monument and dropped Bucher at the entrance to the Smithsonian. "See you at Bremerton," he yelled. But Bucher was already gone.

Neither Harris nor Bucher suspected it, but at this moment a fierce debate was raging within the Naval Security Group about the status of the CT's who would be reporting to *Pueblo*. *Banner's* first skipper, Lieutenant Bob Bishop, had been unhappy with the "detachment" arrangement, under which his research officer reported to the director, Naval Security Group Activity, Pacific, in Hawaii. He felt that he, as skipper, should have *total* control over all officers and men on the ship, and this would be possible, he pointed out, only if the detachment were to be redesignated a department.

Concerned about his reports, officers in Section G-30 at the Naval Security Station studied the problem and concluded that Bishop was right. The detachment arrangement *did* hamstring a commanding officer's prerogatives. Nevertheless, they had no right to change the designation themselves. They could make recommendations, to be sure, but *Pueblo* would be operating under the jurisdiction of the Commander in Chief, Pacific Fleet. The final decision would have to be made in Hawaii.

And to the officers at CINCPACFLT headquarters near Honolulu, these recommendations from Washington made no sense at all. Sure, it would be nice to give a skipper total control, but think of the problems, the loss of flexibility that this would mean for *them*. No longer would they be able to shuffle CT's on and off the ship at a moment's notice to handle fluctuating intelligence requirements. Under a department arrangement this task would revert to the Bureau of Naval Personnel, that bureaucracy in Washington. Even more important, no longer would they exercise control over the funds which had been allocated for the research operation.

The director of the Naval Security Group Activity in Hawaii at the time was Captain Everett B. Gladding, a stout, well-liked, grand-fatherly man whom everyone called Pete. He was nearing retirement; he had no stomach for engaging in jurisdictional disputes, and as far as this argument was concerned, he had no preference one way or the other.

His senior assistants on the staff, Commander Norman Horowitz and Lieutenant Commander Irwin G. Newman, felt differently, however. Washington's recommendations constituted a challenge to their authority. They decided not to give up that authority easily.

13

The 14-mile trip by ferry from Seattle to Bremerton takes just under an hour. The broad reaches of Puget Sound slowly give way to a narrowing channel lined on both sides by dark green arrows of fir and spruce and pine. An old hammerhead crane juts skyward at a bend in the channel. In years past it hoisted gun turrets from the decks of battleships, but the Puget Sound Naval Shipyard hasn't seen many battleships since John Wayne was a young lieutenant, so it stands there today a little awkwardly, like a giant praying mantis, poised to help the shipyard recapture its moments of glory.

There were no such moments during that cold and foggy winter of 1966–67, but this is not to imply that the yard was idle. Quite the reverse was true, for the accelerating demands of the war in Vietnam had plucked many smaller ships—destroyers, oilers, and ammunition carriers—out of the mothball fleet and had sent them to Bremerton for refurbishing. The aircraft carrier USS *Ranger* steamed in for overhaul. Construction of six new ships—USS *Detroit,* USS *Seattle,* and USS *Samuel Gompers* among them—was proceeding at a furious pace, and soon it seemed that every man in the yard—rigger, pipefitter, welder, machinist—was laboring overtime, for Washington wanted these vessels out on the line as soon as possible; there was a "priority" tag on almost every project.

But not on *Pueblo* or *Palm Beach.* For the past few months they'd shuffled from one pier to another to provide more room for *important* ships. Yard personnel had completed the "ripout" process; they'd changed the bulkheads, installed cabling, examined the steering, and tested the engines. The word from Washington had been that *Pueblo* and *Palm Beach* were identical; what fit on one would fit on the other, and all they'd have to remember was to convert both ships in the same way that they'd converted *Banner.*

How ridiculous that was. Anyone could see that *Pueblo* was smaller and lighter than *Palm Beach;* that *Pueblo* had a high, flared bow and a deep well deck, while her sister ship's deck was absolutely flush; that *Pueblo*'s interior design was a mishmash compared to the layout on *Palm Beach*. But they couldn't do much about it until they'd received some guidance from the Naval Ships Systems Command in Washington. And even if they'd wanted to push ahead on their own, there was no money to pay for their efforts. As Christmas neared, the number of men assigned to both ships dwindled to a handful.

On January 4, 1967, Gene Lacy stepped off the Bremerton ferry, entered the shipyard, and asked directions to *Pueblo*. The first few people he approached had never heard of her, but he persisted and finally found someone who pointed knowingly toward Pier 3D. *Pueblo* and *Palm Beach* were moored together, but the tide was out that morning, and all Lacy could see above the level of the pier was four stubby little masts. At first he thought they all belonged to the same ship.

Although he'd seen AKL's before the sight of *Pueblo* still came as a shock. He couldn't believe that the Navy was really planning to convert such an old and tiny ship—or one in such an obvious state of disrepair. Huge swatches of rust pancaked her sides, her superstructure was pitted, and she didn't seem to have many watertight compartments. For the past eighteen months Lacy had served aboard USS *Burton Island,* an icebreaker whose thick hull had been designed for cruising in Arctic waters. He wondered if *Pueblo* would encounter ice on her patrols. Her skin was so thin that it seemed as if a man could poke a hole through it with his bare fist.

As the first officer to report aboard, Lacy was responsible not only for overseeing the ship's conversion but also for initiating much of the necessary precommissioning paperwork. So every day, when he left the pier, he climbed the creaking stairs to the second floor of Building 50—the oldest building in the shipyard—and entered the small ship's "office."

The Navy had designated *Pueblo* AKL-44, and outfitting agencies throughout the country were forwarding crates of equipment—a towing cable, booms, and topping lifts—designed especially for an AKL. Lacy realized immediately that *Pueblo* was no ordinary freighter. He wanted to requisition supplies and publications commensurate with her new duties, but he wasn't sure what those duties were.

Pueblo clearly belonged to a new class of ship—one for which he could find no guidelines. Because she'd once belonged to the Army, he couldn't rely on standard allowance lists or inventories of spare parts. He wanted to speak to someone about this but didn't know where to turn. "All the civilians had been told was that *Pueblo*'s operations were highly classified and therefore none of their business," he recalls. And Lacy himself had instructions not to discuss the ship's mission— even in general terms—over the telephone. If he wanted to write a letter, he had to stamp it "top secret."

Slowly, in twos and threes, *Pueblo*'s crew members reported aboard. Their ages, experience levels, and family backgrounds differed widely. Ralph Bouden, a lean, conscientious chief communications technician from Enid, Oklahoma, had spent fifteen years in the Navy and had served at stations in Guam, Morocco, and Turkey. This would be his first duty at sea. Until recently Roy Maggard had been laying tile for a company in Olivehurst, California. Earl Phares had played tenor saxophone for the one-hundred-and-fifty-member Chaffey Tiger Marching Band in Ontario, California. He'd left a job with the General Electric Flat Iron plant there to enlist in the Navy.

Seaman Ramon Rosales was born in the Smeltertown area of El Paso, Texas. He had eleven brothers and sisters; his father had worked as a waiter in an El Paso hotel for twenty-seven years. Peter Langenberg had dropped out of Princeton after one year "to find myself." His father was a stockbroker in St. Louis, Missouri. Peter Bandera was the son of a card dealer at the Nugget Club in Carson City, Nevada. Rodney Duke was the son and grandson of Methodist ministers in Mississippi; he hoped to become a clergyman himself.

"Army" Canales had requested cancellation of his orders to a destroyer in Norfolk, Virginia, because he "wanted to move West." Charles Law was serving on a tanker, USS *Tolovana,* when one of his shipmates received orders to *Pueblo.* Law had just completed a tour on an AKL, USS *Mark,* in Vietnam. He volunteered to take his friend's place. "But this ship didn't resemble an AKL at all," he recalls. "I felt something was funny." For Storekeeper First Class Policarpo (Pepe) Garcia, *Pueblo* would be his seventh ship. His wife, Myda, had always cried before when he'd received orders to go to sea. This time, inexplicably, she hadn't seemed upset.

Pepe wouldn't have blamed her if she had become angry, for the Navy had just decided that *Pueblo*'s eventual home port would be Yokosuka, Japan. Therefore, any crew members who wanted to bring their families to Bremerton would have to do so at their own expense. Most of the married men arrived at the yard alone.

Tradition dictates that a skipper is among the last officers to report aboard a new ship. Bucher's briefers in Washington had assured him that *Pueblo* was set for commissioning in February, so when he reached Bremerton on January 30, he was dismayed to find that the ship's conversion was less than 80 percent complete and that her commissioning date had been set back to March or April.

"They had finished the structural work, but none of the guts were in there," he recalls. "None of the research spaces, none of the mess decks. And they weren't working on it. There was just these two or three guys who went down to the ship every day and farted around. And this had been going on for weeks."

Bucher called on Rear Admiral Floyd B. Schultz, the shipyard's commander. "The admiral told me he didn't know much about the program," he remembers, "and said he didn't want to know. He gave me every indication that he wasn't very damn interested."

An AKL carries a crew of about thirty men. *Pueblo* would carry nearly three times that number—certainly more than the sixty-four personnel already allocated. But where were these people supposed to eat and sleep? Most ships that have to maneuver adroitly control their speeds directly from the bridge. So why should *Pueblo* be saddled with an antiquated system of ringing up bells to the engine room? Any ship which carries complex electronic gear provides space for the bulky test equipment. *Pueblo* didn't have this space. Nor was there any room set aside for the stowage of publications or any provision for ventilation in the research area. "It was obvious to me that no thinking person was involved in the planning," Bucher says. "No one who'd ever gone to sea, no one with any idea of what this ship was supposed to do."

Usually, whenever a ship is undergoing conversion, the Navy sends its crew to precommissioning school to acquaint them with standard operational and administrative procedures. Sailors from other ships at the yard were attending such courses already; roughly 50 percent of *Pueblo*'s personnel had never been to sea before, so Bucher wrote to the Commander, Service Forces, Pacific Fleet and asked when they might undergo similar training. There wasn't enough time, he was told. On-the-job training would have to suffice.

It took him about a week to inspect the ship thoroughly, and at the end of this time he had decided to conn the ship from the flying bridge. This was an unorthodox location, to be sure; it lacked the communications capabilities of the pilot house. Still, to Bucher it seemed the most logical place. The pilot house was so small and cluttered that he couldn't step from one wing of the bridge to the other without changing course like a broken field runner. Furthermore, a direction-finding antenna on the 0-1 level restricted his view from the pilot house. He'd rather be on the flying bridge.

The crew's initial impression of Bucher was, for the most part, highly favorable. Larry Strickland brought him coffee one morning and remembers noticing "the most beautiful pair of bloodshot eyes I'd ever seen." Bill Scarborough was pleasantly surprised to find that "he knew quite a bit about machinery. I didn't have to go over my problems five or six times." Charles Law's first thought was, "Look at that wild-eyed SOB. He had one helluva head of hair—just like one of them *teen-agers*. But he stepped right in and took command. He let everyone know that he was going to be the skipper."

Some of Bucher's policies soon prompted concern. "He didn't respect rates too much," Law continues. "He put out the word that everyone on *Pueblo* would have to carry an equal load. I'd never been on a ship before where the first class [petty officers] had to chip paint. And he had a lot of submarine thoughts and habits which he tried to apply to the ship. He was always talking about the forward battery or the torpedo room or the chief of the boat."

One of Bucher's most important tasks was to write the ship's "organization," a one-inch-thick manual akin to the bylaws of a club, which covers the commanding officer's relationships with his department heads, lists his leave and liberty policies, includes some general regulations—sleeping in bed with your shoes on is prohibited—and assigns crew members by rates to duty stations for every conceivable "evolution." Which watches, for example, are to be stood, and by whom, while the ship is under way? Which watches while the ship is in port? And which personnel are supposed to do what during the standard fire, man overboard, repel boarders, and general quarters drills?

His conversations in Washington had been reassuring. *Pueblo*'s CT's would constitute a *department,* not a detachment, so he would exercise total control. This would be an advantage in preparing the organization. At the moment, with no guidelines to follow, he planned to pattern these bylaws after a submarine organization. And why not? A submarine was small and operated independently. So was—and would —USS *Pueblo*. Actually, Navy policy stipulated that the first ship of any new class bore responsibility for developing this basic doctrine. But Lieutenant Bob Bishop hadn't written anything which even recognized *Banner*'s new tasks and capabilities. Bucher and Lieutenant Commander Albert D. Raper, the skipper of *Palm Beach,* would have to start from scratch. *Banner*'s commander had simply been too busy to worry about any paperwork.

From the inception of the AGER program, the Navy had wanted to operate *Banner* only off the coast of the Soviet Union. The Russians it reasoned, would never attack the ship on the high seas. A *quid pro quo* existed here. They had too much to lose. But the hydrographic and intelligence "take" from her first half-dozen missions had exceeded everyone's expectations. As they reviewed this data, officials at the National Security Agency in Fort Meade, Maryland, became a little greedy. They wanted to "task" *Banner* against North Korea and China. The Navy said this would be dangerous. It would alter the original concept. The North Koreans and the Chinese had no intelligence collection ships of their own. The *quid pro quo* would no longer apply.

NSA officials pressed their case. Incredibly, instead of dealing through the chain of command in the Pentagon, they contacted CINCPACFLT headquarters in Hawaii *directly* and suggested that *Banner* include North Korea and China on her itinerary. Officers at CINCPACFLT *assumed* that Washington had approved this change and relayed the word to COMNAVFORJAPAN in Yokosuka. Lieutenant Ed Brookes wrote a three-page "concept memo" which said, in effect, *"Banner* is now a flexible platform. She can go anywhere."

Late in 1966 *Banner* prepared for a voyage to the East China Sea. Although she had been subjected to constant harassment by the Soviets, Rear Admiral Frank L. Johnson, Commander, Naval Forces, Japan, didn't think these encounters represented serious threats. His concerns were more mundane. *Banner* might lose her engines and drift into hostile waters. She might even be involved in an accidental collision. Nonetheless, because he was a cautious, conscientious man who tried to prepare for any eventuality, Johnson had established what he would later describe as a procedure for "on call" support. He had no forces of his own to protect *Banner,* but he told his staff to inform Fifth Air Force headquarters at Fuchu as well as the commander of the Seventh Fleet about the ship's proposed patrols. If they viewed her "track" as especially sensitive, they could request Fifth Air Force to provide planes on a strip alert and ask for surface support from Seventh Fleet.

They made no such request for any of *Banner's* first eight patrols. But mission number nine in the East China Sea prompted concern. "I personally was unhappy about the geographical location," Admiral Johnson has said. "I didn't trust the area; I didn't trust the foreign countries involved . . . I didn't know what the reaction would be."

A few days prior to the ship's departure, Lieutenant Ed Brookes and his boss, Captain Thomas L. Dwyer, discussed the mission's risk. They agreed that Chinese trawlers would probably place *Banner* under surveillance; they might even harass her severely. But the odds in favor of a fatal collision, an attack, or a boarding attempt seemed very low indeed—less than one in ten.

Ideally, they would position one U.S. destroyer—perhaps even two —just over the horizon about 30 miles away. And they would have aircraft ready at a moment's notice. Yet even if such support were available, Brookes and Dwyer agreed, it was hardly feasible economically. It placed too high a price tag on intelligence collection. One step further and they might as well load their electronics equipment onto a warship.

Nonetheless, because of the sensitivity of mission number nine, they asked for that destroyer 30 miles from Shanghai. The Seventh Fleet said the best it could do was to place the destroyer 450 miles—or sixteen hours' steaming time—away. Fifth Air Force was more cooperative. The 313th Air Division at Naha, Okinawa, provided a covey of F-102's armed with air-to-air missiles and 2.75-inch rockets on five-, thirty-, and sixty-minute runway alerts.

"That was quite a flap," recalls Lieutenant Colonel James F. Dugan, a balding former high school history teacher who was then on the operations staff at Fifth Air Force headquarters. "The boat was out on the mission before we ever got into the act. And the Navy's request had a very short fuse; it was all push, push, push."

The reason was that *Banner* was being subjected to severe harassment off Shanghai by eleven metal-hulled Chinese trawlers. As it turned out, however, there was no need for the Air Force to launch its planes. Lieutenant Bob Bishop skillfully extricated *Banner* from the surrounding trawlers and steamed back to Yokosuka. Bishop was then transferred to Vietnam. Lieutenant Commander Charles R. Clark assumed command, and now—in January, 1967—he was preparing for mission number ten, a voyage that would send *Banner* close to the North Korean coast en route to her primary operating area near the Soviet port of Vladivostok.

In conjunction with Captain William H. Everett and Lieutenant Commander Al Wilson from the COMNAVFORJAPAN operations staff, Lieutenant Brookes and Captain Dwyer began refining their plans for this patrol. The mission seemed routine; they decided not to request an Air Force strip alert.

The commander of the Fifth Air Force—indeed, of all U.S. forces in Japan at the time—was Lieutenant General Seth J. McKee, a brusque, hard-eyed former fighter pilot, a winner of the Silver Star and the Distinguished Flying Cross. McKee was a worrier, and he was especially concerned about the PARPRO, or reconnaissance, flights which the United States conducted near the North Korean coast. The North Koreans, he knew, had attacked and damaged an RB-47 several years before. They were constantly scrambling their fighters whenever lumbering EC-121 aircraft veered toward their coastline, and just a few weeks ago one of their shore batteries had blasted a South Korean patrol craft out of the water. So when he discovered that *Banner* planned to loiter off the North Korean coast during mission number ten, he decided to make sure that her new skipper, Charles Clark, understood the "on-call" support arrangement.

"If there is a war," he began, *"Banner* wil be the first to know, the first to go, and maybe the cause of it." Then he stressed his eagerness to provide help. "If you ever call on us, we'll come out there shooting. We'll always be ready. We'll go balls to the wall."

"I won't call you directly," Clark replied. "I'll contact my operational commander, and he'll do it. But come shooting anyway, because by that time we probably won't be around anymore to know the difference."

The more he thought about *Banner*'s track, the more General McKee worried about her safety. The Navy's reassurances sounded a little too pat; it wouldn't hurt to take extra precautions. Without informing the Navy, he sent a message to Brigadier General John W. Harrell, Jr., commander of the 314th Air Division at Osan, South Korea. The gist of the message: Place U.S. and ROK Air Force planes on alert.

"Colonel [Robert O.] Fricks and I came out one Saturday and wrote up the 'frag' directives for mission number ten," Lieutenant Colonel Dugan recalls. "We told them to pull the bombs out of the mountain and get live ammo available for immediate use. They had six birds on alert at Osan, all F-105's—'nickels,' we call them—plus two or three training birds."

As the commander in chief of United Nations Forces in Korea and, indeed, of the U.S. Eighth Army as well, General Charles H. Bonesteel III shouldered enormous responsibilities. He seemed an ideal choice for the post. A Rhodes scholar, an engineer, and a former special assistant to the Under Secretary of State, he had evidenced great personal courage. Several years before, glaucoma had left him with detached retinas and had threatened him with total blindness. Doctors had saved his right eye and placed a black patch over his left. He could have retired and drawn disability pay, but Bonesteel spurned the thought. He felt he could still make a contribution to his service and country; he decided to remain in uniform. His friends referred to him affectionately as "Tick."

Normally the calmest of men, Bonesteel was livid when he discovered that General McKee had placed those aircraft on alert. Only a few weeks ago the North Koreans had sunk that ROK patrol boat north of the military demarcation line. The ROK's had wanted to retaliate immediately, had even launched aircraft, and it had required all of Bonesteel's considerable skills to persuade them to return to their bases. General McKee was free to do what he wanted with U.S. planes. But here he was telling the ROK Air Force to help protect an *American* ship—and this after Bonesteel had said they couldn't try to save one of their own. The political consequences were potentially staggering.

His first impulse was to demand an explanation from General McKee. But this was a sensitive area. Such was the crazy-quilt nature of the U.S. command structure in the Far East that McKee, although his subordinate in rank, still maintained operational control over aircraft in his, Bonesteel's, jurisdiction. He contacted General Harrell and told him to cancel the ROK portion of the Air Force alert. Then he wondered how best to prevent this sort of thing from recurring.

To Bonesteel it was obvious that the Navy was behind all this. Apart from the political risks, didn't the Navy appreciate the sensitivity of the Wonsan area? Had the Navy forgotten how just a few months ago North Korean fighters had "flushed" on U.S. reconnaissance planes near Wonsan? He summoned Rear Admiral Donald G. Irvine, Commander, U.S. Naval Forces, Korea, and asked him what was going on.

But Irvine couldn't say. He'd heard about *Banner,* of course, but only in general terms, and nobody had bothered to tell him specifically about mission number ten or the Air Force alert. This was not surprising. His staff was so tiny that his civic affairs officer also had to serve as the staff aviator and then, when he found time, as the intelligence officer, as well. And Irvine's communications facilities were practically nonexistent. "Often messages that were specifically directed to me didn't reach me," he recalls, "and sometimes my messages never got through, either." Had the Navy requested this strip alert, and if so, why hadn't anyone informed him? Irvine knew where to find the answers.

Within hours after they received the admiral's summons, Captain Thomas L. Dwyer and Lieutenant Ed Brookes boarded a jet at Tachikawa Air Base and flew toward South Korea. Fog had closed the airport at Seoul; they had to land at Osan and didn't reach General Bonesteel's headquarters until the following morning. "I mentioned the general's special concern about the Wonsan area," Admiral Irvine recalls. "I told Captain Dwyer how upset he was about the alerts for this mission. I stressed that I didn't want to inhibit the possible use of U.S. planes in an emergency—just South Korean planes. I said we had to consider all the political ramifications before we ever asked them for help."

Dwyer said he understood perfectly; in the future he'd make sure that the admiral was kept informed of all intelligence ship operations in the COMNAVFORKOREA area. He and Brookes flew back to Japan. Two years later neither officer would be able to say how much this session in Seoul influenced his feelings about requesting air support for future missions along the coast of North Korea.

Banner left Yokosuka on January 31, entered the Sea of Japan, and steamed toward North Korea. "My impression was that it was a quiet area," Commander Clark recalls. "I couldn't get any action out of them. I paralleled the coast until I was about forty miles east of Wonsan; then I headed directly to the hundred-fathom curve at top speed and stopped about twenty miles from shore to lower a Nansen cast. There was one radar that tried hesitantly to lock onto us. Several extremely fast patrol boats—they may have been hydrofoils—raced by at between four thousand and six thousand yards, but they didn't show any interest. We finished the cast and moved north about ten miles. We spotted two fishing boats there, so I maneuvered around and conducted man overboard drills, but they paid no attention, either."

Banner chugged north toward Siberia, arrived at her operating area, and lowered a Nansen cast. A Soviet nuclear submarine surfaced 2,000 yards astern and slowly cruised past. Three guided-missile destroyers steamed out from Vladivostok, joined the submarine—which promptly submerged again—and began conducting an exercise, zigzagging progressively closer to *Banner*.

Less than forty-eight hours before, Clark had been complaining that no one seemed interested in him. Now a destroyer on his port bow flashed "Alpha, Alpha"—identify yourself. The destroyer leader lay directly across his bow about 1,000 yards out. The third destroyer sliced within 75 yards of his starboard side. Then a lookout shouted that the submarine was coming up; her bow was underneath *Banner*, her conning tower 20 feet away.

"I peered over the rail," Clark recalls, "and saw a dark, square shape with a five-foot pole sticking up in the middle. It looked like a submarine sail. Then I looked through the binoculars, and nothing was there. I looked again with the naked eye, and sure enough, I saw this big square shape. The temperature was about seven degrees; there was a lot of sea fog, and I realized that this shape was just the shadow of our deck house and the forward mast. So I lit my pipe and strolled to the other side.

"The destroyer on my starboard side was closing very slowly. I could hear chain falls and people running and yelling, breaking out boarding pikes and cutlasses, and a high whining sound like a missile being trained on target. He stopped abeam and started swinging his bow toward my stern.

"I got under way at one-third speed. The destroyer leader edged directly into my path, so I veered twenty degrees to the right, and this continued until I made a one-hundred-eighty-degree turn. Another destroyer came around and followed me with its search lights glaring, and I had visions of them trying to drop anchor on my ship. It was sort of like being on a freeway in a go-cart with a Greyhound bus roaring up behind you.

"One destroyer remained with us for several days. We tried to photograph him in the morning, but he stayed about a mile away against the sun. And every night he'd come screaming by at thirty knots and miss us by less than fifty yards." Clark spent three days and nights on the bridge with almost no sleep. If this harassment continued much longer, he thought, he'd steam south near Wonsan again, where conditions weren't so tense. At any rate, he'd have quite a story to pass on to his friend Pete Bucher.

14

Early in March Rear Admiral William F. Petrovic relieved Rear Admiral Floyd B. Schultz as the shipyard's commander. Petrovic had a high enough security clearance to know the details of the intelligence collection ship program, but he also had $275,000,000 in new ship construction to worry about at the same time. "*Pueblo* was just another job," he recalls, "and a minor one, at that." Her conversion continued at its normal pace.

Which was agonizingly slow. From an organizational standpoint, *Pueblo* fell into the administrative bailiwick of the commander, Service Force, Pacific Fleet in Hawaii, and he in turn had delegated responsibility to the commander, Service Group One in San Diego. The trouble with this neat-sounding arrangement was that the only man who seemed to possess a high enough clearance even to discuss the ship was Rear Admiral Edwin B. Hooper, COMSERVPAC himself, and Lieutenant Commander Bucher was not about to telephone Rear Admiral Hooper every time he encountered a problem.

And these problems multiplied. Lacy worried about the ship's inherent lack of damage control. He wanted watertight hatches leading into the forward berthing compartment and the office spaces. Request denied. He felt that *Pueblo* desperately needed a set of damage control plates and a damage control book. The Naval Ships Systems Command decided that ships smaller than 220 feet wouldn't require these plates or that book. Request denied. Bucher wanted to improve the crew's living quarters and mess decks. Request denied. He wanted his men to go to fire-fighting school. Request approved—provided that he could persuade the skipper of some other ship to help pay the bill.

The ship's internal communications system was a mess. There was was a 1MC, or public address system, but it couldn't function if the general alarm was ringing. Nor could the men in the research spaces hear this 1MC, for regulations prohibited placing a speaker there. A special "secure" link tied these spaces to the captain's cabin and the pilot house effectively enough, but the primary communications system aboard ship was a 1JV sound-powered telephone circuit which the Army had installed before the end of World War II. It boasted thirty-odd outlets, and Bucher knew that in an emergency maneuvering or general quarters situation the resultant "wire flooding" would impede his ability to receive reports and issue orders.

All Navy ships today use several types of sound-powered communications links. Bucher requested a new 1JV circuit, a second circuit for damage control, a third for navigation, and an intercom to link the pilot house with the engine room. These requests, as well as a plea for a collision alarm, were denied. His only hope was to try to acquire this material from a submarine that was awaiting decommissioning and to see if he could install it himself.

Bucher was even more concerned about his ship's stability. The lengthening of the forward mast, the addition of the research spaces on the main deck—all this extra weight had decreased *Pueblo*'s "righting arm" to the point where she might easily capsize. One way to compensate for this would be to provide ballast. Nothing had been done about that. Another means of lowering the ship's center of gravity would be to get rid of the whaleboat. He didn't need it, anyway; he had life rafts for ninety men. Shipyard officials told him to keep the whaleboat.

He couldn't blame those officials. They were only following orders. Washington kept insisting that there was no money or time for improvements, that *Pueblo* was due for commissioning at any moment. So work which might have required only five weeks to complete was never even begun.

Bucher turned to Lieutenant Commander Carroll S. (Deke) Jones, the program's "action officer" at the Pentagon.

"He had some squawks, but he'd been briefed before he went out there that this was an austere program," Jones remembers. "He seemed to forget that. He asked for a lot of things that were frosting on the cake—a rudder angle indicator on the wing of the bridge, improvements to the mess decks, additional bodies—things that weren't in keeping with the game at all."

Jones' counterpart at the Naval Ships Systems Command, the man primarily responsible for drawing up the ship's specifications and submitting them to Bremerton, was a stocky, curly-haired civilian named Al Johnston. Although Johnston was spending at least 25 percent of his time "running around trying to obtain equipment with high priority for an AKL," his efforts were of little benefit, for, incredibly, no one in the Navy hierarchy had ever told him that *Pueblo* was not a standard AKL.

Thoroughly frustrated by the responses he was receiving, Bucher telephoned a senior captain at the Pentagon. The captain listened politely and then inquired, "What are you trying to do—make a Cadillac out of a rust bucket?"

"Army" Canales was beginning to wonder if he'd made a mistake in passing up those orders to the destroyer in Norfolk. His job here wasn't working out; he was having trouble setting up the ship's office. The forms and publications that all ships were supposed to receive automatically hadn't arrived. At the captain's request, he wrote several letters to COMSERVPAC. ". . . although designated as an AKL, we are not. Please send us appropriate directives. . . ." Those directives never came.

He didn't want to bother the captain about his problems, for he could see that Bucher had enough to worry about already. He noticed that no matter how discouraged the captain became, he never criticized his superiors in front of the crew. He maintained that the situation was bound to improve, and every morning he entered the office in Building 50 with a smile on his face and a box of sugar-coated rolls in his hand. "Here, Yeo," he'd say. "Have some." Canales thought he was the friendliest skipper he'd ever known.

To Lieutenant j.g. David (Teddy) Behr, the treatment that *Pueblo* was receiving was downright disgraceful. A short, muscular, high-cheekboned bachelor, a graduate of the California Maritime Academy, Behr had reported aboard as the ship's operations officer and had agreed to serve as the acting XO until someone else arrived. He didn't care for *Pueblo,* but he was determined nonetheless to do his best for the ship. He wasn't adverse to leading "raiding parties" to cumshaw vitally needed supplies, nor was he shy about making demands on shipyard personnel—feeling no qualms, for example, in approaching the master of a shop and raising hell about this or that. On several occasions his vehemence almost brought him to blows with Lieutenant Commander Leo Sweeney, the lean, easy-going Boston Irishman who served as the ship's superintendent. No one faulted Behr's motives—he was only standing up for what he believed to be right—or his basic ability. But everyone questioned his tact.

Some of his personal habits irritated his shipmates, as well. He strolled about in shower shoes, was a sloppy dresser, and on occasion left classified material where anyone could pick it up. Although he seemed to have unlimited funds—he rarely cashed his paychecks—

Behr was continually bumming cigarettes from the crew. "Hey, Mack, what you smoking?" he'd ask, and the tall, bespectacled photographer would reach instinctively for his pocket.

Behr could be arrogant, as well. Late one evening, coming off liberty, he approached the quarterdeck watch. "I want a call at six o'clock," he said. "Do you know how to call an officer? Will you wake me at six?"

The sailor replied that he'd be off watch himself at that hour, but he'd pass the word along.

"Tell him to wake me up," Behr continued. "But don't touch me. Don't lay a hand on me."

Behr disagreed with Bucher's plans to pattern *Pueblo*'s organization along submarine lines and, characteristically, told him so. "I pointed out that submariners as a group are much more skillful than anyone else in the Navy when it comes to fundamentals," he remembers. "We had people aboard that ship who didn't know the front end from the back. I told Pete that he was overestimating the crew's capabilities. He didn't see it that way."

Steve Harris arrived at Bremerton on the cold, clear evening of March 12. His duties as research officer wouldn't begin until the ship's commissioning, so he "volunteered" to relieve Dave Behr as the acting XO. Harris was willing enough and competent in his specialty, but he knew very little about organizing a ship. "I liked Steve," says ship superintendent Leo Sweeney. "He wasn't afraid to ask questions. He just didn't impress me as a nautical person. He didn't have the saltwater touch."

Bucher felt the same way, and from time to time he lost his temper: "Steve, why can't you do this right?" "Steve, don't you have a brain in your head?" "The stuff never got done," Bucher adds. "I really couldn't chew him out, because it wasn't his job in the first place."

But Harris persevered. "Very early in the game," he recalls, "I learned that whenever Pete said he wanted something done, I'd better write it down and give it to the right person to handle, because he wouldn't forget about it. He'd expect it to be done automatically, and he'd be pretty upset if it wasn't."

Nonetheless, to Harris Bucher still represented a paradox. The captain was obviously a humanist who cared deeply about his crew. He'd even let his hair grow long—so he could "associate with the kids," he said—and he was sincerely trying to better their living and working conditions. Yet at the same time he could be so very demanding, so totally oblivious to the inconveniences he was causing other people. He seemed to assume that other people were always thinking exactly what *he* was thinking, and if he decided he wanted ice cream at three o'clock in the morning, well, didn't *everyone?* It was amazing how Bucher could rage at a man all day and then, promptly at five o'clock, stroll up with a grin on his face and say, "Let's get to the club and have a beer."

"For the first couple of days I'd go up and drink with him at the officers' club," Harris recalls, "but it would always drag on to eight or nine o'clock, and that's not my idea of a good time. So I started looking for excuses to be somewhere else."

On Friday, March 17, St. Patrick's Day, Bucher asked if he could borrow Harris' car. He didn't say where he wanted to go, and Harris didn't ask. Next day the Bremerton *Sun* carried the following story on page one:

> Twenty persons were arrested today on charges involving prostitution and gambling after 15 Bremerton police officers and two policewomen made an early morning raid on a downtown Bremerton hotel. The raid, the end result of several months of investigation, . . . began about 1 a.m., Detective Sgt. Edwin (Ed) Schlie said today. . . .
>
> Those who were suspected of gambling at the time of the raid were charged with illegal gambling, while those who were found in the room where gambling was taking place, were charged with frequenting a gambling place. . . .
>
> "Charges of gambling were set against . . . Lloyd M. Bucher, Puget Sound Naval Shipyard. . . . Bail for those arrested for gambling was set at $300.

Bucher explained the circumstances to Admiral Petrovic, the yard's commander. He had arrived at the hotel less than an hour before the raid; he had no idea that any illegal activities were taking place. On March 22 he forfeited his $300 bail. No further disposition was made of the case.

Ever since the middle of February technicians from Ling-Temco-Vought's ElectroSystems Division had been preparing to install the complex electronic gear in the research spaces of *Pueblo* and *Palm Beach*. They had no detailed specifications to follow—the Navy had said there wasn't time to develop any, had in fact listed its requirements only in terms of capabilities—but they were sure nonetheless that they could handle these installations just as successfully as they'd handled the one on *Banner*. They reserved space in a permanent building at the shipyard; they used a small, gray, portable work shack filled with desks and drafting tables down on the pier itself, and now, under the direction of a genial Texan named Jim L. Shuler, they began assembling antennae and making their cable runs. By the end of March they had completed 90 percent of the work on *Pueblo* and 50 percent on *Palm Beach*.

Because he was acting as XO, Harris hadn't had time to oversee the installation on a daily basis. Nor was he that familiar with the equipment from a nuts and bolts standpoint. Yet now he began to see "things taking place in the spaces which were suspicious; they didn't seem right." Bucher agreed with him.

"I wanted to know what the hell provisions were going to be made for the operators," Bucher says, "where they were going to sit. I wanted to put sub tracks in there and a bench that could slide back and forth. LTV used straight-backed chairs with straps to hold the chairs in place, and I knew those chairs wouldn't stay in one spot longer than three seconds when we were under way. If a storm came up, those guys would have to hold onto the gear just to stay alive."

There were no grab bars overhead; there was no stowage space for test equipment or magnetic tapes or boxes of photographic and recording paper. Even the little comforts provided on *Banner*—ashtrays and coffee cup containers built into the equipment—were missing on *Pueblo*. What upset Harris and Bucher even more was the lack of human engineering. The power supply gauge for one piece of equipment had been installed at chest level. In order to operate that equipment, however, a CT would have to get down on his hands and knees. This configuration made no sense. Yet LTV was not to blame, for there it was, all spelled out in the book of plans that Washington had just approved.

The project officer for the research spaces on *Pueblo* and *Palm Beach* at the Naval Security Station in Washington, D.C., was a stocky, dark-haired, rather handsome lieutenant named Richard C. Yeck. He knew very little about modern electronics. And he had never been to sea on Security Group operations. "I had those plans on my desk a long time," he recalls, "and I looked at them a little every day. Something was bugging me about those plans."

Unable to explain his uneasiness, he asked a friend in another section, Lieutenant John P. Arnold, to review the plans. A blond, bespectacled former enlisted man, a forthright and conscientious fellow who liked to peruse sophisticated electronics publications in his spare time, Arnold had once been a "knob-twister" himself, and he could flip through sets of blueprints and see things in their third dimension as easily as another man might read the sports pages of the Washington

Post. "Toss them on my desk," Arnold replied, "and when I get a moment, I'll take a look.

"I thought at this stage that they were still proposals," he says. "There was no indication that there was any contract or that the work was in progress. I made quite a few notes and put question marks in the margins, and I told Dick Yeck that I wouldn't buy those proposals for all the tea in China. He sort of choked. He said not only had they been bought, they were almost finished. And I said well, if that was true, we really had problems."

At Yeck's request, Arnold flew to Bremerton on April 25. A thorough inspection of the research spaces confirmed his fears. The equipment had been installed in a manner befitting Rube Goldberg. Nowhere in the spaces was there any provision for destruct equipment. What would *Pueblo* do in an emergency? Bucher said he'd already written several letters about this but hadn't received any replies. Arnold showed him a sketch of an incinerator that REWSON had proposed for the ship, a 55-gallon drum bolted to the fantail.

"I said I felt like an ass even giving this to him," Arnold remembers. "We agreed right away that it was ridiculous. You wouldn't be able to use it in an emergency because of the likelihood of enemy gunfire. So I suggested using some void spaces within the stack for a fuel-fed incinerator. Bucher and I thought this plan was quite workable, really, but the shipyard said no. *Banner* didn't have anything like that. It would take too much time and cost too much money."

Arnold stayed in Bremerton four days and drew up a list of some 200 deficiencies—120 of them pertaining to problems in the research area, the rest dealing with such general ship items as the cramped mess decks and the lack of bunks in the forward berthing compartment. "I gave Bucher a copy of this list," Arnold says, "and told him my recommendation to Washington was going to be: 'Take care of everything or don't sail the ship.' He said he felt the same way."

At ten o'clock on the morning of May 8, in the third-floor conference room at the Naval Security Station, Arnold presented his findings and urged that steps be taken to correct the deficiencies. He suggested that many of the classified documents aboard ship be placed on microfilm. This would minimize their bulk and simplify emergency destruction. Lieutenant Dick Yeck agreed with him; so did Yeck's boss in the Fleet Support Section, Lieutenant Commander Denny M. Carder.

They ran into opposition immediately. "The people at that meeting couldn't believe so much could be so wrong," Arnold recalls. "The whole thing was hard to swallow. I'd been at the station less than six months, and I knew they were thinking, 'Wow, what a troublemaker this guy is.' I was putting a lot of people in a jam, all the people who had 'chopped off' on these proposals. It was a very touchy situation.

"The general consensus was, 'We aren't concerned with the ship; we'll just worry about the shack.' So we went down the list, and they kept saying, 'We're not interested in this; that's not our responsibility; we don't care about that.' We placed the items in three categories: 'mandatory,' 'nice to have,' and 'luxury.' The rest, they said, 'Don't bother yourself with them.' "

The man who dominated that meeting—and led the opposition to Arnold's suggestions—was a burly, outspoken, retired Navy chief from Colorado named Daniel Preecs. As the project coordinator for *Pueblo* and *Palm Beach* in the REWSON section of the Naval Ships Systems Command, he had helped draw up the plans that LTV was using. He thought of *Pueblo* as "just another old ship, just another job." He maintained that a destruct system wasn't necessary "because it would create horrendous design problems." He insisted—and still insists today—that the installation of the gear in the research spaces was satisfactory; that it was perfectly acceptable to ask a CT to get down on his hands and knees to operate a piece of equipment. And he maintained that the ship's stability and habitability were simply not his concerns.

Preecs was not an engineer, but such was the force of his personality that no one questioned his technical competence. As the meeting continued, Commander Richard A. Weiner, Arnold's boss, sided with Preecs. So did other officers. Finally a compromise was agreed upon. Arnold would return to Bremerton to reassess his findings. And just to make sure that he didn't miss anything, Preecs would accompany him.

15

At three o'clock on that same afternoon of May 8, Lieutenant Edward R. Murphy, Jr., reported aboard *Pueblo* as her executive officer. Tall, bespectacled, cheerful, and very poised, he impressed everyone as a competent, unflappable man who would help Bucher enormously.

A third-generation Californian, or—as he liked to point out—a direct descendant thirteen times removed of one of the *Mayflower*'s passengers, Murphy grew up in the small town of McKinleyville, where his family operated a general store. In 1953, at sixteen, he entered the Principia Upper School, a private, Christian Science–oriented institution in St. Louis. "Ed was a good organizer, a good manager, the kind of guy you could always rely on," a classmate remembers. "He was a very ethical person, very fair."

Although he had been accepted by the University of Pennsylvania, Murphy enrolled instead at Principia College in Elsah, Illinois, just across the Mississippi River from St. Louis. He majored in sociology but, "because I wasn't serious enough about my studies," dropped out after his sophomore year to help his father at the store in McKinleyville.

In the fall of 1958 he returned to Principia, leaving temporarily once again to study ecology at the University of Mexico City. And so respectable was his analysis of the Mercado Merced, the central market, that he was invited to present papers on the subject by several colleges and universities. He left Principia in June, 1960, with a degree in sociology and a military obligation to fulfill.

His grandfather had been a general in the Army; several other relatives had chosen Army careers, as well, but Murphy had always been attracted by the sea, and he enrolled at Officers' Candidate School in Newport, Rhode Island. "Newport was a challenge," he remembers, "and I love a challenge. I've always been amazed at how easy something falls when you challenge it."

He filled a succession of standard junior officer billets: communications officer on USS *Guadeloupe,* assistant navigator on the destroyer USS *Twining,* navigator on the guided-missile destroyer USS *Robison.* To a surprising degree, the officers and men who served with him during those years use the same words and phrases to describe him: "fair," "ethical," "methodical," "a gentleman," "a straight arrow," "he always relied on his senior petty officers' judgment." Not everyone appreciated his dry sense of humor—one former colleague recalls that "he wasn't even up to nineteen-forties jokes"—and some interpreted his quiet certitude as self-righteousness.

Although he fully enjoyed the Navy and, indeed, planned to remain on active duty, he still felt tempted by a career in retail merchandising. During his tour on *Twining* he had had opportunities to attend Junior Chamber of Commerce meetings in the Philippines and now, back in the United States again awaiting deployment on *Robison* to Yankee Station, off the coast of Vietnam, he worried about the problems his family was having with the store in McKinleyville. He had just married an attractive, strong-willed girl, a fellow Christian Scientist named Carol Danks; children would be coming along in a few years, and he wasn't at all sure that he could provide for them on a junior officer's salary. Besides, he even *looked* like he belonged behind the counter of a store. No matter where he went as a customer—to Shafer's Hardware, say, in Eureka—people were always approaching him to ask the price of this or that. *Robison* was due to sail momentarily. He would worry about the future later.

His tour on *Robison* ended abruptly. His father died; his mother was having trouble holding onto the store. He applied for and received shore duty at the Naval Facility in Centerville Beach, California. One morning in March 1966, he and another officer swam out through frigid, pounding surf to rescue three fishermen whose boat had smashed against the rocks. His "prompt and courageous actions" won him the Navy and Marine Corps medal. As base maintenance officer and building engineer, he was responsible for overseeing the lighting, refrigeration, and sewage treatment at twenty-four Capehart houses. But Centerville Beach was close to McKinleyville. He spent several hours a day managing the store, trying to stave off bankruptcy.

"This was one of the busiest times of my life," he recalls. "We had a brand-new baby, and I was working hard at two jobs and not getting much sleep. I was selected to go to postgraduate school in engineering sciences, but I decided I just couldn't do it. Then I got orders to take over as XO on *Pueblo*. I thought I'd experienced the excitement of my life already. I left Centerville ready to relax."

Up to this point in his career, Murphy had served under seven commanders and six captains, and he'd considered all of them as "fairly serious officers." One glance told him his new skipper didn't fit into that category. Bucher was dressed in khakis, his hair was long, and he seemed so very informal, referring to people by their first names immediately.

"Ed seemed ready to go to work," Bucher remembers, "and I was delighted to have him because I thought the Navy had been remiss in not giving me an exec to start the damn thing with, to organize that ship. I gave him a rundown and asked him what the status of his clearance was and when his family was arriving. He said he still had some personal matters to attend to, and I replied that we might be able to work that out, but the commissioning was only five days off and we really had work to do. I told him how much I'd written on the ship's organization and said I wanted him to honcho the thing and get a tickler system set up. I told him in general terms the way I wanted things done.

"We were in the office in Building Fifty there, and Gene [Lacy] came in, and I said, 'Well, let's all go up and get a beer.' Ed said he didn't drink, and I thought he was kidding me, so I said, 'Well, come on, you can have a *beer*.' He said, 'Nope.' I still thought he was kidding me. We went up to the O Club, and Gene and I ordered a beer. Ed had a Coke, and he didn't really seem to want to talk much at all. Most people, they're going to be serving together—particularly in a CO-XO relationship—they want to get to know each other. But Ed was a little stand-offish.

"After he'd gone—he just excused himself and left—Gene said to me, 'Jesus, this is going to be some kind of wardroom with six people and an XO who won't even have a beer with the boys.' I didn't say anything to Gene then, but I was thinking about it."

Early in May Vice Admiral J. B. Colwell, the Deputy CNO for Fleet Operations and Readiness, ended several months of arguments by deciding that *Pueblo* should be designated an AGER. Her new classification, however, wouldn't take effect until June 1, and she would have to go into commission as AKL-44. To *Pueblo*'s officers the delay seemed ridiculous. It would cost at least $1,000 just to change the beads on her hull from AKL to AGER—not to mention the cost of reordering ship's emblems and stationery. Furthermore, the city officials of Pueblo, Colorado, had gone to the trouble of embronzing a plaque with the ship's name and the letters AKL; no one could tell them those letters no longer applied.

Dave Behr was having difficulty writing the blurb for the commissioning pamphlet. Murphy had asked him to find out if *Pueblo* rated any special theater ribbons or unit decorations. He called the Army Historian's office, but no one there seemed able to help. He had to write *something* about the ship's function, but at the same time he had instructions to avoid any phrases which might attract publicity.

He found some glossy photographs of President Lyndon B. Johnson, Vice President Hubert H. Humphrey, Secretary of Defense Robert S. McNamara, and every admiral within a radius of 500 miles. Together, they ought to fill half a dozen of those pages. Behr was an "anchor-clanker," an expert ship-handler, not a gifted writer at all. But suddenly, with true inspiration, he thought of a way to describe *Pueblo*'s responsibilities: "The United States Navy has been a world leader for many years in the conduct of oceanographic research," he wrote. ". . . *Pueblo* joins the fleet proudly in the knowledge that the research operations she will conduct will be an aid to the Navy and mankind. . . ."

Just after dawn on the windy, overcast morning of May 13, Bucher stepped down to the ship. The joint commissioning ceremony for *Pueblo* and *Palm Beach* wasn't scheduled to begin until eleven o'clock, still more than four hours away, but he hadn't been able to sleep well, and now—with the excitement of a child surveying his presents under the tree on Christmas morning—he stood at the end of Pier 6 and gazed at his prize. His first command. A rather ungainly tub, he had to admit, but immaculate inside and out; he had seen to that. The bunting and banners along her sides rippled easily in the breeze.

The ceremony itself would be closed to the public, but this restriction hardly mattered, for the people whom he cared about most would watch him assume command. Rose and his eldest son, Mark, had arrived at the shipyard and were staying with him at the guest house there. Just the other night—after an interval of twenty-two years—he'd managed to get together with Frank Roe, his old friend and classmate from Boys Town; Frank would be an honorary "plank-owner" this morning. And even more wonderful, Father Nicholas H. Wegner, the spry and kindly priest who had succeeded the late Father Flanagan as director of Boys Town, would deliver the benediction. Bucher walked back to the guest house and slipped into his dress blues. He'd have to borrow a chestful of medals from someone, but everything else seemed in order. He put on a pair of white gloves and attached the long sword to his belt.

By ten o'clock Ron Berens had finished hosing down the whaleboat. He reached forward to secure its canvas cover, lost his balance, and tumbled over the side. Steve Harris saw the splash and wondered if it signaled an omen. Berens rushed below to change his uniform. In a few minutes he'd have to blow the whistle to set the first watch. Suddenly, the bugler sounded "attention"; the band played ruffles and flourishes, then swung into the "Admiral's March." A Navy chaplain stepped forward to deliver the invocation.

To Dr. James A. Crutchfield, a professor of economics at the University of Washington, the invitation to present the commissioning address had not come as a surprise. Rear Admiral William E. Ferrall, the commandant of the 13th Naval District, had explained that *Pueblo* and *Palm Beach* would conduct oceanographic research, and Crutchfield had long specialized in the economic development of fisheries; he had, in fact, set up fisheries centers for the United Nations in Africa. Furthermore, as the son, brother, and nephew of Annapolis graduates, he felt a strong attachment to the Navy. But Crutchfield was also an amateur radio operator, and one glance told him *Pueblo* and *Palm Beach* were no ordinary research vessels.

"Say, Lieutenant," he remarked, a puzzled expression on his face, "that's not fishing gear sticking out over there." Dave Behr quickly explained that none of the oceanographic equipment had arrived yet, and Crutchfield, reassured, rose to stress the importance of this kind of Naval research in developing food from the sea. Food from the sea! Standing in ranks on the pier, a few of the CT's pinched themselves to keep from laughing.

The rest of the ceremony proceeded more or less according to schedule. Murphy forgot to introduce one of the admirals, who, after a significant pause, introduced himself. The public address system on *Palm Beach* sputtered and failed—just as her executive officer was posting the first watch. Then Bucher stepped up to introduce Father Wegner. "If it had not been for Boys Town, I wouldn't be taking command of this fine ship today. . . ." He paused; he saw tears forming in the old priest's eyes. His voice began to crack. For a long moment he could not continue.

Traditionally, whenever a ship is undergoing conversion, the commander of the unit to which she will be assigned visits the yard to inspect her himself. The skipper of Service Squadron Seven in San Francisco had assigned the task to some junior officers on his staff. Now Bucher sent a message to SERVRONSEVEN headquarters: *Pueblo* was in commission; he was reporting for duty. His telephone rang almost immediately. The officer on the other end of the line sounded perplexed. "But *Pueblo* doesn't belong to SERVRONSEVEN," he began.

"Well," Bucher replied, "if you'll read the SERVPAC Monthly Administrative Bulletin, you'll find out we do."

There was a pause. "Jesus, you're right," the officer exclaimed. "But I don't think that's correct. I think you should be with SERV-GRUONE."

Lieutenant John Arnold flew back to Bremerton with Dan Preecs on May 16. As soon as he entered the research spaces, Preecs' normally ruddy complexion paled. He had experienced heart trouble some years before, and Arnold feared that he might suffer another attack. "It was obvious to Dan that we did have problems," Arnold recalls. "He had 'chopped' the plans originally, but so had quite a few others, and it upset him so much that he let me talk everything over with the contractor while he went back to the motel."

As Arnold went down his list of discrepancies, Jim L. Shuler and L. D. Turner of Ling-Temco-Vought's ElectroSystems Division slapped a price tag on each one. They'd need more than $250,000 to relocate, augment, and rewire the electronic gear on *Pueblo* and *Palm Beach,* and this estimate covered only the "mandatory" items. Such "luxury" or "nice to have" additions as grab bars for the CT's to use during stormy weather were out of the question.

"I viewed *all* these items as mandatory," Arnold says, "but half a loaf was a lot better than none." There was no time to lose. Until Washington renegotiated the contract, LTV's technicians were obliged to meet their original milestones—and this would cost the Navy an extra $4,000 a day. Lieutenant Dick Yeck quickly secured permission to modify the contract to correct the boo-boos. Arnold flew to Texas over a weekend to hammer out details with the contractor. By the following Tuesday Yeck had a printed proposal from LTV to show his superiors.

Early on the morning of June 2 *Pueblo* eased away from her pier and chugged into Puget Sound for the first of her informal sea trials. The first test on the schedule entailed dropping the "hook," a relatively simple task. Unfortunately, the anchor chain didn't fit the anchor windlass; it jumped off the "wildcat" and flapped about. A second test was designed to determine the engines' reaction time. How quickly could *Pueblo* reach her flank speed of 13.1 knots? How long would it take her to attain emergency backing speed?

Bucher ordered left full rudder as the ship was backing up. Suddenly the cable slipped off its drum and—under 30,000 pounds of stress—mangled some pieces of steel next to the quadrant so badly that they looked like they'd been hit by cannon fire.

"We started going around in circles," Gene Lacy recalls. "The CO was very cool. He acted as if this sort of thing happened every day." Bucher could steer the ship with the engines alone, but at this point it wasn't advisable. There was some traffic in the sound, and in order to steam back to the yard he'd have to pass through Rich's Passage, where the currents are tricky. He decided to call for a tug.

Most Navy ships use hydraulic steering systems. *Pueblo*'s was elec-tromechanical, the product of an elevator company which had gone out of business after World War II. No spare parts were available. Bucher had long suspected that this system would cause trouble, and now, as he reached the yard, he didn't attempt to hide his anger. He wanted it fixed immediately. Yard officials said the problem lay in gauging correct settings for the two limit switches; they'd put their best electricians to work on it at once.

Bucher was concerned as well about the lack of response to his repeated requests for a destruct system. On June 9 he wrote the Chief of Naval Operations.

"The scope of security sensitive equipment aboard . . . renders their quick destruction impossible using conventional means; i.e., fire ax, sledge hammer, destruction bags. An explosive destruction means should be provided to the ship which will enable [me] to thoroughly destroy all sensitive classified materials quickly should the need arise. . . ."

His third major problem involved his relationships with Behr and Murphy. Behr was so adamant in his demands that he was alienating the yard's work force. "I ate Dave's ass out several times," Bucher re-calls. "He actually broke down and cried. He said he was sorry and he apologized profusely and then he'd go out and do the same damn thing all over again."

His problem with Murphy was more difficult. He and the tall XO argued constantly. He wanted to conn *Pueblo* from the flying bridge, where he had better visibility. Murphy insisted that the pilot house was a far better site; it offered better communications and afforded pro-tection. Murphy had wanted to drop the hook in the anchor drill at one location; Bucher had opted for another. Murphy quickly realized that he could never win such arguments and tried to do his job as best he could without confronting the skipper. This only aggravated Bucher further.

"Ed was unsat almost from the beginning," Bucher says. "Any time I could corner him, I'd ask him how these projects were coming—I'd have them all written down, A-B-C-D, and he'd say, 'Well, they are coming along; we're working on them.' And I'd say, 'Show me what you've done so far,' and he'd say, 'Well, I'm still thinking about them.' And the work never got done. It was a very unpleasant relationship. I didn't know what in hell I could do."

Over the past several weeks Bucher had become increasingly impressed by the quiet competence of Lieutenant Carmen Angelosante, the dark-haired, twenty-eight-year-old executive officer on *Palm Beach*. Angelosante was a producer, and he was unflappable, too; he hadn't seemed flustered when the public address system quit on commissioning day. One night, over a drink at the officers' club, Bucher proposed a deal: if he could arrange for Murphy's transfer, would Angelosante consider becoming *Pueblo*'s new exec?

Angelosante hesitated. *Palm Beach* was a larger, more comfortable ship, and Lieutenant Commander Raper was an outstanding skipper. Bucher seemed able enough, too; an inspiring leader, perhaps, but was he really serious about this offer? Angelosante didn't know. He decided to stay where he was.

Largely as a result of Lieutenant John Arnold's persistence, the Navy approved the $250,000-plus "reconfiguration package." The ship would have to remain at the yard for at least five extra weeks. Bucher thought this delay would afford enough time to improve the mess decks, as well.

Up to this point all of his pleas for help in this area had been denied. Visiting Bremerton just a few weeks earlier, Al Johnston, the civilian project officer from the Naval Ships Systems Command, had agreed that the conditions were poor. But there was no money or time to remedy the situation, he said, and no personnel to do the work. Bruce Towne, the short, gray-haired design program manager at the shipyard, echoed Johnston's negativism. During one stormy meeting he'd even referred to *Pueblo* as "that tub," infuriating Bucher and rendering the possibility of their future cooperation even more remote.

The five-week delay clearly invalidated all of Towne's and Johnston's arguments. Still, Bucher knew better than to approach them directly. He asked a retired chief, a hospital corpsman, to inspect the mess decks. The chief decided that, as presently configured, they constituted a health hazard. Then, at Bucher's invitation, the commander of the Puget Sound Naval Supply Center visited the ship. He agreed with the chief's diagnosis and sent a letter to COMSERVPAC. Within two weeks Bucher had the $65,000 he'd sought.

With the help of the skipper of USS *Ranger*, Bucher had been able to send a few of his men to fire-fighting school. Now he requested permission to send additional crewmen to schools in San Diego. At first, the commander of Service Group One resisted the idea—who'd ever

heard of an AGER? Then, reluctantly, he agreed. The twelve *Pueblo*
CT's who attended the damage control elements school earned an
achievement rating 5.5 points higher than the Navy average.

Shipyard workers and LTV technicians swarmed over the research
spaces and mess decks. Until their tasks were completed, *Pueblo*'s crewmen didn't have much to do, and Bucher set a liberal leave and liberty
policy.

Almost every weekend Duane Hodges climbed into his old Pontiac
and headed south to tiny Creswell, Oregon, where his older brother,
Marion, had just started a contracting business. Hodges' father remembers that during one of these visits home, his son seemed worried. "It
doesn't look good, Dad," he explained. "They're loading on all this
electronics equipment."

John (Tiny) Higgins had another concern. "We've got more guns
in our home," he told his father, "than we have on the ship." He was
almost right. The Higgins family arsenal consisted of two rifles, three
.22 caliber pistols, and four shotguns. *Pueblo*'s allowance included four
carbines and seven .45 caliber pistols—the standard prescription for an
AKL. Bucher and *Palm Beach*'s skipper, Lieutenant Commander
Raper, wrote a joint letter to the Chief of Naval Operations, and in
short order they received a new allowance: one carbine, seven .45 caliber
pistols, ten Thompson submachine guns, and fifty "antiswimmer"
grenades.

By the spring of 1967 Admiral Horacio Rivero, Jr., the peppery
Vice Chief of Naval Operations, had become concerned about the lack
of armament on many ships, which in his view "might . . . subject
[them] to being overpowered by even a very minor craft." He asked the
Deputy CNO for Fleet Operations and Readiness, Vice Admiral J. B.
Colwell, to look into the problem, and Colwell recommended that all
except hospital ships receive .50 caliber machine guns.

Then, in June, Israeli planes and torpedo boats attacked USS
Liberty off the Egyptian coast, killing thirty-four in her crew and
wounding seventy-five others. Rivero promptly decided that .50 caliber
machine guns would no longer suffice; all ships had to carry "at least
.20 mm guns."

The admiral's order filtered down through the chain of command,
and by the time it reached Bremerton, the .20 mm provision had been
expanded somehow to stipulate three-inch .50 mm guns. The trouble
was that *Pueblo* would probably sink under the weight of a three-inch
gun. Bucher recommended instead that the shipyard install twin
.20 mm or .40 mm guns in tubs with adequate shielding. The yard's
planning department conducted a study and—without showing Bucher

its report—forwarded its suggestions to Washington. The Naval Ships Systems Command decided that *further* study was necessary. Bucher was never able to find out what had happened to his original recommendations.

Meanwhile, seemingly oblivious to Admiral Rivero's order, the commander of Service Group One sent a chief gunner's mate to Bremerton with two .50 caliber machine guns. Dave Behr wrote a job order requesting the shipyard to mount them. Yard officials rejected it. These guns, they said, constituted the new allowance for an AKL. But *Pueblo* was no longer an AKL; she was an AGER, and no one had decided yet what an AGER's weapons authorization should be. Behr would have to return the guns to COMSERVGRUONE in San Diego.

16

In the halcyon days just prior to World War II, the nickname for the Navy's Combat Intelligence Unit at Pacific Fleet headquarters in Hawaii was "Station Hypo." (Even then, Washington was known as "Negat.") Hypo was, as Walter Lord points out in his excellent book *Incredible Victory*, a small, seemingly disorganized but highly effective operation presided over by "a tall, thin, humorously caustic man in a red smoking jacket and carpet slippers"—a brilliant cryptologist named Joseph J. Rochefort, Jr.

In the summer of 1967, however, Commander Rochefort would not have recognized the place. The Hypo nickname had long since faded into oblivion, and the Intelligence Division at CINCPACFLT headquarters had split into four large branches located on both decks of the sprawling, white-stucco building at the end of Makalapa Drive. The 21 branch was Plans and Policy, 22 was Current Intelligence, 23 was Reconnaissance and Indications, and 24 was Target Intelligence. Each of these branches, in turn, had split into several sections. The number of officers and men in the Intelligence Division had ballooned accordingly—from twenty-four in 1941 to nearly eighty in 1967. And the assistant chief of staff for intelligence at the time was not the sort of fellow to stroll about in a red smoking jacket and carpet slippers.

This is not to imply any criticism of Captain John L. Marocchi, who was—and is—one of the U.S. intelligence community's most respected Soviet analysts. A lean, sad-eyed Annapolis graduate, holder of a master's degree in engineering administration as well as in international relations, he was a modest, unassuming fellow who frowned upon ostentation. His only bow toward relaxation consisted of his regular Wednesday and Saturday afternoon golf games; although he could never cut his handicap below 15, he took the game very seriously.

And when he left the links, he always returned to the office. He agonized over the morning intelligence briefings for the admiral, pouring over the slides and charts and shunning rambling dissertations in favor of meaningful details presented concisely. Above all else, John Marocchi was an orderly man.

As such, he wanted to run a smooth operation. For in addition to keeping the admiral informed, he had to make sure that every U.S. ship in the First and Seventh Fleets, indeed, in the entire Pacific, received the intelligence support she needed to accomplish her mission. And this was what concerned him in the summer of 1967. The turnover on his staff was so high that inexperienced officers—ensigns and lieutenant j.g.'s—were being asked to step into billets of great responsibility. Even more disturbing, there seemed to be a clash brewing between two of the most competent officers in his Current Intelligence Branch. He'd have to settle this dispute before it affected the branch's production.

The problems in the Current Intelligence Branch had first begun festering several months ago and by now were almost beyond therapy. Their origins lay in a simmering stew of constant pressure, overwork, and conflicting personal ambitions, and if there is honest disagreement even today as to who was at fault, there is at the same time reluctant admission that the turmoil retarded the flow of intelligence data to ships operating in the Western Pacific—operating, for example, in the Sea of Japan.

Late in November, 1966, a twenty-five-year-old lieutenant j.g. named Donald Whortley moved into the Navy section of the Current Intelligence Branch. The son of a grape grower in California's Napa Valley, a graduate of Berkeley, Whortley was responsible for familiarizing himself with "all Naval personalities in the Pacific area," for processing data on ships of friendly nations, and for briefing his superiors on the progress of Operation Seadragon, a junk-intercept program that the Navy was conducting off the coast of South Vietnam. In addition, he was supposed to "handle" the navies of Indonesia, North Vietnam, and North Korea.

Whortley had no background in intelligence work. Nonetheless, he scored notable successes in predicting North Vietnamese naval activity, and by April, 1967, had somehow found time to compile a 120-page analysis of the North Korean Navy complete with maps, photographs, and information on ships' characteristics.

No one in the Navy section thought more highly of Whortley's effort than Lieutenant Commander Richard A. Mackinnon, a tall, thirty-three-year-old product of Exeter and Harvard. Mackinnon had spent some time worrying about the North Koreans himself. He understood their penchant for secrecy and realized how difficult it was to compile accurate information on them.

For the past several months Mackinnon had been specializing in the Chinese Navy, approaching the task with characteristic zeal. His superiors considered him to be an able fellow—"probably one of the most competent analysts you could ever find for slow, detail work," one of them later explained—and if they faulted him, it was because he sometimes had difficulty meeting deadlines and expressing his thoughts clearly.

To such complaints Mackinnon would always respond that the processing of intelligence, especially intelligence concerning the Chinese or North Vietnamese, was a time-consuming chore, that it was unrealistic to expect anyone to send information out to the fleet on an assembly-line schedule. And his immediate boss, Commander William E. Nyce, would always support him.

"The CIA people used to come around and thank Dick profusely," recalls Lieutenant John U. Canning. "Some people in the shop didn't like the fact that Dick was always working on publications. They wanted him to concentrate on briefings for the admiral. They said that any long-range studies should be done in Washington. But I got the impression from these CIA people that no one in the world was doing anything about China except Dick Mackinnon at CINCPACFLT."

In April, 1967, Commander Frank Butler, the chief of the Current Intelligence Branch, died of a heart attack. Nyce moved up from his job as director of the Navy section to replace Butler. And into Nyce's billet stepped a sandy-haired lieutenant commander named P. David Moke, who until recently had been specializing in Soviet Navy activities. Mackinnon's troubles were about to begin.

Although he had once spent two years as a China analyst at another post, Moke seemed to view most Orientals with contempt. "Gracious," he'd say, *"they're dirty."* He did admire the Germans— "They sweep the fields in Germany"—and he reminisced constantly about Iceland, where he'd served a recent tour in counterintelligence.

Early in June Don Whortley left Hawaii and got out of the Navy. "Just before I left, the last week there, I was sure glad I hadn't extended," he recalls. "My desk was right behind Mackinnon's. He was pretty discouraged. Things were really building up between him and Moke. Dick was producing good information on the Chinese, but Moke didn't see the importance of this. He had no interest in China at all."

At first the Navy didn't assign a replacement for Whortley. Then Moke told Mackinnon to handle the North Korean and North Vietnamese navies as well as the Chinese. During the relatively short time that Mackinnon bore this responsibility, not a single piece of intelligence on the North Korean Navy was either originated or passed along by CINCPACFLT.

The reasons for this remain unclear, enmeshed in a web of charges and countercharges, for, as historian Barbara W. Tuchman has pointed out, "Truth is subjective and separate, made up of little bits seen, experienced and recorded by different people. It is like a design seen through a kaleidoscope; when the cylinder is shaken, the countless colored fragments form a new picture."

Moke says that Mackinnon's "attention to detail was lacking" and admits that he "did have disagreements with Dick over the content of the material he produced." Moke's superiors in the Current Intelligence Branch noted that "he was not reluctant to point out the fairly frequent errors of fact and interpretation which Mackinnon made" and that "he gave everything back to Mackinnon to write until it was clear."

"All Moke could think of was static intelligence, number counting," Mackinnon maintains; "the ship, the pennant number, the order of battle. A country's intentions didn't faze him at all. He established a policy that intelligence on Oriental navies wasn't all that important and needn't be disseminated outside the command. He kept saying that the Soviets were the bigger threat, and I'd say, 'Sure. But they're not shooting at us right now. These other guys in fishing boats—*they're* shooting at us.' "

Mackinnon was constantly requesting pictures and data on the Chinese and North Korean navies, but when this material arrived, Moke intercepted it and set it aside, sometimes for as long as a week, while he processed routine reports. Mackinnon responded by rifling through Moke's desk at night and removing the packets addressed to him.

"It was a very unfortunate situation," Lieutenant Canning recalls. "Dick would write messages and give them to Moke to chop. Some of the messages wouldn't get out at all. Others, well, Moke liked to change things just for the sake of changing them. He seemed to feel a need to assert his authority."

On July 13, Commander Bobby R. Inman relieved Commander William Nyce as chief of the Current Intelligence Branch. A slender, very competent officer, an excellent briefer who had been selected for promotion ahead of his "year group," Inman attempted to mediate the quarrel between Mackinnon and Moke. His peace-making efforts were unsuccessful.

Late in July Mackinnon went directly to Captain Marocchi and, in an emotional meeting, accused Moke of incompetence and dishonesty, of suppressing vital information and even changing the reports that went to the fleet. If he had to work for Moke any longer, he said, he'd wind up in the mental ward of a hospital.

Marocchi and Inman felt that Mackinnon's charges were groundless, the result of a personality clash. Still, because they valued his ability, they asked him to remain at his desk. Mackinnon agreed to do so on one condition: that he no longer had to report directly to Moke.

"I said that the information I wanted disseminated simply had to go out," he recalls, "and that it shouldn't be stopped because Moke considered the Chinese and North Koreans to be minor threats. I said that if what had been going on was allowed to continue, then someday something was going to happen to a U.S. ship or aircraft, and I couldn't live with that on my conscience."

It was Mackinnon's word against Moke's, a zealous if unorthodox analyst with a sea-going background versus a seasoned if highly opinionated intelligence professional who had spent his entire career ashore. Mackinnon had complicated the equation by insisting on his "condition." Marocchi arranged to transfer him to a less taxing job—counting SAM missiles in aerial photographs. No one with any experience was left to monitor the North Korean Navy on a day-to-day basis.

17

Early in August *Pueblo* set out again to complete her informal sea trials. She steamed north through Puget Sound, then spent hours circling a red and white buoy in an attempt to determine the amount and pattern of radiation emitting from her antennae. As she eased toward the Coast Guard station at Port Angeles, Washington, someone threw a line. A dog on the pier clenched it between his teeth and trotted up to the bollard.

Port Angeles was *Pueblo*'s first liberty stop and almost everyone trekked over to the club on the base to hoist a few beers. By the time Bucher decided to leave, it was past midnight. Because he was due to stand the midnight to four o'clock watch, Steve Harris had refrained from drinking at the club. Now he stood in the pilot house as *Pueblo* chugged homeward through Admiralty Inlet. The sky was clear; there was a slight breeze and although the forward mast obscured his vision somewhat, he still could see, off in the distance, whitecaps stepping every which way in the moonlight.

Willie Columbus Bussell stood at the helm; Charles Law was taking bearings on buoys. Suddenly, Harris spotted a salmon boat dead ahead. *Pueblo* couldn't veer to starboard; the water was too shallow. The salmon boat advanced slowly on a collision course. Harris called for Bucher, who was asleep in his cabin. Then he ordered a turn to port. The salmon boat countered, incredibly, by swinging to her starboard. "It was pretty hairy," Harris recalls. "That guy came down along our port side, and he was almost close enough to shake hands. Pete never said anything to me about this later, but from that moment on he insisted that everyone had to stand watches on the flying bridge."

The lackadaisical routine of the early summer was over. Soon *Pueblo* would undergo the rugged Board of Inspection and Survey (INSURV) tests. Bucher began demanding perfection from his crew.

He wore white gloves, carried a flashlight, and got down on his hands and knees to examine machinery or peer under bunks during his frequent and detailed inspections. "I want that engine room shining like a penny," he said. Nor was he any less exacting in his personnel inspections. "I don't give a damn how you guys look when you're out at sea," he declared, "but when we're in port, you're going to be squared away. That means a haircut and a shave every day."

"One time he told us that liberty couldn't begin until the ship was completely clean," recalls Communications Technician Second Class Elton A. Wood. "We started about seven or eight o'clock that morning and finished up at four or five o'clock that afternoon, and Chief [Communications Technician Charles D.] Wallace, the Master at Arms, reported that everything was ready for inspection. The skipper terminated that inspection at six thirty. He said we didn't pass. Someone had accidentally dropped a grape on the deck of the forward berthing compartment, and it had rolled under a bunk. We had to clean the ship all over again. I was stripping the wax, removing it, rewaxing, and buffing the deck until eleven thirty that night. The captain came down wearing white gloves, and yet when we were finished, white gloves could be used. That ship was spotless."

Ever since June 9 Bucher's plea for a destruct system had been bouncing from one command to another—from Commander, Service Group One in San Diego to Commander, Service Force, Pacific Fleet and Commander in Chief, Pacific Fleet in Hawaii and finally to the Chief of Naval Operations in Washington. On July 5 the CNO had written a letter to the Chief of the Naval Matériel Command asking him to review the desirability of "installing an explosive system." CHIEFNAVMAT in turn referred the letter to the Commander, Naval Ships Systems Command.

"A destruct system is considered highly desirable," the NSSC's commander replied on July 18. "However, accomplishment in the installed equipment would provide doubtful effectiveness . . . charges added to existing equipment may provide only partial destruction . . . the equipment itself must be designed around the charge. . . . It was learned that the Army has developed and proven an acceptable incendiary system. . . ." No action should be taken, the letter concluded, in effect, until the Navy found time to study the Army's device. And this might take several months. Meanwhile, *Pueblo* would just have to go without.

In all other respects, the ship's conversion seemed to be progressing satisfactorily. The new mess decks were a vast improvement over the cramped, unhealthy spaces of a few months ago, and in the forward berthing compartment modern "cruiser" bunks had replaced the tiers of canvas-bottom bunks. The refurbishing of the research spaces had been completed, as well; Dan Preecs reported that LTV's technicians had finally positioned all of the equipment correctly.

As soon as he heard that *Pueblo* was about to begin her INSURV tests, Lieutenant Commander Denny Carder suggested that his colleague, Lieutenant John Arnold, fly back to Bremerton just to make sure that all the "mandatory" items had indeed been included in the spaces. Arnold agreed to do so. Then Commander Richard Wiener, Arnold's boss, intervened. "We can't afford to have him go back out there," he said in effect. "He might find something else wrong." Arnold remained in Washington.

The INSURV tests began on August 23 and continued for three days. A team of nine officers from the Board of Inspection and Survey's office in San Francisco combed the ship thoroughly, examining her engine room, machinery, hull structure, habitability, electronics capabilities—even her medical facilities. A 42-page shipyard report summarized the problems:

> . . . Stability of *Pueblo* is markedly less than that of *Palm Beach*. . . . The adequacy of stability of *Pueblo* appears deficient . . . Excessive rolling is a common complaint . . . bilge keels should have been incorporated in conversion of *Pueblo*. . . . Chairs are loose and unsecured to the deck. . . . In heavy weather serious damage is very likely to occur to valuable materials, as well as possibility of injury to operating personnel. . . . Present whaleboat is not suited for emergency use . . . [it] was not intended by design and was chosen contrary to ship's plans or warnings given. . . . Steering gear unreliable and failed repeatedly during trials. Full power ahead and astern steering trials not satisfactorily demonstrated. Rudder hangs up and sticks . . . when shifting from hard left to hard right and vice versa. . . .

> The steering yoke is unshielded and constitutes a personnel hazard. . . . The emergency steering arrangement is ineffective . . . Present 1JV sound-powered phone line is a potential danger during sea details because of the many stations on the line which have opportunity to block or garble vital engine and line handling commands. . . .

> There is no reliable means of communication between the navigator's chart desk and captain's open bridge conning station. . . . The 1MC system power amplifiers are . . . not suitable for shipboard use. . . . Word passed and alarm passed cannot be heard in many areas. . . .

Commanding Officer's stateroom . . . is below standards . . . habitability environment for other officer staterooms is below . . . standards . . . CPO berthing and living environment is unsatisfactory . . . quarters are cramped and congested. . . . No washbasin provided. No separate head and washroom. . . . There is no Sick Bay/Pharmacy aboard.

Yeoman's desk in ship's office vibrates excessively even at normal standard speeds. . . . Existing pilot house/bridge windows are unsatisfactory and unsafe for inclement weather/heavy seas operations. . . . Water leaks from flying bridge deck into pilot house. . . . Boat compass has deviation errors in excess of twenty percent. . . . The heat blower system puts a great amount of dirt into the research spaces, presenting a maintenance problem . . . repair parts, equipage, plans, publications and technical manuals designated critical by the Commanding Officer are missing. . . . Ship's stack should be secured. . . . At present, top of stack is held in place by baling wire. . . .

And on and on. The INSURV team listed 462 separate deficiencies and stated that 77 of them "must be corrected" before *Pueblo* left the yard. Most of these "critical" problems were the same ones that Bucher had been shouting about for the past seven months.

On August 28 the Chief of Naval Operations sent a message to the Chief of the Naval Matériel Command which elaborated on Admiral Rivero's order of July 24: "A decision has been made to install defensive armament [no less than .20 mm guns] on commissioned Navy ships not now so equipped. . . ." The message specifically cited AGER's. Unaccountably, it failed to reach Bremerton.

Shipyard workers corrected most of the "critical" deficiencies, and at noon on September 11 *Pueblo* chugged out of Bremerton en route to San Diego for her shakedown training. She had ninety-one officers and men and only eighty-four bunks. A sixth officer, Ensign Timothy L. Harris, had just reported aboard. The son of a chief petty officer, Harris was a natural athlete, a russet-haired, fair-complexioned fellow with an engaging grin and a manner so informal that many crew members found it difficult to address him as "sir." Only twenty at the time, he had been graduated from Jacksonville (Florida) University a few months before with a degree in business administration; he had attended flight school at Pensacola and then dropped out to become a supply officer. He had never set foot aboard ship before, and now, as he listened to "The Lonely Bull" over the 1MC, he wondered whether all Navy ships had similar theme songs.

The ship's recreation committee had purchased fishing gear, and next afternoon, by the mouth of the Columbia River near Astoria, Oregon, Bucher stopped to try to catch some salmon. The sea was too rough. From time to time, standing on the flying bridge, Bucher raised his .22 caliber pistol and took potshots at occasional seagulls. The seagulls were very safe.

Bucher was becoming concerned about the ship's steering apparatus, which was failing regularly—several times a day. To be sure, he could always dispatch two men to the helm and rely on manual steering, but that was no way to guide a ship across the Pacific. He'd have to have it checked again once he reached San Diego.

Pueblo stopped in San Francisco on September 15 for a three-day liberty call, and over that weekend Bucher received word that he had been selected for promotion to commander: scrambled eggs on his cap and an extra $160 per month. He hadn't expected it; he had, in fact, estimated his chances at no better than one in fourteen, and what was so surprising was that some of the officers who'd beaten him out for submarine commands the year before had been passed over for promotion. Perhaps there was some justice in the system, after all.

Pueblo steamed south again toward San Diego. At dusk on September 21 she lay off the coast near La Jolla. The steering gear was malfunctioning now on an hourly basis and half the crew was seasick, but Bucher still couldn't get permission to enter port. Harbor officials said he was too early and told him to wait outside another day. Bucher decided to have some fun.

Harry Lewis had just dumped the garbage over the fantail; he reported sighting a shark. Bucher picker up his .30 caliber carbine and told him to dump more garbage. Lewis took some rotten meat from the reefer, attached it to a grappling hook at the end of a quarter-inch line, and lowered it over the side. The shark slashed toward the hook and ripped the meat away before Bucher could squeeze off a shot. Lewis baited the hook again.

At nine o'clock that night Elton Wood was standing on the fantail talking to Earl Kisler and Jim Layton. He held the line in his hand. Suddenly he saw three shadows four or five feet below the surface. One of them churned toward the bait and caught the hook in the side of its mouth.

Wood, Layton and Kisler pulled at the line and lifted the shark's nose up to the rail. He was a monster: thirteen or fourteen feet long. If they could get him on deck, they could photograph him and make necklaces from his teeth. Bucher was pumping slugs, but the shark kept flapping its tail and refused to die. Murphy leaned over the side. Bucher fired again. Blood splattered Murphy's uniform. "Excuse me, Ed," Bucher said, "I didn't see you there."

Wood, Layton, and Kisler yanked the line again. Too hard. The shark's jaw ripped loose from its body, which fell back into the sea. As he watched the shark's companions devour the bloody carcass, Larry Mack wondered what explanation Bucher would have if someone slipped and fell overboard.

Three thousand miles away, at the St. Anthony Club on East 64th Street in Manhattan, Skip Schumacher was having drinks with some old friends. He'd just finished an uneventful tour as communications officer on USS *Vega;* in a few days he'd have to report to a new ship, USS *Pueblo,* and he knew this night would be one of the last he'd spend in New York for a long time. Thus far the evening had progressed awkwardly. One of his friends, an amateur astrologer named Mike Lutin, was obviously ill at ease; he had nothing in common with the rich, sophisticated people at the table. Schumacher tried to bring him into the conversation.

"Mike sort of looked at me," he recalls, "and said, 'Something terrible is going to happen to you. I don't know what it is.' We joked for a couple of minutes, then he became very quiet. He said, 'No, I'm serious. Something very horrible, and I can't see how it's going to end. But I don't think you'll die.' Then he got up and left. He was very worried."

Lutin's concern was, of course, ridiculous, for up to this point in his life Schumacher had led a comfortable, silver spoon existence untroubled by calamities of any kind. And he couldn't think of anything that might upset the pattern. Son of a prosperous insurance executive in St. Louis, Missouri, he had attended the Country Day School there, joining the drama and debating societies and managing the track team. His grades were mediocre; still, he was accepted at Trinity College in Connecticut. He joined St. Anthony's Hall and became one of its most popular members. He served as a coeditor of the college yearbook. He impressed his teachers as an intellectually capable but somewhat diffident student. He graduated in the lowest third of his class. He talked about spending the next three years at Chicago Theological Seminary but wasn't sure in his own mind that he had the compassion a minister needs. So he decided instead to enroll at Officers' Candidate School in Newport, Rhode Island, and spend three years in the Navy "figuring things out." His father, a Navy officer in World War II, had been enormously pleased and had given him an expensive watch as a going-away present.

Now on this foggy morning late in September, he drove his silver-gray Porsche along Harbor Drive in San Diego, parked by the Anti-Submarine Warfare School pier, and set out to find *Pueblo.* The ship was only one-fourth the size of USS *Vega,* but this didn't upset him. He remembers thinking "she was unique and very special." He joined the officers for lunch in the wardroom. "One of the first things I noticed about the captain was his eyes," Schumacher recalls. "The pupils were very dark, almost black. They held a slight question mark, as if he were asking himself, 'Who is this guy and how's he going to fit into the picture?' you know."

In the days that followed he began to understand the reasons for Bucher's puzzlement. It was obvious that although the captain liked Steve Harris personally, he couldn't rely on him to help prepare the ship. Nor did he seem to depend on Murphy. Schumacher noticed that Dave Behr was bypassing Murphy in the chain of command and dealing directly with Bucher and that Bucher didn't seem to mind. One afternoon Behr warned him, "Watch out for the XO." "I sensed a real power vacuum on that ship right away," Schumacher says. "I decided to play it cool and not get involved in wardroom politics."

Although he wouldn't officially relieve Behr as operations officer until the end of October, Schumacher had no time to relax. "There was so much to do because this was a new type of ship," he recalls. "Any standard reference publication I'd go to to find the answer to a problem, well, it wouldn't cover an AGER." Behr had returned the two .50 caliber machine guns to Service Group One headquarters. Schumacher received custody of the other weapons on board and noted that Behr had qualified everyone in firing the Thompson submachine guns and .45 caliber pistols. But he noted also that Behr's operations department had failed its preunderway training readiness inspection, a test to verify that the ship was following standard Navy procedures and fleet directives. He had to straighten out that department as soon as possible.

Schumacher's attitude and ability impressed everyone. "I needed a producer," Bucher recalls. "Skip was a producer, and he really delighted me." Adds Larry Strickland, "He had a good sense of humor; he didn't bum cigarettes like Dave Behr, and he knew how to assert his authority. I never once heard him raise his voice to chew anyone out. And he was really cool when the ship was under way. The captain would give him instructions and start to repeat them, and Skip would say, 'I got it, Captain.' He made the right moves. And he never stuck around for congratulations. He knew he'd done a good job, and that was enough."

At the moment, Schumacher's main responsibility was to coordinate plans for *Pueblo*'s underway training. He found the task enormously frustrating. To be sure, some of the drills on the schedule were routine: damage control, fire-fighting, general quarters, man over-

board, repel boarders, and abandon ship. There were simulated colli-
sions and machinery breakdowns, and tests of the ship's reporting procedures. There was gunnery practice, as well—involving some floating
oil drums.

The trouble was that most of the other drills ignored the fact that
Pueblo was an AGER. Some were designed for a ship of the line, others
for an AKL. "The training was very confused," Schumacher recalls,
"plagued by the limited number of people who were cleared to know
what our mission was. I had a general idea, although I couldn't get any
details. I wasn't supposed to know. I couldn't imagine an AGER ever
being involved in a fighting war, but they were trying to put us through
drills aimed at a fighting war."

One communications drill, for example, tested *Pueblo*'s ability to
coordinate with other ships in a large task force. Schumacher realized
that *Pueblo* would operate independently—away from the rest of the
fleet. The plotting exercise was designed for a ship with a combat information center, a capability for generating a strategic picture of a
developing battle. *Pueblo* didn't have a combat information center.
Another drill was supposed to test *Pueblo*'s reaction in the event of a
nuclear blast. At the other extreme, *Pueblo* was called upon to conduct
a towing drill with an AKL and an underway replenishment exercise
and a precision navigation test with a DLG (a guided missile frigate).
Then she was to engage in a highline transfer, an evolution for which
she didn't have the necessary equipment. Schumacher spoke to the
training supervisor, Lieutenant j.g. Paul V. Huebner, about this, but
Huebner wasn't cleared to know what the ship's mission was, either; he
couldn't help. Neither could Murphy. Schumacher turned to Bucher.

Bucher discussed the problem with Rear Admiral David Lambert,
commander of the Training Group. Lambert offered him little encouragement. "The battle problem was supposed to be designed
around your mission," Bucher says. "A simulated harassment situation
would have been ideal for us; a realistic approach would have included
something of this nature. I told the admiral this and said that our
battle problem as set up wasn't very realistic, but he and his staff had
no concept of what our mission was, and there was really no way to talk
about it. We couldn't talk to them, and they couldn't talk to us."

On September 29 Bucher received a message from Captain Everett
B. (Pete) Gladding, director, Naval Security Group, Pacific. Contrary
to what he had been told during his visit to Washington back in
January, *Pueblo*'s CT's would *not* constitute a department, after all.
They would function as a detachment. Steve Harris would report

"for technical guidance" directly to Gladding in Hawaii. And there was nothing that Bucher could do about it.

Ten days later Harris flew back to Washington for briefings at the Naval Security Station and the National Security Agency. "The location of the first mission hadn't been decided upon," he recalls, "but I was sure we were going to do some productive things. So I selected a list of countries which I thought were significant, and I went around to various offices at NSA and talked to people about them. North Korea was on my list. I remember feeling, 'Well, we might go by there.' "

At six-thirty every morning *Pueblo* steamed out to her assigned training area to conduct her drills. Bucher tested his officers on the "rules of the road" and on their use of the radar and loran. In a few weeks Lacy would qualify as an officer of the deck; so would Tim Harris and Charles Law, whose skill and leadership abilities were becoming more and more apparent.

Bucher tried to mold his officers and men into a cohesive unit. "I never could interest Ed Murphy in coming along, but the rest of us in the wardroom would go out for dinner and drinks together almost every night," he recalls. "I even managed to get football tickets three weekends in a row." Bucher took special delight in introducing Tim Harris to San Diego night life. One evening they conspired to steal a painting of a nude woman from the Ballast Tank Club. While Bucher diverted the bartender's attention, Harris sneaked behind the bar, grabbed the painting, and fled. It didn't matter that their prank was discovered, that they had to return the painting next morning. Bucher and Harris had shared an experience that they'd be able to chuckle about for months.

Yet the incident which did the most to weld the crew behind Bucher wasn't preplanned at all. Early one evening Earl Kisler, Elton Wood, and Tony LaMantia were strolling west on Broadway in front of the YMCA. Navy regulations prohibited wearing blue jeans in San Diego and specified that enlisted men's shirts had to have collars. Kisler wore blue jeans, Wood's shirt lacked a collar, and he and LaMantia needed haircuts.

"Hey, sailor."

Kisler turned and saw two Shore Patrolmen approaching them. He nudged Wood. "They walked us back, demanded to see our ID cards, and searched us," Wood recalls. "They said they were going to report us and shoved us in the back of the truck. They talked for a few minutes, and then one of them said, 'Go get haircuts and buy some proper clothing.' We felt there was nothing wrong with our attire, so we refused. They took us to the station and threw us in separate cells and kept us there until two, three o'clock in the morning. Then they gave us back our personal belongings and took us to the ship. I kept saying, 'There's going to be trouble about this'; I was going to press charges. And they said, 'Keep your mouth shut.'

"I went to the captain's stateroom, but he hadn't come back yet, so I went to forward berthing. Just then the quarterdeck watch reported that the captain had come on board. He and Tim had been out partying, and he was really high, but when I told him what had happened, he became very serious. And mad. He saw nothing wrong with our appearance. 'They're not gonna pull that shit on any of my boys,' he said. 'You guys get ready. We're gonna go into town and have us a little fun.' And he kept repeating, 'We're gonna go right now; we're gonna go right now.' "

Bucher herded Tim Harris and the three CT's into a white 1958 Ford station wagon, drove out the main gate, and headed along Harbor Drive. "Tim," he said after a while, "you know, if this thing had some lights, we might be able to see a little better."

"I'm sure they're right there on the dash," Harris replied.

"You know, Tim," Bucher said, "I don't want these people to think we were out on an all-night blast."

"They won't, Captain," Harris said.

As the car pulled up in front of the Shore Patrol headquarters building, Harris turned to the three CT's. "Now let the captain do all the talking," he said.

Bucher stormed into the office and threw his hat down on the desk of a startled lieutenant j.g. "I'm Commander Bucher," he said. "What's going on here? I want to know what you're doing with my men."

The lieutenant j.g. insisted that he didn't know what Bucher was talking about. Bucher noticed a second-class petty officer standing by the door. There was a grin on his face.

"Hey, sailor. You keep yourself squared away?"

The grin disappeared. "Yes, sir, Commander, I'm always squared away."

"Are you sure, sailor?"

"Yes, sir, Commander, I'm sure."

"Well, sailor, do you know that your shirttail is sticking out?"

"Yes, sir, Commander, my shirttail is sticking out."

A lieutenant commander entered the room to see what the fuss was about. Bucher pressed his attack, demanding to know why his men had been picked up, comparing the Shore Patrol's tactics with those of Nazi Germany, insisting that no U.S. sailor should ever have to suffer the sort of indignities that Kisler, Wood, and LaMantia had suffered.

"I pointed out," Bucher recalls, "that the instruction they pulled those guys in under also says that no one's allowed to wear Bermuda shorts in a public place. Well, I'd been at the Navy Exchange and seen high-ranking officers in shorts, so I said, 'If you're going to enforce the rule on a couple of enlisted men, why don't you start picking the admirals up, too?' "

The Shore Patrol officers didn't answer his questions, and next morning Bucher was still fuming over the incident. He told Larry Mack to take some color Polaroid pictures of the men wearing the same clothes they'd worn the night before.

"But I don't have any color film," Mack replied.

"Dammit, why don't you?"

"Sir, it isn't in the ship's allowance."

"Well, order some anyway," Bucher said.

Mack knew his request would be turned down. He mentioned the problem to Dave Behr, who gave him a five-dollar bill. "Here," Behr said, "take it. It'll be easier in the long run."

Bucher enclosed Mack's photographs in a letter to the commander of Service Group One. A few days later he received his reply—a summons to report to COMSERVGRUONE headquarters. The chief of staff of the 11th Naval District had directed that he be censured for "imprudent" conduct.

"The skipper never said one thing to us about it later," Wood recalls. "He never said, 'I got my ass in a sling for you guys.' But we found out. Any other captain would have agreed with the Shore Patrol and put us on report. When he stood up for us like that, we figured we had the captain of all captains."

"Army" Canales was in a quandary. Dave Behr had told him several weeks ago that the captain wanted him to send out those forms requesting security clearances for Alvin Plucker and the other men on the navigation team. Yet every time he started to work on those forms, Behr told him to put them aside for awhile and concentrate on the weekly deficiency reports that had to go back to the Naval Ships Systems Command in Washington. They had priority, Behr said. Canales was spending thirteen or fourteen hours a day in the ship's office already, yet the harder he worked, the more paperwork he seemed to accumulate.

Schumacher noticed his problems and mentioned them to Murphy one day. "I said, 'Canales has got things pretty well screwed up down there,' " he recalls, "but nothing happened. Murphy just walked away." His own relations with Murphy were deteriorating rapidly. At Bucher's request, he'd drawn up a list of excess publications; he had requested and received permission to eliminate them from the ship's allowance. Murphy had put some of them back aboard without telling Bucher.

Another time, again at Bucher's request, Schumacher and Behr had drafted letters requesting some publications pertinent to an electronics exercise.

"I typed them in the rough for chopping and put them in the XO's basket," Schumacher says. "Next day the captain asked about them. I said we'd given them to Murphy for approval, and he said fine. But Murphy just sat on the letters. As it turned out, we had to drop the exercise because of an equipment malfunction. But I wrote Murphy a little note anyway requesting an explanation. He made some snide little comment like '*You* are asking *me?*'

"The captain and Murphy were still arguing about the ship's organization. The captain wanted to pattern it after a submarine organization. Murphy held out for a standard destroyer organization. I wasn't sure in my own mind which would be the better system. There was a lot of inflexibility on both sides. The captain didn't want to change his position at all, and Ed didn't want to go along with the captain's recommendations at all, and this resulted in a total lack of communication. Then they evolved a bastardized organization which was neither one nor the other. And one or the other would have worked."

The steering system was still malfunctioning regularly, and no one in San Diego seemed to know how to fix it. Then Bill Scarborough had an inspiration. He tied strings to the electrical contacts and jiggled them in such a way as to prevent short-circuiting. For awhile the failure rate decreased.

Some crew members thought *Pueblo* was a jinxed ship, anyway. A steward named Ochoa declined to wash and iron Bucher's shirts. Confronted with a direct order, he responded by "accidentally" tearing holes in the shirts. Bucher succeeded in swapping him for another steward, Rizalino Aluague, who was then on USS *Seminole.*

As he watched Ochoa depart, Ralph Reed felt a twinge of envy. For the past several weeks he had sought a transfer himself, had even volunteered to serve in Vietnam. But all his chits had bounced back disapproved. He had to serve on *Pueblo* for a year, Murphy said. Only then could he request another assignment. Reed knew he wasn't as good a cook as his friend Harry Lewis, but every man was entitled to some small successes in life, and he hadn't had his share. No matter how hard he tried, he couldn't produce a decent pineapple upside-down cake. "It never worked out for me," he says. "It was just one of the things I couldn't handle." One afternoon, thoroughly frustrated by the failure of his umpteenth effort, he carried the cake up from the galley and threw it over the side. It sank to the bottom immediately.

The underway, or shakedown, training ended on October 20, and six days later officers from COMSERVGRUONE conducted a predeployment readiness inspection, a final check of *Pueblo*'s capabilities in such areas as operations, communications, and engineering. Although they lacked sufficient clearance to enter the research spaces, they rated *Pueblo*'s performance as "good." "They said she was one of the finest ships," Bucher recalls, "that they had seen come through the training program in some time."

Pueblo moved from the Anti-Submarine Warfare School pier to the destroyer pier at 32nd Street for a ten-day "upkeep" period. Steve Harris returned from his briefings in Washington. Dave Behr removed all the uncashed paychecks from his stateroom, turned his duties over to Schumacher, and left the ship. Bucher said farewell to old friends.

At five o'clock on the morning of November 6 *Pueblo* sailed for Hawaii. Rodney Duke was seasick for the first three days. So were John Grant and Tim Harris. Communications Technician Second Class Larry J. Taylor thought *he* might die. He lay flat on his back for most of the trip. The steering system was causing trouble again. Murphy decided he wanted some "evidence" to show shipyard officials at Pearl Harbor. He told Larry Mack to examine the logs and record every steering "casualty" the ship had suffered since her commissioning. Mack complied and filled two large sheets of paper.

Despite her steering problems, *Pueblo* had following winds and a quartering sea; she arrived at Pearl Harbor on November 14. Elton Wood strolled through the International Market Place hunting for souvenirs. Norbert Klepac, Frank Ginther, and Michael Barrett rented a car and explored the island of Oahu. John Grant and some of his buddies checked out the bars along Hotel Street in downtown Honolulu. He remembers that he spent $90 that night "and I didn't even get drunk."

Bucher had long been a fan of entertainer Don Ho, so he proceeded to take the members of his wardroom to Duke Kahanamoku's for dinner and drinks. The $20 each officer threw into the hat was gone before the start of the second show. "Ed was very upset at having to put more money into the kitty," Bucher says. "Although the unpleasantness was always there, I tried to overlook it. I sort of drove right by it."

Bucher, Murphy, Steve Harris, and Lacy returned to the ship at 5 A.M. A few hours later Schumacher and Tim Harris appeared. Harris was barefoot; someone, he said, had stolen his shoes. Crew members noticed their bloodshot eyes and smiled to themselves. "We said those guys must be okay," recalls Ron Berens. "From then on it was 'Skip' and 'Tim.' "

Bucher called on Rear Admiral Edwin B. Hooper, Commander Service Force, Pacific Fleet, and mentioned his steering problems. Hooper had 67,000 personnel and 120 other ships to worry about at the moment but said nonetheless that his force maintenance experts would do what they could. Then Bucher walked to the CINCPACFLT head-quarters building on Makalapa Drive.

A primary function of the Current Intelligence Branch in CINCPACFLT's Intelligence Division was to provide analyses of Asian navies to its sister branch, Reconnaissance and Indications, as well as to the ships in the fleet. Since the transfer of Lieutenant Commander Richard Mackinnon a few months before, the Navy section of the Current Intelligence Branch had lacked an experienced analyst on North Korea. In volume, the number of items on China and North Korea which flowed to the R&I branch and the fleet exceeded Mackinnon's output. In substance, however, there was no comparison. "It wasn't the kind of thing you noticed right away," says Lieutenant John Canning. "Don Whortley and Dick Mackinnon had built such a good foundation that it was possible for anyone to coast along for a while on it."

Mackinnon's initial replacement was a thin, bespectacled lieutenant j.g. named Albert E. Morris. A former aviation cadet, he had dropped out of flight school because "I was too nervous to be an RIO [radar intercept officer] in an F-4," and just prior to filling Mackinnon's billet he had served briefly as a target analyst. His formal training in Naval intelligence consisted of a six-week course at a school in San Francisco.

Although Morris was a conscientious fellow, he simply didn't have enough time to follow the navies of China, India, North Vietnam, and North Korea on a daily basis by himself. In the fall of 1967 he received an assistant, an ensign named Charles Hall, Jr., who took over responsibility for North Vietnam, North Korea, and "approximately a dozen other Pacific navies, as well."

A husky graduate of the University of Denver, Hall had no experience in intelligence work, either. Furthermore, he seemed more interested in swimming during his lunch hour every day or in sailing his small boat on Kaneohe Bay than in processing information. "C. B. came in like cold," Morris remembers. "He was in the wrong place—no doubt about it. He didn't like what he was doing. I had my work to do, and I'd have to do his, too. You couldn't tell from one minute to the next what he'd come up with. He'd miss things, say they weren't important. There was a real lack of intelligence on North Korea."

One of the officers who received Hall's analyses was the deputy chief of the R&I branch, a pudgy, balding, gravel-voiced lieutenant commander named Ervin R. Easton. More than anyone else in the Intelligence Division, Easton was responsible for planning and monitoring AGER operations, and over the past several months he'd earned a reputation as an extremely hard-working and competent fellow. Now, on November 15, he and his counterpart from the Operations Division, a burly South Carolinian named Jim C. Hayes, began to brief Bucher in general terms on the type of mission *Pueblo* would undertake. Easton handed him USS *Banner*'s patrol reports and said that although no final decision had been made, *Pueblo*'s first cruise would probably be off the coast of North Korea.

"What happens if we get out there and into a situation that's untenable?" Bucher asked. "And they actually start shooting? What the hell happens then?"

"I don't have the answer," Easton replied, "but I'll take you up and introduce you to the man who does."

The assistant chief of staff for operations at the time was Captain —now Rear Admiral—George L. Cassell, a stocky Texan with a bulldog manner whose heroism in World War II had earned him a Distinguished Flying Cross. Cassell listened quietly as Bucher repeated the question.

"Commander," he said finally, "if something like that does happen, there's very little possibility that we can do anything for you. But I'll tell you what we will do." Cassell leaned forward. "We've got *plans* written. You can be reassured that there will be retaliation within twenty-four or forty-eight hours—in force."

"Erv and I talked about this later," Bucher recalls. "I was impressed that Cassell had a finger on the problem. I went away feeling that there was some definite plan to take care of contingencies."

Although *Pueblo* was supposed to spend only two days in Hawaii, Admiral Hooper's maintenance people decided they'd need an additional forty-eight hours to complete their work on the steering apparatus. Bucher realized that many officers on the CINCPACFLT staff, particularly in the Operations Division, had never seen an AGER before, so he asked them to inspect the ship. Captain Cassell accepted the invitation; so did lieutenant commanders Hayes and Easton.

"I was pleasantly surprised to see the ship so squared away," Easton remembers. "And I was impressed by the equipment they had in the research spaces. The only thing that didn't ring true to me was the attitude of the XO. When you go to sea, you know, you just don't complain anymore. You shift over to a positive attitude. The XO still thought he was back in the shipyard."

Commander Norman Horowitz and Lieutenant Robert E. Nisbett from the Naval Security Group staff inspected the research spaces and provided Steve Harris with further guidance on his electronic equipment. Mike Alexander reported aboard to replace the chronically seasick Larry Taylor. "I was standing on the well deck and I could see this guy in a flower shirt, Bermuda shorts, and shower shoes," Alexander recalls, "and I turned to one of the guys and said, 'Who in hell is that?' And he said, 'That's the captain.' And I said, 'You must be kidding.' "

The steering repairs were almost completed. Bucher sent his wife some talisman roses for her birthday. Fireman Duane Hodges wrote home to Creswell, Oregon. He sent his mother a Bible.

Something went wrong with the 1MC. Bucher wasn't able to play "The Lonely Bull." Nonetheless, at four o'clock on the afternoon of November 18 *Pueblo* steamed out of the Pearl Harbor Channel and rounded Barbers Point. Her routing was standard for that time of year: by rhumb line to 29 degrees north and 150 degrees east, then by rhumb line directly to Yokosuka.

On the second day out the steering system failed again. John Grant and Ken Wadley rushed to the pilot house to help man the helm. Sometimes repairs took less than five minutes. Sometimes. Alvin Plucker was having trouble mastering the loran. He'd worked with loran before on an aircraft carrier, USS *Hornet,* and had never had any problems. He couldn't understand what he was doing wrong now. Then someone noticed that the loran was mounted on a table that was vibrating excessively. Murphy ordered the table secured; the loran began to function properly. Below in the fo'c'sle, John (Tiny) Higgins stood over the laundry machine. It hissed and rattled and finally overflowed, soaking Higgins and several of his shipmates. On the mess decks, projectionist Stu Russell was getting ready to show a movie. Its title was *The Losers.*

Cotton-white clouds scudded across the sky. The sea was calm. Standing on the bridge, Charles Law spotted "whales and schools of porpoises." In the berthing compartments forward and aft a few of the men played poker or pinochle. Others played Monopoly. James Sheppard seemed to land on Boardwalk or Park Place every time.

Bucher was pleased with his crew's performance. "People were beginning to get their sea legs," he remembers. "Become familiar with the ship, and know just what is expected of them by me, what my policies were and how I wanted watches stood. We had matured with respect to operating the ship."

Bucher insisted that Murphy wake up half an hour before sunrise every day to plot the morning stars "because that was his job—navigator." Some crew members wondered if there wasn't more to it than that. Thanksgiving Day approached, November 23. The younger officers wanted to spike the mince pie with brandy. Murphy suggested a compromise: Add alcohol to half the pies, and leave the others plain. "Hell, no," Bucher said.

The head in the first class berthing compartment was always backing up, spreading urine and feces over the deck. Monroe Goldman and his assistant, Rushel Blansett, couldn't seem to fix it. They nicknamed it "the Shooter." *Pueblo* had other hygienic liabilities as well: There were only four shower stalls and six wash basins for eighty-three men. Bucher decided to stop the ship for a "swim call," designed as much for cleanliness as for recreation. A few crew members jumped over the side. Peter Langenberg watched them from the rail. Someone gave him a push. He landed on Radioman First Class John D. Mullin's back. Mullin cried out in pain.

His injury seemed serious. There was little that "Doc" Baldridge could do to help him. The seas were kicking up. *Pueblo* began to pitch and roll. USS *Samuel Gompers,* a destroyer tender, was steaming nearby. She had a doctor aboard. Bucher sent a message.

At nine o'clock on the morning of November 25 crewmen placed Mullin in the whaleboat and set out for *Gompers,* now only 500 yards away. A crane hoisted the boat on deck. Richard Arnold remembers that "none of us had shaved in a week. The men on the *Gompers* were squared away. They looked at us like we were pirates or something." One of *Gompers'* officers complained about the 5-degree rolls. *Pueblo's* rolls had exceeded 35 degrees.

Arnold and his companions traded movies, picked up supplies of ice cream and cake, and chugged back toward their ship. A sudden squall enveloped the whaleboat. "It was cold and raining so hard we couldn't even see," Arnold says. "We ran into the side of the ship, backed off, and sat there about twenty minutes. Then we tried again. They waved us off. We made it the third time."

Bucher decided to break out the grog: Every man in the whaleboat or out on deck received a two-ounce bottle of brandy. "This boosted morale about 600 percent," says John Grant. "We knew the old man hadn't forgotten us."

Pueblo's CT's were having trouble receiving messages; already they'd missed several "broadcast numbers," and Bucher worried about it. On the seventh day out a generator caught fire. Engine room personnel doused it quickly. Then the lube oil coolers clogged. "The temperatures on the engines were running high—one hundred ninety or two hundred degrees," Darrell Wright recalls. "They shouldn't go higher than one hundred seventy-five. Once the oil gets too hot, it breaks down, loses its ability to clean the metal, and wipes out the bearings. We thought for awhile that we'd have to secure one engine."

The cooks abandoned their efforts to produce hot meals. They passed out peanut butter or ham and cheese sandwiches instead. The "bubble" on the inclinometer in the pilot house registered a roll of 47 degrees. "It sounded like we were going to crack up," Richard Arnold remembers. "We just sat there and shook, quivered for two minutes, and nobody said anything." Michael Barrett wrote his wife that the ship would probably roll over someday. Frank Ginther shared Barrett's concern. "I found myself praying a lot," he says.

Late on the cold, overcast afternoon of December 1, *Pueblo* steamed into the Yokosuka Channel. Her electrical steering system failed again, for the sixty-second time since leaving San Diego. There seemed to be some problems with manual steering, as well. Extra men dashed to the helm. *Pueblo* was supposed to tie up at Pier 8 South, and some of Bucher's old friends from the SUPFLOTSEVEN staff were there to meet him: Chief Quartermaster Peter Trone, Lieutenant Commander James K. Jobe, Lieutenant Angelo E. (Flip) DiFilippo, his wife, Sanna, and their little girl, Maria, who was born on the day Bucher had left, almost a year before.

Normally, whenever a new ship docks at Yokosuka, high-ranking officers from the COMNAVFORJAPAN staff welcome her. DiFilippo spotted Lieutenant Commander Al Wilson from Operations and Lieutenant Ed Brookes from Intelligence, but he saw no commanders, captains, or admirals. That's odd, he thought. Then he noticed that *Pueblo* was aiming for the wrong pier. "We thought Pete was lost. We started waving and yelling to him out there." Pusher boats sped out to intercept the ship and guided her back to Pier 8 South.

One of the "deck apes" threw the first line over the side. Michael Barrett glanced at his watch: 7:42. He had won the anchor pool: $100 and four days' basket leave. He decided to take the money now and postpone the leave. He'd have plenty of time for that when *Pueblo* returned from her first mission.

As the AGER "project officer" at COMNAVFORJAPAN, Lieutenant Ed Brookes had received all of *Pueblo's* "casualty reports" since her departure from Pearl Harbor, and now he stepped aboard to see what help he could provide. "We talked about the steering system, the engines overheating, even a liberty schedule for the crew," he recalls. "Steve Harris needed assistance in upgrading the competence of his detachment. He said his people hadn't been trained. They couldn't copy the fleet broadcast. That was unbelievable.

"I got the impression that the officers were disturbed by how hard Bucher had pushed them coming across the Pacific. They looked pretty haggard. But Bucher looked worse than any of them. I said I wanted all his officers to attend a two-week course in intelligence collection—publications and photos for the most part—at COMNAVFORJAPAN headquarters. We'd tried to do this for *Banner,* but we're not really set up to be a training command, and there'd always been the problem of her officers' getting enough free time. Bucher said he might send one man. He wasn't sure. He just had too many other things to worry about."

Bucher told Murphy to make sure that everyone had the necessary papers for one month at sea, that the entire crew was familiar with the ship's organization and participated regularly in fire-fighting and damage-control drills. He said he wanted Murphy to acquire the necessary charts and read the intelligence publications covering the order of battle of the North Korean Navy. He told Schumacher—who had recently been promoted to lieutenant j.g.—to prepare his "recognition codes" and handle weapons training. Then he told Steve Harris to see to it that his detachment was thoroughly prepared. Harris promptly sent six CT's to the Electronic Intelligence Center at Fuchu for training in ELINT intercepts and analysis and the rest to the Naval Security Group Activity at Kamiseya.

The remaining ship's company set about scraping and painting the hull, scrubbing the bulkheads, and, inevitably, polishing brass. Scarborough tore down one of the generators, repaired it, and put it back together. Charles Law and the men in his navigation team tested the loran, the radar, the bearing circles, the sextants, and the fathometer. The Mark 18 Sperry gyro showed a consistent error of 1.5 degrees east; they checked it twice a day on morning and afternoon azimuths. This deviation, they reasoned, wasn't important so long as it was predictable.

The steering, of course, was quite another matter. Bucher wanted the entire system replaced. Ship Repair Facility officials examined it and agreed that it was old and unreliable. But *Banner,* they pointed out, used a similar system and she hadn't experienced that many difficulties. *Pueblo's* would function well enough with adequate repairs. Bucher requested a windscreen, a plexiglass canopy to replace the canvas dodgers on the open bridge and afford his watch-standers better protection from wind and weather. COMSERVPAC in Hawaii had denied this request. But Rear Admiral Frank L. Johnson, Commander, Naval Forces, Japan, told his chief of staff, Captain Forrest A. (Buster) Pease, to reconsider it. Pease visited the ship and promptly approved the request.

"I don't think any ship in the Navy ever received better support," Lieutenant Brookes says. "Other ships have to steal from a yard or a land repair facility. *Pueblo* didn't have that problem. It was Admiral Johnson's desire that these AGER's didn't want for anything."

Although most skippers restrict overnight privileges in port to senior enlisted men, Bucher granted "overnights" to everyone in the crew. Few men hit the beach more frequently, or with more predictable results, than "Doc" Baldridge. Late one evening he staggered back to the ship, then changed his mind and decided he needed another drink. The officer of the deck ordered him to go to bed.

"Murphy and I were in our banks," Steve Harris recalls, "and Doc came storming into our stateroom demanding to be taken to a hospital. 'Mr. Murphy,' he said, 'I want a sobriety test, and I want it right now, and I want to go back on liberty.' Somehow we got rid of him and told the quarterdeck watch not to let him go."

On another occasion the Shore Patrol hustled him back to the ship. Gene Lacy ordered him below. Baldridge refused to budge; he said he wasn't going to let Lacy chew him out as if he were an ordinary seaman. Lacy put him on report. Baldridge stepped below—and entered Bucher's stateroom. "Skipper," he said, "they won't let me go ashore."

"Go," Bucher said.

"Sir, I need some money."

Bucher gave him 5,000 yen (about $16), rolled over, and went back to sleep.

Lacy was furious. So were Murphy and Schumacher. Next morning Tim Harris called Baldridge aside. "Doc," he said, "you acted disgracefully last night."

"Go to hell," Baldridge replied.

Harris reported this insubordination to Bucher, and Baldridge was summoned to see the captain immediately. "I apologized," he remembers. "I told the captain I'd had a couple of drinks, and I said maybe I shouldn't have asked for that money. The captain said, 'Well, the thing that really teed me off, you didn't wait for me. I was going to go with you.' "

For a while Bucher had thought of bringing Rose and the two boys back to Japan. Then he abandoned the idea. Mark and Mike had both taken up surfing, and they were happy at school in San Diego. Furthermore, now that he'd made commander, his time aboard ship would be limited. He'd be leaving for another assignment soon. Steve Harris, Gene Lacy, Tim Harris, and eight or nine enlisted men, however, did plan to bring their wives and families to Yokosuka. So did Ed Murphy.

Over the past few weeks, Bucher's relations with his executive officer had deteriorated even further. He seldom attempted to hide the fact. "When the skipper chewed the XO's ass out," recalls Charles Law, "he didn't take little bites. He tore out huge chunks."

"I heard Pete chew Murphy out many times," adds Larry Mack, "jump him often for minor things when it wasn't justified. You shouldn't do that in the presence of enlisted men. One thing I'll say about the XO. He didn't fluster. He stayed cool. He never let anything get to him."

From time to time Murphy might comment that "there's no two men always in complete agreement. If they were, they would not be individuals," or that Bucher was "not the most thinking skipper I've ever served under, not the most intellectual." But other than that he would remain silent, and in retrospect, it seems clear that his stoicism coupled with what Bucher felt was his attitude of moral superiority only fanned the dispute. If Murphy had ever pounded his fist on the table or otherwise vented his anger, he might have been able to clear the air. But he was not the sort to engage in theatrics.

"My relation to him was one of contempt," Bucher says. "He wasn't doing his job, and I don't get along with people who can't do their jobs. His relation to me was one of studied absence. He did his best to avoid me. I had to chase that guy down anytime I wanted to see him. He never came to me voluntarily about anything. He couldn't bear to look me in the eye. He knew every time I looked at him that he had things that hadn't been done from *May*. He never did get that tickler file set up. Then we had a pair of binoculars missing from a locked binocular box back in San Diego. I told him to conduct an investigation. It was an afternoon's work. But it never got done. No production at all."

And now, despite the enormous amount of work that remained to be done to prepare the ship for her mission, "Murphy was spending a lot of his time taking care of his personal problems." Bucher was tired of shouting at him. He sought to penalize him in another way. He decided to delay the arrival of all dependents.

More than pettiness was involved, for Bucher was also convinced that the presence of dependents would impede his training efforts. He sent Schumacher to attend a short course in intelligence collection at COMNAVFORJAPAN headquarters. He compiled a list of pertinent intelligence publications and told his officers to read them. He asked Steve Harris to obtain some slides of Soviet and North Korean ships. Harris contacted COMNAVFORJAPAN. "Ed Brookes had a mossy old collection," he recalls; "six slides of the same old rustbuckets that everyone had seen for years in the Sea of Japan." Bucher suggested he try SUBFLOTSEVEN headquarters, and Harris obtained a better set. Almost every evening between six and seven o'clock, Bucher assembled his officers in the wardroom for recognition drills.

Finally, in mid-December, *Pueblo*'s wives and families arrived in

Yokosuka. None of the crew qualified for base housing, and for the most part, the homes they were able to find were cramped and cold and smelled of kerosene. Gerald Hagenson, for example, had managed to rent—for $150 a month— a small house near Hayama. His wife, Mercy, took one look at it and—exercising a woman's prerogative—pronounced it unfit. "I'm not staying," she declared. "Start looking for another place."

Christmas Day was chilly and overcast. That afternoon *Pueblo* hosted a party for twenty-six Japanese orphans. Projectionist Stu Russell showed Donald Duck and Mickey Mouse cartoons; someone else dispensed cakes and ice cream. Charles Law snuggled into a borrowed Santa Claus suit and passed out presents which the crew had chipped in to purchase. Bucher presided over the affair, and at his instructions, all the officers were present. "Ed Murphy had his home in Hayama with Carol, who was pregnant again, and their little boy, and he was kind of upset that he was going to have to come in," Steve Harris recalls. "He didn't make an issue of it, but he expressed disappointment, disapproval of the whole thing. I didn't think it was such a great idea, either, but you know, Pete was going to make a splash."

Although he was in familiar surroundings, Bucher was still desperately lonely, as much for his own wife and family as for the camaraderie of the SUBFLOTSEVEN days. Some of his oldest friends—Jim Jobe, Phil Stryker, "Flip" DiFilippo—were still at SUBFLOTSEVEN, and during Christmas week he shuttled back and forth among their homes. On Christmas Eve he delivered presents to the Jobe's three little girls and to Stryker's children. He gave DiFilippo's daughter, Maria, a tiny blue and white checkered dog; she called him Uncle Pete. Her father gave him a yard ale glass inscribed with submarine dolphins. He told DiFilippo about his problems with Murphy.

"He said, 'Flip, just between you and me, that guy's not going to make it,'" DiFilippo remembers. "So I volunteered to be his XO. I meant it, although I realized it could never be. Then I suggested he ought to be thinking about his next assignment. He didn't want shore duty back in Washington. He said he'd be happy only at sea, doing what he knew best."

"I volunteered to go as his XO on *Pueblo*, too," Stryker adds. "The guy was just tremendous at sea. He had such a love for the sea. If he hadn't been a sailor, I don't know what he ever would have done with his life. But he was so disheartened over the fact that he'd missed his sub tour that he didn't really care where they sent him next. I suggested he try for the battleship *New Jersey*, maybe as navigator. He called the bureau and asked if there was a chance. They said all the commander billets were already filled."

18

Since his first encounter with the Soviets back in February, Lieutenant Commander Charles Clark had conducted six additional missions on *Banner*—four in the Sea of Japan and two in the East China Sea. And he'd been harassed consistently. "The Soviets, they almost considered me part of their forces," he says. "They missed me when I was in port. Generally they'd stay between one hundred and two hundred yards away for a three-week period. They'd frequently point their guns and order me to leave. And there were quite a few that would head directly for me, pretend to ram, and make course changes at the last minute. I couldn't get too much sleep."

Actually, Clark had grown rather accustomed to the harassment. His main complaint was that he wanted to see a movie, *The Ipcress File*. But every night that he'd settle back in the wardroom to watch it, he'd receive a call to rush to the bridge. On one occasion a Chinese trawler approached to within 5 yards of *Banner*. Another time a Soviet Kotlin class destroyer signaled, "You are in territorial waters. Heave to or I will open fire." Clark checked his radar: He was 18 miles from shore. He'd already ordered "all stop," but he was damned if he was going to let the Soviets think he was following *their* instructions. He ignored the signal, puffed on his pipe, and told the engine room to proceed on course at one-third speed. The Soviet destroyer steamed north over the horizon and disappeared.

That was the thing about the Soviets—they were so bloody unpredictable. One evening an amphibious ship sent him a message: "You are in territorial waters. Advise catch. Barometer is falling." How was a man to respond to that? And then there was the auxiliary ship which shadowed *Banner* on mission number eleven and reappeared on mission fourteen. As the ship approached, Clark ordered his men to "harassment quarters."

"He came up along our side," Clark recalls, "and his off-duty crew was standing on deck in bathing suits, waving and smiling. Some of them got out their musical instruments and played us a Sunday afternoon concert, and we applauded after each number. We had a large country and western contingent on board, so we responded with a few Buck Owens tunes."

The moment the concert ended, however, the Soviet ship resumed her belligerency. She churned directly toward *Banner*. Clark didn't budge. He'd been watching the Soviet skipper for several days and considered him to be an excellent ship-handler. The auxiliary passed 20 yards from *Banner*'s stern, steamed out, and promptly collided with her relief.

From time to time Clark wondered what he would do in the event of a similar emergency. *"Banner* has only one evolution," he used to say, only half joking. "Abandon ship. If anyone had wanted to, he could have rammed and sunk us in short order. Any hole below the water line would have done the job. I did consider the risk of being seized on the high seas. I lived with it for a full year knowing it could happen. But everything was being done completely in the open, in accordance with international law. It was just inconceivable that any country would ever go out and pull a stunt like that."

Clark's concerns were more basic. Although he'd removed the whaleboat, his ship was still top-heavy. She frequently experienced rolls of 50 degrees or more. A Naval Ships Systems Command study concluded that with any appreciable icing *Banner* would capsize in a 40-knot beam wind. And *Banner* carried no steam hoses. Whenever ice threatened, she had to steam south. On one mission mountainous seas forced Clark to leave his station two days ahead of schedule. He tried to reverse course and steam back toward Yokosuka along the coast of Honshu, Japan's main island. But so severe were the rolls that for a long time he couldn't even turn around. And he was drifting farther and farther out to sea. He sat in the pilot house and wondered which land he'd spot first: Hawaii or San Francisco. Finally he managed to swing *Banner* back on course. In the next twenty-four hours he progressed 23 miles.

Banner lost electrical steering "only four or five times a trip." Engine failures occurred more frequently. A fuse in the air compressor unit kept blowing out. The ship utilized an air-operated clutch, and once air pressure was lost, there was no way to tie the engines to the screws. *Banner* wallowed helplessly.

"Our principal means of navigation was loran," Clark remembers. "Many times at night it would completely fall apart." The radar wasn't reliable, either. Clark told his officers not to approach within 18 miles of land unless he was on the bridge.

Clark was convinced that the quantity of classified material he was supposed to carry was excessive and that his means of destroying it in an emergency were grossly inadequate. His incinerator was tiny; he didn't even have any paper shredders. What upset him even more was the problem of communications.

"We had a peculiar communications system that other naval forces don't have," he explains with marvelous understatement. "Initial communications were always very difficult. When I felt I had to get a message out, it might take ten or twelve hours."

Or even longer. On one occasion *Banner* lay 100 miles out of Yokosuka en route to Sasebo when water seeped into her fuel tanks. Both engines stopped. Clark sent a message to COMNAVFORJAPAN: "DIW [dead in the water] with no engines." He received no reply. Somehow he managed to start one engine. Yokosuka remained silent. He tried to establish contact for twenty-four hours before giving up in disgust. Then he lost both engines again. Finally, he limped into Sasebo. The communications failures, it seemed, were endemic. Alerted at last to his predicament, the Navy dispatched a tug to find him. The tug steamed out, unaware that he was already in port, and spent the next two days searching for him.

On December 20 *Banner* returned to Yokosuka from a mission in the Sea of Japan and tied up next to *Pueblo*. Two days later Clark and Bucher went to see Admiral Johnson, who told them to effect "a complete exchange of information at all levels, from the commanding officer through all the officers and the key enlisted men."

The more Bucher listened, the more concerned he became about his ship's lack of destruct devices. *Pueblo* would encounter harassment. Clark played too many tapes and projected too many slides for him to harbor any illusions on that score. Clark maintained the best thing to do in a harassment situation was to follow the rules of the road. But what if the Soviets or North Koreans didn't play by those rules? What if he had to get rid of his classified documents and gear in an emergency?

He didn't want to write another letter on the subject, "because I had already been officially turned down, and there wasn't enough time, anyway. I was thinking, well, I would be told, 'Didn't I read the letter I had received?' Every time you get into a pissing contest with people who've already told you no, it sort of ruins your career."

He mentioned the problem to Captain Forrest A. Pease, the chief of staff at COMNAVFORJAPAN. Pease didn't know where he might find any destruct devices and told him to contact Captain Daniel R.

McComish, commanding officer of the Naval Supply Depot. McComish replied that all he could offer was a pile of weighted bags and suggested Bucher get in touch with Commander John W. Ryles, Jr., at the Naval Ordnance Facility. Ryles shuttled him back to Lieutenant David M. Chism at the Naval Supply Depot. And Chism told him to call a chief warrant officer at the Naval Ammunition Facility on Azuma Island.

Exasperated by all the buck-passing but still determined to acquire some sort of destruct devices, Bucher telephoned Azuma Island. He seemed to be in luck. The warrant officer said he had a lieutenant on the staff, an explosives expert named Lynn F. Pickard, who would be happy to inspect the ship next morning. Bucher "sanitized" the research spaces and waited for Pickard.

But Pickard didn't appear. Bucher waited one day and called the warrant officer again.

Next morning Pickard toured the ship. "I showed him the various racks of equipment we had," Bucher remembers. "I said I wanted something to enable me to destroy the equipment in the event I had to. What did he recommend?"

Pickard suggested ten or twelve chemical thermite bombs.

Then Bucher discovered that Navy regulations specifically prohibited carrying thermite aboard ship. Still, he was prepared to ignore these regulations if he could convince himself that thermite didn't constitute an unacceptable risk. He debated the pros and cons for the next several hours. He could strap the thermite bombs at the top of each rack, and these devices, he knew, would destroy the equipment in seconds. But he wouldn't have positive control. There was no way to make sure that someone else, by accident or design, didn't pull one of those pins. Reluctantly, he decided thermite wouldn't do.

All submarines carried satchel bombs, small kegs of TNT which could be set off at the flick of a protected switch. Perhaps he could find some 50-pound cans of TNT with time fuses and primer cords and stow them aboard ship. COMNAVFORJAPAN didn't have any TNT. He went to SUBFLOTSEVEN headquarters and requested help from his old friends Phil Stryker and "Flip" DiFilippo. Might he borrow TNT from a submarine that was due to return to the United States? Stryker and DiFilippo couldn't oblige him.

Harris and Schumacher didn't favor TNT, anyway. They were convinced that it would only serve "to toss a lot of things around." Bucher abandoned his efforts. "I figured perhaps I was making too much noise about a very small matter," he recalls.

Late in December a message arrived from the Chief of Naval Operations directing the immediate installation of .50 caliber machine guns on all AGER's. Rear Admiral Frank L. Johnson didn't like the idea. Nor could he understand what had prompted it. *Banner* had already completed sixteen missions in an unarmed status. "I considered this to be a good basis for continuing this type of mission unarmed," he has said. "On several missions *Banner* had been closed by unfriendly forces. They had pointed their guns at *Banner*. I was not particularly happy about the thought of my captains having armament of their own, having them manned and pointing back in return."

With this directive, Washington was clearly altering the original AGER concept. If the CNO insisted on this change, he should at least provide the ships with better means of protecting themselves. "The addition of [these machine guns]," Johnson added, with typical under-statement, "did not appear to me to provide a significant defensive capability." Nonetheless, he told Lieutenant Ed Brookes to handle the matter.

"I called [Lieutenant Commander] Al Wilson [the Operations Division's AGER project officer] and told him we were in the shooting gallery business," Brookes recalls. "He said he was busy, so I agreed to honcho things. Then I called [Lieutenant] Dave Chism at NSD [Naval Supply Depot], and I said, 'Dave, you got any spare cannon lying around?' I told him I needed six .50 caliber machine guns and all the ammo he could spare, five or ten thousand rounds for each."

Chism was only able to find four of the six machine guns, and they were in questionable shape. He delivered two to *Banner,* the other two to *Pueblo.* "Ed Brookes and I joked about the idea," he remembers. "We knew both those ships would roll in a bathtub, and we were sort of wondering what installing those guns might do to their stability."

It was ridiculous, Bucher thought. He had three mounts but only two guns. He asked the Ship Repair Facility to build some gun tubs to protect his men. SRF officials explained that there wasn't enough time.

Not that Bucher had much confidence in the weapons, anyway. A Marine Corps lieutenant had cautioned him that they were "very subject to misalignments"; his gun crews would have to make constant adjustments to the firing pins in order to prevent jamming. Then, too, the lieutenant had said that rapid firing, fourteen or fifteen shells in one burst, would probably melt the barrels. The gunners would have to remember to squeeze off no more than two or three rounds at a time. Brookes and Schumacher arranged for about fifty crew members to spend several hours at a Marine Corps firing range. Not nearly enough time for anyone to become familiar with operating the guns, but probably sufficient for *Pueblo*'s needs. Bucher couldn't envision

Pueblo's ever coming under attack. He couldn't imagine ever having to depend on those guns, and besides, once the ship left Yokosuka, he'd be able to give his men all the practice they required firing at tin cans.

As they watched the Japanese workers installing the mounts, some crew members became concerned. "There was quite a few of us who felt funny about the whole thing," Stu Russell remembers. "We knew the captain didn't want those guns, and we couldn't figure out, well, if everything was going to be so hunky-dory, why we needed them aboard."

Although he had received word of his promotion to commander several months before, Bucher still hadn't had time to host a traditional "wetting down" party. On December 28, in the ABCD Room of the officers' club at the Yokosuka Naval Base, he remedied this oversight. Wearing Hush Puppies, lemon-colored slacks, a bright red vest under a candy-striped jacket, a bow tie and a straw boater on his head, he dashed about dispensing thick black cigars. In one hand he held a small gadget which Elton Wood had designed for the occasion. "Here," he said, "take a look at my new transistor radio." And then he pressed it to his unsuspecting victim's ear, grinning mischievously as the tiny siren emitted a blood-curdling wail. A small button nestled in his lapel. Red letters on a white background spelled "POETS." "It means 'Piss On Everything,' " Bucher explained, " 'Tomorrow's Saturday.' "

Hundreds of multicolored balloons hugged the walls and ceiling. In the rear of the room stood several bowls of black velvet punch, a potent brew containing equal parts of Bock beer, champagne, and sparkling burgundy. Faint wisps of smoke from the dry ice below curled over the tops of the bowls.

Steve Harris had never tasted such a delicious punch. He started toying with the balloons. By rubbing them on the rug, he found, he could generate static electricity. *Very interesting.* He noticed most of the wives were wearing nylon stockings. What would happen if he were to sneak behind them and place the balloons at ankle level? Would they rise up under the skirts? The subjects of his experiments seemed shocked. They didn't appreciate his sense of humor. Harris mumbled apologies, grabbed some more balloons, and made another discovery. If he placed the glowing tip of a cigar against the side of a balloon, he could create the most extraordinary noise. "I saw Pete break into a laugh over this," he recalls, "so I just continued doing it, stuffing the cigar back in my mouth every time, playing innocent but obviously guilty."

"It was the first time in all those months that I'd ever seen old Steve show any real signs of life," Bucher recalls. He glanced at his watch: almost eight o'clock. Jimmy-san was still hammering away at the old piano, but some of the guests were about to leave. And where was Murphy? Here he'd gone to all the trouble of providing a bowl of nonalcoholic punch for his XO. The least Murphy could do was make an appearance. At that moment Murphy arrived. Bucher hid his anger and summoned his officers to the piano for a song:

> "Here's to *Pueblo*—she's a fine ship;
> Here's to *Pueblo*—she's a peach;
> Bumyackle, bumyackle, bumyackle,
> Bumyackle, bumyackle, bum. . . ."

Murphy downed one glass of punch and left a few minutes later. The party broke up; Bucher, Schumacher, Tim Harris, and Lacy moved out into the main bar. Steve Harris spotted Photographer Larry Mack and offered him a ride back to the ship. "I assumed he'd been having a ball, and I expected him to be loaded," Mack remembers. "But he had control of himself. He started talking about the party. He said, 'Generally, Mack, I don't go for that sort of stuff. I don't like all the bullshit. I've got too much to worry about to stand around and drink.' "

The trip across the Pacific had exposed some glaring personnel weaknesses in the research spaces. And what was worse, some of Harris' better men would miss the ship's first mission; Charles Wallace, for example, had just received orders to Scotland. And Communications Technician Second Class Joseph Fejfar was in a hospital recovering from an appendectomy.

Harris requested assistance from the Naval Security Group Activity at Kamiseya, and a chief warrant officer named Vernon I. Bowen selected replacements: James Kell for Wallace, Ralph McClintock for Fejfar. Although the station at Kamiseya was supposed to have seven Korean linguists on its rolls, it had only three, the others having been detached to monitor the conversations of North Korean pilots engaged in the Vietnam War. Now Bowen tapped two of the three, Bob Chicca and Bob Hammond, for duty aboard *Pueblo*.

On five occasions over the past eighteen months, Chicca had volunteered to serve in Vietnam. All his applications had been rejected. This assignment discouraged him further. "The orders said I was to provide 'direct support of operations,' " he recalls, "but I'm not stupid. I knew what they needed. I didn't think I was qualified. I knew my Korean wasn't good enough." His wife, Ann, was eight months pregnant, and "when she heard I was leaving," he adds, "she just about went into hysterics. She said, 'You're not going to Vietnam, are you?' and I said, 'No, I wouldn't do a thing like that.' I promised I'd be back before the baby came, but she was still worried, so I thought about taking her down to Yokosuka to show her the ship. Then I saw the ship myself. It was *so* small. I figured I'd better wait until I got back and off that thing for good before I let Ann take a look."

At his apartment in Suitland, Maryland, Harry Iredale was stuffing clothes into his suitcase. Only a few days before, he had received word that he and his friend "Friar" Tuck would be sailing on *Pueblo.* They'd have to report no later than December 30. "I thought it was just another job," he recalls. "Actually, I knew I'd have to go out there later in the year. I volunteered for the winter trip because I was due to be in a wedding at home that summer. My orders ran to June 1. I'd take the first three missions and have some time to break in my replacement."

Iredale closed the suitcase. Suddenly he remembered the small framed picture of his family that his parents had just given him. He started to open the suitcase, then hesitated. He remembers thinking that "something was going to go wrong this trip." Better to leave that picture at home.

New Year's Eve was cold and windy. Shortly before eight o'clock Charles Law stepped into the Tophat, a small bar near the main gate of the Yokosuka naval base. As a semiconfirmed bachelor, and a sensible fellow, besides, he shunned the city's more raucous clubs with their ubiquitous B-girls; he much preferred the company of sailors from *Pueblo,* the destroyer USS *Hollister,* or the guided-missile cruiser USS *Providence.* Nonetheless, he had to admit he felt an attraction to Emiko Nagachi, the Tophat's mama-san. He had known her since 1961; she was buxom and boisterous but shrewd. Never underestimate the business sense of the Japanese woman. Over the years she'd saved her Tophat earnings; already she owned two other bars and was about to purchase a third.

Above all else, Emiko Nagachi enjoyed a good party, and on this final night of 1967 she didn't feel like stopping her celebration at the ridiculous curfew hour of 1 A.M. She'd have to close the bar then, of course. But perhaps Charles Law and his friend Jim Layton would like to stop by her house afterward? Layton volunteered to bring along a case of Scotch. Law vacillated. He had duty back aboard ship in a few hours, and he wanted to remain reasonably sober. Still, it was New Year's Eve. And who could tell? Someday he might even ask Emiko to marry him.

At the Bar Betty, just around the corner from the Club Alliance, John Shilling was telling one of the girls that *Pueblo* was really an aircraft carrier. The girl wasn't buying a word of it. "She asked me if I knew *Banner,* and I said yes," he recalls. "Then she said, 'Your ship is like *Banner,* and you're leaving in a few days.' "

In a corner booth nineteen-year-old Larry Joe Marshall, the youngest member of *Pueblo's* crew, suddenly realized that he had just spent $40 on drinks for himself and one girl in less than two hours. The girl asked for more champagne. Marshall was broke. Earl Phares saw the girl leave Marshall's booth and move in his direction. With an operator like that he wouldn't stand a chance. He gave her 2,000 yen (about $6) and returned to the ship.

Shivering despite their pea jackets, Norman Spear and Peter Langenberg were standing watch on the quarterdeck. Sailors from the Coast Guard cutter *Winnebago* had stepped aboard to offer them some eggnog. A few minutes more and the watch would change; they'd be free to enjoy it. In his stateroom Steve Harris was finishing a letter to his friend Lieutenant Richard H. Fine, research officer on *Palm Beach.* Since leaving Bremerton back in September, *Palm Beach* had steamed through the Panama Canal and crossed the Atlantic. Harris suspected that she might already be operating against Soviet targets in the Baltic. Below decks in the aft berthing compartment Frank Ginther was reading in his bunk. Suddenly he heard whistles and sirens erupting from every ship in the harbor. He swung out of bed, pulled on his clothes, and rushed to the bridge to add *Pueblo's* welcome to the New Year. Then he saw that Lacy had already beaten him to it. Ginther didn't know Lacy very well. Few crew members did; the stocky, black-haired warrant officer's natural reserve precluded the sort of easy banter they struck up from time to time with Tim Harris, Schumacher, even the captain himself. Yet no one denied Lacy's ability. He was an unspectacular man, to be sure, but very solid, very dependable. Ginther thought he was one of the best officers on the ship.

And Bucher agreed. He had said as much in writing Lacy's fitness report. Lacy was due for promotion to chief warrant officer (W-4). Perhaps that report would give him the little push he needed. Bucher was pleased as well with the performances of Schumacher and Tim Harris. He felt he could trust them completely as officers of the deck. Now that they'd finally received their Secret Intelligence (SI) security clearances, they had access to the research spaces. He could rely upon them even more.

The Naval Security Group's insistence on designating the ship's CT's as a detachment instead of a department still angered him. Here was Steve Harris, his *subordinate,* maintaining operational and administrative control over the research spaces. On *his ship!* Bucher recognized that the setup created problems for Harris, as well. And forgetting for a moment their constant disagreements about Harris' right to bypass him in the chain of command, ignoring the fact that their personalities had not—indeed, could never—mesh perfectly, he had to admit that Harris' performance was satisfactory in almost every respect. He would receive a fine fitness report.

That left one report outstanding—Murphy's. Was he riding his XO too hard? Was he placing too much emphasis on the tiny irritations —the discovery, for example, that Murphy was having his laundry done free, a privilege normally reserved for the captain? Was he criticizing unfairly the man's eccentricities, like keeping a box of animal crackers in a drawer in his stateroom? Animal crackers! He hadn't believed it possible. Was he faulting the navigator for personal habits—his abstinence from cigarettes and liquor—which other captains might find commendable?

He decided to delay submitting his evaluation until the end of the first patrol. "I showed Ed the notes I'd made on him for fitness report purposes," Bucher recalls. "I'd also prepared a letter to have him relieved, and I told him about that. I said this trip was going to have an awful lot to do with his future in the Navy and that he'd better shape up. He said he understood."

But this was not the night to worry about his XO. This was New Year's Eve. How odd it was that no one in Yokosuka had invited him to a party. Each of his friends had probably assumed that he'd already accepted another invitation. And so he'd come to Tokyo by himself and had tried to get into the party at the Sanno Hotel, but it was a mob scene over there; he'd turned away and then, quite by chance, found this delightful bar not far from the Soviet Embassy. Someone was strumming a banjo and there were lots of Americans by the piano and one of them passed him a funny hat and someone else blew a horn in his hear and the din was just unbelievable. He knew he'd be leaving Japan on his first mission in a few more days, probably steaming toward North Korea. He couldn't say for sure. Washington still hadn't approved the specific mission proposal, and until that approval arrived, *Pueblo*'s destination was anybody's guess. Perhaps some word would be waiting when he returned to Yokosuka. But now all the Americans were thumping on tables and blowing on horns and linking arms around the piano to sing "Auld Lang Syne," and there was only one thing a sensible man could do. Bucher waved his hand back and forth and shouted above the clamor: "Bar—tend—er."

19

I don't want intelligence people approving operational stuff; they're too enthusiastic.
—Admiral David L. McDonald, former Chief of Naval Operations

★   ★   ★

In the spring of 1929, shortly after becoming Secretary of State, Henry L. Stimson made a rather disturbing discovery. In conjunction with the War Department, State was helping to maintain a hush-hush cryptanalytical division in New York City, the so-called "American Black Chamber." Stimson withdrew his department's support immediately. "Gentlemen," he explained, "do not read each other's mail."

"The hell we don't," one of his successors, Dean Rusk, was reported to have said some thirty-five years later. "We read anything we can put our hands on."

The Secretary's remark seems less a comment on changing mores than a backhanded acknowledgment of the need for a free society to acquire intelligence—by *whatever* means are available—in order to protect itself in a nuclear age. For, as President Nixon has pointed out, "When a war can be decided in twenty minutes, the nation that is behind will have no time to catch up."

Responsibility for ensuring that this country never falls that far behind is vested in the United States intelligence community, a vast and interlocking network of agencies which employs an estimated 100,000 men and women around the world and spends between five and seven billion dollars every year. Through its Bureau of Intelligence and Research the State Department belongs to this community. So, too, in a literal sense do the departments of Justice, Treasury, and Commerce and the Atomic Energy Commission—all of which have branches which dabble in intelligence. For practical purposes, however, real power is exercised by a muscular triumvirate. And of its members the most important—certainly the most conspicuous—is the Central Intelligence Agency.

At its headquarters building in Langley, Virginia, the CIA employs some 12,000 people, most of whom work in one of three major divisions. The Clandestine Services Division, sometimes referred to as the Department of Dirty Tricks, concerns itself with espionage as well as—to quote the late Allen Dulles—"activities belonging in the category of political or psychological warfare." The Intelligence Division, which rather resembles a large publishing house, gathers and evaluates information and is responsible for compiling the top secret intelligence summary which President Nixon reads each morning. The Research Division specializes in the new and esoteric field of technical espionage. Apart from these is the Office of National Estimates, a section of fewer than fifty people who furnish the "educated guesses" which influence the formulation of U.S. foreign policy.

Although it is less than twenty-five years old, the CIA has become for much of the world's population a sort of acronymic bogeyman. The hullabaloo is unfortunate, for it precludes an appreciation of the agency's contributions to American security (and there have been many), while at the same time diluting the thrust of much well-deserved criticism. The U-2 episode exposed some shocking weaknesses; the Bay of Pigs fiasco unveiled even more. Yet there is much to be said for the thesis that, in recent years and under the able direction of an ex-newspaperman named Richard Helms, the CIA has abandoned the freewheeling gambits that spiced its adolescence and has taken up stodgier, more bureaucratic pastimes. Columnist Stewart Alsop, who knows as much about the intelligence game as any reporter in Washington, refers to this metamorphosis as the "triumph of the prudent professionals."

Even larger than the CIA—in budget and personnel, if not in prestige—is the National Security Agency, which employs between 14,000 and 15,000 men and women at its headquarters complex in Fort Meade, Maryland, and thousands more throughout the United States and overseas. As a former director has explained, somewhat cryptically, NSA operates "within but not [as] a part of the Defense Department." Through its major operating components—the Office of Research and Development (R/D), the Office of Communications Security (COMSEC), and the Office of Production (PROD)—NSA devises and breaks intricate codes; it eavesdrops on the communications of foreign powers; it takes measures to protect U.S. codes and communications.

From time to time senior CIA officials will brief selected members of the press on a background basis or will "leak" their version of a controversial event—the Green Beret murder case is a recent example—to the Washington *Post* or New York *Times*. NSA frowns on such ostentation. So thick is its carapace of secrecy that even the 1952 executive order which established the agency remains under wraps. And reporters who attempt to contact NSA officials are apt to receive a telephone call from Roy Banner, the general counsel, an amiable-sounding fellow who explains once again, as he has for years, that interviews with agency personnel—no matter what the ground rules—are simply out of the question.

Up until 1941, as Stewart Alsop points out in his excellent book *The Center,* "there was no serious intelligence agency in the Government; the War and Navy departments' intelligence sections were run by elderly ladies with a penchant for pince-nez glasses who filed the gossipy reports amassed by the military and naval attachés on their social rounds." World War II changed that, of course; the military services established their own intelligence branches, which even after the end of the war continued to proliferate like the mythological Hydra.

In the intelligence business, as in anything else, competition is healthy, and these intelligence branches—the Army's G-2, the Air Force's A-2, and the Navy's Office of Naval Intelligence (ONI) — competed against each other vigorously. The only problem was that they seemed to be spending millions of dollars to acquire information on the same subjects, often from the same sources. In October, 1961, Secretary of Defense Robert S. McNamara lumped sections of them together to form the final member of the triumvirate—the Defense Intelligence Agency.

If the idea behind the creation of DIA—to coordinate and supervise military intelligence requirements better—was an excellent one, and almost everyone agrees that it was, then it's also true that the plan has failed in its execution. The agency hasn't lived up to its expectations. "DIA was born old," says one former official. "McNamara just gathered the drones and put them all in one building."

Several buildings, to be precise. So fast has the agency grown, so inexorably has it accumulated staffs of experts on political and economic as well as military intelligence, that its 6,000 personnel utilize office space today not only in the Pentagon but also in, among other locations, the Mather Building in Washington, D.C., and Pomponio

Plaza, the Tyler Building, the Lynn Building, the Cafritz Building, and Arlington Hall Station, all in Arlington, Virginia. The number and geographical diversity of these sites are worth noting, if only because excessive size and lack of internal coordination rank high among the agency's problems.

Not long ago a subcommittee of the House Appropriations Committee elicited testimony to the effect that DIA didn't know what to do with all the information it collected; that, specifically, the office responsible for monitoring Southeast Asian affairs simply hadn't gotten around to processing data which, in bulk, equaled 517 linear feet of file-drawer space. There were some other fairly juicy revelations, as well—all of which prompted Representative Jamie Whitten (Democrat, Mississippi) to turn to Vice Admiral Vernon L. Lowrance, DIA's deputy director, and exclaim: ". . . the management of your intelligence assets is in a state of complete disarray."

Whitten and others maintain that DIA is too sluggish, too unresponsive. Whenever a message arrives at the Alert and Warning Center in the Pentagon, for example, clerks promptly put it on microfilm, thereby insuring that they'll be able to prove they received it if questioned about it later by a "Murder Board"—a panel of military or Congressional investigators. In theory, the precaution makes sense. Unfortunately, it often means that the person to whom the message is addressed doesn't see it for hours.

DIA's most serious fault, critics assert, lies in its composition—and in the nature of the military system. During his tour with the agency a Navy commander, for example, is in a position to say no to this or that Navy proposal. But if he is a normal fellow, he is ambitious. He realizes he will be leaving DIA after a few years, and he would like to become, say, the senior intelligence officer on the Seventh Fleet staff, a billet which virtually assures him a captaincy. If he says no to *too* many Navy requests, he will not join the Seventh Fleet at all; instead, he will wind up counting blankets in some Aleutian warehouse. The result of such subtle pressures, of course, is that DIA's officers tend to project and protect their own services' viewpoints—which is precisely the sort of situation that Secretary McNamara was trying to avoid in the first place. The problem is real, and at this moment no one in Washington seems to know quite how to deal with it.

Because the members of this triumvirate are all engaged in the same business, there is quite naturally some overlap in their acquisition effort—an area where CIA's Clandestine Services Division, NSA's PROD, and DIA's Office of Special Activities are apt to want to use the same means to elicit the same information. Contrary to popular mythology, these means seldom include James Bonds—or even Mata Haris—anymore. As former Secretary of Defense Clark M. Clifford pointed out in a 1969 speech, somewhat ambiguously, to be sure, "Penetration is a practical impossibility today through the use of the human agent." The intelligence community considers men and women—no matter how dashing—simply too fallible.

"Machine spies," to use the argot of CIA Director Richard Helms, are far more satisfactory. From its Western Test Range at Vandenberg Air Force Base in California, the Air Force—in cooperation with the CIA—launches SAMOS (Satellite and Missile Observation System) vehicles into orbits 100-odd miles above the Soviet Union and China. The coverage is constant—and expensive. In 1968 the U.S. orbited 36 of these "ferrets," which logged at least 234 days of baby-sitting time over the Soviet Union alone (the Russians responded in kind for at least 200 of those days). And the cost of such surveillance? Knowledgeable sources maintain that $2 billion per year is not too high a figure.

The "take" is substantial. High resolution cameras focus on military installations. Infrared photography provides early warning of Soviet missile launches. Sensitive listening devices eavesdrop on radio traffic and play back their tapes upon command. Electromagnetic pulse detectors monitor radar signatures and ascertain nuclear tests. Until recently analysts had to rely on different satellite "packages" to acquire all the data. But so rapidly have photography and sensor technology advanced that today a single package can fulfill almost every demand. The name of this supersnooper is the "integrated" satellite—Program 949.

Aging U-2's still soar over Cuba on routine "weather research" patrols. The U-2's successors, the YF-12A and the SR-71, swoosh along the periphery of the Communist world at speeds of about 2,000 miles per hour and altitudes of more than 70,000 feet. The Air Force keeps at least twenty of its lumbering "flying ear" planes—EC-121's and the like—in the air at all times.

But satellites and aircraft are costly; they can't remain on station very long. And there is a need for the type of information they can't collect. Enter the Navy. Submarines cruise the Baltic, filter from the Mediterranean into the Black Sea, glide toward the Arctic ice cap and the northern tier of the Soviet Union. Occasionally, they even play tag with their Soviet counterparts. Destroyers, such as *Maddox* and *Turner Joy*, pick up their mobile vans of electronic equipment and steam out on "De Soto" patrols. Oceanographic ships conduct "legitimate" research around the globe. They also find time to compile a sonar "atlas" detailing the salient characteristics of the Soviet Union's 400-odd submarines.

The number of reconnaissance missions that the United States conducts around the world every year is a well-guarded secret, but some indication of the program's scope can be gleaned from the fact that in 1967 there were some 1,500 flights near the borders of North Korea *alone*. At his comfortable home in suburban Maryland, a senior advisor for national security affairs shakes his head and says in a soft, almost resigned tone of voice, "These missions just increased and increased until now there's this fat book of them every month. It's an accepted fact in government—an article of faith, you might say—that they must go on."

Pearl Harbor caught everyone by surprise. So did the Korean conflict; not until eleven hours after North Korean troops marched into South Korea was U.S. intelligence even sure that an attack had taken place. Data which can forewarn of such disasters are of inestimable value today. "This is a mean, difficult, onerous, dangerous, twenty-four-hour-a-day business," say former Secretary of Defense Clark Clifford. "We are in it because we have to be, from the standpoint of our survival."

There's little doubt that some of these missions have enhanced that survival. During the 1962 Cuban missile crisis, for example, as Admiral Thomas H. Moorer, the Chief of Naval Operations, has pointed out, "electronic intelligence acquired by surface ships led to the photographic intelligence which gave us undisputable evidence of the . . . Soviet missiles in Cuba." A second justification is that such missions—no matter who conducts them—provide a nervous world with a measure of stability. During the Arab-Israeli War in 1967, Egypt's President Nasser and Jordan's King Hussein charged that planes from the U.S. Sixth Fleet were aiding the Israelis. Washington officials feared that the Russians might believe the story and enter the conflict on the side of the Arabs. Soviet "fishing trawlers" in the Mediterranean promptly assured Moscow that U.S. planes hadn't left their carriers' decks.

Some observers even maintain that these reconnaissance efforts *save* money. "Intelligence can tell you that you don't have to prepare for certain contingencies," says one. "It lets you cut your costs." Yet there are other costs *aside* from those inscribed in the budget. There have been a number of "incidents." Since 1950 at least 225 United States personnel have been killed or captured while participating in such missions.

One humid afternoon last summer, relaxing at his home in Washington's fashionable Cleveland Park, former Under Secretary of State Nicholas DeB. Katzenbach attempted to put the issue in perspective. "Look," he said, "take the last couple of years. The record will show something like nine thousand seven hundred and twenty-six missions with the loss of three planes and one vessel. That's a pretty good record. Any large insurance company would take that risk."

And the Joint Chiefs of Staff would agree. Still, some nagging and interlocking questions remain. The uproar over the U-2 affair in May of 1960 sabotaged a summit meeting. Even worse, it etched scars in the government's credibility. So it seems fair to ask: Are these missions worth risking political—to say nothing of military—confrontation? Are they worth risking that loss of public confidence? In short, do the losses the United States incurs from this handful of "accidents" outweigh the gains achieved from all the others?

To be sure, it's pleasant to acquire some of this "nice to know" information. But even supposing that X ship, Y aircraft, or Z satellite succeeds in picking up everything it's asked to get; what *difference* will it make? How is this information apt to change United States policy toward the Soviet Union, China, or North Korea? In short, how vital are the requirements? As the posters used to ask during World War II: Are all these trips really necessary? Are these missions laid on to satisfy a vital need for certain information, or—hints of heresy—is the motivating factor merely a bureaucratic desire to *use the resource,* a feeling that "we've got the ship, the airplane, the satellite—now let's put them to work to justify the cost"? Does the need determine the hardware, or is it the other way around? In short, does technology dictate policy?

And if this is so, what are the implications? A former administration official says, "These things are so darned technical that we civilians just haven't been able to keep up with them. For all we know at our level, the CIA or the military might be requesting permission to go into Leningrad Harbor with their listening devices. You can't expect a [Walt] Rostow or a [Dean] Rusk to sift through and evaluate all the requirements himself; they're too complicated. And that's the trouble: The people who have the knowledge don't have the authority; the people who have the authority don't have the knowledge." Is the decision-making machinery as it's presently constituted too rusty to cope with the challenge?

The answers to at least some of these questions emerge from an account of the way that the *Pueblo* mission proposal was first concocted, then approved, and finally executed.

Ever since March of 1967, the intelligence staff at COMNAVFOR-JAPAN headquarters in Yokosuka had known that *Pueblo* would be

USS *Pueblo*—"The Lonely Bull"; the beads on her hull indicate she is the second in a class of General Environmental Research vessels.

Official photographs, U.S. N

A Soviet-built North Korean submarine chaser (SO1) of the type
that led the attack on *Pueblo*.

A Soviet-built North Korean P-4 torpedo boat, which is capable
of speeds in excess of 45 knots.

Official photographs, U.S. N

Official photograph U.S. Navy

North Korea's senior negotiator, Major General Pak Chung Kuk (left), with aide at Panmunjom.

Commander Bucher, his wife, Rose, and their eldest son, Mark, enjoy a steak dinner at the Balboa Naval Hospital in San Diego on Christmas Eve, 1968.

Right: Quartermaster First Class Charles B. Law, Jr., receive plaque from actor John Wayne at a party in San Diego followi the crew's return. "The citizens of the United States," the plac read, "will always remember the *Pueblo.*"

Official photograph U.S. Navy

Above: Lieutenant j.g. F. Carl (Skip) Schumacher (center), *Pueblo*'s operations officer, confers with Commander Bucher (left) and Lieutenant Murphy shortly after the crew's return to San Diego.

Official photograph U.S. Navy

Official photograph U.S. Na

Waiting for a session of the court of inquiry to begin are (from left) Commander William E. Clemmons, associate counsel; Captain William R. Newsome, counsel for the court; and Commander Richard W. Bates, a security officer.

Right, Lieutenant Stephen R. Harris, the Harvard-educated officer in charge of *Pueblo's* research detachment.

Below. A "fisheye" lens provides a panoramic view of the *Pueblo* court of inquiry. The members of the court are (from left) Rear Admiral Richard R. Pratt, Rear Admiral Marshall W. White, Vice Admiral Harold G. Bowen, Jr., Rear Admiral Edward E. Grimm, and Rear Admiral Allen A. Bergner.

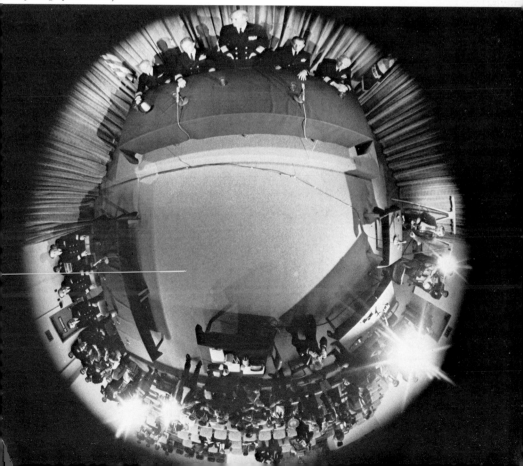

Above: Pueblo's skipper, Commander Lloyd M. Bucher (left), and executive officer Lieutenant Edward R. Murphy, Jr., salute the colors after receiving Purple Hearts at a San Diego ceremony.

Below: Bucher prepares to testify before a closed session of the *Pueblo* court of inquiry. Facing camera are his civilian counsel, E. Miles Harvey, and his military attorney, Captain James Keys.

joining *Banner* in conducting operations off the coasts of China, the Soviet Union, and North Korea. The *modus operandi* had been agreed upon. While she was out on a mission, *Pueblo* would fall under the operational control of Rear Admiral Frank L. Johnson, who bore the fancy title of Commander, Task Force 96, as well as that of COM-NAVFORJAPAN. In port, however, she would revert to the operational control of Vice Admiral William F. (Bush) Bringle, the white-haired, soft-spoken commander of the Seventh Fleet. Administrative control of the ship would remain in the hands of Rear Admiral Norvell G. Ward, Commander, Service Group Three, who was based in Sasebo.

Admiral Johnson wasn't expected to protect *Banner* and *Pueblo;* these were, after all, the only ships under his control. If they needed help, he could rely upon his "on-call" support arrangement with Fifth Air Force and Seventh Fleet. Johnson's main responsibility was to determine his area's intelligence needs and propose to CINCPAC-FLT missions designed to acquire the information.

Any surveillance mission, of course, has a capability for satisfying a spiderweb of Specific Intelligence Collection Requirements (SICR's), and this simple fact lay at the heart of Admiral Johnson's problems. The National Security Agency wanted to target the ships solely against "national" requirements and viewed the Navy in much the same way that Howard Hughes might view his chauffeur. For its part, the Navy was much more interested in achieving its tactical objectives; it thoroughly resented these NSA "intrusions." Eventually, a fragile compromise was struck. On some missions *Banner* and *Pueblo* would be "available to DIRNSA [Director, NSA] for primary tasking"; on others the Navy would call the shots. Under a third mode of tasking the ships would try to satisfy Navy and NSA requirements on an equal basis.

Throughout the fall of 1967 Admiral Johnson's intelligence staff attempted to hammer out a six-month schedule for both ships that would please everyone. The geographic area these men had to consider was enormous—stretching from the East China Sea north to the Sea of Japan, North Korea, and Vladivostok, then east to the Kurile Islands, the port of Petropavlovsk, and the Kamchatka Peninsula.

As the "surface intelligence support officer," Lieutenant Ed Brookes pretty much ran the show. Each mission, he knew, would require a separate proposal message, but he wanted to send out the six-month schedule anyway, circulate it informally among his peers at CINCPACFLT and COMSEVENTHFLT "and start all the people in the chain of command thinking in the same direction." The time frame would allow for nine missions. NSA would demand primary tasking on at least five of them. *Pueblo*'s first mission, though, would be a Navy affair. She would tackle NSA requirements only on a "not to interfere" basis.

On several occasions in October and November Brookes called meetings in the spook locker to determine where to send her. Captain Thomas L. Dwyer, the assistant chief of staff for intelligence, attended most of these sessions. So did Lieutenant Commander Duane L. Heisinger, a clean-cut, conscientious Naval Academy graduate from Fresno, California. As did Lieutenant Commander Carl L. Hokenson, Jr., a stout, balding, and thoroughly unflappable former enlisted man who was forty-two at the time but looked at least ten years older. Brookes wanted to give *Pueblo* a productive assignment, yet at the same time didn't want to overtax her capabilities. Her crew needed more experience.

The officers looked at their maps and quickly selected four possibilities: the North Pacific, the Tsushima Strait, the East China Sea, and the Sea of Japan. Foul winter weather ruled out the North Pacific immediately. Political considerations eliminated the East China Sea. Ever since *Banner*'s run-in with those metal-hulled trawlers near Shanghai, the State Department's Bureau of Intelligence and Research had been extremely queasy about conducting intelligence missions off the coast of China. That left the Tsushima Strait and the Sea of Japan.

Soviet warships patrolled the Tsushima Strait constantly. *Banner* had already photographed most of them; there wasn't much that COMNAVFORJAPAN still needed to know about them. "Originally, we talked about a Tsushima Strait mission all by itself," Captain Dwyer recalls. "We knew the take would be minimal, but we wanted a good break-in mission, a good conditioner. Finally we decided it wouldn't be exciting enough.

Dwyer suggested a compromise: *Pueblo* would spend half her time in the Tsushima Strait, the other half in the Sea of Japan. Brookes held out for a 25–75 split. A few weeks before, he had received a letter from Lieutenant Commander Richard Mackinnon, his friend in Hawaii. Mackinnon had explained the circumstances surrounding his own fall from grace and complained bitterly that no one at CINC-PACFLT seemed to care about China or North Korea. Brookes had been impressed by Mackinnon's arguments. "I was convinced that having the ship steam around in the Tsushima Strait would be an absolute waste of the resource," he explains. "The cost-effectiveness would be so poor. It would be so much more profitable to go for some valuable intelligence against the North Koreans. There wasn't much intelligence available on those people, and there we had a real potential enemy. I said, 'Let's see if we can put the ship up there.' "

Before they could submit the mission proposal up the line for approval, Brookes and his colleagues had to evaluate the risk and, in doing so, take into account such factors as the following: What was the nature and scope of the intelligence task? How long would *Pueblo* remain in which areas? How close would she venture to the North Korean coast? What was the long-range weather forecast? How frequently did the North Koreans send out patrols at that time of year? How much harassment had *Banner* received in that area? How near were the first available United States support forces? And what was the current political climate in North Korea?

On October 13, 1966, North Korea's chunky premier, Kim Il Sung, had delivered an uncompromising speech stressing his intention to "reunify" the peninsula—by force if necessary. Then President Lyndon B. Johnson visited Seoul to reaffirm United States backing for South Korea. That visit apparently infuriated Kim Il Sung; in the next ten days his troops killed more United Nations Command personnel than they had in the previous thirteen years. The number of serious incidents along the DMZ skyrocketed from 37 in 1966 to 445 in 1967. North Korean patrol craft captured 50 ROK fishing boats and detained 353 of their crewmen. Radio Pyongyang's nightly diatribes were becoming infinitely more threatening.

None of these trends seemed to alarm intelligence analysts at COMNAVFORJAPAN. *Banner*'s presence off Wonsan several months earlier, they remembered, hadn't elicited any reaction at all. The North Koreans didn't seem to operate many patrols in the winter. Furthermore, *Pueblo* would be steaming in international waters; one hundred sixty-one years of U.S. naval tradition dictated that no foreign power would ever dare to threaten her freedom of movement. And if one did? Well, there was a *quid pro quo*. Communist trawlers were awfully vulnerable, too. The United States would retaliate in kind. "We looked at the peaks and valleys of North Korean moves," Brookes recalls. "We decided they wouldn't affect the ship at all."

There were, of course, some other factors to be considered here. The nature of the system presented the risk evaluators with a cruel dilemma. They wanted to use the ship to collect intelligence against a potential threat. Before they could do so, they had to receive approval from higher authority. Because of the Vietnam War, higher authority was reluctant to provide any backup support for an AGER; was even reluctant, in fact, to approve any mission proposal at all unless it came in labeled as "minimal risk." Without that approval, *Pueblo* would linger in port for weeks, maybe months. Brookes tagged the mission proposal "minimal risk."

While the intelligence staff was reaching this conclusion, the operations division at COMNAVFORJAPAN was gearing up to provide the necessary logistics support, laying out the mission's "track" and estimating the amount of food and other provisions *Pueblo* would need for a thirty-day voyage. The AGER project officer was a lieutenant commander from Atlanta, Georgia, named Al Wilson. An aviator and former intelligence specialist himself, he had been "surprised" to find upon his arrival in Japan that he would be working in operations. "I didn't know too much about ships," he says. Nonetheless, he rather enjoyed the job and, from all accounts, performed creditably indeed. He completed his analysis of the ship's requirements and passed the mission folder to Captain William H. Everett, the assistant chief of staff for operations. Everett approved the proposal and, in turn, sent it on to Captain Forrest A. Pease.

For the past seventeen months Pease had been serving as the chief of staff, the second most important billet in the COMNAVFOR-JAPAN hierarchy. A short, bald, seemingly gruff New Englander, he had been a champion wrestler in the 165-pound class at Brown University in 1937, and even now he retained a wrestler's characteristics: the thick neck, the slightly cauliflowered ears, the bouncy side-to-side walk on the balls of the feet. Almost everyone called him Buster.

Although he approved of the AGER program in general terms, Pease still harbored some reservations about it. "This was a real hush-hush program," he recalls, "a little side deal, and only a few people here were ever allowed to get involved in it." Nonetheless, the mission proposal seemed perfectly straightforward to him. The intelligence and operations staffs had obviously coordinated well and had prepared for contingencies. If anything unexpected occurred—if the North Koreans turned nasty—well, there was always that "button" to push, that "on-call support" to request. He signed the proposal and gave it to Admiral Johnson.

Johnson had never disapproved any of *Banner*'s sixteen mission proposals, and he saw no reason to object to this *Pueblo* proposal now. He thought about the risk evaluation. "I was aware of the increase in incidents along the DMZ, and I was aware over the past year of certain actions taken by the North Koreans." Nonetheless, "I did agree that the risk was minimal, and I personally made the final decision." On December 14, Johnson sent the mission proposal with a formal request for approval to CINCPACFLT headquarters in Hawaii.

There it received "shotgun" distribution; everyone who was due to have "a piece of the action" got a copy immediately. As the AGER project officer in the Reconnaissance and Indications Branch of the Intelligence Division, Lieutenant Commander Erv Easton was primarily responsible for steering the proposal through the layers of command. He agreed with the need to acquire new information on the North Koreans. He wanted to "exercise the capability," as well, and, reviewing the record of *Banner*'s sojourns in the area, he found no fault with the threat assessment. Still, he wanted to get an up-to-date reading on North Korean naval activity from the Current Intelligence Branch.

At each step of its progression all the way back to Washington, the mission proposal was supposed to receive an independent risk evaluation. If Lieutenant Commander Richard Mackinnon had remained at his desk as the North Korean analyst, he would have handled this task. But ever since his bitter fight with Lieutenant Commander Dave Moke, he'd been spending his time counting SAM missile sites in aerial photographs. So in his absence the assignment fell into the lap of Ensign Charles B. Hall, Jr. He tagged the proposal "minimum risk." "At that time I did not see the North Koreans as a direct threat," Hall remembers. "I had no reservations because I frankly didn't know enough about it to have any."

Reviewing Hall's assessment a day or so later, Lieutenant j.g. Albert Morris felt "uneasy." "I couldn't say I *didn't* agree with it," he remembers. "It was just that I approached this sort of thing with a healthy skepticism anyway. I knew about the DMZ activity—I'd never trusted those North Koreans. *Banner* had been harassed before by the Soviets and the ChiComs, and, well, anytime we had this sort of mission, I felt this harassment was probably going to happen again." Yet "because there was such a lack of information on the area," Morris swallowed his misgivings. He gave the proposal to Easton, who in turn sent it to Captain John L. Marocchi, the assistant chief of staff for intelligence.

"These evaluations were in no sense rubber stamps," Marocchi maintains. "The North Koreans were pushing bodies across the DMZ. They continued to seize South Korean ships and accuse them of being spy boats. What we saw and heard didn't seem any different from what we had been seeing and hearing for the past ten years. The Koreans, up to that point, had done nothing to our ships, while the Russians had harassed them. The mission looked like it would be quiet and safe. The logic was in the message. It took me about as long to approve it as it did to read it."

The assistant chief of staff for operations, Captain George L. Cassell, agreed with his counterpart's analysis. "Everything the intelligence people had we examined. There was nothing contained in any of that [data] which would have substantiated any risk assessment other than minimal, as far as I'm concerned. The mission was no more hazardous than we normally would expect in going to sea." Then Cassell added the fatal presumption: "It didn't follow that these people, although they were attacking our people across the DMZ, would do anything across the water."

Noting that both Marocchi and Cassell had raised no objections, Vice Admiral Walter H. Baumberger, CINCPACFLT's chief of staff, okayed the mission proposal on December 17 and sent it a few miles away to Camp H. M. Smith. There, at the headquarters of Admiral U. S. Grant Sharp, Commander in Chief, Pacific (CINCPAC), Captain Erman O. Proctor submitted it for further review to the intelligence and operations staffs. Proctor viewed the request as "routine." He didn't question it because "the whole deal [had been] handled by Fleet already. We were just sort of, you know, like the handle on the teapot." He "massaged" it up through CINCPAC's chief of staff to Sharp himself.

A wiry, taciturn Montanan who had spent nearly forty-five years in the Navy, Sharp had between 400 and 500 ships and "about a million men" under his direct command. Nonetheless, he took an active interest in the AGER program and on one occasion had even changed *Banner*'s "track" out of concern for her safety. Yet now as he watched his briefers leaf through their charts and listened to them explain the *Pueblo* proposal, he couldn't find any reason to fault the risk assessment. On December 23 he referred the paper to the Joint Chiefs of Staff and requested their approval.

Commander Victor B. (Chris) Wolke had been expecting this formal proposal for the past week. As the surface reconnaissance action officer for the AGER program in the Joint Reconnaissance Center (JRC) of the Joint Chiefs of Staff, he was primarily responsible for determining that the intelligence requirements which COMNAVFOR-JAPAN had laid out were, in fact, worth acquiring. He also had to decide whether or not *Pueblo* possessed sufficient tools to gather this data. On December 17 he had received an information copy of the message which Vice Admiral Baumberger at CINCPACFLT had sent to Admiral Sharp at CINCPAC; already he had discussed the mission with his fellow action officers from the various services as well as with representatives from NSA and the State Department's Bureau of Intelligence and Research.

Now Wolke decided he needed a new risk evaluation from DIA. In its brief history DIA had rarely—if ever—disagreed with a minimal risk assessment from the field, and Wolke didn't expect any static this time. He called in the liaison officer between JCS-JRC and DIA, a soft-spoken lieutenant commander named Harry K. Cook, and asked him to handle the matter. As was his practice, Cook waited until he had several dozen separate proposals. Then he sent them via "guard mail," or courier, to a twenty-eight-year-old Army major named Donald Alexander who worked in the DIA office responsible for North Korean affairs.

That office at the time was located on the second floor of Building B at Arlington Hall Station, a ten-minute bus ride from the Pentagon. This fact alone gives some indication of its place in the pecking order. Nonetheless, Don Alexander, a tall, rather handsome graduate of Texas A&M, was an extraordinarily busy fellow. As North Korean military analyst he had to contribute to DIA's "daily publication." He had to update his estimates of North Korea's order of battle on a regular basis. He had to cope with dozens of other requirements, as well. The J-3 (Operations) staff of the JCS, for example, might be working on a paper to increase the number of U.S. aircraft at bases in South Korea. It would need an estimate of North Korean reaction to such a move. J-6 (Communications-Electronics) might be preparing to introduce a new communications system in South Korea. It would need to know whether or not the North Koreans could intercept its messages. J-4 (Logistics) might forward an Air Force request to substitute 750-pound bombs for 500-pound bombs on its planes in South Korea. It would need new data on North Korean air defenses to support this change.

Alexander had just returned from a tour as an adviser to the South Vietnamese Army. He had considered that billet grueling enough. Now hardly a morning went by that he didn't have to wade through fourteen to sixteen inches of new paper, most of it crammed with technical data. He found he was spending between ten and fourteen hours in the office every day. Free weekends seemed to be rare luxuries. Gamely he kept chipping away at the mountain of paper. Just clearing his desk—even temporarily—was a major accomplishment. He didn't have time to ask the basic questions.

Before coming to any conclusions about the risk to *Pueblo*, Alexander was supposed to consider "five specific anticipated reaction criteria and five anticipated sensitivity criteria." He had very little to go on: The CINCPACFLT message simply assessed the risk as "minimal" without providing any elaboration. And he had a deadline to meet.

Alexander declines to say whether or not he weighed these criteria. Nor will he estimate how much time he spent on the proposal. "The way it probably worked in this case," says one former DIA official, "is that he got the book on his desk one morning at nine o'clock with orders to return it by noon. That book is the size of a Sears, Roebuck catalogue. It would be a physical impossibility for him to study each mission in detail."

Nonetheless, Alexander estimated the risk as "minimal." So did his superiors in the office of North Korean affairs. Lieutenant Commander Harry Cook retrieved the proposal and gave it back to Commander Chris Wolke.

The procedure by which the members of the Joint Chiefs of Staff approve a reconnaissance mission is choreographed as formally as a Balanchine ballet. Now, with DIA's blessing in hand, Wolke set out to follow the ritual. He gathered the "inputs" of his fellow action officers, summarized all the pertinent facts about *Pueblo*'s mission on a piece of white paper called a "flimsy," and bucked it to his superiors on the Joint Staff. No one logged any objections, so Wolke repeated the process, turning out a buff-colored "consolidated working paper" and circulating it among officers at an even higher level. Again—a few minor additions and deletions, but no serious objections. Wolke changed the color of the paper to green.

Now the approval cycle quickened. The *Pueblo* proposal joined hundreds of others inside a fat notebook—the "Monthly Reconnaissance Schedule for January 1968." Air Force Brigadier General Ralph D. Steakley, the balding, cigar-smoking chief of the Joint Reconnaissance Center, picked up where Wolke had left off. He sent the notebook to the various services for their formal concurrence. He got it almost immediately. Then he dispatched it to CIA, NSA, and the State Department's Bureau of Intelligence and Research.

Back in April, 1965, the State Department's "Geographical Bulletin #3: Sovereignty of the Seas" had noted that "the itinerary of any naval vessels close along a foreign coast or through strategic waters may be tantamount to creating tensions and precipitating crises, even among otherwise friendly states. . . ." And since the inception of the AGER program, the Bureau of Intelligence and Research had been wary about giving the military *carte blanche* on these missions, had even forced the cancellation of a *Banner* voyage into the Yellow Sea. In response, officers in JRC referred to the I&R liaison man as the "resident pants-wetter."

So R. Robin DeLaBarre felt misunderstood. A tall, bespectacled somewhat diffident fellow, he liked to point out that he was the son of a Navy officer, that his wife was an admiral's daughter. He didn't *enjoy* giving the military such a hard time; still, he had a job to do. On December 26 he began "walking the book around." He'd have to show it to Thomas L. Hughes, director of the Bureau of I&R, and then to Nicholas deB. Katzenbach, the Under Secretary of State. "The sensitivity of the mission was recognized," he remembers, "and pointed out to all clearing it." At CIA and NSA his counterparts followed suit.

At eleven o'clock on the morning of December 27 the service action officers—the representatives from JRC, CIA, NSA, DIA, and I&R, maybe two dozen men in all—gathered in Room 2E924—the "tank"—of the Pentagon to resolve any differences of opinion either about the mission or the risk evaluation. But there were no differences of opinion. Everything was strictly routine.

The members of the Joint Chiefs of Staff usually meet three times a week—on Monday, Wednesday, and Friday afternoons—inside the "tank," a large rectangular room with yellow drapes and carpeting and a thick walnut table surrounded by sixteen red leather chairs. Before these formal sessions begin, each Chief is supposed to receive a briefing about each item on the agenda. If he still harbors questions about, say, the monthly reconnaissance schedule, he can ask Brigadier General Ralph Steakley, the chief of JRC, to discuss that schedule in detail at one of the meetings.

"Steakley would show us the number of missions requested and the number he'd approved," recalls Admiral David L. MacDonald, the former CNO. "If there were something unusual, he'd flash it on the screen. We'd all look, and the chairman would say, 'Any comment?' We didn't usually make any comment. This wasn't a request for approval *per se*. It was sort of 'Look here—here's what's going to be done unless you fellows want to do something about it.' "

"The JCS usually interjects itself on a policy level to question the desirability of a particular program or mission," General Earle G. Wheeler, its chairman, has said. "Unless there was some event which would cause us to really focus on it, we would say, 'Well, last month this particular program went off without incident.' There would be no reason to expect, or require, a detailed examination. We look at them, I might say, in chunks."

The members of the JCS did *not* convene to review the monthly reconnaissance schedule for January, 1968. For during that busy week between Christmas and New Year's Day, General Wheeler was away on leave. General Harold K. Johnson, the Army Chief of Staff, was visiting Southeast Asia and would not return until January 5. General Wallace Greene, Jr., Commandant of the Marine Corps, was set to retire in a few days. So the fat notebook with its hundreds of missions was approved, Wheeler has noted, "by each Chief's telling his operations deputy that he had no dissatisfaction with the program, thereby giving him permission to release it at the operations deputies' meeting which was held on Friday morning, the twenty-ninth of December."

How much time the Chiefs of Staff or their operations deputies actually spent in reviewing the *Pueblo* proposal—if, in fact, they reviewed it at all—is a matter of speculation. General Wheeler has said, "I was fully aware of the mission of the *Pueblo*. . . . General Steakley informed me of this at one of my morning briefings, and I offered no objection to it." Yet by his own account, Wheeler was not in Washington at the time the JCS considered the monthly reconnaissance schedule. It strains credibility to assume that upon his return he would receive a briefing on this particular mission, one of hundreds in the "package," one which *everyone* considered to be routine.

Similar doubts exist about the testimony of Admiral Thomas H. Moorer, the Chief of Naval Operations. Although he would later assure Congress that "everyone was aware of the mission," Moorer would also acknowledge, "I don't recall having delved into it as a specific mission. . . . I don't recall being briefed [about it] in the final review. . . ."

Moorer's right-hand man at the time, his operations deputy, was Admiral Waldemar F. A. Wendt. And Wendt does not remember approving the *Pueblo* proposal either. "Only those missions which were considered in the possible risk category or the possible reaction category," he says, "would have been specifically briefed by the operations staff to me. The [*Pueblo*] operation was considered . . . routine and would not therefore have been brought to my specific attention."

Nonetheless, on Friday, December 29, the *Pueblo* proposal was approved by the JCS, CIA, NSA, and the State Department. Then it was approved by Paul H. Nitze, the Deputy Secretary of Defense, an extraordinarily able man who had once been Secretary of the Navy and who in the months to come would argue persuasively for a deescalation of the American effort in Vietnam. "The proposals I paid attention to," Nitze recalls, "were the ones where there was a difference of opinion. This was not one of them."

One final hurdle remained: the hush-hush 303 Committee, the Senior Interdepartmental Group—or SIG—of the U.S. intelligence community. Late that Friday afternoon its members (Nitze, Katzenbach, and Walt Rostow among them) gathered in the White House to review the January schedule. They found no fault with it.

The fat black notebook returned to the Pentagon. A green sheet of paper marked TOP SECRET stretched across its cover. Down the right-hand border of that paper ran the red stripe which indicated that everything inside had been approved. At any other time, Brigadier General Ralph Steakley, the chief of JRC, might have contacted CINCPAC in Hawaii to say that the mission could proceed immediately. CINCPAC would have relayed the news to CINCPACFLT, which in turn would have passed it on to COMNAVFORJAPAN. But this was late Friday afternoon, the start of the long New Year's weekend. Steakley locked the notebook in a file cabinet inside his office, Room 2D 921G. There was no hurry; he could send that message on January 2.

20

On the wall of General Steakley's outer office hangs a framed cartoon from the Washington *Daily News*. Two men, unshaven and clad in rags, are standing on a desert island. One of them is pulling a note out of a bottle which has just floated up to the beach. "Hey," he says, "it's a message from the Joint Chiefs of Staff—for the *Liberty*."

Military communications aren't as chaotic as that cartoon would indicate. The Chiefs and other high-ranking officials seldom rely upon bottles. Yet at the same time it's naïve to believe that—as former Secretary of Defense Robert S. McNamara once assured Congress—"all theater commanders can be contacted by voice and/or teletype in less than thirty seconds to execute emergency action." So immense is the volume of traffic—800,000 messages a *day* pass over the Armed Forces Communications Network—and so fallible are the human beings who funnel it into this or that channel that mistakes *do* occur. Messages sent to the Mediterranean, as in the case of USS *Liberty*, wind up in the Philippines. If they materialize at all. The consequences of such mistakes are troublesome enough; their implications are frightening.

At the National Security Agency's headquarters at Fort Meade, Maryland, that Friday afternoon, a retired Navy chief who shall be known as Hank still worried about the *Pueblo* proposal. He couldn't quite bring himself to agree with the "minimal risk" assessment which the services, DIA, the State Department's Bureau of I&R—almost everyone, in fact—had already settled upon.

But at this point what could, or should, he do about it? NSA was not responsible for determining the risk of these reconnaissance missions. That was DIA's job. NSA didn't have the authority to question DIA's judgment. Furthermore, NSA was happy with the overall "tasking" arrangements, which decreed that in the months to come *Pueblo* and *Banner* would spend more time collecting against its requirements than working for the Navy. Hank didn't want to ruffle the Navy's feathers by questioning its judgment. And yet—he couldn't dismiss his qualms. He mentioned them to his superiors.

The deputy to the assistant director of PROD at the time was a tall, blue-eyed civilian with a strong chin and a habit of using his hands to punctuate his sentences. The more this man—known here as Efon—listened to Hank's concerns, the more convinced he became that something ought to be done. In all the years that he had monitored these reconnaissance missions, he had never sent out a "warning message." Yet now, for all he knew, the JCS was still considering the *Pueblo* mission proposal. He decided to send a message, addressing it "for action," to the JCS:

> . . . the following information is provided to aid in your assessment of CINCPAC's estimate of risk. . . . The North Korean Air Force has been extremely sensitive to peripheral reconnaissance flights in the area since early 1965. . . . The North Korean Air Force has assumed an additional role of Naval support since late 1966. The North Korean Navy reacts to any ROK naval vessel-ROK fishing vessel near the North Korean coast line . . . internationally recognized boundaries as they relate to airborne activities are generally not honored by North Korea on the east coast of North Korea. . . . The above is provided to aid in evaluating the requirements for ship protective measures and is not intended to reflect adversely on CINCPACFLT deployment proposal. . . .

At 10:28 that night Efon's message, carrying the signature of the director of NSA, arrived at the Defense Intelligence Agency Signal Office (DIASO) in Room 1D884 at the Pentagon. A clerk sent it upstairs to the National Military Command Center in Room 2D901A. The officer on watch, Commander Victor B. (Chris) Wolke, scanned it and decided to refer it to Brigadier General Steakley, the chief of the JRC. Additionally, he thought he'd furnish a copy to the CNO. But instead of addressing this copy correctly, he attached the prosign "Zen," a signal that it had already been mailed to him. As a result, the message would get lost inside the building; the CNO wouldn't see it for another thirty days. Wolke's was only the first in a series of mistakes.

As soon as he returned to JRC on January 2, Steakley saw the NSA warning. Although it dealt with risk assessment and deserved, therefore, to be routed to DIA, Steakley did not send it there. Nor did he bring it to the attention of the Joint Chiefs of Staff or the members of the 303 Committee. Instead, he changed the message's priority from "action" to "information" and sent it to CINCPAC headquarters in Hawaii. "I didn't specify the retransmittal [to any particular officer there]," he explained later. "[I] just sent it to CINCPAC, period. It gets to the right office. It wanders its way down."

Shortly after one o'clock that afternoon the message from the JCS approving the mission proposal arrived at the Joint Reconnaissance Center in CINCPAC headquarters. So when—at 4:01 P.M.—this second message, from NSA, which Steakley had passed along, showed up at the same location, the officer on watch assumed it was superfluous, that its contents had already been taken into consideration by the JCS. "That timing sequence was probably as unfortunate a situation as you'll ever run into," says Commander Kelley Sims, the former action officer for the AGER program in the office of the CNO. "Had it arrived any earlier, those people might have taken a different approach to it."

If General Steakley hadn't changed the priority tag from "action" to "information," the NSA warning message would have landed on the desk of Air Force Major General Chesley Peterson, the assistant chief of staff for intelligence; it might even have merited Admiral Sharp's personal attention. But as it was, the watch officer in CINCPAC's JRC noted the "information" tag, decided that there was "no need to show this to the boss," and relayed it to some junior officers on the intelligence staff. These officers concluded that the message contained "no new information. Accordingly, no further action was . . . necessary." They didn't inform the JCS, or anyone else, of their decision.

Two opportunities remained for that warning message to reach someone who might act on it. The first was quashed in the Pentagon. An officer in the NMCC spotted the message, realized that no one had sent it to DIA, and proceeded to do so on his own. The message apparently disappeared in the great paper swirl.

The bungling of the second chance is even harder to understand. The director of the Naval Security Group, Captain—now Rear Admiral—Ralph E. Cook, had received the message informally over a "back channel circuit." Cook was unaware that Steakley had changed the priority. He assumed that senior officers on the CINCPAC intelligence staff would consider the message's implications and discuss them with their counterparts at CINCPACFLT. And CINCPACFLT would then bring Cook's representative, Captain E. B. (Pete) Gladding, the director of Naval Security Group Activities, Pacific, into the conversation. If Cook could alert Gladding to this possibility, he'd be helping him to stay one step ahead of the game.

In doing so, Cook faced a problem—one which stemmed from the unorthodox way he'd received the message himself. "Since it wasn't officially addressed to me," he recalls, "I couldn't officially readdress it to anyone." He sent the message to Gladding informally—under the table, so to speak.

Gladding at the time wore three separate hats: as officer in charge of the Naval Security Group Detachment in Hawaii and as special assistant for Naval Security Group matters, he was responsible in the chain of command directly to Admiral John J. Hyland, Commander in Chief, Pacific Fleet. But as director, Naval Security Group, Pacific, he *didn't* come under Hyland's jurisdiction. He reported instead to Washington. If as DIRNAVSECGRUPAC, for example, he received a message stating that *Pueblo* carried 43 pregnant kangaroos and 14 tons of green cheese, he wouldn't be under any *obligation* to mention this to anyone at CINCPACFLT.

This distinction is more important than it appears, for what happened to Captain Cook's message after it left Washington is still a matter of some dispute. It was addressed to Gladding as DIRNAVSECGRUPAC. Gladding says he never received it. Other officers insist that he did. The fact remains that neither Gladding nor the CINC-PAC intelligence officers nor anyone else ever told CINCPACFLT that the NSA warning message existed.

On January 3 CINCPAC relayed the JCS's approval message to CINCPACFLT, which in turn contacted COMNAVFORJAPAN. The estimated risk remained "minimal." COMNAVFORJAPAN should prepare the sail order. *Pueblo* should leave Yokosuka as soon as possible.

One of the first officers at Fifth Air Force headquarters to receive a copy of the *Pueblo* mission proposal was a bespectacled, curly-haired lieutenant colonel on the intelligence staff named Robert Orcutt. As he had done with all the *Banner* proposals, he discussed this mission with Lieutenant Colonel James Dugan, the former schoolteacher from the operations staff, and Commander Tom McDonald, the Navy's liaison officer at Fuchu. The three of them noted that COMNAVFOR-JAPAN had not requested an Air Force strip alert; they wouldn't have to make any special preparations. Still, there was something odd about that proposal. Dugan said he'd call Lieutenant Ed Brookes in Yoko-suka.

"He said, 'There appears to be an impossible situation here,'" Brookes recalls. 'You have the ship going through the Tsugaru Straits [which separate Honshu from the northernmost island of Hokkaido].' I said, 'It's been changed to the Tsushima Straits.' Then he said, 'Are you asking for a strip alert?' I said, 'No. We're just passing this info to you so you can tip off people.'

"We didn't want to get the Air Force too excited," Brookes ex-plains. "We didn't want them to go to a strip alert and get their frag orders out. We knew what the situation was over in South Korea. There was just a small number of planes, and they were configured for nukes. We didn't want to work a hardship on those people."

But there was another reason as well for the Navy's decision: the confusion resulting from *Banner*'s trip off North Korea the previous February. "The flap with General Bonesteel certainly was a factor," Brookes admits. "I'd be a liar if I said it wasn't. It lingered in our sub-conscious—what might happen if we asked for a strip alert. You're going to do it if you think it's necessary, but, well, you get burned once and you're perhaps a little reluctant to do it again. We were con-cerned that there be no difficulty over this."

Nonetheless, even though he hadn't requested a strip alert, Brookes felt sure that the Air Force would place some planes on a ready status anyway; that they'd be able to wing to *Pueblo*'s aid should an emergency develop. Hadn't the Air Force done just that *without* a formal request ten months before? "There was an agreement," he says. Then he pauses. "Sometimes the liaison broke down. Sometimes the distance seemed a million miles away."

★   ★   ★

On January 3 Bucher received word that the mission had been approved. For nearly a year he had been jousting with all the petty bureaucracies, trying in every way he knew to prepare his ship. Soon he and that ship would face their first test. He knew his relief, Lieuten-ant Commander Theodore R. Kramer, would be reporting aboard in May. So if he was ever going to excel, he'd have to do it now.

But what could he hope to accomplish off North Korea? "I was a little disappointed at having to go up there at that time of year," he says. "There was nothing to read that would give me a really good in-dication of what to expect. It'd be so goddamn cold, and I figured so unproductive, and I did look forward to the end of the trip, getting down there with the Russians in the Tsushima Straits, getting some indication of why they'd been there so long and what they were doing."

The ship would be leaving in less than forty-eight hours, and there was still so much to do. Bucher worried about icing, so he told Schumacher to obtain 600 pounds of salt from the Naval Supply Depot. But NSD couldn't oblige him; he had to purchase the salt on the local economy. He asked Steve Harris if he'd received all the data he needed on the location and frequencies of North Korean radars. He ordered Murphy to make sure that the crew's records were placed aboard ship. Finally, a formality: He invited Admiral Johnson to inspect *Pueblo*.

Johnson accepted that invitation on January 3. "I talked with Bucher," he has said, "with the idea of trying to encourage him to conduct all the training and drills that he could on the damage control and emergency destruction bills he had. I asked Bucher if there was any further assistance I could give him or his ship and whether he had any problems. As I recall, he answered in the negative."

Although the .50 caliber machine guns had been delivered to the ship, they hadn't yet been mounted on deck. Johnson seemed concerned about them. "He said I shouldn't uncover them unless it was absolutely necessary," Bucher adds, "that they were to be used only in the event all else failed in extricating ourselves from a harassment situation. He was quite sure they'd never be needed."

Now only thirty-six hours remained until the ship's departure. Norman Spear wrote to his parents in Portland, Maine. "Anything can happen on this trip," he said. Don Bailey had just received orders to *Pueblo*. Although he had gone on similar missions before, he sensed this one would somehow be different. He decided to grant his wife power of attorney. "She had just had a baby," he recalls, "so when I came home and gave her the papers, she got excited. She wanted to know why I was doing this." Murphy, his wife, Carol, and their son, Eddie, were all recovering from the flu. Murphy knew the ship was due to return to Yokosuka on February 4. Still, for reasons he can't explain, he bought a Valentine's Day card and left it in a sealed envelope on a buffet table at home. He told his wife not to open it until February 14.

Larry Mack was depressed. A passport mixup had delayed his wife's arrival from the United States. She wouldn't reach Yokosuka until after *Pueblo* sailed. He hadn't filled out the papers to give her a monthly allotment. And Bucher had ordered all the crew's records to be carried aboard ship. Without access to those records, Mack's wife wouldn't be able to pay the rent or buy groceries for herself and the four children. He spoke to Murphy about this; Murphy seemed sympathetic. He said he'd leave the records in Yokosuka. He didn't tell Bucher about this decision.

Before a submarine left port on a mission, Bucher knew, its officers always received a formal presail briefing which covered all aspects of its operations. For *their* last-minute instructions, however, *Banner's* skippers had usually had to rely upon the detailed message from NSA through DIRNAVSECGRUPAC to the research officer. Bucher requested one. Lieutenant Ed Brookes said he'd take care of it.

At CINCPACFLT's instructions, COMNAVFORJAPAN was supposed to make sure that *Pueblo* carried an up-to-date destruction bill, as well as ample tools to demolish her classified documents and equipment. But no one had ever assigned this responsibility to a specific officer. Brookes "made it my business" to look into the matter informally.

He was aware that even before the ship left Bremerton, Naval Security Group inspectors had examined the research spaces. He knew, too, that the other inspectors had come aboard in San Diego. He thought it odd that these inspectors had not provided COMNAVFOR-JAPAN with copies of their reports. There was only one logical explanation: They had seen no need for this; *Pueblo* had passed all her tests satisfactorily.

Brookes noted that *Pueblo* had an incinerator and two paper shredders. He counted the fire axes and sledgehammers. He checked to make sure that the destruction bill was posted properly. But he did not conduct a formal inspection. It occurred to him that the destruct gear was "not designed for a combat situation." He didn't worry about that. "You figure, well, he passed inspection, so you just assume he has an adequate destruction plan," Brookes explains. "You don't want to be rude to him."

The trouble with this assumption was that the ship's preparations had not passed muster at all. Inspectors had noted that *Pueblo's* destruct plans should be "more specific"; they'd granted the ship only an interim authorization to carry Secret Intelligence (SI) material. Why the inspectors kept their conclusions to themselves remains a mystery.

In the absence of word from Brookes or anyone else to the contrary, Steve Harris assumed that *Pueblo's* emergency destruction provisions were adequate. Still, he was worried about what he considered to be an excessive number of publications aboard the ship. The trouble had started in San Diego several months before, when COMSERV-

PAC had goofed and had given *Pueblo* the standard allowance for an AGMR—a converted escort *carrier*. And no one since then had been able to straighten out the mess. Since *Pueblo* "belonged" to COM-SEVENTHFLT for at least part of the time, she had received a huge wad of classified documents that *it* thought she should carry. CINC-PACFLT had added to the pile; so had COMNAVFORJAPAN; and so, it seemed, had every naval facility in the entire world. (Some of these people still thought *Pueblo* was an AKL.) And there was no one to coordinate or control the flow of all this material. *Pueblo* was fast becoming a floating paper repository.

Banner, Harris knew, had faced a similar predicament about six months before and solved it by requesting a hazardous duty allowance, a dispensation permitting her to offload much of the excess material. Yet Harris disagreed with *Banner's* allowance. He thought she was carrying some publications she didn't need and leaving behind some that she did. Initially, he'd planned to work on *Pueblo's* allowance after the end of the first mission. But so staggering was this paper invasion that he had to do something immediately. He decided to speak to Brookes about it at the presail briefing.

The briefing was scheduled to begin at nine o'clock on the morning of January 4. *Pueblo* would be leaving in another twenty-four hours. Harris, Bucher, Murphy, and Schumacher piled into an old Studebaker Lark from the motor pool and drove from the pier to COMNAVFORJAPAN headquarters on the hill. "I assume you've got all the pay records on board," Bucher said.

Murphy shook his head. He said he hadn't and began to explain why. There was this problem with Mack, the photographer, and . . .

"Pete got all unglued about this, really steamed up," Harris recalls. "He kept repeating, 'You know, we may never come back to Yokosuka.' We all thought this was ridiculous. Where else would we go?"

The car pulled up outside the red-brick administration building, and they climbed the stairs to the spook locker on the third floor. Brookes began the briefing with a report on the North Korean order of battle. He identified the North Korean coastal defenses on a map. He cited the tension in the DMZ, the North Korean reaction against ROK fishing boats. He discussed what *Banner* had done in harassment situations. He provided a long-range weather forecast. *Pueblo,* he said, would probably encounter North Korean patrol craft which would probably harass her. They weren't likely to do anything more.

"We got strictly *military* intelligence," Bucher says. "What little they had. I felt there was a definite lack of interest because this was just something to let us work out the kinks. There was an opportunity that we might be able to confirm a few things and, if so, well and good. But none of these people indicated that they seriously expected us to find anything worthwhile. In fact, they indicated just the opposite. There would be nothing. It was designed that way."

Someone brought up the subjects of guns. They shouldn't be positioned in such a way as to show aggressive intent. They should remain covered at all times. Bucher should use them only in an emergency, only if someone else were already shooting at him. Commander Charles Clark stood up and said, well, orders were orders, but he'd rather not carry guns on *Banner* at all. It wouldn't do for an AGER to seem provocative. The other officers nodded their agreement. "How about a boarding party?" Bucher asked. "Should I use them in a situation like that?"

"Yes," Captain Dwyer replied.

"How about emergency destruction? Should I begin that in a boarding situation?"

Dwyer said yes again.

What support might *Pueblo* receive if she were attacked?

Dwyer and Brookes handled that question together. No surface forces would be available. Fifth Air Force headquarters would be kept informed and could be called upon for assistance. Its pilots would need two hours or more to react effectively.

Harris said he thought the ship was carrying too many classified publications. Could *Pueblo* be granted the same sort of hazardous duty allowance that *Banner* had received?

Brookes was surprised by the request. *Pueblo* had been in Yokosuka for more than a month, and this was the first time Harris had even mentioned the problem. "We had no control," Brookes remembers. "We didn't even know what [intelligence] pubs he had in his research spaces, what he'd been given by NSA and NSG. It wasn't really in our province to reduce those pubs." Perhaps he could compile a hazardous duty allowance covering operations and communications publications. *So little time* remained before the ship's departure. Still, he said he'd try.

The more he talked to Chuck Clark and reviewed *Banner*'s patrol reports, the more concerned Bucher had become about *Pueblo*'s communications. "If there was one thing that did bother me," he says, "it was the possibility of having an encounter which I couldn't report because I couldn't get anyone to accept our traffic." He'd contacted senior officials at the Naval Communications Station in Yokosuka and had mentioned the difficulties he'd had coming across the Pacific, how his men had missed all those broadcast numbers.

On the afternoon of January 4 Bucher, Schumacher, Steve Harris, and Clark drove over to NCS to meet with those senior officials. "They were aware of the problem," Bucher says, "but I was not satisfied the solution was in their hands. I didn't come away feeling that we would be able to effect rapid communications."

Bucher was still fuming at Murphy when he returned to the ship. "It's your job to make sure that everyone makes out an allotment to his wife," he stormed. "Why didn't you do that? Why?"

Murphy walked back to his stateroom. Larry Mack was waiting for him. "Is it okay to leave the records ashore?" Mack asked.

"No, you've got to bring them aboard."

"Well, what about my *wife*, Mr. Murphy?"

"He said this was the captain's orders," Mack recalls. "He said he was pretty darn disgusted about the whole thing. I heard him say, 'This kind of breaks my back. I'm going to resign from the Navy.'

"I was irate myself, so I went down and talked to the captain. I said, 'My wife doesn't have any funds or anything. I'd like to make a provision for her to draw on my pay records.' I'd previously gone down to disbursing and squared this away. He said the reason he didn't want records left ashore was that the ship might be rerouted. It happened all the time with submarines. Our pay would be held up for months. I kept saying, 'That's fine, but what about my wife and kids?' He finally gave in and said he'd make an exception. He'd let me keep the records in Yokosuka."

Dusk fell. A cold breeze rippled the waters of the harbor. Harry Lewis was checking the reefers, making sure that all the provisions he'd ordered had arrived on board. The tenderloin steak was there; the chicken, the ham, the roast, the duck, the liver. He'd been wise to order those extra gallons of ice cream. The captain seemed to want ice cream at the oddest hours. Ralph McClintock was cursing his own bad judgment. Here he'd been scheduled to sail on USS *Enterprise* and then receive thirty days' leave at home in Massachusetts. He'd turned that down because he had only four more months to serve in the Navy; he wanted to get it over with as soon as possible. Then he'd been offered a trip on a destroyer escort with leave in Hawaii. But he'd already been to Hawaii. Finally, he'd volunteered for *Pueblo*, "which I'd never heard of before." He'd come down from Kamiseya to see the ship and "nearly died."

Now he determined to "get drunk out of my mind." A fragment of an old conversation kept spinning around in his head. A friend of his at Kamiseya, a former CT on *Banner,* had told him about a threat to that ship. If *Banner* ever sailed around the west coast of North Korea, the "gooks" were going to board her. His friend had stated this as gospel. McClintock dismissed the idea. He was sailing on *Pueblo,* not *Banner.* And he didn't think she was going anywhere near the west coast of North Korea.

Bucher, Schumacher, and Steve Harris went to the officers' club for dinner and drinks. Harris said he wanted to return to the ship by eight o'clock to receive some new publications from Kamiseya and also to help Lieutenant j.g. Will Little inventory the "pubs" for his hazardous duty allowance. Other problems remained, but Bucher and Schumacher were through worrying about them. This was their final night in port, and they were going to have a good time.

At seven thirty Murphy approached the table. He told Bucher that he'd just talked to Lieutenant Lynn Pickard, the young explosives expert at the Naval Ammunition Facility on Azuma Island who'd inspected the ship a week before. Pickard had finally located some dynamite charges which *Pueblo* could use. Murphy told Schumacher to bring the charges aboard.

Harris said he thought the charges were dangerous. Bucher agreed. He countermanded Murphy's order. Murphy left the table. Harris returned to the ship. Bucher and Schumacher each ordered another drink. Hours passed. At his home in Yokosuka, Lieutenant Commander Charles Clark was mulling over the afternoon's events. He and Bucher had left the meeting at NCS and had stopped to talk for awhile at the foot of Pier 8. Clark wouldn't be able to say good-bye in the morning; he had to take his men to a firing range. They'd talked about contingencies. Clark had mentioned boarding parties, and suddenly Bucher had made an odd remark, characteristic of his bullishness, perhaps, but also apocalyptic, as if he had already resigned himself to some fateful encounter in northern latitudes. "You know, Chuck," he said, "if those bastards come out after me, well, they're not going to get me."

★ ★ ★ PART THREE

21

★   ★   ★

Norbert Klepac had run the line through the chock and placed it over the bit. Now he felt very cold. He watched as the North Koreans jumped from the deck of the P-4 onto *Pueblo*'s stern. They wore heavy boots, thick fur hats, and dark blue uniforms—Charley Browns—with quilted thermal jackets. The officers carried pistols. The enlisted men brandished AK-47 automatic rifles. They started advancing toward him. "I figured my best bet was to go back to my battle station," he says. "I started walking there. Then one of the soldiers hollered at me. I stopped."

Bucher stepped forward and identified himself as *Pueblo*'s captain. "I still did not know what they intended to do," he remembers. "I considered it a strong probability that they intended to capture the ship, but I was not completely convinced of that."

A North Korean officer aimed his pistol at Bucher's waist and motioned for him to climb the ladder to the 0-1 level and enter the pilot house. Some of the men had already gathered forward on the well deck. The North Korean signaled the others to move to the fantail.

Murphy was just stepping out of the head between his cabin and Bucher's. A North Korean "took me at gun point and gave me a quick kick to get me moving. I went up the ladder by the wardroom on the 0-1 level. He jabbed the weapon in my back." Murphy stumbled toward the fantail. The P-4's, he noticed, were bobbing just off *Pueblo*'s stern. Sailors manned their guns.

Lee Hayes had left the radio shack to find a fire ax to destroy his transmitter. "This North Korean looked at me and waved his hand. He was really perturbed. I figured they'd blindfold us, shoot us, and push us over the side."

Don Bailey climbed to the main deck and saw a North Korean directly in front of him, pointing an AK-47 at his chest. He had been kneeling beside the teletype so long that his feet "felt like two-by-fours." He noticed ice on the deck; he hoped the guard wouldn't slip and accidentally squeeze that trigger. The guard prodded him toward the fantail. "I couldn't get this one question outta my mind," he says. "Where the hell is the rest of the Navy? Where is the Air Force? When are they gonna get here?"

★   ★   ★

At Fifth Air Force headquarters in Fuchu, Commander Tom McDonald rushed into the office of Major Robert W. Dees and told him what he had heard in the hallway seconds before from Major Ray Priest.

"Let's go to Stallings," Dees said. They stepped across the hall to find Colonel Herbert D. Stallings, the square-jawed physical fitness buff who was then assistant director of operations and training.

"We've got a real flap," McDonald began. "The North Koreans are attacking the *Pueblo*."

"Gee," Stallings said. "We've got to get Guynes in on this." Stallings, McDonald, and Dees raced next door to see Colonel Joseph B. Guynes, the assistant deputy chief of staff for operations.

Guynes stood before a large map of the world and began firing questions: Where was the ship? What planes did the Air Force have in South Korea? How long would it take to load and launch them?

The telephone rang, and someone handed it to McDonald. Al Wilson was calling from Yokosuka. "He said, 'What are you guys doing to save the ship?'" McDonald recalls. "He thought that all we had to do was 'push the button.' I told him to back up that dad-gum thing with a flash message and get it on up here. You couldn't start a war on the basis of a lieutenant commander's phone call."

Stallings was still trying to answer Guynes' questions. Guynes cut him off. "We gotta tell the old man on this," he said.

For the past nine minutes Lieutenant General Seth J. McKee, commander of the Fifth Air Force, had been sitting in his second floor office listening to a briefing on—of all things—accident prevention. The subject bored him, and he glanced at his watch. It was 2:10.

Guynes, Stallings, McDonald and Dees rushed down the hall and entered McKee's outer office. Guynes turned to the general's aide, Captain Roy M. (Ike) Ikeda. "I've got to get in right away," he said. "I've got something critical."

Ikeda opened the door and announced that Guynes was there on an urgent matter. McDonald remembers thinking how formal the procedure was, even in an emergency; how each officer in the chain of command had to be notified in his proper turn.

Forty-five minutes had elapsed since Wilson first picked up the phone to call Fifth Air Force headquarters. McKee looked up from his charts.

"Tom here says the *Pueblo* is under attack," Guynes began. "The North Koreans . . ."

An expression of amazement crossed the general's face. This was clearly not a part of the briefing on traffic safety. In the entire headquarters complex, there was only one secure phone. It was 300 feet away. "We've got to go to the Command Center," McKee snapped. "Got to get Hawaii in on this." He hurried down the hall.

Lieutenant Colonel Robert Orcutt, the deputy assistant chief of staff for intelligence, was standing by the door of the Warning Center holding a copy of a "critic" which had just arrived. He gave it to Guynes, who passed it to McKee. The general brushed past two armed guards, entered the Command Center, and stepped to a large desk on a raised podium. To his left nestled the red, secure telephone. On the wall facing him were maps of Asia and charts with pins denoting the location of all U.S. forces.

The Air Force had seven F-4's at bases in South Korea. Theoretically, they could streak to Wonsan in less than thirty-five minutes. But they were configured to carry nuclear weapons. The racks they'd need for conventional bombs were stored in Japan; reconfiguration would require several hours at best.

The South Korean Air Force consisted of fewer than two hundred planes—F-5's at Suwon, Osan, and Kunsan and F-86's at Kimpo Airport near Seoul. Defense Secretary Robert S. McNamara had purposely limited its size and striking power on the theory that any North Korean attack would be signaled by a period of "strategic warning"; the United States would have plenty of time to fly in reinforcements. The F-86's were nearly twenty years old; the F-5's boasted no air-to-ground capability. They carried only Sidewinder missiles and air-to-air rockets. McKee knew they were no match for the North Korean

MIG's. Not that the ROK's wouldn't want to go anyway. The State Department had its hands full already trying to restrain them from avenging the Blue House raid; when they heard about *Pueblo,* they'd be even more eager to fight. McKee remembered the flap with General Bonesteel about a year before and decided not to alert them on his own. He would inquire about their availability. But Bonesteel would have to make the final decision.

This left Japan and Okinawa. The Air Force maintained F-105's at Yokota. But the 41st Air Division there was in the process of substituting F-4's for its F-105's. The 39th Tactical Fighter Wing at Misawa, on the northern tip of Honshu, flew F-100's. But it was involved in the same transition to F-4's. The flight time to Wonsan from these bases was only eighty minutes. Because of the transition, however, these planes would need at least three hours before they could even get off the ground. The Air Force base at Tachikawa boasted no combat planes. The base at Itazuke was on a "caretaker" status; it had no planes at all.

The Navy kept aircraft at Atsugi, but they were lumbering EC-121's. The Marine Corps had four A-4's and four F-4's at its air station at Iwakuni, but they were undergoing repairs. Furthermore, they were under the stewardship of the Commanding General, Ninth Marine Amphibious Brigade. And he was in Okinawa. Iwakuni was not plugged in to the right communications network. Its officers wouldn't even hear of *Pueblo* until sometime the next morning.

McKee toted up the figures. Although the United States maintained six fully operational air bases in Japan, it had only twenty-four attack aircraft. And none was combat-ready. The nearest available planes were F-105's—and they were several hundred miles away at Kadena, Okinawa. He knew he'd have to alert General John D. (Jack) Ryan, Commander in Chief, Pacific Air Forces, at his headquarters in Hawaii. He'd also call Brigadier General John W. Harrell, Jr., commander of the 314th Air Division in South Korea. Harrell might just be able to "download" those seven F-4's in time to help. And he could approach General Bonesteel about requesting aid from the ROK's. "Get me Ryan," McKee barked. "Get me Harrell at Osan. Get me the CO of the Eighteenth at Kadena."

Ryan was not in his office in Hawaii, and it would take at least twenty minutes for him to reach a secure phone. But the commander of the 18th Tactical Fighter Wing, Colonel Monroe S. (Saber) Sams, was on the line from Kadena. McKee lifted the receiver. This phone was insecure. He couldn't be too specific.

"General McKee advised that I should prepare F-105's for deployment to a peninsula," Sams remembers. "Information as to precise location and events taking place was not discussed. Configuration of aircraft—number and types of external fuel tanks, bomb pylons and racks and ammunition loads—was left to my discretion. This placed me in a rather difficult position, as I could not imagine what disturbance had occurred."

Of the twenty-four F-105's assigned to the wing at the time, only nine were ready, and they were outfitted with 450-gallon external fuel tanks, centerline bomb pylons, and outboard wing pylons—a standard configuration for the training exercises scheduled for that afternoon. Four of the planes, in fact, were airborne already, and two more were taxiing for takeoff. Sams recalled them all to the parking ramp. McKee had promised to call back on the secure phone and send a TWX explaining the crisis. Sams couldn't make any specific plans until that message arrived.

McKee drafted the TWX and sent it to Sams: "You are to launch all available aircraft. Proceed to Osan, refuel as soon as possible, proceed to the scene at Wonsan and strike in [*Pueblo's*] support." McKee knew that Sams would have to mount rails on his F-105's in order for them to carry missiles. "I didn't want to take the time," he says. He told the colonel to arm the first six planes with 20 mm cannon instead.

Now an enlisted man said that General Harrell was on the line from South Korea. McKee told him to begin downloading the F-4's there and replace their nuclear weapons with 3,000-pound conventional bombs. The racks would arrive shortly.

Another telephone rang inside the Operations Control Center. The flash message had just arrived from Yokosuka, and Captain Everett was calling back to find out what steps the Air Force was taking.

McDonald took the call. "I knew they were really expecting things they could see in the sky," he remembers. "So I said, 'Quit asking us to react with the speed of light. I think we're going to make it, but not immediately. It'll take two or three hours.' "

"What about the Air Force alert?," Everett asked.

"I said, 'There isn't any alert,' " McDonald recalls. " 'You never asked for one.' I could sense surprise in his voice. I had the distinct impression that he was shocked."

Inside the spook locker at Yokosuka, Lieutenant Ed Brookes was sending out "lateral" critics as fast as he could. The facts at his disposal were frustratingly vague. "The line in the message from *Pueblo*

—'small wound in rectum'—we weren't sure whether that was Bailey or Bucher," he remembers. "And the '. . . one man with leg blown off . . .'; we didn't know whether that was as a result of gunfire or emergency destruction."

Brookes passed copies of his messages to Lieutenant Anthony Celebrezze and asked him to hand-carry them to the command cave. Celebrezze hadn't had so much exercise in months. He was determined not to give any appearance of panic. "I was hurrying, but I wasn't sprinting," he recalls. "There was a certain amount of decorum necessary."

Commander Schoenherr and Lieutenant Commander Wilson were studying maps on the wall of the command cave, trying to pinpoint the ship's position and estimate her course and speed. Captains Pease and Everett were making and directing telephone calls. Lieutenant Brookes wanted to send a message requesting assistance from the Seventh Fleet. Pease vetoed the idea. He was sure that Seventh Fleet had already received word from Washington. "I figured there were too many messages out already," he remembers. "We'd only be throwing more traffic on the keys." Of all the decisions Pease made that afternoon, this was the most unfortunate.

At 2:20—almost an hour after receiving the first critic—Al Wilson telephoned CINCPACFLT headquarters in Hawaii and asked to speak to the duty officer there.

22

In the narrow, rectangular intelligence plot in the basement of CINCPACFLT headquarters in Hawaii, Lt. Commander Erv Easton had just received a phone call from CINCPAC's Indications Center. Now Wilson was calling from Japan with the same information. *Pueblo* was in trouble. "A very odd feeling" swept over Easton as he realized this was not just any ship; this was Pete Bucher, his old friend and fellow submariner. He was at the huge plot table at the far end of the room and glanced at the clock on the wall: 7:25. He would have to move quickly. He telephoned Commander Robert T. MacOnie, chief of the R&I Branch; Commander Arlo J. Jensen, chief of the Target Intelligence Branch; and Commander Bobby R. Inman, chief of the Current Intelligence Branch. Then he decided to call Captain Marocchi at his home on Halawa Drive.

"The phone was insecure and Erv couldn't say very much," Marocchi recalls, "but he did get the message across that there was trouble. I should come in. I didn't gather it was that urgent." Marocchi finished his dinner, brushed his teeth, and set out at a brisk walk toward the intelligence plot several hundred yards away.

MacOnie and Inman had arrived within the first five minutes. Easton had pulled out the navigation charts; he had summarized all the available information and set it on a clipboard. MacOnie began to read the messages. "It took me quite a while to realize how late we were running time-wise," he recalls. "The critics were still coming in, and there was this sense of immediacy—of things happening where *you* were. It was very difficult to realize that there was a delay, that we were not operating in anything like real time."

At 7:43 the first follow-up message to the original critic chattered over the teletype from Japan. Two minutes later another message

arrived. Easton saw the words ". . . open fire on us now. . . ." At
7:50 Marocchi entered the room. "Things were becoming excited,"
he remembers. He telephoned the Operations Control Center on the
third floor, then turned to Easton. He'd need to have copies of all the
messages and a suitable set of charts if he was going to brief the
admiral.

At that moment on this warm Monday evening, January 22, Admiral John J. Hyland, Commander in Chief, U.S. Pacific Fleet, was
hosting a dinner party in his quarters at 37 Makalapa Drive in honor
of Vice Admiral Thomas F. Connolly, the DCNO (Air), and members of his entourage, who were stopping in Hawaii en route to Southeast Asia. Connolly was "an old and special friend," and "Floss" Hyland, an attractive and gracious hostess, had "made an extra effort to
have a special meal," finally settling on chicken Florentine with an
exotic fruit dessert.

A steward announced that dinner was served. A few of the guests
lingered on the lanai, continuing a conversation about the air war in
Vietnam. The tinkle of ice in their cocktail glasses melted into the
soft night air. Then a telephone rang in an anteroom off the main
foyer. The steward handed it to Captain Paul E. Pugh, the deputy for
current operations on the CINCPAC staff. Pugh listened quietly as
Captain Leslie J. Barco, the battle staff watch chief at CINCPAC
headquarters, explained that *Pueblo* was being boarded by the "people from the North."

Pugh whispered the news to Captain George L. Cassell, his counterpart on the CINCPACFLT staff, and Admiral Hyland himself. He
told his wife he didn't know when he'd be back and raced to his 1960
Austin-Healey roadster. The CINCPAC battle staff watch area was
located on the third deck of a concrete, windowless building at Camp
H. M. Smith, several miles away. Normally, he would need fifteen
minutes to drive there from Makalapa. This evening he would arrive
in ten.

Marocchi, MacOnie, and Commander Jim Hayes from the CINCPACFLT operations staff had passed the two white elephant statues at
the entrance to Hyland's quarters and were just stepping up the green-canopied walkway as Pugh dashed out the door. They knocked. A
steward went to fetch the admiral, who appeared about a minute
later. "He said, 'All right, what is it?'" MacOnie recalls. "He was
aware that something was up and that it involved the *Pueblo*. He
wanted the details. I held the charts while the captain briefed him
there in the front foyer. He said, 'Oh, my God,' and asked a couple of
questions. Then he turned and went back inside and started telling
people what to do."

Hyland had inspected *Banner* several months before but he had never seen *Pueblo*. "*Pueblo*'s presence in the Sea of Japan was in my consciousness," he says. "I knew she was there, but if someone had come in before all this happened and asked me, 'Where is she now?' I'm not certain I'd have been able to say."

Bravely, Mrs. Hyland tried to keep her dinner party on course. Cassell was dashing out every few minutes to call the Operations Control Center and coming back to confer with her husband. And some of the other guests had already left.

"I decided the best thing to do was wait for some more information," Hyland says. "We were still trying to find out what in the dickens had happened. *Pueblo* was being towed into Wonsan—that was the last word we got. I just couldn't think of anything we could do. We just sat there and looked at each other and we thought, 'How is that possible?' "

★   ★   ★

The guided-missile cruiser USS *Providence*, flagship of the Seventh Fleet, was churning through the waters of the Tonkin Gulf. She had spent the last several weeks on Yankee Station off the coast of Vietnam. Her officers and men had their shopping lists ready and were eagerly anticipating liberty in Hong Kong.

Shortly after noon on January 23, in his tiny office on the 0-1 level, the ship's communications officer, Commander Jon C. Woodyard, noticed some operator chatter from USS *Pueblo*; the ship was being harassed somewhere in the Sea of Japan. A few minutes later he saw a message on the flash net, and this was followed almost immediately by another flash. He tried to "patch" directly to *Pueblo* but wasn't able to get through. He patched instead to the Naval Communications Station in Yokosuka and asked a chief warrant officer there what was happening. "He told me it appears that the North Koreans are boarding *Pueblo*," Woodyard remembers. "I thought, 'There goes my lunch hour.' "

Woodyard called Captain Joe P. Moorer, the Seventh Fleet's operations officer, then notified Captain P. Anthony Lilly, the chief of staff. "The atmosphere was rather surprised," he says. "This was a kind of miraculous thing." Moorer and Lilly decided immediately to alert Vice Admiral William F. (Bush) Bringle, the Seventh Fleet's commander.

The white-haired admiral was stunned by the news. He kept rubbing his hands against the sides of his head. *Pueblo* was only one of hundreds of ships which at one time or another fell under his operational control. He was "not personally aware of the specifics of [her] mission," and did not know that she was operating off Wonsan. Incredibly, instead of dispatching a copy of her sail order to him through normal communications channels, COMNAVFORJAPAN had relied on the Armed Forces Courier Service. That sail order wouldn't arrive for another four days.

Bringle set up a "flap watch" in the flag plot and told his staff to compile a running situation report. Then he decided to change course. The seas were relatively calm; the ship's four boilers were all on line. *Providence* swung around and headed east at nearly 30 knots. "I could see right then," Woodyard recalls, "it was going to be a long time before we got to Hong Kong."

★   ★   ★

At 2:30 that afternoon the nuclear-powered aircraft carrier USS *Enterprise*, the largest flattop in the world, was 510 miles south of Wonsan. Accompanied by the nuclear frigate USS *Truxton*, she was steaming south at 27 knots toward Subic Bay in the Philippines, where she planned to conduct flight training before deploying for combat duty in the Tonkin Gulf.

In her air wing were 59 attack aircraft: twenty-four F-4B Phantoms with a speed of Mach 2 and a range—under ideal conditions—of more than 1,500 miles; twenty-three A-4E Skyhawks with a speed of 700 miles per hour and a range of 1,000 miles; and twelve A-6A Intruders, night fighters with a speed of 650 miles per hour and a range of 1,500 miles. Also perched on the hangar decks below were RA-5C Vigilante reconnaissance planes and KA3B Skywarrior refuelers.

Shortly after lunch Rear Admiral Horace H. (Spin) Epes, Jr., Commander, Carrier Division One and Task Force 71, stepped into the ship's "war room" on the 0-3 level. The daily briefing on flight operations in Vietnam was about to begin. Because it covered so much material—today's targets as well as yesterday's results—it normally lasted one or two hours.

At 2:31 the officer in charge of the ship's security detachment interrupted that briefing and handed Epes a copy of *Pueblo*'s "Pinnacle One." Nine minutes later he returned with "Pinnacle Two." Epes had never heard of *Pueblo*. "The first thing I did," he remembers, "was to call for a publication to find out what kind of ship she was. I found an AGER in the publication. But it was *Banner*, not *Pueblo*."

Epes sent for charts to plot *Pueblo*'s position and told his intelligence staff to gather all available photos and publications on North

Korea. He had to know the order of battle of North Korea's air force, the location and order of battle of its missile and antiaircraft batteries. He asked his meteorologist for a new weather report and an estimate of the time of darkness at Wonsan.

The skipper of the *Enterprise,* Captain Kent L. Lee, often attended the daily briefings on the air war in Vietnam. But he had gone to the bridge to check on the ship's navigation. Now Epes asked him about the status of the carrier's planes.

Because of corrosion (*Enterprise* had encountered storms crossing the Pacific) and insufficient repairs, only thirty-five of the fifty-nine strike aircraft—ten F-4B's, nineteen A-4E's, and twelve A-6A's—were listed as "operationally ready." Four of the F-4B's were on a standard five-minute alert, their pilots already in their cockpits; four more were on a thirty-minute alert. But these planes only carried air-to-air ordnance, Sparrow missiles, and Sidewinder rockets, and their pilots weren't trained in air-to-surface operations. Furthermore, it would take time to fuel and arm the additional planes, time to provide pilots with a skimpy briefing—*Enterprise* carried no mission folders for the Wonsan area—and, most important, time for the pilots to streak to the scene.

Still, *Enterprise* could have reacted. "If, at two thirty, we had been told 'Prepare to launch,'" says Captain Lee, "we could have had twenty planes in the air in maybe an hour and a half." Epes adds that if he'd received a plea for help from either COMNAVFOR-JAPAN or COMSEVENTHFLT, it "would have changed" his thinking. But *Enterprise* had received no requests for assistance. The messages Lee and Epes had seen had not even been addressed to them; they had, in fact, reached the ship on "back channel" circuits. And they were so highly classified that Epes couldn't discuss them with his air crews. He certainly couldn't use them as the basis for a positive response.

In the absence of any instructions, Epes considered his shrinking alternatives. *Pueblo,* it seemed, was already in North Korean hands. The distance to Wonsan was a factor; so was time—darkness would fall in a few hours. His meteorologist said 5:41. North Korean air defenses were formidable indeed. There were SAM missile sites and antiaircraft batteries and swarms of MIG's to worry about. "What can I do for a ship that's already in the hands of another country and inside of its territorial waters?" Epes asked himself. "What risk would I be putting my air wing in to go to a place of overwhelming odds—the possibility of starting another Korean War?"

It was almost three o'clock. Reluctantly, Epes concluded that "by the time we could get any aircraft there, it would be too late." *Enterprise* remained on course, steaming away from Wonsan at 27 knots.

Inside the Command Center at Fifth Air Force headquarters in Fuchu, an enlisted man signaled that General Ryan was on the line from Honolulu. General McKee picked up his red telephone. Standing beside him and listening to his part of the conversation, Commander Tom McDonald was impressed by McKee's resolve. "I'm changing the ordnance configuration of our F-4's in Korea," he remembers the general saying; "I've also sent word to Okinawa—the Eighteenth Tactical Fighter Wing. Unless you direct me otherwise, I'll launch and attack if I can."

"Okay," Ryan said, "but whatever you do, make sure you do it in international waters."

"Yes, I understand," McKee said. "I understand." Then he suggested that *Enterprise* was in the area, perhaps even closer to Wonsan than his planes in Okinawa. Ryan might want to contact Admiral U. S. Grant Sharp at CINCPAC headquarters there in Honolulu and confer about using the carrier's planes. Ryan said he'd look into the matter. McKee hung up and repeated the conversation to his assembled staff. He had full authority to launch planes to save the ship, but not to attack North Korean bases. He couldn't do anything once *Pueblo* lay inside North Korea's waters.

It was 2:47. There was still time. "Get me General Harrell again," he barked. Even if he managed to launch the F-4's in Korea, he wouldn't be able to arm them with anything more than those 3,000-pound bombs. If they encountered any MIG's, they'd be helpless. He'd have to tell Harrell to call General Bonesteel to see if the ROK's could assist.

Inside the large red-brick building which served as headquarters for the U.S. Eighth Army in Seoul, General Bonesteel was leafing though some routine reports. The South Korean papers, he noted, unhappily, were whipping up public indignation over the Blue House raid; they could cause some problems. An intelligence officer appeared at the door with a copy of *Pueblo*'s "Pinnacle Two" message. Bonesteel recognized its importance immediately. He stepped next door to the Tactical Operations Center, a low-slung, Quonset-like building, and began to summon his staff.

At his quarters several hundreds yards away in the Yongsan Compound, Rear Admiral Donald G. Irvine, Commander, Naval Forces, Korea, was stretched out on a living room couch. He hadn't been feeling well for the past several days. He'd run a temperature that morning, and his chief of staff, Captain John A. Gray, Jr., had suggested he go home for a rest. Gray would keep an eye on the office. So when the admiral saw the official car pull up next to the curb, he knew that something drastic had happened. He slipped on a jacket and, five minutes later, entered the war room in the Tactical Operations Center. Bonesteel was sitting at a long table studying messages which someone had yanked off the teleprinter.

"Sorry I had to pull you away from a sickbed," the general said, "but this looks pretty important."

Irvine studied the messages. He had no forces which could possibly help the ship. There was nothing he could do. He decided to alert Rear Admiral John V. Smith, the senior negotiator for the United Nations Command at the Military Armistice Commission.

Smith was in his office reviewing his plans for the MAC meeting which had been scheduled at Panmunjom at eleven o'clock on January 24. He wanted to protest the Blue House raid in the strongest possible terms and had arranged to show a filmed interview with a captured infiltrator. He felt it was important to establish a strong case—if only for the record. Then his telephone rang.

"Admiral Irvine called me," he recalls, "and he said, 'Guess what'?"

"I said, 'What?' Then he told me. I didn't even know what *Pueblo* was. I wasn't cleared for that information."

A call came into the war room from General Harrell. He said that General McKee wanted to know how Bonesteel felt about requesting help from the ROK's. Bonesteel hesitated. There were those tricky policy questions to consider. The ROK's were under United Nations— not United States—command. It was important to preserve that distinction. And this was obviously not a UN matter. Then, too, Bonesteel had been trying to convince them not to avenge the Blue House raid. How would they react if he asked them to help *Pueblo?* Would they conclude that the United States considered this little ship more important than the life of their *President?*

Finally, there were some practical considerations. The ROK airfields were located in the western portion of the peninsula. Wonsan was on North Korea's east coast. The F-86's at Kimpo were clearly inadequate to tangle with MIG's. The F-5's at Kunsan, Osan, and

Suwon weren't adequately armed, either, and their range was limited. "If there was any possibility of their being effective, I think we would have gone for broke—and started a nice hassle for sure," General Bonesteel recalls. That possibility seemed awfully slim. Bonesteel told Harrell that he had decided not to request aid from the ROK's. Still, he'd double check with Washington. He'd discuss that decision when he talked to General Wheeler.

★   ★   ★

By 12:45 on the morning of January 23 Walt W. Rostow, the President's Adviser for National Security Affairs, had decided that this was a serious crisis indeed. Alerted nearly an hour before by a call from Jim Brown in the White House Situation Room, he had remained at his home on Lowell Street, N.W., and spoken on the phone with Secretary of Defense Robert S. McNamara, Secretary of State Dean Rusk, and Assistant Secretary of State William P. Bundy. Finally he decided to drive to the White House himself.

Then fifty-two, Rostow was a Yale graduate and former MIT history professor who had first come to Washington seven years before as an assistant to McGeorge Bundy, President John F. Kennedy's Adviser for National Security Affairs. Shifting to the State Department's Policy Planning Council, he had returned to the White House again soon after Bundy's departure. An extremely intelligent, articulate, and cheerful man, he was the father of "Walt's Plan Six"—the scheme which introduced American combat troops into Vietnam in 1965—and even though this plan had not produced its expected results, he remained boundlessly optimistic. This quality infuriated his critics in Congress and the press. It endeared him to Lyndon Johnson.

At 1:05 Rostow entered the Situation Room. His shirttail was hanging out and his tie was askew, but he was not the sort of man to worry about that. For the past hour messages from Japan had been flowing onto Bud Denner's desk. Rostow studied them. Although they weren't as garbled as the first critic, they were still frustratingly vague. He telephoned Rusk and McNamara, who advised him not to wake the President until he had more information. Then he asked Jim Brown to contact Admiral Sharp at CINCPAC headquarters in Hawaii. Sharp was on an inspection trip to South Vietnam. Brown asked to speak to the chief of staff, Army Lieutenant General Clare E. Hutchin, Jr. He wasn't available, either. Finally Brown reached Air Force Major General Royal B. Allison, the deputy chief of staff for plans and operations. He nodded to Rostow. The circuit to Honolulu, usually flawless, was crinkled with static, and Rostow had trouble understanding what Allison was saying.

"General," he repeated, "can you tell us what happened to the *Pueblo?*"

There was a pause. More static. Then Allison replied, "Well, sir, you know, it's a long way from here to there."

23

In the pilot house Bucher was alone with his captors. One of the junior officers drew heads with long noses on a sheet of paper and placed a question mark beside them. How many men were aboard ship? Bucher stepped out on the 0-1 level and shouted to Canales below.

"About eighty," Canales replied.

"What do you mean, 'about'?" Bucher snapped. "Don't you know?"

"Eighty-three," Peppard said.

Suddenly, one of the guards squeezed off a burst of automatic rifle fire. It passed directly over the men on the fantail. They hit the deck. The North Koreans told them to sit there with their knees tucked up against their chests. Some of the guards found sheets in the berthing compartments below and shredded them with bayonets. They passed out the narrow white strips and signaled the men to blindfold themselves.

Schumacher noticed that Rosales was sitting in front of him. "He was shivering like mad. I said, 'Don't worry. Everything's gonna be all right.' He said, 'I don't care about that. I'm just freezing to death.'"

Mitchell was shaking, too. He felt a hand on his helmet and heard a voice saying something in a strange language. He thought it was Korean. Then he realized it was Rogelio P. Abelon, the Filipino steward, praying softly in Tagalog.

The North Koreans searched Ron Berens, confiscated his pocket knife and, discovering that he was the helmsman, sent him back to the pilot house. They grabbed Lacy's watch and moved toward Hayes. The sandy-haired radioman hadn't slipped on his blindfold yet. He glanced around and noticed that he was the only sailor wearing a white hat. Then the guards cuffed him across the back of the head, and for awhile he couldn't see anything.

On the well deck, Larry Strickland was thinking, "Well, we really got ourselves into it now." He hadn't written a will; he had little life insurance, and Mimi, his wife, had no power of attorney. He wondered what would happen to her and the baby. He had borrowed "Tiny" Higgins' foul-weather jacket and he was still very cold. Higgins was wearing a thin dungaree shirt. He could imagine how Higgins felt.

McClintock was sitting next to Layton. "Okay, Jimmy," he said. "We're going on liberty in Wonsan."

"Yeah," Layton said. "Do you know any numbers in Wonsan?"

McClintock tried to laugh but couldn't.

The guards were moving among them now, passing out blindfolds. Grant saw a knife in Maggard's belt. He plucked it out and flipped it over the side. He was sure someone had seen him, and he waited for the blow. But it never came.

Scarborough was slipping a blindfold over Law's eyes. "I was shaking. I was pretty cold and pretty scared," he remembers. "I thought, 'This is it,' and I just wasn't going to sit there and get murdered. Charlie and I were whispering back and forth. If we heard a shot, we were gonna get the hell out of there, you know, start running toward those guys and jump over the side. We figured we might be able to take one of them with us."

Steve Harris clutched the Bible which he'd taken from his cabin only minutes before. He was wearing Hush Puppies, wash khakis, and a leather flight jacket. He'd left his cap behind, and the North Koreans hadn't identified him as an officer. From the well deck he could see the "Request medical assistance" and "Protest" flags fluttering on the signal halyards. Somehow they seemed "improper," and for a moment he wondered why Bucher hadn't yet taken them down. Then it occurred to him that the ship's status had changed, that Bucher no longer had absolute authority. The realization was "horrifying."

The North Koreans were trying to open the ammunition box by the forward machine gun. They couldn't do it. One of them walked back to the top of the ladder on the 0-1 level, looked down at the men on the well deck, and made a twisting motion with his hand. "Keys," someone said. Ken Wadley reached in his pocket, pulled out the keys, and tossed them to the guard.

In the engine room Monroe Goldman was thinking about disabling the engines. It wouldn't be too difficult. Hagenson and Blansett were there to help him. Still, he hesitated. "I hadn't received any word to do anything like that." Then, too, the guard looked mean. "I knew we would only get started and he would have shot us—before we got started good."

Pueblo got under way again at one-third speed. Berens stood at the helm flanked by North Korean guards. An officer was using the 1MC to talk to the S01 on the ship's port side. The S01 veered off and sped toward Wonsan. The officer motioned for Berens to follow in her wake. Berens turned and looked at Bucher.

A guard jabbed a rifle butt into Bucher's back and prodded him toward the radio shack. The transmitter was humming. An officer signaled him to shut off the power. "I refused to do so," Bucher says. The officer pushed him aside, ripped the antenna jacks from the patch panel, and yanked the transmitter key from its mount. Then he pointed to the aft machine gun. He wanted Bucher to remove the tarp from the barrel.

The temperature had dropped about 20 degrees since noon. Frigid winds gusted across the deck. The tarp and the lines which held it in place were sheathed in ice. Bucher fiddled with the knots, then shrugged his shoulders as if to say he couldn't untie them. The officer smashed a pistol butt against the side of his neck. Then he told two guards to rip off the tarp. It took them half an hour.

The officer motioned to Bucher to increase *Pueblo*'s speed. Bucher signaled that this, too, was impossible. He still thought the Air Force might appear. "I was going to grab the mike of the 1MC and announce as quickly as I could for my men to attempt to resume control. I thought there was a possibility that we could overtake, overcome the personnel that were on board. Even though they had all the guns, it still would have been entirely possible to be lucky enough to have overcome them if our planes had shown up, and I would have made an attempt to do so. I kept my eyes open and my ears peeled as much as I could."

The North Koreans signaled Bucher to gather his crew in the forward berthing compartment. He walked to the fantail and told the men there to remove their blindfolds. Then he stepped forward to the well deck. "I felt somebody lifting my blindfold," Steve Harris says. "I looked up. It was Pete. He didn't say a word. Then a guard jabbed a bayonet at me. He took my Bible. I followed the others below."

Smoke still filled the passageway. Lee Hayes noticed two large bags of publications near the door to the research spaces. The door was open; he could see other papers inside. He stepped over one of the bags and continued forward. Scarborough noticed the bags, too, and wondered why they hadn't been thrown over the side.

In the pilot house an officer signaled Berens to stop the ship. A P-4 backed down again and a second boarding party jumped across to the deck. Its leader was a stocky senior colonel with a huge scar on the back of his neck. Later, the men would call him Scar. With him were a harbor pilot dressed in civilian clothes and a cocky, black-eyed interpreter who spoke out of the side of his mouth. His nickname became Max.

Scar wanted a tour of the ship. Bucher led him below. Hodges was still alive, lying on a stretcher in the passageway outside the wardroom. Bucher said he needed medical assistance, not only for Hodges but also for the other wounded men. Max relayed his request; Scar ignored it. They stepped onto the mess decks. Scar pointed to the piles of charred and smoking publications and said something quickly in Korean.

"Were you trying to destroy your orders?" Max asked.

"This is where we make ice cream," Bucher said.

The guards kicked him viciously, sending him sprawling across the deck. They picked him up and shoved him forward, first to the engine room, then to the research spaces.

Bucher blinked as he saw the mattress covers full of classified documents, the ones he'd told Steve Harris to throw over the side nearly an hour before. "It did surprise me. I had no prior indication that this material had not been jettisoned or destroyed in some other way."

Scar and Max seemed surprised as well. They stepped past the bags and examined the smashed electronic gear. They jabbered among themselves, then signaled Bucher to move to the crypto room. The teletype was still humming. Bucher could see an occasional letter jumping across the printer.

"Turn it off," Max said.

Bucher refused. The guards pummeled him again. Max yanked out the antenna coupling jacks. The machine was silent.

Piles of ashes and papers cluttered the entrance to the research spaces. Scar said something to Max, who turned and told Bucher to carry the papers inside. He reached down. Although the guards had searched him several times, they hadn't found his cigarette lighter; if he could light one of those papers, throw it inside, then slam the door . . .

Scar must have suspected his plan, for now he barked new orders. Strong hands shoved Bucher against the bulkhead and thrust his arms above his head. A guard dumped the papers inside and then inadvertently shut the door. Bucher knew that without a blowtorch, his captors wouldn't be able to open it again. Unless someone gave them the combination.

The guards motioned him to the forward berthing compartment. His men were sitting silently on the deck and their bunks, blindfolds over their eyes. He wanted to say something, offer them some word of encouragement, but knew he'd be hit if he did. And there was really nothing to say. His back was aching; the pains in his legs and rectum were sending hot flashes through his body. He stumbled forward to the laundry and saw the jagged holes from the S01's cannon shells. Then Scar brought him back and told him to sit in the passageway outside his own cabin.

Tony LaMantia thought his bladder would burst. "Hey, guard," he shouted. Someone laughed. The North Koreans stomped toward him.

"Benjo," LaMantia said—the Japanese word for toilet. The guards understood and let the men out one by one, whacking them across their backs and shoulders.

Hayes worried about his parents in Columbus, Ohio. He'd started a letter in Sasebo to tell them that he'd been transferred to *Pueblo,* but he hadn't had time to complete it. They'd hear the news and think he was still aboard *Mars.* Two guards stood by the ladder. Two more were breaking into the lockers and stealing souvenirs. Hayes heard them shriek with laughter. They must have found some foldouts of nudes from *Playboy* magazine.

Baldridge had ripped the rate off his sleeve. He pointed to the Red Cross marker on his first aid kit and then back at himself. An officer motioned for him to go to the wardroom. Woelk was lying on the deck with his feet propped up on a chair. Baldridge treated him as best he could, then returned to the passageway. He knelt over Hodges.

"He's dead, Captain," Baldridge said.

Bucher nodded. The North Korean pilot had relieved Berens at the helm and had rung up flank speed. Thirteen knots. Bucher could feel the engines throbbing, straining beneath him. It was 3:45. He wondered how long it would take for the ship to reach Wonsan.

★   ★   ★

Rear Admiral Frank L. Johnson was growing impatient. The Army had said its helicopter from Camp Zama would reach Hardy Barracks in Tokyo at 2:25. And it was 2:35 already. Finally, at 2:39, the chopper landed, picked him up and sped toward Yokosuka. At 3:10 Johnson entered his headquarters and climbed to the spook locker.

"I was briefed immediately," he would say later, "and advised again that Fifth Air Force had been requested to provide air support under this concept of on-call assistance. No request had been made to Commander, Seventh Fleet, because there were no forces so positioned that they could have provided assistance. I told the staff that as far as I was concerned, they had taken the proper actions."

Lieutenant Ed Brookes, who conducted the briefing, remembers, "The admiral was still under the impression that the ship had been sunk. He wanted to make sure that the SAR (Sea-Air-Rescue) effort had begun. Then he began to grasp the implications of what had really happened. He said to me, 'AGER's are done.' Everyone was sort of hanging around twiddling his thumbs in shock and frustration. There wasn't much that anyone could do. I felt like a useless spoke in a useless wheel."

Several hundred yards away, inside the command cave, Al Wilson was trying to keep a running track of the ship's location, course and speed. He'd have to advise Tom McDonald at Fifth Air Force headquarters on this as often as possible. He didn't know whether *Pueblo* had been taken under tow or whether she was steaming along under her own power. He figured she'd reach the 12-mile line between 4:20 and 4:30 and the 3-mile line after dark.

Shortly after three o'clock Vice Admiral Bringle on *Providence* sent a message to Rear Admiral Epes on *Enterprise.* "Have received information that *Pueblo* has been boarded by North Korean personnel and is being escorted into Wonsan Harbor, North Korea. For CTF [Commander, Task Force] 77: divert TG [Task Group] 77.5 to proceed at best speed 32.30N—127.30E. Expect TG to consist of *Enterprise, Truxton* with *Collett* joining as feasible *O'Bannon* movements. No TG 77.5 ship or aircraft take any overt action until further informed."

Because the message had to be relayed—first to the Philippines, then to Japan, and finally to *Enterprise,* Epes didn't receive it until 3:50, 44 minutes later. He ordered a new course immediately; the 75,700-ton carrier swung around and began to steam north.

At four o'clock Bringle sent another message, this time to Admiral Hyland in Hawaii. He outlined what he had done thus far, then added, significantly, "Task Group will be held this posit. pending further developments."

A few minutes later Epes managed to contact Bringle directly.

"He was aware he couldn't, he shouldn't do anything," Epes remembers. "The wording of that message indicated his view. *Pueblo* was probably gone. Any use of force on our part would be an act of war—and that was something that higher authority would have to decide."

★   ★   ★

Colonel Monroe S. (Saber) Sams was convinced that his F-105's could take off from Okinawa, attack the North Korean ships, and land in Osan, South Korea, without refueling. But the TWX he'd just received from General McKee in Japan was very specific: His planes were to refuel at Osan and *then* proceed to Wonsan.

He notified his vice commander, Colonel John D. Rosenbaum, and his munitions chief, Major Donald G. Strandberg. He called for pylons, bomb racks, and HEI (High Explosive Incendiary) ammunition for the 20 mm cannon. The aircraft already on the ramp carried "ball" ammunition for training. Reloading would take time and run the risk of gun-jams. The first six planes would just have to launch with ball ammunition.

Inside the 12th Fighter Squadron's operations building, Major Charles E. Bishop was briefing the pilots. This was his first duty day after a hernia operation two weeks before, and he was still grounded; he was cursing his bad luck at not being able to fly himself. He passed out printed flight plans and trimmed his briefing to ten or fifteen minutes. Most of the pilots, he knew, had already been to Osan on typhoon evacuation flights. Now he listed the order of launch.

The squadron's commander, a forty-two-year-old major from upstate New York named Robert T. (Soupy) Campbell, would lead the deployment. His wingman would be a young captain, Carl D. Eliason. Captain Edward D. Nowokunski would take off next. His wingman would be Captain John P. Schoeppner . . .

Campbell and Eliason took off at 4:11. Nowokunski and Schoeppner followed them twenty minutes later. "All kinds of things go through your mind in a situation like this," Nowokunski remembers. "Campbell and I had just finished a tour in Thailand. Flying over North Vietnam. Everything after that is usually pretty anticlimactic. Now, I figured, I'd have some excitement."

★   ★   ★

At Fifth Air Force headquarters it was almost 4:30. Commander Tom McDonald approached General McKee. "General, there's one thing I must tell you," he said. "From now on, they're inside Korean waters."

"Get me Harrell," McKee said. The F-4's in South Korea still weren't ready to launch with conventional bombs. Now it was too late. The first of the twelve F-105's from Kadena would land at Osan at about five thirty. It would be dark by the time they could reach the ship 140 miles away. They should refuel as scheduled. But not attack. McKee would have to notify Ryan that he was aborting the strike. "I was racking my brain, trying to think of something else we could do," he remembers. "I felt bad, very, very bad."

24

The ship passed the big black rock at the entrance to Wonsan harbor. A North Korean sprang to the bridge and hauled down the U.S. ensign.

In the engine room, Rushel Blansett stood by the throttle. One of the guards gave him an order. He didn't understand. The guard's fist smashed into his jaw and sent him sprawling against a bulkhead. Then the guard kicked him and rabbit-chopped him on the side of the neck. Spear watched the beating. "I said to myself," he remembers, " 'Norman, you're dead.' "

In the forward berthing compartment, the men could sense that the ship had stopped. They shifted uneasily and tried to look out from beneath their blindfolds. Once, years before, Schumacher had been involved in an auto accident. He remembered the fear and frustration which swept over him as he braced for the crash. Then he thought about the time he'd lost all his luggage on a European vacation. He'd felt completely helpless and alone, even more so than in that speeding car. He felt the same way now.

The guards prodded the men up the ladder to the deck. They frisked them and tied their hands. Then they dragged and shoved them one by one across a tiny gangway. Leach, the signalman, whispered something to the man behind him. A rifle butt crashed into his mouth; he stumbled and fell to his knees. Someone kicked Harry Lewis in the leg. He looked around instinctively. "Then some woman hit my head. I couldn't understand what she was saying because she was making these odd, funny noises. But I figured, these people—they really hate Americans." Joe Sterling kept his head down and tried to walk straight ahead. The North Koreans were spitting at him and screaming invectives. He recognized the words "Kill Yankee."

In the engine room, a guard knocked Hagenson's glasses off and shoved him toward the ladder. Blansett turned to follow him. He knew the guard was watching him closely. He kicked the switch which turned off all the lights on the ship. The guard screamed, pummeled him viciously, and forced him to turn them on again.

In the wardroom a North Korean officer was standing over Steve Woelk, ordering him in English to get up and walk off the ship.

"He can't walk," Baldridge said. "He needs a stretcher." The officer spun around and told Baldridge to put his hands against the bulkhead. He grabbed a towel from the wardroom table, cut it in half, and placed it around the corpsman's head. Then he tied Baldridge's wrists. Baldridge motioned to his first aid kit. He wanted to take it with him. The officer picked it up and threw it across the wardroom, spilling its contents on the deck.

Several high-ranking officers were waiting in Bucher's cabin. He couldn't tell if they were generals or admirals. He tried to explain through Max that *Pueblo* was conducting oceanographic and electromagnetic research, studying sunspot activity. He demanded that his crew be kept together and asked what treatment the North Koreans intended to give his wounded men.

"I never did receive a reply," he says. "Instead, I was only asked why were we spying on Korea? Were we members of the CIA? Were we trying to start another war with Korea?" Bucher was the last man off the ship. The North Koreans tied his hands, blindfolded him, and marched him toward a waiting bus. His blindfold slipped, and he could see "several hundred if not a couple of thousand Korean civilians lining the sides of the road, and they were shouting at us." He noticed that any civilian who reached out to strike one of his men was pummeled in turn by the guards.

He entered the bus. Max reappeared and ordered him back to the ship and told him to open the door to the research spaces. "I told him that I did not know how and insisted that I didn't, and I was told I would be shot. I refused to open the door."

An officer walked back to the bus. "Is Lieutenant Harris here?"

"I had no idea how they knew I was in charge," Harris says. "They dragged me back to the ship and took my blindfold off and ordered me to open up the spaces. I said I didn't know the combination. That was true. I didn't. They threatened me, and I said, 'You'll just have to shoot me.' They sat me on a box of tiles between the bulkhead and the Coke machine, and I can remember hearing the hum of the refrigeration unit. The captain was there, too. The interpreter was very bad. He kept saying, 'Why don't you have key?' and it was obvious that this was a combination lock."

The first bus pulled away from the pier and bounded along a bumpy road. Canales had banged his shin a few minutes earlier. He bent forward to rub it with both hands. A guard whacked him across the side of the head. He bit his lip to keep from crying out. Chicca's blindfold was loose. He saw one of the guards rip the watch from Woelk's wrist and throw it into a gunny sack. The guard moved down the aisle, forcing the men to stand while he searched them, then beating them back to their seats. Chicca wondered what would happen when they discovered that he could speak Korean. Then the bus stopped. Someone pushed him toward the door. He stumbled about 20 feet over rough gravel and followed the others through an entrance and down a long passageway. The building smelled of straw.

Richard Rogala thought it was a police station. Someone kicked him in the testicles; he fell to the floor. Pepe Garcia was slugged in the face. Soldiers pulled his hair and shouted at him in Korean. He cried, "Filipino, Filipino." They didn't believe him. Larry Strickland's head "felt like it had been used for a cue ball." A guard was dragging him forward by his thumbs. He heard an interpreter say, "Don't look up. Don't talk and we shan't kill you. You have broken our laws. You are criminals and you must be punished." He was afraid his blindfold would slip. "I knew if it did that I'd had it," he says.

Max led Bucher and Harris to the second bus, which was still waiting by the ship. A guard removed Bucher's wallet but allowed him to keep his watch and his sapphire ring. Then Max came back and prodded Bucher toward a waiting staff car. Bucher's hands were tied; his blindfold was tight. He mentioned the Geneva Convention.

Max laughed. "I was informed that we would be tried in accordance with their laws for espionage," Bucher says. "We would all be shot." The staff car reached the building. Bucher stepped inside. "I could hear some of my crew being beaten. I insisted that the beatings be stopped. I was shoved into a room where I could no longer hear any beatings."

The room was six feet square. There were some chairs and a small table. Max tried again. Why was *Pueblo* spying on North Korea? Why was she carrying South Korean agents? Why was the United States trying to start another war?

"All I'm required to give you is my name, rank and serial number," Bucher said. "I am Lloyd Mark Bucher, commander, United States Navy, serial number 582154. We were conducting electromagnetic research. My primary mission was to observe sunspot activity. I demand that my crew be kept together and returned to the United States together with the ship at the earliest possible moment. . . ."

Max led him out of the room and back to one of the buses. The caravan bounced to a railroad station. The thongs around Bucher's wrists were so tight that he lost feeling in his hands. Guards placed him aboard a waiting train and shoved crew members in after him. The train began to move.

Steve Harris' jaw was aching from a beating he'd received on the bus. The guard hadn't liked the way he'd been sitting. The train was cold. He shivered and stamped his feet to revive their circulation. "If they're going to kill us," he thought, "they're taking us a long way to do it."

A guard stood over Larry Marshall and said something in Korean. Marshall shrugged. The guard kicked him and punched him in the nose. Then he spoke in Russian. Marshall shook his head again. The guard whacked him across the shoulders and moved to the next compartment. Marshall slumped over in his seat. Earl Phares nudged him. He didn't stir. Phares grabbed his thumbs and yanked him forward.

The North Koreans told Lee Hayes to bow his head. They grabbed his nose and twisted it and laughed. "They gave me some water," he says. "I coughed. It practically burned my throat out. They thought it was funny. The train kept stopping, and I was thinking, 'This is it.' But then we'd take off again."

Schumacher was sitting next to Tim Harris. Bucher and Lacy were facing him. A guard appeared and reached for his wallet. There was no money inside. The guard put it back. No one spoke. Schumacher peeked under his blindfold and saw the bloodstains on his khaki trousers. He hadn't been wounded himself; he didn't know how they had gotten there.

The guards came back for Bucher and brought him to another car. Max continued to ask him why *Pueblo* was spying, kept insisting that he was an agent of the CIA. Bucher repeated his name, rank, and serial number. The first of these sessions lasted about twenty minutes. Guards prodded him back to his seat and struck him with rifle butts. After awhile his hands turned black. Someone loosened the bonds on his wrists and massaged his hands. Feeling returned to them. Then the guards pushed him forward again.

Woelk was lying on a stretcher across the aisle from Murphy. He was moaning softly. Murphy asked the guards to give him water. They did. Then, from somewhere in the next car, Murphy heard the interpreter's questions. And Bucher's answers.

The train rolled on.

25

Floss Hyland's dinner party had collapsed like an overweight soufflé. The telephone had been ringing constantly for the past several hours, and most of her guests had rushed to their offices. Shortly after nine o'clock the admiral himself decided he needed a "better feel" for what had happened. He left his quarters with Captain Cassell and walked to the OPCON center on the third floor of the CINCPACFLT headquarters building.

"The information I received was that *Pueblo* was already captured," he remembers. "So there was no point in any sort of panic reaction. I began to wonder what in the dickens we could do. Perhaps it was a mistake. Perhaps the North Korean government would deny it. Perhaps the U.S. would issue an ultimatum."

He talked to COMNAVFORJAPAN on the secure phone. The Fifth Air Force, he learned, had been asked for assistance. Its planes could not arrive in time. The Seventh Fleet's commander, Admiral Bringle, had already ordered *Enterprise* to steam north. He had started to reposition his other forces, as well. Hyland stepped down to the basement and entered the intelligence plot. He conferred again with Captain Marocchi, who had been trying to find out if any North Korean ships were operating on the high seas. He talked to the CNO, Admiral Moorer, in Washington. Then he sent a message to Admiral Bringle:

"Take steps to place and support destroyer off Wonsan immediately outside 12 mile limit. Be prepared to engage in operations which may include towing *Pueblo* and/or retrieval of *Pueblo* crew. Provide air cover as appropriate and feasible."

Hyland talked to Cassell about sending planes to bomb the ship in Wonsan harbor. A pinpoint strike would obliterate her classified documents and equipment before the North Koreans had a chance to remove them. But Hyland couldn't order an air strike without approval from Admiral U. S. Grant Sharp, Commander in Chief, Pacific. And Sharp couldn't move without approval from Washington. Hyland took the only option that was available to him. At 12:37 he sent a second message to Bringle: "Be prepared to conduct photo reconnaissance Wonsan first light."

Admiral U. S. Grant Sharp had left Danang and flown in a Navy COD to the aircraft carrier USS *Kitty Hawk*. He studied the message traffic, talked to Bringle on *Providence,* then sent a sitrep to the JCS in Washington. *Enterprise* was racing toward the western entrance of the Tsushima Strait. *Truxton* accompanied her. The destroyers *Higbee, Halsey, O'Bannon, Osborn,* and *Collett* would join the task force as soon as possible. The first of these ships would reach Wonsan late the next afternoon. *Higbee* would be assigned to enter the harbor and bring out the crew.

"Recommend this latest and most flagrant disregard for rights of US property and lives on high seas," Sharp concluded, "be met with stern protest and demand for immediate return of ship and crew, full explanation this brazen act of piracy and indemnity all damages."

Bringle received Hyland's message and ordered Epes to ready the planes on *Enterprise* for morning reconnaissance flights. Then he sent another message to Hawaii: "*Enterprise* prepared to execute air strike against suitable military target or take other action as authorized by higher authority."

In the Situation Room Walt Rostow was still gathering data for the intelligence report he'd have to place outside the President's bedroom door at 6:30 A.M. Art McCafferty, the chief of the Situation Room, was helping him. So were Jim Brown and Bud Denner. Rostow had called the President shortly after two o'clock to give him an "advisory"; he hadn't been able to supply too many details.

For there were still so many unanswered questions. The ship had maintained radio silence for a full ten days, had not submitted position reports until just prior to the incident. Had she at any time

violated waters claimed by North Korea? This was one of the first
questions the President had asked. And Rostow hadn't been able to
say. It was difficult enough from reading those confused messages to
ascertain *Pueblo*'s position at the time of boarding. But why hadn't
she made a run for it? Why hadn't she fought back? Throughout the
night, Pentagon aides had insisted she carried destruct devices. So why
was Bucher saying that destruction had been "ineffective," that several
publications would be "compromised"? Which ones? There was no
sense trying to guess about that. Already, the word had gone out to
United States posts around the world: Change codes immediately.
Rostow trimmed the report to one page and sent it upstairs.

McNamara left his home on Kalorama Circle and reached the
Pentagon shortly after seven o'clock. He called in his military and
civilian advisors. "There was a sort of stunned silence," remembers
Richard C. Steadman, the Deputy Assistant Secretary of Defense for
International Security Affairs. "*Pueblo* was in port. Nobody really
knew what had happened or what to do about it. He told us to re-
construct the incident, prepare a chronology of events." McNamara
left the building and headed toward the White House. A few minutes
later, at 8:40, a Pentagon news release announced the ship's capture.
It estimated her position at the time of boarding as 25 miles off the
North Korean coast.

The first of the "crisis meetings" had already started in the White
House basement. Rostow was still in his shirtsleeves. Rusk, Katzenbach, and William P. Bundy, an Assistant Secretary of State, were
seated at the long table in the conference room. So were McNamara
and Paul Nitze, the Deputy Secretary of Defense. General Maxwell D.
Taylor had just entered the room with his aide, Lieutenant Colonel
Robert S. McGowan. General Wheeler was doing most of the talking,
flicking his pointer from the spot on the map where the ship had been
boarded to the location of the task force churning north through the
Sea of Japan.

Sixty-four years earlier, in 1904, a Moroccan bandit chief named
Raisuli had seized an American citizen named Perdicaris. And Secretary of State John Hay had dispatched that famous cable: "Perdicaris
alive or Raisuli dead." But governments couldn't react that way anymore. This nation had grown so powerful and, more important, so
aware of its power and of the consequences of its use, that, in a sense,
this knowledge bound it, like Prometheus to his lonely mountain. Most
of the men in this conference room had weathered the Cuban missile
crisis and learned the value of moderation. Then, too, in 1964 they
had deliberated the United States' response to the North Vietnamese

"attack" on Navy destroyers in the Tonkin Gulf. They had discovered the pitfalls of a rash reaction.

And to these men it seemed clear that sending a lone U.S. destroyer with air cover into Wonsan harbor as Admiral Sharp had suggested was very rash indeed. North Korea had undoubtedly placed her four-hundred-odd MIG's on alert; sixteen antiaircraft batteries and SAM missile sites ringed the port city. "No one ruled out a military response at that first meeting," one participant recalls. "But we had one war on our hands already. We had to have more information before we committed ourselves to a course which might start another."

The President entered the conference room at ten o'clock. At 10:25 General Wheeler telephoned Admiral Hyland in Hawaii, where it was 5:25 in the morning.

Hyland had been waiting all night for the United States to issue an ultimatum. Now it occurred to him that "nothing like this was going to happen." Sadly, for he felt that his superiors were making a grave mistake, he relayed Wheeler's orders in a series of messages to Admiral Bringle: "It is desired that no show of force be deployed in area of *Pueblo* incident. Hold all forces south of 36-00N [a line extending east from the coast of South Korea] until further advised. . . ." And then, two hours later, "JCS has directed that fleet units proceed no further north than present positions. *Higbee* remain in company of *Enterprise* and *Truxton*. Do not, repeat, not send *Higbee* to take position off Wonsan."

Ever since leaving the Navy section of the Current Intelligence Branch several months earlier, Lieutenant Commander Richard Mackinnon had been marking time, counting SAM missile sites in aerial photographs. But then, inexplicably, he'd been reassigned to the R&I Branch as an assistant to Lieutenant Commander Erv Easton. January 23 was to be his first day on the job. Although delighted by the transfer, he still hadn't planned to drive to work earlier than usual. Just after midnight he received a cryptic phone call from a Marine Corps officer who shared in his car pool. There was a crisis, the officer said. Could Mackinnon come by for him at 4:30? So now, well before dawn, Mackinnon left his home in Kailua. Later that morning he would receive his first assignment: Assess the intelligence loss resulting from *Pueblo*'s capture.

At his apartment in Honolulu Ensign Charles B. Hall, Jr., the officer who had replaced Mackinnon as the North Korean analyst, stepped into the bathroom and started to shave. Music purred from the radio on his night table. Then it was time for the five o'clock news. ". . . has been seized by the North Koreans," the announcer was saying. "Pentagon spokesmen identified the ship as the USS *Pueblo.* . . ." Hall stared blankly into the mirror. Blood was trickling from a cut on his chin. "I didn't finish shaving," he remembers, "for I probably would have had many self-inflicted wounds had I continued." He dressed as fast as he could, ran outside to his green Volvo, and sped to the office.

Inside the reseach spaces on USS *Banner,* Communications Technician Third Class Patrick J. Biesemeier was monitoring incoming traffic. As was his practice, he ripped and set aside only those messages addressed specifically to *Banner,* crumpling the others into little balls and tossing them into a trash can. At that moment, early on the morning of January 24, *Banner* was steaming north along the east coast of Honshu en route to her primary "op area" off Siberia. Everything was quiet, and Biesemeier started reading a book. Suddenly, he noticed something extraordinary on the teleprinter. "I saw the word 'critic,'" he remembers. "You don't normally get that on a broadcast." It had to be a mistake, he thought, "an hallucination." He tore it from the machine, threw it aside, and returned to his novel. But he couldn't concentrate. Suppose there *really was* an emergency? He plucked the message from the trash can and read it again. Then he set out to find the research officer, Lieutenant Anthony W. White.

White glanced at the paper, then ran to wake up the skipper, Commander Charles Clark, in his cabin. "We sat there all night reading those messages as they came in," Clark recalls. "I was relating them to our own previous harassment and thinking, 'What would I do in this situation?' Then it got to a point beyond my experience. I thought, 'There but for the grace of God go I.'"

Hours later, *Banner* received an order from Admiral Johnson: "Discontinue Ichthyic II operations and return to. . . ." The message was garbled, but Clark had no doubts about its intent. He swung the ship around and steamed back toward Yokosuka.

Aboard USS *Kitty Hawk,* Admiral Sharp read a copy of the message that Bringle had just received from Hyland in Hawaii. He was "convinced we needed to do something . . . and we thought at least we ought to have a ship up there that would reassert our right to do that patrol. . . ." He sent a message to General Wheeler and urged him to reconsider the JCS decision. He never received a reply.

In Room 167 at the Bahia Motor Hotel in San Diego, Rose Bucher was alone. She had sent her two sons off to school minutes before; now she fixed a cup of coffee and settled back to watch the last half hour of the *Today* show. She had been living at the motel for the past several months, ever since *Pueblo* steamed down from Bremerton, and if the apartment was more expensive than her budget could really afford, it was also extremely comfortable, a pleasant place to stay until May, when Pete returned from Japan. The newscaster was reading a bulletin: ". . . the ship has been identified as the USS *Pueblo.* . . ."

For several seconds she stared at the screen numbly, disbelievingly. Her older brother, John, a Marine in World War II, had been taken prisoner by the Japanese. She knew what this could mean. She hurried to the phone and called her mother in Jefferson City, Missouri. "Pray for him," she said. "Pray for him."

26

The train began to slow down. Woelk was still moaning, pleading for water. The guards moved through the compartments, untying the men's hands and removing their blindfolds. Sheets covered the windows. An interpreter said the men would arrive at their destination soon. Woelk, Crandell, and Chicca would remain in their seats until they were ordered to move. The others would follow the captain.

Bucher stumbled down the steps and limped onto the platform. He raised his hands above his head. The maze of lights and popping flashbulbs blinded him; he could hear cameras clicking and whirring, and for a few seconds he lowered his hands. Then he felt a rifle butt in the small of his back. He raised them again.

The clock on the steeple atop the station read 6:40. Just below it, in a gold frame with a red background, was a portrait of Kim Il Sung. This, Schumacher thought, has to be Pyongyang. He stamped his feet on the platform to keep them warm. Someone shouted at him. He turned and followed Bucher toward the two buses 150 yards away.

Steve Harris had seen the clock, too, but he had lost all track of time. He didn't know whether it was morning or evening. It was just dark. The guard had told him to lower his head. There was no sheet over his window, and now as the bus began to move he rubbed his hand against the glass to clear away the frost. He saw some trolley bus wires overhead but almost no traffic. He noticed the dull gray limestone buildings set back from the road, the rows of shops and apartments. They all looked the same.

The buses entered what seemed to be a military compound and lurched to a stop outside a rectangular, four-story building with a dark tile roof. Later, the *Pueblo* crew would call this building "the Barn." Someone shoved Bucher outside, and almost immediately one of the guards kicked him in the back; another in the legs. "I went after this guy," Bucher remembers, "and before I could reach him I was grabbed by three or four other Koreans and thrown to the ground, thrown forward toward the building."

At bayonet-point he entered the Barn and climbed the stairs to the third floor. A guard pushed him into a room and shut the door. The radiator didn't work, and the room was very cold. A blackout curtain covered the window, which had been nailed shut. A naked light bulb hung from the ceiling on a thin cord tufted with dust. There was a small table and a straight-backed chair and, against the wall, a cot with a course muslin sheet, a brown wool blanket, and a pillow filled with rice husks. He was exhausted and in pain, but he could not sleep. He worried about the contents of the mattress covers he'd seen in the research spaces and blamed himself for not making sure that they'd been thrown overboard. He could hear his men crying out as they climbed the stairs, and he could imagine how the guards were pummeling them. He blamed himself for their predicament, as well.

Now the guards kicked open the door and marched him to an interrogation room. Max, the interpreter, sat behind a small table. The litany continued. Why was *Pueblo* spying on North Korea? Was Bucher a member of the CIA? Bucher's answers remained the same. He fully expected U.S. retaliation. Hadn't Captain Cassell in Hawaii assured him this would be the case? He knew it might result in his death, but at that moment he didn't care. He sensed that Max was worried about it and told him that he had radioed *Pueblo's* position to U.S. authorities. Max sent him back to his room. Guards appeared with a plate of boiled turnips, bread and butter, and sugar. Bucher shook his head. He could not, he would not, eat.

A few minutes later, at 8:30, the guards came for him again and took him to see a senior major whom everyone later called Squint. Bucher blinked as he recognized his service jacket on the table in front of him. Squint was reading the personal history page. How old was he? Where was he born? What were the names of his wife and children? He knew that Squint had all the answers; he didn't deny a thing. Squint frowned. Bucher had attended Combat Information Center School in Glenview, Illinois, in 1954. CIC—wasn't that the same as CIA? They couldn't be serious. Bucher insisted again that *Pueblo* was only an oceanographic research ship. The guards began kicking him in the back and legs. The pain was so great that he couldn't remain standing much longer; he would fall, perhaps pass out.

But then the guards prodded him into the hall and marched him to a large room at the far end of the building. His officers and Tuck, the senior oceanographer, followed quietly. It was 9:45.

The room was dimly lit. A jowly, bull-necked officer with deep-set eyes sat at the center table. His yellow-green tunic was buttoned to the throat, and the two silver stars glittered against the red and gold collar boards as he bobbed back and forth. He looked like Oddjob and was obviously a general. Max sat in a chair to his right.

"Give your name and your job aboard ship," Max said.

Bucher complied. So did Murphy. Schumacher said merely, "First lieutenant," and sat down again in a straight-backed chair. The general was a caricature. Hollywood, he thought, had prepared him well for this experience.

Did Bucher know that 500,000 American troops were stationed in South Korea? The general was shouting now. So was Max. Why were those troops there if not to start a new war?

"Because the South Korean Government requested them," Bucher began, "to provide assistance in the defense of their country. . . ."

A colonel at the table to his left jumped up and drew back his hand. The general barked an order. The colonel sat down again. The men of *Pueblo*, the general continued, had no rights under the Geneva Convention. They would be treated as spies.

"How do you want it," Max asked, "one at a time or all together?"

Bucher got to his feet. "Shoot me, sir, but let my crew take the ship and go home."

"The ship belongs to us," the general stormed. "It was caught in the act of espionage."

"Our ship, you captured our ship in international waters, where we had every right to be. Your act was an act of war against the United States. . . ."

Max gave a signal. A guard punched Bucher back to his seat.

"Do you admit to spying?"

Bucher shook his head.

"You, executive officer, what do you say?"

Murphy maintained that *Pueblo*'s mission was oceanographic research, that the ship had not violated North Korean waters. So did the others. As each officer sat down, the general repeated a phrase to Max.

"You will be shot at sunrise," Max said. Then Max and the general laughed.

27

Rear Admiral John Victor Smith felt sure that North Korea wanted war, that Kim Il Sung would welcome U.S. retaliation. First the Blue House raid, then this *Pueblo* incident. The cable from Dean Rusk had reached him in Seoul several hours earlier: "Is there a meeting scheduled? If there is none, call one." He had made the arrangements already. He received last-minute instructions from U.S Ambassador to South Korea William J. Porter and the embassy's political expert, Richard Erickson. Then he rushed to the helicopter that would whisk him to Panmunjom, 42 miles away.

Smith had never felt comfortable at the truce village. The armistice agreement had stopped the war fifteen years earlier, but the passage of time hadn't softened North Korea's belligerency. It was easy to think of the North Koreans as children. Who else would insist so petulantly on raising their flag an inch or so higher than the United Nations banner in the Joint Security Area? Who else would keep that camera trained on him constantly—hoping, no doubt, to photograph him falling asleep, wiping his eyes, or picking his nose. In other respects, Smith thought, these people were savages. Dangerous and unpredictable. He was convinced they'd hidden a machine gun in the "ice cream parlor" which overlooked the row of blue and green buildings. He didn't rule out the possibility of their firing on him someday or even trying to kidnap him. Back in 1934 the Annapolis yearbook had described him as a man of "tact" and "conversational ability." Well, his six-month tour would end in May. He was glad about that.

Now, at eleven o'clock on the morning of January 24, he entered the metal-roofed meeting hut, sat down at the green-felt covered table, and stared across the DMZ at Major General Pak Chung Kuk. The North Korean negotiator, a thin, dark-haired man with Occidental features and a mole beneath his right eye, stared back at him. Some of

Smith's aides referred to Pak as "Frog Face," and over the past few weeks Smith himself had become proficient in blowing cigar smoke into Pak's face. "He had no counter," the admiral remembers. "Although he chain-smoked cigarettes, these had insufficient range. He would often get excited and light a second cigarette with the first one still burning in the ashtray. It gave me fiendish delight."

Because the UN Command had called this two hundred and sixty-first meeting of the Military Armistice Commission, Smith was entitled to speak first. He protested the "heinous" Blue House raid and played a tape of the captured assassin's confession. Pak fidgeted uneasily in his chair.

"I want to tell you, Pak, that the evidence against you North Korean Communists is overwhelming. . . . I now have one more subject to raise which is also of an extremely serious nature. It concerns the criminal boarding and seizure of . . . *Pueblo* in international waters. It is necessary that your regime do the following: One, return the vessel and crew immediately; two, apologize to the Government of the United States for this illegal action. You are also advised that the United States reserves the right to ask for compensation under international law."

Smith looked up from his paper. The North Koreans were laughing at him.

"Our saying goes, 'A mad dog barks at the moon,' " Pak began. "I cannot but pity you who are compelled to behave like a hooligan, disregarding even your age and honor to accomplish the crazy intentions of the war maniac Johnson for the sake of bread and dollars to keep your life. In order to sustain your life, you probably served Kennedy, who is already sent to hell. If you want to escape from the same fate of Kennedy, who is now a putrid corpse, and of Johnson, who is a living corpse, don't indulge yourself desperately in invectives. . . ."

Pak shuffled his documents. "Around 1215 hours on January 23 your side committed the crude, aggressive act of illegally infiltrating the armed spy ship *Pueblo* of the U.S. imperialist aggressor navy equipped with various weapons and all kinds of equipment for espionage into the coastal waters of our side. Our naval vessels returned the fire of the piratical group. . . . At the two hundred and sixtieth meeting of this commission held four days ago, I again registered a strong protest with your side against having infiltrated into our coastal waters a number of armed spy boats . . . and demanded you immediately stop such criminal acts . . . this most overt act of the U.S. imperialist aggressor forces was designed to aggravate tension in Korea and precipitate another war of aggression. . . ."

Pak listed his government's demands. The United States must admit that *Pueblo* had entered North Korean waters, must apologize for this intrusion, must assure North Korea that it would never happen again.

"I will investigate any reasonable allegations," Smith replied, "but I will not be diverted by your tactics. I propose a recess."

"I accept your proposal for a recess," Pak said.

Pak and his aides stood up and marched out one end of the building. Smith and his aides turned and walked out the other.

"It's a goddamn disgrace," one admiral said. "I'll tell you what I would have done. I would have headed zero-nine-zero [due east] as fast as I could and opened up on the first patrol boat and put it out of action. I would have gone down fighting."

"I just can't believe that this man Bucher would not have tried to fight—no matter what his orders were," another admiral exclaimed. "I'd have scuttled the ship if I couldn't do anything else. A Navy ship just shouldn't have to go down in defeat that way. I'd rather see it sunk."

Lieutenant John Arnold was stunned when he heard the news. Then his mind flashed back to all the troubles the ship had encountered at Bremerton. "It was predictable," he thought. "The whole evolution was a fiasco."

Twenty-four hours had passed since the first critic reached Washington. At the Pentagon, members of the Joint Staff had held the first of literally dozens of meetings to consider a wide range of possible responses. Officers there, at NSA, and at the Naval Security Station on Nebraska Avenue were still trying to find out what classified documents and equipment *Pueblo* had carried. The ship had received a hazardous duty allowance, someone discovered, just prior to leaving Japan. Had she offloaded all those publications? Well, no, Yokosuka replied in effect. Why not? No one could say.

At the State Department Rusk had already instructed U.S. Ambassador to Moscow Llewellyn Thompson to ask if the Soviets—in the interest of protecting freedom of the seas—would intercede with Pyongyang. Thompson would seek an audience with Deputy Foreign Minister Vasily Kuznetsov. Under Secretary of State Nicholas deB. Katzenbach huddled with William P. Bundy, the Assistant Secretary for East Asian and Pacific Affairs. Bundy was spending every available moment on Vietnam, and he didn't see how he could afford to worry about *Pueblo,* as well. He suggested that the job of handling the crisis on a day-to-day basis be given to his deputy, a former ambassador to South Korea named Samuel D. Berger. Katzenbach agreed.

Then fifty-three, "Silent Sam" Berger was something of an anomaly in diplomatic circles. Short, balding, and blunt—often to the point of rudeness—he played his cards close to the vest and rarely took subordinates into his confidence. Throughout his career he had shown an independent streak, a willingness to challenge conventional wisdom. In 1946, for example, he had served as a junior officer at the embassy in London. His colleagues in the political section hobnobbed with Britain's Conservatives, blithely assuring Washington that Churchill's party couldn't lose the postwar elections. Berger disagreed and culti- vated friendships in the opposition Labor Party. The "upset" occurred; Labor triumphed at the polls, and as one former associate puts it, "Sam was the only man in the embassy who knew all those guys by their first names."

Now this independent streak led Berger to make a rare mistake. Increasingly, in recent years, State Department officials have reacted to major crises by establishing "task forces" and housing them in the seventh-floor Operations Center. The rationale is that this procedure gathers everyone involved in a crisis at a single location, provides them access to communications, and releases them from normal bu- reaucratic binds. Furthermore, it imbues them with a sense of urgency. Berger decided he would not move to the Operations Center. He would handle *Pueblo* like any other routine matter—from his own desk. He summoned Ben Fleck, the "country director" for South Korea, and asked for situation reports at six-hour intervals. Then he called in a bespectacled, brown-haired woman named Brynhilde Rowberg and placed her in charge of the "third country" effort. She began drafting cables to more than one hundred nations requesting their help in effecting a diplomatic solution.

At six o'clock that Tuesday evening, January 23, the leaders of both major political parties, members of the Senate Foreign Relations Committee and the House Foreign Affairs Committee—about two dozen lawmakers in all—filed into the Fish Room of the White House. The President greeted them perfunctorily and then, as the briefing began, leaned forward on the end of a couch, his chin resting between the thumb and forefinger of his right hand, his eyes staring morosely ahead. "I've never seen him so serious and curiously unfriendly," one Senator told *Newsweek* magazine. "He didn't have the old self-con- fidence. It was clear to me . . . that he wasn't quite sure of just what was happening."

A map of the Sea of Japan rested against an easel. General Wheeler pointed to the two little red crosses—the first denoting the ship's position at the time of the first critic; the second her location when the North Koreans stomped aboard. McNamara sat to his left, supplying occasional comments and answering questions. Thirty minutes later, the President stood up and said that he would send the Senate a message in the morning requesting a three-year extension of the Arms Control and Disarmament Agency. That message would include his views on the nuclear nonproliferation treaty. Some legislators viewed his reference to disarmament at that point as "surprising." Others termed it a shrewd ploy to tone down the crisis atmosphere.

"We ought to keep our shirts on and not go off half-cocked until we know more about the details of this incident," warned Senate Majority Leader Mike Mansfield. Good advice, but hard to follow now, for passions—in Congress and elsewhere—had already been aroused. It was one thing for the United States to back away judiciously from nuclear confrontation with the Russians over Cuba in 1962. But it was something else entirely for this country to allow its nose to be tweaked by a dinky ministate like North Korea.

"North Korea's bold seizure of the *Pueblo* is not nearly so outrageous," stormed the Milwaukee *Sentinel*, "as . . . the pusillanimous American reaction to it. Our official bird is not eagle, hawk or dove. It is chicken." South Carolina's Representative L. Mendel Rivers, chairman of the House Armed Services Committee, said the United States "should declare war if necessary. . . . If they don't turn back the ship, I'd turn loose whatever we have out there on them. . . ." Even "moderate" legislators joined the chorus. "The ship must be returned at once with all Americans aboard," said Idaho Senator Frank Church, a dove on Vietnam. "Our national honor is at stake."

Rostow spent the night in the Situation Room. So did McCafferty. "The President was on the horn quite frequently," McCafferty remembers, "calling down to speak to Walt and me. He'd say, 'What's new on *Pueblo?*' or just the one word, '*Pueblo?*' He was concerned about the safety of the men, and he was mad as hell. One time he asked me, 'Why wasn't I called immediately [when the first critic arrived]? You know you can call me anytime. I was still awake.' And the only answer I could give him was, 'Mr. President, we could have called you and said, "Sir, here's what we have. But please don't ask any questions. We just don't know the answers." ' "

★　　　★　　　★

A junior officer had brought him a pitcher of milk and a plate of cookies. "If you don't eat," the North Korean said solicitously, "you will ruin health." Bucher shook his head. The officer went away. A few minutes later some guards stomped into his room. They punched and kicked him for no apparent reason. Then they left. He got to his feet and paced back and forth. The room was 22 feet long and 12 feet wide. There was a bucket of water next to the table in the corner. There were eight panels in the green door. There was a transom above it. He thought he heard a muffled scream. And a sharp crack. A door slamming? A rifle shot? Then he heard footsteps. Coming closer.

The guards pushed him toward a small room at the end of the hall. The officer who'd almost clouted him several hours before, during the session with the general, was standing behind a large desk smoking a cigarette. He was tall and thin with oversized front teeth. He wore a fur hat and a heavy gray overcoat with red lapels and large, squared shoulder boards that sloped up and away from his neck. The total effect was almost comical, and yet there was something about this man, some intangible quality which suggested power and cunning and erudition. Bucher noticed four silver stars on each shoulder board and guessed that he was a senior colonel. Soon he would refer to him as "Super-C."

Max was gone and in his place was another interpreter, a lean man with hollow cheeks, horn-rimmed glasses, and a receding hairline. Super-C began to shout at the top of his lungs. The interpreter coughed as he tried to keep pace. Later he would be known as "Wheezy."

"We have proof that you were spying on our country," Super-C was screaming, "that your purpose was to start another war."

Bucher denied the charges and demanded again that he and his men be treated in accordance with the Geneva Convention.

Super-C slammed his fist on the desk. "You are not military prisoners of war. You have no such rights." Then Super-C handed him a typewritten confession. "Sign this."

Bucher refused.

Super-C shouted an order. The guards dragged Bucher back to his room, punched him and kicked him and threw him against the wall. Forty-five minutes later they came back and took him to the long, dark conference room where he'd seen the general that morning. There on a long table were stacks of classified documents. He blinked as he noticed copies of the *Banner* patrol reports that Erv Easton had given him in Hawaii. Then he saw a copy of his own narrative, the one Schumacher prepared on the ship every morning.

"Do these not prove that you were spying?" Super-C was grinning, waving the papers in his face.

The documents carried the name of his ship. They bore his signature as having read them. He agreed that *Pueblo* had been collecting intelligence.

Super-C handed him the confession again. The CIA, it said, had promised him "a lot of dollars" if he was successful in this "sheer act of aggression," the purpose of which was to start another war.

"Sign it," Super-C said.

"No." The guards took him away again.

Hours passed. His window was broken, but it was so high that he couldn't reach it, and the Koreans had warned him not to try. He paced back and forth in the cold. He knew he would be beaten again but didn't know when, and in a way the uncertainty was worse than the punishment itself. Although the walls were very thick, he could hear the sounds of chairs smashing, the screams of his crew. From time to time, interpreters entered his room. What was happening to his men? Could he see them? The North Koreans didn't even acknowledge his questions. How much of this could a man stand? What was the breaking point, the line beyond which nothing mattered anymore? Would they rip off his fingernails one by one, or jam a hot poker into his rectum, or thrust it into his eye? Or would they begin with subtler methods? Would they try water torture?

He looked at his watch. Almost time for sunset. He thought of his wife and his sons, and he wished he'd somehow been able to prepare them for this. Rose was a strong girl; she'd make it all right. And his friends would be there to help. If only he had thought to say in one of his messages to Japan that he had not entered North Korean waters, that he had remained faithful to his orders throughout the mission. His friends would know that, but would the Navy? It was ironic. Once the North Koreans translated that narrative, they'd realize that he had accomplished almost nothing on this mission, that he had succeeded mainly in chipping a lot of ice.

They came for him at eight o'clock. Super-C was waiting with Max in the room at the end of the hall. The guards pointed AK-47's at his head. An officer drew his pistol. Super-C began by explaining through his interpreter, quite calmly at first, that North Korea wanted peace. In order for peace to be maintained Bucher would have to sign that confession. Then he and his men could go home.

Bucher shook his head.

"Well, do you deny that you had materials on board your ship for spying on our country?"

"I saw the documents that you showed me this afternoon. Certainly the narrative was mine."

Super-C told him to kneel and face the wall. The officer drew back the slide on his pistol and stood behind him. "You have two minutes to decide whether to sign this confession," Super-C said, "or you will be shot."

A wave of relief surged through his aching body. There would be no torture. He closed his eyes and waited and didn't mind the cold.

Two minutes passed. Super-C looked up from his watch. "Are you ready to sign?"

"I will not sign."

An officer in front of him stepped out of the line of fire.

"Kill the son of a bitch," Super-C said.

He heard a *click:* the hammer striking the firing pin.

"Well, it was a misfire," Max said.

"You were lucky the last time," Super-C said. "You will have another two minutes. This is your last chance."

Bucher heard the slide on the receiver draw back. The officer was placing another bullet in the chamber. He closed his eyes again. And waited. Suddenly, it occurred to him that the misfired cartridge hadn't fallen to the floor. This was just a *game.*

"Do you agree to sign?"

"I refuse."

Super-C motioned to the guards. "You're not worth a bullet," he said. "We will beat you to death."

The guards smashed their rifle butts into Bucher's back. They kicked and punched him and knocked him to the floor. He raised his hand to shield his face. He felt a sharp pain at the base of his neck. Then he lost consciousness. They dragged him down the hall and threw him into his room.

He came around a few seconds later. His head was throbbing, his jaw ached, he had to go to the bathroom. A guard marched him to the head. He urinated blood. They could do whatever they wanted now; he no longer gave a damn. He elbowed the guard out of the way and limped back to his room. He was too tired to pace the floor. He sat at the table and stared at the wall.

An officer whom he'd later call Chipmunk entered his room at ten o'clock. He held a pistol in his hand. "Now," he said, "you'll see what happens to spies." Bucher got to his feet. Guards led him down three flights of stairs and pushed him through a door and into the back seat of a waiting car. He thought he saw Max up front near the driver. In the darkness he couldn't be sure.

The car stopped ten minutes later. He got out and stumbled down half a flight of stairs into a semibasement. "Look," someone shouted. And there, strapped against the wall, three spotlights playing on his body, hung the figure of a man. He was still alive. His right arm dangled grotesquely from his side; Bucher could see the bone protruding from his elbow. His face was the color of raw meat. He had bitten completely through his lower lip, which drooped over the side of his chin. His right eye was gone. Black matter was trickling slowly from the socket.

Bucher felt his knees buckling beneath him. The North Koreans were shouting, but he could no longer hear them. The man's body seemed to be turning around and around. Then he blacked out.

"You see what happens to spies. You are spies. You can expect the same treatment." Super-C was standing over him again, fidgeting with his cigarette lighter. He sensed he was back in the end interrogation room, but didn't know how long he had been there. "You will sign this confession."

Bucher shook his head. "No."

"We are through fooling around with you. Do you know that you are responsible for the lives of your crew?"

"Yes, and you are responsible for the treatment of my wounded. You murdered one of my men. . . ." He saw the guard's fist coming at him out of the corner of his eye. He tried to duck; his muscles wouldn't respond. The blow knocked him across the room.

Super-C droned on as if he were lecturing an errant schoolboy. Bucher had to sign the confession so the world would understand the imperialistic designs of the United States. All he wanted Bucher to do was confess to what he had *already admitted,* that documents on board the ship assigned him to collect intelligence off the coast of North Korea. It was as simple as that. He held out the paper again.

Bucher refused.

Super-C slammed his fist on the desk. "You will sign this; I assure you that you will sign it." He said something quickly to one of the guards. Bucher thought he recognized the name of one of his men. The guard rushed out of the room. "We will now begin to shoot your crew one at a time until you sign. If you do not sign by the time the entire crew has been shot, I will see that you sign anyway." He smiled thinly. "You know that we have the means to persuade you to do so."

He sensed a note of desperation in Super-C's threat. The North Koreans had played one game with him. They could not afford to play another without losing face. They obviously felt they needed something to justify this act of piracy. There was no doubt in his mind that they would do anything to get it. They were animals.

Did they know how he felt about these men, how he almost considered them part of his *family*? Were they that smart? He looked up at Super-C and down at the paper again. They were going to shoot the youngest man first and had already sent for Fireman Apprentice Howard E. Bland. Was Bland the youngest? He wasn't sure. Bland or Marshall, one of the two. Such innocent kids. What did they know about this? He couldn't bear to look them in the eye as they came into the room, to hear them scream, to watch them as the bullets ripped into their bodies, to sit there all the while and know that he was responsible for their deaths. He couldn't bear to be the last man to die himself.

Super-C was watching him intently. Seconds passed. He raised his head. "I will sign the confession," he said.

The guards escorted him back to his room. Someone brought him a tray with bread and butter and turnips and eggs. He could not eat. His mind kept flashing back to those bags full of classified documents in the research spaces, to the stacks of papers he'd seen on the table that afternoon, to the limp form of the South Korean "spy" in that awful dungeon, to the confession he had just signed. They had broken him in less than thirty-six hours. Could he have held out any longer? Would it have made any difference? He knew that confession would embarrass the United States. And they would be after him for more; a public appearance perhaps, a radio broadcast. He hadn't slept since leaving the ship. His body ached, but he still felt mentally alert. He realized they weren't going to kill him. They needed him.

He noticed the bucket in the corner. It was almost full. He knelt above it. A thin crust of ice had formed. He knocked it away. He plunged his head into the bucket, down, down, clutching the pail with both hands. Thirty seconds, one minute—he felt his lungs about to explode. He . . . he could not do it. He fell to the floor gasping for breath and lay there for a long time. He got to his feet and stumbled toward the chair. He stared at the bucket. Then he fell asleep.

He felt the guard tug at his shoulder and woke with a start. It was five o'clock in the morning. Super-C wanted him to alter the confession, to admit that *Pueblo* had intruded into Korean waters. That wasn't true, Bucher maintained. He was in international waters. They couldn't prove otherwise.

"Well, it's not where we brought you under attack," Super-C went on. "But you did follow us in toward Wonsan, did you not?"

"Yes."

"Where did we finally board you? Would you estimate that you were within the twelve-mile line at that time?"

How could he say for sure? It seemed so long ago, and so many thoughts were spinning around in his brain. Why were these supposed intrusions suddenly so important? Bucher remembered seeing an island—Ung-do? Nan-do? Yo-do?—they all sounded the same—through the afternoon haze. But when? Before the firing started or later, as the ship approached Wonsan with the Koreans on board? He heard his voice responding, dully, mechanically, "I am sure that I was inside of the twelve-mile line."

"That's all we are asking you to say, that we boarded and actually captured your ship inside our territorial waters."

Super-C was smiling now. Bucher hesitated.

"Do we have to go back and start all over?"

Bucher looked at the new confession. It said *Pueblo* had been captured 7.6 miles from Yo-do island. The long black sock that he had wrapped around his ankle on the ship was caked with blood. The wounds in his leg and rectum were throbbing. No bones were broken; still, he knew from the trouble he'd had at the toilet that he was hurt internally. "No," he said, finally. "That will not be necessary. I will agree."

He limped back to his room. Two hours later, at eight o'clock, Super-C summoned him again. He had confessed to espionage; he had admitted that *Pueblo* was captured inside the 12-mile line. Now he must link these "crimes" together. He must say that he had entered the territorial waters of the Democratic People's Republic of Korea for the *purpose* of spying.

But he would have been *told* if the ship had ever crossed over that line during the mission, Bucher said. He would have been one of the *first* to know.

Lieutenant Murphy had already acknowledged this fact, Super-C continued. Was Bucher calling his navigator a liar? Would he like to read Murphy's confession?

He shook his head. He knew they could break Murphy as they had broken him. He was responsible for his crew. If he refused to go along with the North Koreans, his men would die. For no reason. There was no exit. He said he would include whatever Super-C wanted in his confession.

He sat at his table and stared at the typewritten pages. He had to copy them in his own hand. Was this just the beginning? How many times would he have to add new "facts" to suit his captors' whims?

Does a man come to believe the lie if he repeats it often enough? He was aware that a photographer was watching him from the door. He didn't look up; his pen moved slowly across the paper:

> I am Commander Lloyd Mark Bucher, Captain of the USS *Pueblo* . . . who was captured while carrying out espionage activities after intruding deep into the territorial waters of the Democratic People's Republic of Korea . . . the U.S. Central Intelligence Agency promised me that if this task would be done successfully, a lot of dollars would be offered to all crew members of my ship. Particularly, I myself would be honored. . . . I have no excuse whatsoever for my criminal acts. . . . The crime committed by me and my men is entirely indelible. . . .

28

"This alleged 'confession' is a travesty on the facts," a Pentagon press release maintained on January 24. "The style and wording of the document provide unmistakable evidence that this was not written or prepared by any American. Typical of the propaganda sham is the suggestion that the CIA had promised Commander Bucher and his crew 'a lot of dollars.' . . . No credence should be given this contrived statement."

Throughout the first few days of the crisis, Pentagon and White House spokesmen tried to clarify what had happened and, in doing so, kept tripping over their own feet. "Press reports which imply that the captain of the *Pueblo* made a number of calls for help are wrong," another release began; "the facts are that the only time the *Pueblo* requested assistance was when she was actually boarded." Reports that the United States lacked the forces to respond to the seizure immediately simply weren't true, either, Defense Department officials maintained. Pentagon spokesmen refused to confirm that *Pueblo* was in Wonsan harbor. They wouldn't acknowledge that *Enterprise* had been diverted to the Sea of Japan. They *did* admit that—instead of being 25 miles from the North Korean coast, as they had claimed initially—*Pueblo* had been 16.3 miles away at the time of her capture. "The position of this government is that the ship was in international waters when it was boarded," said Presidential News Secretary George E. Christian. Did this mean that *Pueblo* had *never* entered North Korean waters? "I'm not going to get into fine lines," Christian replied.

"The administration must realize," the Washington *Post* pointed out, "that public tolerance in this country for the unexplained and the inexplicable is wearing thin." And in the New York *Post*, columnist Murray Kempton went one step further. "It is painful and embarrassing to me both as a person and a citizen to say so," he wrote, "but I cannot believe anything my government says about the *Pueblo*."

Armed with chronologies for both the Blue House raid and the *Pueblo* incident, Rusk spent the morning of January 24 on Capitol Hill briefing the members of the House Foreign Affairs Committee. The day before, he had termed the seizure "a matter of utmost gravity." Now, emerging from a conference room in the Rayburn Building, he said, "It is a very harsh act. I would not object to characterizing it as an act of war. . . . My strong advice to North Korea is to cool it."

News Secretary Christian announced that a "regular" meeting of the National Security Council would be held at one o'clock that afternoon. Reporters noted that the last such "regular" meeting had taken place nearly two months before—on November 29—and groused anew about the credibility gap. Christian emerged from the meeting to say, "We have not abandoned diplomatic efforts toward settlement of the matter. . . ."

Answers to Brynhilde Rowberg's cables requesting third country assistance were beginning to come in from around the world. Their contents were discouraging. The news from Moscow was particularly gloomy. Deputy Foreign Minister Vasily Kuznetsov had rudely dismissed Ambassador Thompson's plea for Soviet help in dealing with Pyongyang. Had the Soviets engineered the incident? No one could say for sure. At the very least, they could be expected to take full advantage of it. In a day or so, U.S. intelligence would report that dozens of Soviet technicians had flown to Wonsan and boarded the ship.

Even before their presence further complicated matters, the prospects for a U.S. military strike against North Korea had diminished considerably. Beginning on Wednesday evening, January 24, and continuing on for the next several days, the members of an informal "Planning Committee" held a series of meetings at the White House and State Department. Among those attending one or more of these sessions were Rostow, Rusk, McNamara, Wheeler, Katzenbach, U.N Ambassador Arthur J. Goldberg, General Maxwell Taylor, CIA Director Richard Helms, Deputy Secretary of Defense Paul Nitze, and Assistant Secretary of State Sam Berger. Paul C. Warnke, the Assistant Secretary of Defense for International Security Affairs, had just flown in from Okinawa. He arrived with his chief aide, Richard Steadman. Yet the man who by all accounts influenced these meetings the most held no official position at all. His name was Clark Clifford, and he was soon to become Secretary of Defense.

"If you ever get into trouble," President Johnson once told a friend, "if you ever get arrested and need somebody to help you, get ahold of Clifford." As a Navy commander in 1946, the tall, urbane attorney from St. Louis had helped President Harry S. Truman draft his State of the Union message. Columnist Drew Pearson referred to him as "a new power in President Truman's entourage," and political experts credited him as the brains behind Truman's upset victory in 1948. Even among Washington attorneys, an extraordinarily skillful breed, Clifford was *sui generis*—and not only because of his fondness for double-breasted suits. Over the years he'd represented such blue-chip firms as General Electric, RCA, Phillips Petroleum, E. I. du Pont de Nemours, Hughes Tool, and Standard Oil. He had served as John F. Kennedy's personal counsel, as well, and although he had twice declined President Johnson's request to become Attorney General, he had always been available to offer advice in a crisis.

The Planning Committee discussed a list of options which the Joint Staff—at the President's request—had compiled. The Air Force or Navy could bomb the ship, or raid Wonsan or Pyongyang, or knock out one of the larger military installations in North Korea. The Navy could shell Wonsan from outside the 12-mile line. The ROK's might be encouraged to stage a battalion-sized raid across the DMZ.

"Nobody stood up in favor of any of these proposals," Steadman remembers. "There were no lunatics at these meetings."

An air strike would be costly—"You don't fly planes over North Korea without losing planes," Warnke pointed out—and it would probably result as well in the death of the crew.

"The crew is expendable," Katzenbach said, "but you don't want to expend the lives of eighty-two men and still not accomplish anything. That would be a disaster."

Rusk and McNamara counseled moderation. So did Clifford, who pointed out that if Great Britain had been faced with this situation one hundred years ago, she would have sent in her fleet immediately. Life was so simple then—and so complicated now. The United States was so bogged down in Vietnam. How could anyone predict what the Soviet Union or Red China would do to help North Korea? Pyongyang had flouted international law; its action threatened the principle of freedom of the seas all over the world. Clifford conceded that. But his colleagues, he suggested, should stop asking, "What have we got to hit them with?" and ask instead, "What are this country's objectives?" If they decided their objective was to teach the North Koreans a lesson or to reassert the principle of freedom of the seas, well, so be it. But as far as he was concerned, nothing was more important than the safe return of the crew. A military response would not advance that objective. It would lead only to further complications, perhaps even another war.

"This was the first time I'd ever seen Clifford operate," Warnke recalls. "He was superb. I remember being struck by the fact that this was one helluva lot different than the Tonkin Gulf deliberations. Tonkin Gulf, as I understand it, the idea was that if you showed firmness, the Reds would back off. Now everyone figured this sort of approach didn't work with Asian Communists." The Planning Committee's members tabled a military response. They looked at other possibilities.

On involved placing *Banner* on station off Wonsan with an armed escort. This would demonstrate U.S. determination to continue using the high seas and prove to both the North and South Koreans that the U.S. had not been intimidated. Rostow, Nitze and Wheeler favored the idea. Katzenbach and Warnke expressed misgivings and called it "showboating." Rusk opposed it, too, "because it didn't seem to have any intelligence purpose." Clifford pointed out that it didn't further the main objective of retrieving the crew; it merely placed another ship in jeopardy. "Why," he asked, "just issue another challenge?"

Someone suggested seizing a North Korean ship—"the queen of the North Korean sardine fleet."

"Aw, come on," McNamara said.

Pyongyang had already ordered most of its vessels back into port. The ships that remained on the high seas were owned jointly with the Poles and manned by sailors from several nations. This presented legal as well as logistical problems.

A third proposal involved a salvage operation. Divers would attempt to retrieve the gear and documents which *Pueblo*'s crew had presumably thrown overboard. This would provide a logical excuse for marshaling large numbers of ships in the area; it would prove the incident had occurred in international waters, and it might give the intelligence community a better feel for the extent of its loss. The military always likes to demonstrate its capabilities, and the Joint Staff favored the idea. The Navy was sure it could come up with something. Warnke agreed, with reservations. Steadman said that if it couldn't be implemented immediately, it shouldn't be considered. Nitze and Katzenbach questioned its practicability. The waters off Wonsan were deep and, in January, very cold. Clifford thought of it as "provocative." The North Koreans could be expected to harass any such effort. It wasn't clear at the time how much there was to be salvaged. If the divers found nothing, the United States would have spent a large sum of money needlessly. Even worse, Washington's claim that it knew precisely where the ship had been captured would look rather silly.

How about blockading North Korea? This would be costly and very dangerous. Furthermore, it wouldn't be very productive. North Korea conducted most of its trade overland with the Soviet Union and China; it really wasn't vulnerable to economic sanctions. Someone suggested slapping a blockade on Wonsan alone, saying, in effect, "Until you release *Pueblo,* nothing moves." But in order to accomplish this, U.S. ships would have to move in close—within range of Russian-built Styx missiles. The idea fell of its own weight.

The discussion turned to "gambits." The Navy could scramble planes off its carriers in the Sea of Japan and give Pyongyang a case of the jitters by "spooking" its radar. Katzenbach considered the plan "ingenious" but finally agreed that "it would get you nowhere. After a while they would realize they were being spooked." The military pointed to the risks involved: There would be a possibility of air-to-air combat. Rusk and McNamara objected. So did Clifford. "I jumped on that idea with both feet," he says.

At that moment the aircraft carrier *Enterprise* lay off the South Korean coast. A Soviet intelligence ship, the *Gidrolog,* was shadowing her diligently. This gave Rostow an inspiration. Why not lure *Gidrolog* into South Korean waters and then encourage the ROK's to seize her?

"Walt was all excited about it, hopping around," Steadman recalls. "He kept referring to the 'symmetry' of this response."

Katzenbach thought this was "a nutty idea." "If you really want to escalate," he said, "that's the way to do it."

Clifford said he was "not able to see the logic" in that proposal.

Over the past several years Rusk and Rostow had disagreed occasionally over the scope of their respective roles in determining foreign policy. Both men held essentially the same view about the war in Vietnam; still, relations between them were "correct." Now the Secretary of State looked directly at Rostow. "The only symmetry," he said, "is its equal outrageousness."

Although no formal votes were taken, the Planning Committee's members had—by the end of that first round of meetings—effectively ruled out the blockade, the "spooking" proposal, and the scheme to seize a Soviet ship. The other ideas generated no real enthusiasm, but they would be considered again. "We kept them alive, I suppose, because we felt so frustrated," Katzenbach recalls. "We all thought *something* had to be done."

On Thursday, January 25, the third day of the crisis, the North Koreans instigated six clashes along the DMZ; several American soldiers were wounded. Two squadrons of MIG's flew sorties 5 miles north of the border; normally they remained at least 30 miles away. And Radio Pyongyang declared, "The criminals who encroach upon others' sovereignty . . . must receive deserving punishment . . . the Korean people . . . are completely ready to deal a hundredfold, a thousandfold retaliation. . . ."

The President listened to Clifford, who once again counseled restraint. He sought advice from his "Wise Old Men": Dean Acheson, McGeorge Bundy, and George W. Ball. He asked Ball to chair a special committee and gave him his first assignment: Find out how this incident could possibly have happened and suggest steps to prevent a similar disaster in the future. He ordered a chronology from the Pentagon and, when it arrived, called it useless. Angrily he turned to Art McCafferty and told him to compile a new one from scratch. "I figured, 'He's the President and he's up tight,'" McCafferty remembers. " 'He has to vent his spleen somewhere, and it might as well be at me.' He was in and out of the Situation Room. He'd see what there was and listen to any information we had. Then he'd express dismay, issue orders, turn and walk out."

"He wanted to do something pretty quick," another former White House aide says, "but he was in the position of not knowing, not finding anything that looked like a very good thing to do." He talked to McNamara, Rusk, Rostow, Clifford. He telephoned Sam Berger in the middle of the night. His message: Give us more ideas, more alternatives; think them out.

The United States was already flexing its muscles in the Far East. Aircraft from Hawaii, Japan, and Okinawa were flying to bases in South Korea. The Navy was assembling its task force in the Sea of Japan. By noon on Thursday, all the destroyers had left Yokosuka; the submarines had slipped away. Only one combat ship, the guided-missile cruiser *Canberra,* remained in the harbor. And she would soon be gone.

Throughout the course of the Vietnam War, the President had refrained from calling up the reserves—wary, presumably, of the political consequences. Now he activated fourteen Air National Guard units, eight Air Force Reserve units, and six Navy Reserve units—a total of 14,787 men. The call-up was the largest since the Berlin crisis of 1961, and News Secretary Christian hinted that this might be just the beginning, that Army and Marine reservists might be summoned, as well.

The President's action threw jitters into the stock market. The index on the New York exchange dropped 43 cents. Most reservists were told to report in less than twenty-four hours. In 1967 relief hurler Darold Knowles had appeared in sixty-one games for the Washington Senators. Now, as Airman First Class Knowles, he pondered his future as a typewriter jockey with the 113th Tactical Fighter Wing of the District of Columbia Air National Guard. In Frankfort, Kentucky, a thirty-seven-year-old State Senator named Richard Frymire paraphrased Abraham Lincoln. "I'm too old to cry," he said, "but it hurts too much to laugh." Caught up in the spirit of the moment, a man named Marko Jukica stepped into a recruiting booth in New York City to volunteer his services. He had experience, he said, as a gunner for the Austro-Hungarian fleet. The what? Marko Jukica was seventy-nine years old.

In retrospect, the call-up seems to have been sparked almost entirely by psychological considerations; a consequence, perhaps, of the President's desire to appear to be doing *something*. Months later, Rear Admiral Frederick H. Michaelis would assert, "Our units were recalled without deployable equipment. They were not in a position to be immediately responsive." In other words, they couldn't have gone to war for months.

On Thursday afternoon the President asked Ambassador Goldberg to request an "urgent session" of the United Nations Security Council. No one seriously expected the UN to accomplish anything. The Soviets could veto any resolution which condemned North Korea or called for the return of the ship and her crew. Still, it was a good idea to establish a strong case at the international forum.

But how strong was Washington's case? This, at first, was what worried Goldberg. He told the President that he didn't want to be in "another Bay of Pigs situation"; to assert U.S. innocence as Adlai Stevenson had done seven years before and then come to find out that the administration had not been telling him the truth. So was the Pentagon *absolutely sure* that *Pueblo* had been captured in international waters?

The answer lay in a series of "intercepts" which U.S. listening posts had just forwarded to Washington. The S01, the North Koreans' own broadcasts revealed, had radioed her position to headquarters at least a dozen times on the day of the incident. Just before noon, when she sighted *Pueblo*, her position was 39 degrees, 25 minutes north latitude and 127 degrees, 56 minutes east longitude; in other words, 15.3 miles from the island of Ung Do and 25 miles from Wonsan. Ten minutes later she added: "We have approached the target here. The name of the target is GER 1–2. Get it? GER 1–2. Did you get it? I will send it again. Our control target is GER 1–2." At 1:50 the S01 reported that she was 21.3 miles from the nearest land. "According to present instructions we will close down the radio, tie up the personnel, tow it, and enter port at Wonsan. We are on our way to boarding. We are coming in. . . ."

Reassured by these recordings Goldberg telephoned his request for a Security Council meeting to UN Secretary General U Thant and Ambassador Agha Shahi of Pakistan, the council president. Then he asked: Could he cite these intercepts as evidence in his speech? The Pentagon protested. The North Korean messages, it claimed, were highly classified. With the issue unresolved, Goldberg flew to New York to file a formal request for the council meeting.

That night the President hosted a formal dinner in honor of Vice President Hubert H. Humphrey, Chief Justice Earl Warren, and House Speaker John W. McCormack. In the East Room of the White House, Carol Lawrence and Gordon MacRae entertained guests with songs from the Broadway musical *I Do, I Do*. As the party broke up, Supreme Court Justice Abe Fortas borrowed a violin from a Marine Corps musician, tucked it under his chin, and proceeded to play *Eine Kleine Nachtmusik* by Mozart. The President led the applause.

In Moscow, Ambassador Thompson was set to make a second appeal for Soviet assistance, this time to Foreign Minister Andrei Gromyko. Even as he moved, Tass, the Soviet news agency, was denouncing President Johnson's call-up of the reserves as "a threatening act." On Capitol Hill reporters asked Dean Rusk to comment on North Korean assertions that the crew of *Pueblo* would have to be punished. "Reprehensible," Rusk replied. The escalation of words continued. "I'd select a target," South Carolina's Representative L. Mendel Rivers told United Press International. "I'd do like Truman did—let one of them disappear."

By Friday morning, January 26, Assistant Secretary of State Sam Berger had finally realized that he couldn't handle the crisis routinely from his desk in the Bureau of East Asian and Pacific Affairs. The situation was too confused; no one seemed to know what anyone else was doing. Katzenbach had urged him to establish a special task force, and he had done so, belatedly, summoning Edward Doherty, his former deputy chief of mission at the embassy in Seoul, to serve as his deputy again and calling on Ben Fleck, the "country director for South Korea," to act as his exec.

Outside the Operations Center on the seventh floor, a cafeteria-like menu board noted the "crises of the day": Peace, *Pueblo,* Czecho-slovakia. The members of the task force passed the news tickers, the "crisis clocks" on the wall (UAR-Israel, Saigon, Peking, Moscow), and the map of divided Berlin, then set up shop in a series of austere, windowless offices. They sent out a new batch of cables. One, to U.S. Ambassador Roger Tubby in Geneva, Switzerland, told him to request assistance from the International Red Cross. "We under no illusion that ICRC intervention will succeed. However. . . ."

President Johnson addressed the nation Friday afternoon. His manner was subdued; he seemed exhausted. "This week the North Koreans committed yet another wanton and aggressive act," he said. "Clearly, this cannot be accepted. . . . We shall continue to use every means available to find a proper and peaceful solution. . . . We have taken and are taking certain precautionary measures to make sure that our military forces are prepared for any contingency. . . . I hope that North Korea will recognize the gravity of the situation they have created. . . . I am confident," he concluded, "that the American people will exhibit in this crisis, as they have in other crises, determination and unity."

Even as the President spoke, Ambassador Goldberg was polishing the text of his address to the UN Security Council, trying to incorporate the flood of corrections, additions, and deletions he was receiving over the scrambler phone from Washington. His first draft hadn't mentioned the North Korean intercepts, which the Pentagon still maintained were too secret to reveal. Dissatisfied, he had talked to the President, insisted that he needed to cite this evidence to make a strong case. And the President had agreed.

Now, just after four o'clock, he entered the council chamber. Clutching a pointer, he stepped before a large map. His delivery was ineffective; he kept referring to "territorial" when he meant to say "international" waters. But there was no mistaking his tone. The seizure of *Pueblo,* he said, was "no mere incident, no case of mistaken identity, no case of mistaken location." It was "nothing less than a deliberate, premeditated armed attack on a U.S. vessel on the high seas. It is imperative that the Security Council act with the greatest urgency," he added. "This course is far more preferable to the other remedies which the charter reserves to member states. . . ." No one had to be reminded that this was a reference to article 51—the clause which grants authority, in cases of self-defense, for unilateral military action.

★ ★ ★

A U.S. task force was churning through the Sea of Japan. The flagship of the Seventh Fleet, USS *Providence,* had refueled at Subic Bay in the Philippines and then steamed north—"as fast," remembers Commander John Woodyard, "as I've ever seen that light cruiser go." Woodyard had been given the job of assigning a code name to the operation. He selected "Formation Star." "We had to be careful," he explains. "We didn't want to give anyone the impression that this was war."

No euphemism, however, could veil the fact that this was the largest task force the United States had assembled since the Cuban missile crisis of 1962. In the days and weeks to come it would include three cruisers, *Providence, Canberra,* and *Chicago;* six carriers, *Enterprise, Ranger, Yorktown, Kearsage, Coral Sea,* and *Ticonderoga;* and eighteen destroyers. It would also include *Banner.*

One evening, as *Banner* wallowed around in the cold, her skipper, Lieutenant Commander Charles Clark, saw the nuclear-powered frigate *Truxton* bearing down on him at full speed. *Truxton*'s searchlight caught *Banner* amidships; she passed 20 yards from *Banner*'s stern, then flashed a message to a nearby carrier: "I have a Soviet intelligence ship in the middle. . . ."

"Hey, *Truxton,*" the carrier said, in effect, "knock it off. That's our buddy."

Truxton's suspicions were perfectly understandable. The Soviet Union had long considered the Sea of Japan to be its special preserve, and Soviet ships were steaming south to monitor the U.S. fleet. "We had a pretty sporting time out there with the Russians," remembers Rear Admiral Horace H. (Spin) Epes, Jr., the task force's commander. The Soviets positioned their vessels—Kotlin and Kashin class destroyers, tankers, submarines, and a lone AGI—close to the American units. They illuminated each U.S. ship as it passed through the narrow Tsushima Strait. They sent aircraft overhead constantly.

"Those were Badgers," Admiral Epes adds; "some equipped just for reconnaissance and others armed with air-to-surface missiles. At first they'd just fly down to take a look. We'd intercept them, and they'd turn back. Then they started going through our formation toward the Tsushima Straits. One day they conducted thirty "raids" al all altitudes, a few as low as thirty-five or forty feet off the deck. That gave us a rather full schedule of flight operations ourselves."

The weather worsened; the temperature dropped below freezing. Near Wonsan, North Korean MIG's were still flying sorties. United States listening posts recorded their pilots' questions: Where is *Enter-*

*prise? Where is *Enterprise?* The mighty carrier was poised for any contingency. "We waited and trained," remembers her skipper, Captain—now Rear Admiral—Kent L. Lee. "We trained and waited."

"That is not my husband's voice," Rose Bucher said in San Diego after hearing a tape recording of his first confession. "It does not sound in any remote way like my husband."

Sorry, the Pentagon said. It is indeed his voice.

At General Wheeler's request, Captain Henry B. Sweitzer, the former skipper of SUBFLOTSEVEN, prepared an analysis of the *Pueblo* incident. No one, he cautioned, should pass judgment on Bucher's actions until all the facts were in, until Bucher had a chance to give his own account. Captain Charles D. Grojean submitted a paper to McNamara which made the same point. And the Chief of Naval Operations, Admiral Thomas H. Moorer, declared, "From all we know, Bucher behaved well. . . ."

Privately, the Navy was taking no chances. Toward the end of that first week, agents from the Naval Investigative Support Office (NISO) in Yokosuka rounded up Bucher's friends and subjected them to interrogation.

The sessions were held on the second floor of Building B-39A, just below the submarine sanctuary where Bucher had spent so many carefree hours. The agents played tapes of his confession and came to the point. "Most of their questions concerned Pete's sex life," one of his friends remembers. "They were really scraping the bottom of the barrel. They said, 'Can you tell the difference between a Japanese girl and a Korean? Can he?' Then they started making wild charges like, 'This girl at Ohara's says she slept with him; that girl at the Club Bamboo says so, too,' and expecting me to confirm it. I wouldn't have told them even if it was true—which I'm damn sure it wasn't."

So incensed was this officer that he took a swing at one of the agents. Another friend refused to talk. "All their questions were aimed at finding the guy guilty of something," he says. "Any answer I gave them, I was sure they'd take it in the wrong sense. They kept harping on the same theme: Was Pete a traitor? After it was over, this NISO commander sort of apologized. He said, 'We've been given this job to do by Washington, to look into this area. And everyone we've talked to has high regard for this man.' He seemed disappointed."

29

Now it was Murphy's turn. The North Koreans had thrown him into a room with three enlisted men and for the first few days merely toyed with him. He had attended a college called Principia. The last three letters of that word intrigued them: PIA—was that the same as CIA? He had spilled orange juice on his dress blues and left them in Japan to be cleaned. His captors found this very suspicious.

A short, slender junior colonel nicknamed Deputy Dawg told him to admit that *Pueblo* had intruded within the 12-mile line on at least half a dozen occasions for the purpose of spying. The "evidence" he cited was preposterous—the erroneous loran fixes which Mack and the other inexperienced navigators had written in the ship's position log. If only Murphy had thrown those charts and records over the side. But he had been convinced that they would *prove Pueblo's* innocence. Couldn't the North Koreans understand that the lines his men had drawn through those fixes meant that they were mistakes?

They made him strip to his shorts and kneel on the floor. They placed a stick behind his knees and told him to raise his hands. Deputy Dawg, Max, the interpreter, and another officer punched and kicked him repeatedly. Murphy refused to agree that *Pueblo* had intruded. His second major interrogation lasted two hours. If he admitted to the intrusions, the North Koreans promised, he could go home.

"No," he said.

They made him kneel back on the stick again, this time holding a chair above his head. They smashed him in the face and kicked him in the back until he doubled over in pain. He said he'd sign a confession. But after he staggered back to his room, he said he'd changed his mind.

The North Koreans assured him that further resistance was futile. Would he like to hear Bucher's statement? He shook his head. Then, from somewhere down the hall, he heard a tape recording. Bucher's voice? He wasn't sure. There was a "certain hollowness" to it.

He wrote his first confession on the morning of January 29. Super-C was apoplectic. Murphy wasn't "sincere"; he hadn't confessed *Pueblo*'s intrusions. Months later, in a copyrighted series of articles in the *Christian Science Monitor*, Murphy described the conversation that followed:

" 'Are you ready to die?' [Super-C asked.]

" 'Yes, sir, I am.'

" 'You know I have the authority to kill you.'

" 'Yes, sir, I'm sure you do.'

"His pistol was lying in front of him.

" 'I'll give you twenty minutes to write your will.'

" 'I've already written a will.'

"I wasn't bluffing. At that point I had lost my fear of death. And I could look him straight in the eye and tell him to shoot me. . . .' "

At eleven o'clock that night the North Koreans forced him to strip once again and squat on the floor. An officer nicknamed Solutions placed the sticks behind his knees and told him to balance on the balls of his feet. The sticks deadened circulation; his knees began to quiver. The window was open; it was snowing outside. A heavy boot smashed into his mouth and filled it with blood. Another kick split open his ear. His back and sides ached terribly. He pitched forward and lost consciousness at least six times. He remembers waking up and feeling the warmth of the blood on his shorts and the cold of the room at the same time.

The North Koreans were going to get what they wanted eventually; what was the point in holding out if the game was over? Had the others already confessed—as his captors insisted? Why should he be the last man to buckle? He raised his head and whispered that he was ready to say whatever Super-C wanted to hear.

The guards kicked him into unconsciousness again. Then they dragged him to Super-C. He couldn't control his hands. There was a constant ringing in his ears. The right side of his mouth was numb. Super-C asked him if he was ready to sign. He nodded; he couldn't talk. A major nicknamed Spot guided him back to his room and told him what phrases to use in his confession.

Steve Harris heard groaning and thumping and the guards screaming, "Bucher, Bucher." Then the guards came for him. They kicked him and slapped him and warned him he was responsible for the lives of the CT's. He agreed to confess. Schumacher tried to commit suicide by drowning himself in a bucket of water. He couldn't do it. The guards beat him, threatened him, placed bayonets at his temples. He, too, agreed to confess. "I didn't think I could resist the torture," he says, "and I didn't see any point in going through it." He tried to save the other officers. "Tim Harris is very young," he said. "He doesn't shave. He doesn't know anything. Gene Lacy doesn't know anything, either. I've never seen him out of the engineering spaces."

"Where is Washington, D.C.?" the North Koreans asked Harris one day.

"One hundred miles north of Rhode Island."

"Where is the Air Force Academy?"

"In Texas."

"On Johnson's ranch?"

"Of course."

The North Koreans seemed satisfied. They didn't beat him severely. They did, however, turn on Lacy. They flung open his door at fifteen-minute intervals and threw sticks on the floor. They made him strip and assume a squatting position. They shoved the sticks behind his knees and told him to hold a chair over his head. When they tired of beating him, they forced him to sit on a steaming radiator. He agreed to confess.

The guards had placed the enlisted men in twelve separate rooms on the third floor. They'd passed out uniforms—quilted blue pants and jackets, undershorts with drawstrings, pink socks, and green, canvas-top boots—and explained some basic rules. Whenever a guard entered their room, the men would have to spring to attention. If they stood in front of a guard, they'd have to bow their heads. They could not talk to each other in the latrine.

One morning, Communications Technician Second Class Charles W. Ayling used a small pocket comb to tap a message in Morse code on his radiator pipe. From the room next door, Lee Hayes tapped back. A crude link, but the only one available. Quickly they set up ground rules. Whoever tapped last would have to start tapping again. Ayling's call sign would be "Hi"—four dits and two dots.

"Who is this?" Ayling tapped one day.

"Lee," Hayes replied.

Silence. To Ayling, "Lee" might be Korean. Hours passed. Then Hayes tried again. "Who is the carpetbagger?"

On *Pueblo* carpetbagger was a nickname for the man who sold candy bars, the man who was now Hayes' roommate.

"Russell," Ayling replied. Communications resumed.

Russell's glasses had been smashed during the capture. He and Hayes took turns wearing the radioman's pair. Russell held a degree in psychology. They talked about brainwashing. The Koreans had said they'd be shot if they tried to look outside. But maybe a rescue team was on the way; perhaps an "agent" was attempting to signal them. Hayes parted the cloth over the window. Across a parking lot he saw a prefabricated building with an antenna on its roof. That was all. Another night, he heard a commotion: someone shouting, "Please don't hit me anymore." Standing on Russell's shoulders, he turned the transom over the door. Twenty yards away, a group of guards was pummeling Sergeant Hammond. Hayes and Russell made a pact: "Anything that happened we would tell each other right away. We would keep honest with each other."

Several months before, Don Bailey had attended the Navy's Survival, Evasion, Resistance, Escape (SERE) School, and now he told his nine roommates that fear was their only enemy. "Expect to get the hell beat out of you," he said. The guards had searched him, but they hadn't taken his pen or little address book. He thought they'd find it sooner or later, so he inked out each name. Then it occurred to him that they'd want to know why he'd done that. He ripped out the pages and chewed and swallowed them one by one.

The guards would enter Bob Chicca's room, start shivering themselves, then ask if the men were cold. Just from the way they looked at him, Chicca suspected they knew that he spoke Korean. He hadn't admitted it; he hadn't told them he'd served in South Korea. He had to find out what—if anything—his buddy, Sergeant Hammond, had said. He tapped on his radiator pipe. He heard no reply. Conditions in Chicca's room were deteriorating rapidly. He had been wounded in the thigh. Charles Crandell carried shrapnel in the leg. Steve Woelk was lying on a wooden rack, crying out in agony. His wounds had become infected; they were open and draining, and the stench was unbearable. The only man in the room who hadn't been injured was Dale Rigby, the soft-spoken Mormon from Utah.

But now the guards appeared at the door. "Rigby-baker," they said. A junior officer nicknamed Hitler told him to fill out a personal history form; Rigby said he was allowed to provide only his name, rank, and serial number. They made him kneel and hold a chair above his head.

"Sign this form."

Rigby refused. They beat him with a table leg and, when that broke, with a two-by-four. They told him that his friend Norman Spear had already signed.

"No," Rigby said. "You're giving me a line. Spear would never talk."

They pressed the muzzle of a gun against the back of his head. He heard a "click." Then they went at him again with the two-by-four.

He held out for six or seven hours and finally said he would tell them what they wanted to know, what they *already* knew, that he was a baker. He made rolls and pastries and cakes aboard ship. Why would they go to all that trouble to make him admit such things? Rigby didn't know. Did they really *care* how much money the U.S. Navy had spent every day to feed the crew of *Pueblo?* Or were they simply attempting to make him an *example?* He limped back to his room. Bruises and welts covered his body. He didn't want to talk about it, and he was glad when the others didn't ask.

A wave of terror surged through the Barn as the guards stomped into each room with personal history forms. A few of the men remembered the military Code of Conduct and wondered whether it applied in a situation like this. "Army" Canales told his roommates that he hadn't had a chance to destroy their service records. Everything the North Koreans wanted to know was in those records. So what was the point of offering resistance?

"I guess it was just a matter of pride," Bob Hammond remembers. "I was curious to see how long I could last. Eventually, they'd have to give up or kill me, one or the other." The North Koreans kicked him in the face and groin. They hit him with the two-by-four and "bounced me off the floor," and when he yelled, they shoved a towel into his mouth. They got what they wanted after six hours; they continued working on him for another thirteen.

Roy Maggard scribbled all over his form and handed it back to the guard. Then he saw what they had done to Hammond. He filled out the form.

"You are a communications technician," the North Koreans told Earl Kisler.

"No."

"You lie."

"I said I was a line-handler, that I was on the sea and anchor detail and that was my only job," Kisler recalls. "They started asking me about Florida, where I'd gone to school. I said I went down there to learn knot-tying. They slammed a folder down on the desk and started pounding on it. That was my record—*my service record*—right there in front of me." Kisler filled out the form.

The guards used clubs and whipped belt buckles across the

men's eyes and smashed chairs over their backs and made them crawl on the floor until their knees were bloody. All of the men filled out those forms and, in so doing, acknowledged to themselves as well as to others the limits of their own endurance. In the days and weeks to come, some would ask privately, plaintively, "Did I hold out long enough? Was it really that important? Am I *less of a man* because I submitted?" Now they felt only helplessness. And rage. Larry Strickland prayed for the United States to drop a nuclear bomb on North Korea. "We knew we were at ground zero," he says, "but we thought it would be worth it if we could just see that dawgone mushroom cloud." It did not occur to him that he and his shipmates would be dead before that cloud began to form.

In the Operations Center of the State Department the members of the special task force continued their frantic, round-the-clock search for a viable U.S. response. The Joint Staff was still submitting proposals for military action. Ed Doherty rewrote them to include political considerations. A young attorney named George H. Aldrich reviewed their legality. Specialists from the Bureau of I&R added the views of the intelligence community. The drafts went to Ambassador Berger, to Assistant Secretary of Defense Warnke, to Under Secretary of State Katzenbach, to the White House. The White House found flaws in all of them. Walt Rostow and his aides were on the phone constantly, demanding new ideas. Berger drove his men hard. "You could sit in a room with him," one task force member recalls, "and just feel the pressure bouncing off the walls." Doherty began to feel sharp pains in his chest. In a few days, completely exhausted, he would be taken to a hospital.

But now an event occurred which was to render the task force's plans almost irrelevant. At a banquet for some visiting Rumanians in Pyongyang's Ongynu Hall, Kim Kwang-hyop, the Secretary of the Central Committee of the Korean Workers' Party, delivered what at first seemed to be just another scathing attack against the United States.

"That the U.S. imperialists have illegally brought the *Pueblo* case to the United Nations, though there is precedent for the treatment of similar cases at the Korean Military Armistice Commission, is a premeditated intrigue for covering up the criminal act and misleading world public opinion.

"The United Nations has no right whatsoever to intervene in the internal affairs of a sovereign and independent state. . . . It is a miscalculation if the U.S. imperialists think they can solve the incident . . . by military threats or by the method of aggressive war or through illegal discussions. . . . It will be a different story if they want to solve this question by the method of the previous practice. . . ."

Berger and Doherty studied the speech as it came off the Foreign Broadcast Information Service (FBIS) ticker. ". . . there is precedent . . . similar cases . . . the method of the previous practice. . . ." This was an obvious reference to a 1964 incident involving two U.S. Army helicopter pilots who had crossed the DMZ inadvertently and been imprisoned for nearly a year. After a series of private meetings, the United States secured their release. The United States had been forced to sign a paper admitting that they had violated North Korean territory. Pyongyang was sure to demand even more damaging admissions this time. General Pak had already indicated as much in his session with Admiral Smith on January 24. But at least the North Koreans were willing to hold private talks. That was a breakthrough of sorts. Berger conferred with Katzenbach and Rusk, then sent a cable to Admiral Smith: Request a private meeting to discuss *Pueblo* as soon as possible.

Smith was gratified. "I hadn't wanted to talk much in public," he recalls. "I thought there was little useful that could be accomplished that way. What do you say to a Mongolian savage who has eighty-two of your men?" At eleven o'clock on the morning of February 2 he faced General Pak across a round table in the small building at Panmunjom normally used by the members of the Neutral Nations Supervisory Commission.

In the public meetings Pak had been vitriolic and had even threatened Smith with a guillotine. "Just wait, you will find your head chopped off." Now he was businesslike. Smith had referred to his adversary as a "propagandist, a stooge." Now he addressed him courteously as "General."

Pak insisted that the United States had committed a "criminal act" and repeated his earlier demands—the so-called "Three A's" formula, which he would cite again and again over the next several months. The United States must admit that the ship had intruded into North Korean waters for the purpose of espionage; must apologize to the North Korean government for this intrusion; must assure that this sort of thing would never happen again.

Smith denied the charges and pressed for the return of the ship and her crew. Where are the men? Who is wounded? Who is dead?

"The dead body is preserved," Pak replied. "The remaining crew members are getting on in good health without any inconveniences in their life." He refused to provide any names. The session broke up after fifty-one minutes. Smith returned to Seoul and filed his report.

"We are exploring every diplomatic move that is available to us," President Johnson assured reporters on February 3. "Practically every expert I've talked to on Korea and North Vietnam and the Communist operation, all of them, I think, without exception, believe there is a definite connection [between the seizure of the ship and the Communist Tet offensive in Vietnam]."

Some lawmakers and reporters found this logic hard to follow. So did some of the "experts" whose counsel the President had sought.

The real surprise was still to come.

On February 4, at the President's suggestion, McNamara and Rusk appeared together on *Meet the Press*.

"Does the Navy know for sure," asked Max Frankel of the New York *Times,* "that the *Pueblo* at no time entered North Korean waters?"

"No," McNamara said. "I think we cannot say beyond a shadow of a doubt that at no time during its voyage did it enter North Korean waters."

The Secretary added that he believed Commander Bucher had followed his orders, that he was sure the ship had been *seized* on the high seas. The damage had already been done. The *Times* and other papers interpreted his reply as an "admission" that the ship might have intruded, after all.

Ambassador Goldberg was furious. McNamara's statement pulled the rug out from under the U.S. position at the UN. In Seoul, Admiral Smith was unhappy, too. He knew that General Pak would be sure to mention this statement at the next private meeting. It would make his job even more difficult. And at that moment, he and his colleagues had troubles of another sort.

The South Koreans were fuming over the lack of a U.S. response to the Blue House raid. What was the sense in having an ally if that ally wouldn't help in a crisis? Washington seemed concerned only about *Pueblo*. On January 30 a South Korean Foreign Office spokesman had said it was "unthinkable" that the United States would ever conduct bilateral talks with the North Koreans. Three days later, Smith met Pak. This, the ROK's claimed, compounded the insult. The United States was negotiating on *their* soil with *their* enemy, acknowledging the existence of a regime which *they* didn't recognize.

On February 5 Defense Minister Kim Song-un called in General

Bonesteel and complained bitterly that the United States hadn't even told the ROK's about the meetings at Panmunjom. Next morning, the ROK's issued an official protest against Washington's "policy of appeasement." Bonesteel and Ambassador William Porter briefed Premier Chong Il Kwon on the status of the talks. Chong countered with a demand that the ROK's attend. The United States couldn't agree to that and still expect negotiations to succeed. On February 7 hundreds of South Korean students rallied to protest the U.S. position. Newspapers in Seoul began to clamor for war. Government leaders hinted that it might not be such a bad idea. It might give them an opportunity to "unify" the country.

Ever since the Blue House raid, the ROK's had been requesting a Presidential mission from Washington. The State Department opposed the idea. In Ambassador Porter and General Bonesteel the United States already had top-level representation in Seoul. Yet as he read the daily cables from the embassy, an affable, pipe-smoking diplomat named John E. Walsh—now Ambassador to Kuwait—realized the situation was deteriorating. A Presidential mission, he thought, might succeed in easing tensions and preventing the ROK's from launching a foolhardy strike. Katzenbach agreed. So did Rusk. But who could head such a mission? They drew up a list of six or seven candidates and—because they knew he was having trouble with an old back injury—placed the name of the man they favored somewhere in the middle. The President, as usual, selected Cyrus R. Vance.

Then fifty-one, the tall, West Virginia-born attorney had served as Deputy Secretary of Defense under Robert McNamara and had gone on to establish an extraordinary record as a Presidential emissary and troubleshooter. "Cy is one of the greatest negotiators in modern history," says his friend John Walsh, and there is much in the record to bear this out. In 1967 he shuttled between Athens, Ankara, and Nicosia in a grueling though finally successful effort to prevent war between Greece and Turkey over the island of Cyprus. Later, he would join Ambassador W. Averell Harriman in representing the United States at the Paris peace talks on Vietnam. Now he agreed to try to restrain the ROK's. Walsh would accompany him; so would a veteran Korean-speaking diplomat named Daniel A. O'Donahue.

General Bonesteel met them at Kimpo Airport on February 10 and whisked them to Eighth Army headquarters in an open helicopter. Walsh remembers sitting on the general's lap. His teeth were chattering, and he was rueing the inadequacy of his thin overcoat in keeping out the cold. The ROK reaction to their visit seemed, at first, equally chilly. The war fever had heightened. Humiliated by their government's failure to stop North Korean infiltration, the entire ROK cabinet had offered resignations. President Park Chung Hee would not be able to see the Americans right away. He was busy talking to his generals.

Vance, Walsh, and O'Donahue spent their first day in Seoul huddling with Bonesteel and Porter, requesting and receiving answers to more than one hundred questions. They met with Premier Chong Il Kwon. They attended a banquet hosted by the ROK army. "It was a long and fascinating dinner," Walsh remembers. "Everyone I talked to that night had the same story. They tied the Blue House raid and the *Pueblo* together. They said, 'We're blood brothers. When you are hurt, we are hurt,' and they meant it. They were convinced that Kim Il Sung was a bully. The only way to teach him a lesson was to belt him hard."

The ROK's began discussing military strikes. Despite their enthusiasm, the outlook was grim. They had planes at six bases, and all of these fields were "soft." The North Koreans had fifteen fields, hardened and well protected. The ROK air force was no match for North Korea's modern MIG's. Furthermore, the North Koreans had mobilized; they could go on the offensive immediately.

The sessions extended over five days and nights. Vance, Walsh, and O'Donahue pointed out that any military move would be suicidal and might even result in the loss of Seoul. They stressed that by meeting privately with the North Koreans at Panmunjom, the United States wasn't undermining its ally; the United States had a tradition of negotiating with nations or individuals it didn't recognize—the Barbary pirates, Pancho Villa—for the release of its men. They tried to persuade President Park Chung Hee that the United States was not wheeling and dealing or welching on its commitments. Then they played their trump card.

Infiltration from the North was a "manageable problem," they said. If the ROK's had the right hardware, if they adopted a "managerial concept," they could develop a system to handle it themselves. The ROK's warmed to the idea and compiled a list of requirements. The Americans balked. "That bill would have been outta sight," Walsh recalls. But the negotiations had passed their critical point. The ROK's had agreed not to march North, not to object to bilateral talks at Panmunjom. The only quibbling now was over terms. Vance said the United States would provide an additional $100,000,000 in military aid, earmarking most of the money for anti-infiltration efforts. The ROK's seemed satisfied; Vance, Walsh, and O'Donahue sped to the airport.

Although they hadn't slept in over forty hours, they still couldn't relax. The KC-135 took off and flew back toward the United States. Someone passed around a bottle of bourbon, and after a while, Walsh and O'Donahue—two ebullient Irishmen—began to sing. Vance grimaced at their efforts and went forward to try to rest. At eight o'clock on the evening of February 15, the plane touched down at Andrews Air Force Base in Maryland. On the last leg of their journey the three Americans had tried to write a full report. They hadn't been able to complete it. Their mission had been a success—they could assure the President of that. A waiting helicopter ferried them toward the White House. The President had already summoned the members of the National Security Council to the Cabinet Room. The helicopter approached its destination. Vance looked down and saw the Capitol dome, the Washington Monument, and the lights of the city strung out like pearl necklaces. They had never seemed clearer or more beautiful.

30

Bucher slowly abandoned hope that the United States would retaliate. It was too late for that. He and his men would remain in the Barn until—until when? Perhaps they would stay here forever. He had removed the long black sock from around his leg and soaked his wounds in the bucket. They were beginning to heal. He was losing weight. He couldn't eat; he couldn't sleep any more than a few hours at a time. He paced the floor. The guards had carried a stretcher down the hall and stopped in front of his door and let him look at Sergeant Hammond. A sheet covered the young Marine's face; his stomach and groin were puffed and bloody and turning blue. Bucher screamed at the guards. Why had they done this? What were they doing to the rest of his crew? No one would tell him.

He couldn't erase the memory of those bags full of classified documents, those stacks of papers on the table in that dark room. The North Koreans continued to interrogate him, but, incredibly, they didn't seem interested in this material. There was only one possible explanation. The North Koreans realized they couldn't conduct sophisticated interrogations themselves. They were waiting for help from the Russians or Red Chinese.

Yet Super-C had already hinted this was unlikely. The North Koreans, he seemed to be saying, were fiercely independent. They disliked the Russians and Chinese almost as much as they disliked Americans. Over the past several days Bucher had come to regard Super-C as a worthy adversary. The cruel, thin-lipped colonel was an excellent officer who probably would have attained the same rank in any army in the world. He was decisive, he had a fine military bearing, and he was shrewd—no doubt about that. He had read Shakespeare and seemed to know Greek and Roman mythology. Still, he seemed naïve in some respects. He hadn't noticed that Bucher had falsified his serial number in that first confession. He hadn't objected to the "lots of dollars" phrase. Bucher knew that Super-C could *force* him to say anything. Perhaps by pretending to play along he could outwit the colonel. Perhaps he could lace his confessions with so many absurdities that no one at home would believe them. He determined to try.

A dull routine began to emerge. The men woke up at six o'clock and washed in buckets of cold water. Chunky, black-haired women—the "Doughnut Dollies"—brought trays of rice and turnips to their rooms at eight in the morning, two in the afternoon, and eight at night. They seldom looked at the men, and once, when Mike O'Bannon murmured, "Thank you," they backed away and called for the guards.

February 8 was the twentieth anniversary of the founding of the Korean People's Army. The Doughnut Dollies served hard-boiled eggs and salt and milk and cake for breakfast. At lunchtime they returned with another feast: soup, duck, dried squid, rice cakes, candy, apples, powdered milk, and bottles of beer. Super-C was following the camera crews, smiling broadly. Hayes and Russell debated whether or not to drink the beer. "Oh, God," Hayes thought, "if they take a picture of this and send it home, it'll be terrible for my parents. They'll think I'm *collaborating*." They drank the beer anyway; the photographers skipped their room.

Now a guard told Hayes to walk down the hall and clean Bucher's room. Surprisingly, the guard left them alone for a minute. Little red veins streaked Bucher's eyes. His cheeks were hollow. "The CO looked terrible, very old and thin, and I could hardly recognize him," Hayes remembers. "He said we hadn't been in their territorial waters and that he'd had no choice but to do what he'd done. I said we all understood, and I told him where some of the people were in the building. He said, 'We'll get out of here yet,' and he even took a rag and tried to help me clean the light, but the guard came in and pushed him back."

Next morning Hayes and Russell drafted a note to Bucher: They had filled out personal history forms but hadn't revealed classified information. Hayes walked down the hall. The guard turned away. Bucher jammed the note in his pocket. The following afternoon the guard watched them closely. Bucher began tapping his pencil on the table. "I thought he had lost his mind," Hayes says. "Then I realized he was saying something in Morse code: 'Send me all the messages and . . .' I couldn't get the rest. The guard kept telling him to stop and asking me if he was sending a message, and I said, 'No, no, he's just very nervous,' and the guard didn't buy that at all. He grabbed the pencil, and he got so mad I thought he was going to shoot the captain." Later Hayes figured out the rest of the message: ". . . and put them under my pillow." He did not send any more notes. There wasn't anything to say.

Schumacher sat brooding in a room by himself. The guards peered through cracks in the door and at half-hour intervals flung open that door and stomped inside. He remembered that evening in New York several months before when Mike Lutin had said that something awful would happen to him. He had laughed. Everyone at the table had laughed.

At night he dreamed about fraternity parties at Trinity or debutante balls in St. Louis. He would have a few shots of Dewar's under his belt; still, he wouldn't be able to relax. He'd have to leave early and return to North Korea. Then he'd wake with a start. It was hard to dream when they kept the lights on all the time.

He leafed through the propaganda material that he'd received on February 8: a four-hundred-page collection of Kim Il Sung's works, copies of *Korea Today* magazine, and a book entitled *Fortune's Favorites*. A photograph showed two U.S. Army deserters greeting each other in Pyongyang. "What a luck," the caption read. Schumacher laughed. Then he noticed a short item about two U.S. pilots who had apparently been imprisoned in North Korea. The fact that they had been released after negotiations at Panmunjom struck him as enormously encouraging.

On February 13 guards marched the six officers and oceanographer Tuck into a large room at the end of the hall for a press conference. There were bowls of fruit and candy and cookies on the table; there were packs of Kalmaigi and Chollima cigarettes. The questions and answers had been rehearsed carefully; Bucher wasn't able to include any absurdities in his replies. Super-C thought the conference was a huge success; so did the half-dozen North Korean "reporters." Up to this point Bucher had assumed that some, perhaps all, of his officers had either been killed or had committed suicide. The sight of their faces cheered him considerably.

A few nights later, Super-C began haranguing the officers about U.S. "atrocities" during the Korean War. He took a nail and pretended to drive it into the side of his head. Tim Harris started to laugh, sending Super-C into an even more violent rage. Didn't the men understand that they could be shot as spies? Only if they were "sincere," the colonel added, his tantrum subsiding, would they ever return home.

And to prove this sincerity they would have to apologize to the North Korean government and write a petition to President Johnson.

"We cannot have any complaint even should the worst come," the apology declared. "We should be punished severely by the law of the Democratic People's Republic of Korea for our serious crimes. We may expect such a severe punishment as may deprive us of even the possibility of revival. . . ."

As Super-C dictated the letter, Bucher passed his black sapphire ring with a note to Lacy. He sent another note to Schumacher. "It didn't mention suicide," Schumacher recalls. "It was just one of those 'I don't think I'm ever going to get out of here' things. The captain said he considered himself personally responsible for Hodges' death. He wanted me to see Rose and the two boys when I got back. I figured he was thinking of cashing in the chips, so I slipped him a note which said, 'Don't do it. I tried and it didn't work.' " Lacy managed to speak to Bucher several days later and insisted he take back the ring. The captain, he said, had just as good a chance of getting out alive as anyone else in the crew.

On February 19 the officers began the petition to the President. "We have formed the opinion," it said, "that espionage such as we conducted is an unjust infringement on the sovereignty of North Korea. . . ." Colonel Scar was in charge of the effort. Super-C had left the camp. Schumacher thought he might have gone to Panmunjom.

The guards had finally allowed the men to exercise outside in the snow. One evening, before calisthenics, Bucher called them together. "I have great news for all you boys," he began. "I've just received word from the United States. . . ."

The men leaned forward expectantly.

"The Red Cross has notified me that Hagenson's wife has borne him a son. Both mother and boy are doing well. . . ."

"Yeah, that's great," Hagenson said. The men trooped outside in silence.

Super-C returned to the Barn and began berating the men whose confessions had not been "sincere." John Shilling, for example. At the mention of Shilling's name, one crew member turned around and made a wringing of the neck motion—as if to say that his stubbornness was endangering everyone else. Later, this same crew member stood up and praised the North Koreans' propaganda. "I didn't know things were that bad in the United States," he said, "or that I belonged to such a rotten country. . . ." His shipmates eyed him with disbelief. "I took off my crow [petty officer's rating] when I left the ship," this man persisted. "I ain't gonna put it back on until I leave."

Now Super-C decided that the petition to President Johnson was unsatisfactory; it would have to be rewritten. Finally, at two o'clock on the morning of February 29, the draft was deemed acceptable. It cited the six "intrusions," said the men had been treated humanely, and added that they would be released only when the United States admitted committing espionage, apologized for this "hostile act," and assured the North Koreans that it would never happen again.

Bucher did not *order* his crew to sign the petition but said he thought it would be a good idea. As Don Bailey would explain months later, "In my time in the service, whenever a CO makes a request, it's the same as an order to me." Earl Kisler thought to himself, "I sure hope the captain knows what he's doing." And Seaman Apprentice John R. Shingleton said, "If they can force the captain, of all people, to do something like this, well, they can force anybody to do anything they want them to do."

The North Koreans had finally taken Steve Woelk to a hospital. They'd marched Bob Chicca down the hall, placed him on a bare table, and operated on his thigh under a flickering light. He had received only a local anesthetic, and when the operation was over, the doctor told him to walk back to his room by himself. That had been two weeks ago. Since then, he hadn't been able to exercise outside. Still, the wound was healing nicely. He knew he'd be back in shape soon enough.

By this time, he thought, his wife had probably given birth to a child—hopefully, a son—and he was determined to see them. He began planning escape. He would slip out the window and drop to the ground. It would be fairly simple.

Two events interrupted his plans. On March 1 the captain passed word to the crew: "Hold on tight. We're going to be out of here soon. Don't abuse your privileges." Then, on the evening of March 4, a duty officer nicknamed Fetch entered his room and told him to wrap all his belongings in a blanket for "airing" outside. Even pencils and papers? Everything, Fetch said. Hours later, Fetch returned. The men were going away, he said. He didn't know where.

★   ★   ★

By March 4 the United States and North Korea had met ten times at Panmunjom. General Pak had finally provided the names of the dead and wounded. Nothing else had been settled. The United States at first had demanded the return of the ship and her crew. With an apology. The North Koreans laughed. The United States, they insisted, must "admit, apologize, assure"—accept the "Three A's" formula. Admiral Smith replied that he couldn't admit to something which his country hadn't done. He didn't regard crew members' confessions as valid. On February 16 the North Koreans presented their "evidence."

It consisted primarily of *Pueblo*'s navigational records, the logs and charts which "proved" the six intrusions. The Navy reviewed the data and said it was full of holes. One fix placed the ship 32 miles inland; another credited her with a speed of 2,500 knots. Assistant Secretary of Defense Paul C. Warnke wanted to publicize these errors and embarrass Pyongyang. So did Deputy Secretary of Defense Paul H. Nitze. Under Secretary of State Nicholas deB. Katzenbach feared that such exposure might cause the North Koreans to punish the crew. Rusk agreed with him. If the North Koreans put the men on trial, the United States would release its analysis of this evidence. Until then the best thing to do was remain quiet. Katzenbach was sure that someone in the Washington press corps—"anyone who's ever done any sailing"—would take out a pencil, plot the positions against their times, and conclude that all the intrusions were phony. No one ever did.

To a degree which puzzled Katzenbach and his colleagues, both press and public seemed ready—almost eager—to believe whatever the North Koreans said. A Los Angeles jeweler named Benjamin Ellis, the father of a *Pueblo* crew member, wrote President Johnson, "Frankly, I'm convinced that we were in their territorial waters. . . . We have to admit that we were at fault. . . ." And the St. Louis *Post-Dispatch* declared in an editorial that the crew members' joint confession had "an authentic ring to it . . . if the Administration thinks otherwise, it ought to explain why." The editorial closed on a harsh note: "The officers and crew of the ship are being denied repatriation because their own government finds it impossible to admit it was wrong."

For the past month the State Department had tried in every conceivable way to pressure Pyongyang. "If we heard of some North Korean trade delegation visiting anywhere in the world," one official remembers, "we'd ask that country to say, 'We can't deal with you until you return the *Pueblo*.' Some of those people took the North Koreans and really shook them by the lapels."

The lack of progress frustrated President Johnson. "Just about the time you'd want to go to bed, he'd pick up the phone and call down to the Situation Room," Art McCafferty remembers. "He'd ask, 'What's new on *Pueblo*? What's new on Vietnam?' Sometimes he'd add, 'I'm afraid to ask what else is going on.' I remember calling him at one o'clock one morning to say that the North Koreans had just requested another meeting at Panmunjom. He asked what we were doing about it. I said, 'Sir, I believe we're going to take care of it. It's a matter of logistics. We're going to skip a few hours and then make a counterproposal.' He really exploded. 'There are eighty-two men's lives at stake,' he said. 'Doesn't anybody in this government understand that I *mean* what I say, that we will do *anything* to get those men back—including meeting naked in the middle of the street at high noon if that's what it takes? Get State,' he told me. 'Tell them to get that meeting on the road.' "

Toward the end of February the United States proposed new terms for a settlement. Although the United States was sure that the ship had never entered North Korean waters, it was ready to submit the dispute to any impartial body—the International Court of Justice at The Hague, for example—and abide by its findings. If that body ruled in North Korea's favor, Washington was prepared to write a formal letter of apology and "do what is appropriate." Furthermore, the United States would promise that in the future its ships would not violate North Korea's claimed territorial waters.

Early in March, General Pak delivered Pyongyang's reply. The *Pueblo* affair, he said, was a matter of North Korean sovereignty. The U.S. suggestions were "outrageous."

31

The buses pulled away from the Barn and bounced toward another compound on the outskirts of Pyongyang. *Pueblo*'s officers and men filed between two marble columns and entered a grayish-white concrete barracks. It was newer and larger than the Barn. The lighting was better, the floors cleaner. On the walls in the foyer hung paintings of Kim Il Sung standing amid the wreckage of American tanks, and North Korean soldiers charging a U.S. machine-gun nest. Larry Strickland thought the building resembled a courthouse, "that we were goin' to see the judge."

Super-C entered the hall with an interpreter nicknamed Silverlips. They would remain here, he said, until the United States apologized. Guards told the men to exchange their boots for rubber-soled slippers. They led the officers upstairs to private rooms, divided the enlisted men and the civilians into groups of eight and four, and assigned them to quarters on the second and third floors. No sheets or blackout curtains covered their windows, and for the first time since their capture, they could turn off their lights at night.

No longer did they receive their meals alone in their rooms. There was a mess hall on the third floor and—directly across from it—a large room called "the Club," where they saw movies and listened to lectures. They could play ping-pong inside the building and exercise outside. They could play football and volleyball.

But most important, they could communicate, whisper among themselves and pass messages when the guards weren't looking. The chain of command, frayed by the fear and isolation of those days in the Barn, survived and grew stronger. The senior petty officer in each room was responsible for his shipmates; Hammond, the tough Marine, was put in charge of the men on the third floor. Law led the men on the second floor; soon he became responsible for all the enlisted men. Mitchell cleaned the captain's room at least twice a day. He became the liaison between the officers and the men.

From the window of his room Bucher could look out over the countryside. There seemed to be a large number of military installations nearby; hardly a day passed that he didn't see trucks or tanks on the roads. He watched the guards amusing themselves below. They practiced karate every morning, kicking wooden posts, trying to smash boards with their bare hands. They pulled the legs off birds that fell from their nests. They captured toads and split them apart. They searched the sidewalks for small, crawling creatures and tortured them with lighted cigarettes. They dug their boots into the ribs of the mangy dogs that lingered around the compound. And laughed.

Bucher was continuing the marathon sessions with Super-C which he'd begun in the Barn. The North Korean would fidget with his lighter and raise his voice from whisper to shout with no warning. He rambled for hours, discussing mythology, current world tensions, American history. The early American pioneers, he said, had committed genocide by wiping out the Indian race. Did Bucher know that? Did Bucher realize that one United States President—William Henry Harrison—had actually used a razor strop made from an Indian's skin? Was he aware that the United States had stolen its Western states from Mexico?

The American *people* were not to blame, Super-C explained. It was all the fault of the "expansionists," the "imperialists," the same bloodthirsty ruling class whose folly had lost the United States 1,200 ships during the Korean War, whose mistakes even now were responsible for the loss of 12,000 planes a day and 45,000 tanks a week in Vietnam.

Super-C always took forever to come to the point. Which seemed to be that the men of *Pueblo* were hapless victims of the "warmongers" in Washington. They could atone for their sins only if they developed a proper attitude, only if they were "sincere." Bucher still hoped for a chance to discredit North Korean propaganda. He never told the colonel directly that he would "cooperate"—such a statement might arouse too many suspicions. But he did attempt to convey this impression as often as possible.

The North Koreans wouldn't allow him to be alone with his men. He had to rely upon Mitchell to relay his instructions. He told the young seaman how he hoped to undermine the propaganda campaign. He said he didn't want anyone taking foolish risks. But he wanted his men to follow his lead and resist as best they could.

Slowly, deliberately, as much to regain their own self-respect as to

defy their captors, the men began to do just that. They lied constantly—if not consistently—during interrogations, admitting only
to information which they were sure the North Koreans already knew.
"Doc" Baldridge said that as a corpsman he was acqauinted with Doctors Casey and Kildare. Ralph McClintock explained that the members of the National Guard kept all their weapons at home. Even the
tanks? Why, yes, of course. "You want them to be safe. You don't want
anybody stealing the hubcaps."

The North Koreans told the men to write to their families and
public officials. They had to make three copies of each letter to ensure delivery; after all, didn't the CIA intercept all the mail in
America? They could not quote their captors directly, and every paragraph was scrutinized carefully, translated and retranslated over and
over again. Don Peppard sent his regards to "Garba Gefollows"
(garbage follows). Earl Kisler told his parents to say hello to Aunt
Jemima, Uncle Ben, Jack Spratt and his wife. The North Koreans,
he added, were the most congenial people he'd met since his high
school class toured St. Elizabeth's [a mental institution in Washington, D.C.] several years before. Lee Hayes said he hated the color of
his car and wanted to change it as soon as possible. His car was red.
He told Ohio Governor James Rhodes that he "prayed every morning
and prayed every night for the glorious light from home." He meant
the atomic bomb.

One morning in mid-March Schumacher got word that Super-C
wanted to see him. The colonel was in a mellow mood. "He said that
he'd already talked to the captain and Murphy," Schumacher recalls,
"and that he was very sympathetic to my position. I was very young.
I had no wife, only a girlfriend. He talked about broads. City girls
were more sophisticated and open. Country girls tended to hide their
emotions inside of them. I said, 'Yeah.' He went on like this for five
or six hours. He hated to see me get off to such a bad start in life. I
thought he was trying to make an end run on me, some kind of brainwashing appeal.

Schumacher went back to his room, composed a ten-line poem
and called it "The Captain's Lament" ("Instead of victory, sorrow
is our lot;/Trapped by the pirates of the running snot"). He made
sure that the first letter of each line spelled out the words "DPRK
EATS IT." He slipped the poem in a stack of propaganda brochures
and stepped outside to play volleyball. When he returned, it was gone.
He thought the guards had found it and waited for them to punish
him.

The guards in the Barn had been changed every two or three

weeks. Here they seemed to comprise a more permanent detachment. The men assigned them nicknames—The Bear, Stoneface, Cheeks, Foamy, and Fly—and disobeyed their commands as often as possible. "Whenever a guard said 'Open the door' or 'Close the window,' we'd shrug and pretend we didn't understand," Tim Harris remembers. "He'd start screaming, so we'd move the bed or pick up a chair and put it on the table. This used to drive them out of their skulls."

So, too, did the crew's refusal to march the way the Koreans did, swinging their arms with the fists closed, cocking their heads to the side as they turned. "Forward, march!" a guard might shout, and the men would stumble ahead, out of step in a ragged file. "Stop!" and they'd keep going. "About face!"—some would turn to the left, others to the right.

"But you are military men," a guard exclaimed one day, thoroughly exasperated. "Why you not march like soldiers?"

"We're Americans," Chicca replied. "We just don't walk like you."

"Goddamn," the guard said and left.

On March 29 a guard nicknamed Kneehigh stepped into Room 5 and shouted an order at Earl Kisler and Mike O'Bannon. They didn't understand and asked him to explain. Kneehigh began to slap his pocket and grunt like an animal. The sailors laughed in his face.

"He really blew his mind," Kisler recalls. "He took O'Bannon and me out in the hallway and had us face the wall and kicked us a few times, smacked us around. A duty officer came by and asked what was going on. We started telling him we were laughing at each other, you know, but he wouldn't buy any of that. We got dragged down in front of this officer called the Habitability Colonel. I told him it started from a misunderstanding between a guard and myself. He said, 'Which guard?' I said, 'The short one.' Boy, he hit the fan. I was calling the guard short, making fun of him because he was small. I found myself and the whole room in a pile of shit."

Kisler and his roommates lost all their privileges; they had to bow their heads in shame. As a result of their insolence, the crew would no longer be allowed to address the guards in English. They had to learn Korean. If they did not speak it correctly, they would suffer the consequences.

Three nights later, on April 1, Super-C called a meeting in the Club. The men were flouting the "Rules of Life"; they were not "sincere." The men in Room 5 had mocked the guards; they had banged on their door and rattled the lid on their teapot. No sooner had they arrived at this building than they had started a fire in their bunks. And just the other day Joe Sterling and Mike O'Bannon had compounded these felonies by accusing one of the guards of stealing their cigarettes. Did they realize the penalty for such arrogance?

Sterling and O'Bannon apologized for their crimes. But Super-C wasn't satisfied. He pounded the table and started screaming hysterically, castigating the other "ringleaders" in the crew. LaMantia, for example, who had been caught saying "goddamn" to one of the guards. He would let the offended guard practice his karate techniques on LaMantia. Bob Chicca was an "instigator"; he would be punished, too. And so would David L. Ritter, a bright but unpredictable communications technician who had apparently told one of the guards that he would kill himself before he wrote a letter home. "Give me a grenade," he had said, "and I'll do the trick."

"I understand you want to commit suicide," Super-C said. "We have plenty of hand grenades. We'd love to give you one right now. Are you ready?"

"Well, sir," Ritter said, obviously shaken, "death is a little too quick, sir."

Super-C stared at him contemptuously. Then he turned to Steve Harris. "Will you take responsibility for the actions of this man?"

"He's in my division," Harris replied. "As his senior officer, I guess I have to."

Bucher stood up. "I will take responsibility," he said. "Gladly."

The "April purge" began the next day. The guards waited for the men as they stepped into the latrine, kicking them viciously in the shins, punching them in the back, ribs and stomach, always making sure not to cause bruises which might show up in the propaganda films. One guard pummeled James Kell into semiconsciousness for the "crime" of leaving the mess hall with rice in his mouth. Another pressed the muzzle of his submachine gun between Richard Arnold's eyes and fiddled with the safety. A third—whom everyone called "the Imperialist"—beat Schumacher senseless for having a button loose on on his tunic. Schumacher, he said, was "insincere."

The men could hear the squeals of pigs being slaughtered outside. They could see compound dogs pawing at the piles of turnips and cabbages below. Soldiers sat on these cabbages and broke them apart. Then the Doughnut Dollies—Country Cousin and Native Dancer—boiled the slop into a stew and hauled it in buckets to the third floor. The men drank from these buckets and called the liquid "cream of petroleum soup." They ate small portions of rice and turnips and occasional pieces of a stinking fish which they called "sewer trout." Don Peppard found a tooth in his bowl; others found eyeballs and nails and slivers of pork fat covered with hair. Later, they ate grass.

Almost everyone had diarrhea. Some suffered from scurvy, others from pneumonia and hepatitis. Scratches became infected, and the infections spread. Steve Woelk returned from the hospital. The North Koreans had performed an operation on his thigh. He was still weak. Within two days they began to kick him again. Dale Rigby developed a rash over 90 percent of his body. The skin above his waist peeled off; ugly sores formed on his legs. The North Korean doctor wouldn't let him disrobe; the sight might "embarrass" the nurse. He prescribed a mudpack. Rigby's condition worsened. The doctor gave him a liquid ointment. That didn't help, either. Bill Scarborough's feet began to swell. The doctor tried acupuncture. He stuck four needles in one foot and three in the other.

"Doc" Baldridge asked for permission to treat his ailing shipmates. The North Koreans produced a medical dictionary and told him to prove that he was a corpsman. They interrogated him at length about his personal life: Why had he married a Japanese? Then they told him he couldn't help; he couldn't even offer advice.

Bucher was having trouble with his leg. A nurse called Little Iodine jabbed a long needle into his butt. The doctor said this was the first in a series of shots. He'd receive the last one on June 15. That was two and a half months away. Bucher's spirits sank. He begged Super-C to give his men a break, to let them, for example, celebrate Easter. Surprisingly, the colonel agreed. But only after he was convinced that Easter had no political significance, that it was simply —as one of his aides expressed it—"the anniversary of the day that Easter died."

The crew received hard-boiled eggs on Sunday, April 7. Not until much later did they discover that April 7 was Palm Sunday.

Spring came slowly, grudgingly, to Pyongyang. The snows and bitter winds subsided. The rice began to grow and peasants flooded the paddies which surrounded the compound. The duty officers passed out new uniforms: tan, four-button suits with wide lapels for the officers; gray Kim suits with Mandarin collars for the enlisted men. "We thought that after we got rid of those old horseblankets that they weren't going to beat on us anymore," Frank Ginther recalls. "It didn't make any difference to them. Their beatings just hurt a little more because we didn't have quite so much padding."

Along with their uniforms, the men received nail clippers and tiny penknives. Kisler and Strickland whittled a two-inch model of

Pueblo and used matchsticks as masts. They hid it in a toothpaste box. Scarborough found a chunk of wood and sculpted a four-cylinder engine. Peppard carved a six-inch cross. The guards found it. They threw it to the floor and stomped on it and laughed. He picked it up and repaired it. Then they took it away.

In their loneliness and misery, the men prayed. They talked about cars and sports and women. Kisler sat on his bunk and growled to simulate shifting gears. Seaman Stephen A. Ellis polished his golf swing, looking up to follow the path of the "ball" down the "fairway," mystifying the guards. Kell said he was sure that Sandy Koufax of the Los Angeles Dodgers had hurled a no-hitter against the Chicago Cubs on September 9, 1965. His roommates disagreed. It was September 12, they said.

They talked about food. Canales and Blansett, the burly engineman, planned a Mexican dinner topped off by ice-cold bottles of Coors' Beer. Law craved pork chops. Kisler wanted a glass of milk, a piece of German chocolate cake, and a peanut butter, bologna, and mayonnaise sandwich. "But after a couple of months I couldn't remember what it tasted like," he says, "or the smell."

Steve Harris remembered playing with an aluminum train on his grandmother's kitchen floor twenty-five years before. He could still see the train, feel it, hear its metallic "choo-choo." He was very depressed. He worried about Murphy, who seemed to be equally dispirited. The Koreans had just told him that his mother had died. Harris listened, sympathetically, to Murphy's stories about the failure of the family hardware business, to Murphy's account of his difficulties with Bucher. It occurred to him that he was Ed's only friend in the wardroom. Still, he wasn't going to be drawn into the trap of taking sides between the two men.

He talked to Lacy. "I'd ask him, 'What did you do today?' " he recalls, "and Gene would say, 'I started stripping down my 1937 Ford. I'll finish it tomorrow.' And he'd remember. Two or three days later he'd come back to me and say, 'It's almost done now.' "

Some of the men spoke Russian; others knew Japanese, Spanish, and German. Language classes began. Schumacher designed and built a $56,000 home. He was set to "move in" when Bucher warned him about the high property taxes. Chicca offered skin-diving lessons to Woelk. Kisler and Alexander built a 19-foot sailboat and embarked on a cruise around the world.

They talked about escape. Constantly. Kisler lay on his bunk and tried to remember plans from movies he'd seen. How had Steve McQueen broken out in *The Great Escape*? There were no motorcycles here. How about tunnels? Impractical. A man would need time to dig. He and his roommates were allowed outside only an hour or so every day, and then under close supervision. Besides, the guards occupied the building's first floor. He checked the drain pipe outside his window. It was sturdy enough. He figured out which guards were posted where and when and for how long.

Forty-four men lived on the third floor. The guards took head counts before each meal and every morning and evening. They made unscheduled checks throughout the night. Stuffing a dummy under the covers à la Hollywood—that wouldn't work. When the guards came into his room, they counted eight cots, eight warm bodies. The best time to go was between ten o'clock and midnight. He peered out the window and saw those mountains 25 miles away. Some days, they looked so close. There was an irrigation ditch off to the right of the compound. A man could beat feet along that and make it to the foothills of the mountains in a few hours. But what then? Kisler decided the smartest plan was to set out for the Russian border 300 miles to the north. No one would ever expect him to do that. Timing was everything. He would have to wait until the right moment.

Scarborough, Berens, and Layton noticed the power lines outside and guessed that they led to a dam. If they could slip away from the compound, they'd reach the dam and follow the river to the sea. There they'd steal a boat. Scarborough stole food from the mess hall, hid it in his socks, and brought it back to the room. Berens confiscated a straight-edge razor from a duty officer's desk. They, too, were waiting for the proper moment.

Of all the men who plotted escape—and everyone seemed to have a different plan—the most persistent was Chicca. He had been to Korea before, and he spoke the language. He knew survival techniques. The North Koreans had placed Hammond in the same room in this second building. That was a stroke of luck. "He was the first one I approached, and he was all for it," Chicca remembers. "I knew that the first escape attempt had the best chance and that the guys who stayed behind would really be in for some trouble. I was going to take everyone in our room except for Don McClarren and Steve Woelk. McClarren loved to harass the North Koreans, but he was nervous and high-strung. Woelk had been injured pretty seriously, and we needed able-bodied men."

There were two guards on each floor every night. There was a guardpost at the main gate, and others were scattered around the perimeter. There were roving patrols. He wouldn't be able to wear his shoes, which were kept on the first floor. He and the others would slip out the window on a rainy, foggy night. He felt sure they could drop to the ground, evade the guards, and reach the mountains before sunrise. If there was trouble, they'd split up. He'd take one group; Hammond would take the other.

Chicca thought of taking along one of the duty officers. Bloke, perhaps, who spoke with a British accent. Or Fetch, who had this extraordinary interest in sex. He would come into the room and ask for the names of the male and female reproductive organs. Then, grinning self-consciously, he would say, 'How you spell, huh? How you spell, huh?' Someday, he added, when Korea was finally unified under Kim Il Sung, he would go to Hawaii. There he would find "bikinis" and "boobs" and "piece of tail." Fetch always giggled when he said "piece of tail." Chicca wondered what Fetch would say if they told him about their scheme, requested his help, and offered him a girl in return. Then he dismissed the idea. It was much too risky. His only hope was to stick to the original plan. He decided to go in May—time enough for warm weather to melt the snow in the mountains, time for the wound in his thigh to heal completely. He'd need provisions and a map. He and his roommates began to save small portions of rice.

For the first three weeks of their stay in this second building, the officers had been allowed to eat in the mess hall with the crew. Then Super-C had decided that they should dine separately. One evening in April, after a supper of "worms and germs" in their makeshift wardroom, Schumacher told Bucher that Chicca was planning to escape.

Bucher was perturbed. It seemed clear to him that any attempt involving as many as half a dozen men was doomed in advance. Any Caucasian would be spotted immediately. He suggested sending Pepe Garcia, the Filipino storekeeper, to the DMZ. Chicca and Hammond, he said, could teach him to speak Korean before he left.

Schumacher argued that Hammond was a far better candidate. He was small and tough. He could darken his face; he already knew the language.

Lacy said he'd noticed that small planes flew over the compound almost every day. There had to be an airfield nearby. Tim Harris had spent some time at flight school. Perhaps he could hijack one of those planes and fly it to South Korea. Harris said he was willing to try.

Steve Harris thought Bucher's plan was impractical. He was dubious about the others. If they were patient, he said, the United States would find a way to engineer their release. Murphy agreed. He said he opposed the "useless sacrifice of life."

Bucher appointed an escape committee. Schumacher would be in charge; Tim Harris and Lacy would assist him. "We didn't want to be planning to spring one or two men," Schumacher says, "and then find out that someone else was just about to sneak out the other end of the building. At the same time we decided there was a danger if too many people knew about the committee. We decided not to tell everyone what we were doing."

A few nights later, on April 20, Super-C called another meeting in the Club. The Reverend Martin Luther King, Jr., had been shot down, he said—on the orders of President Johnson. Riots flared in every major American city. The United States was losing the war in Vietnam; the dollar was doomed. He rambled on and on: President Johnson had called up the reserves in the days after *Pueblo*'s capture. He had taken the case to the UN Security Council. The Seventh Fleet had been steaming about in the Sea of Japan. The United States and North Korea were holding talks at Panmunjom. . . .

Negotiations: This was tremendous news. Schumacher had no illusions about immediate results, but at least there was a dialogue. This took some of the steam out of the escape committee. Why risk being shot if repatriation was near? Chicca decided to postpone his attempt to the start of the monsoon season in August or September. Enough time for the crops to grow and provide cover. Enough time to judge if these talks were serious.

For the past few weeks the men had seen movies every Friday night. Some extolled North Korean industry, which was growing at the speed of a *chollima,* or flying horse. Others celebrated North Korean "victories" in battles against "the United States imperialist aggressor armies" or followed the fortunes of the North Korean soccer team (which lost to Britain, an interpreter explained, only because the referees were "Israeli expansionists"). There were "feature films," with snappy titles, as well—*The Girl from Diamond Mountain,* for example. The plot was always the same: A lowly bus driver or mechanic felt so indebted to Kim Il Sung—"the peerless patriot national hero ever-victorious iron-willed genius commander"—that he gladly worked overtime. And the dialogue was predictable:

Grandfather: "What do you want to do when you grow up?"
Child: "I want to kill an American."

Toward the end of April the North Koreans supplemented these movies with formal lectures on the glories of socialism. Junior Colonel Specs and Senior Majors Possum and Robot led the discussions. The steady diet of propaganda infuriated Lee Hayes. If there were only some way to find out the truth. Suddenly, he had an idea. Why not build a radio, a simple receiver to pick up broadcasts from Seoul or

Tokyo? As a boy in Ohio he had built several crude sets; he was sure he could find the parts. He drew a schematic and told his roommates what he needed.

Someone discovered a razor blade under a seat in the Club. That would serve as a detector. Someone else suggested using the foil from a pack of cigarettes as the diaphragm. Law found a coil of wire to activate the diaphragm. The two interpreters, Captain Nice and Captain Queer, always used microphones to translate the movies. And in those microphones were tiny transistors. Hayes was sure he could steal one of them and use it as a speaker. He had no trouble finding nails for the voice coil in that speaker. But how could he magnetize them?

Up to this point he had planned to use a loop-wire directional antenna. Functional enough, but difficult to conceal. Outside Chicca's room, though, was a wire which led to an antenna on the roof. If he could tap into that, he wouldn't need the cumbersome device. Two or three weeks after beginning work on the radio, Hayes began to transfer all his components to the men in Room 6. Communications Technician Third Class Angelo S. Strano was competent. So was Chicca. They could finish the job.

Hayes had another motive, as well, for this move. One man in his room, the same man who had praised the North Korean propaganda several months earlier, was becoming increasingly nervous. He quaked whenever the guards approached him. Hayes thought this man would say anything to save his own skin.

32

These men are not, nor will they become forgotten men.
—G. McMurtrie Godley, Deputy Assistant Secretary of State, in a
letter to the parents of *Pueblo* crewman Richard Arnold

★　　★　　★

At the State Department the crisis atmosphere had subsided. The
special task force had moved downstairs, away from the Operations
Center. Assistant Secretary Berger had left to become the deputy
United States ambassador to South Vietnam, and in his place Rusk
had appointed another former envoy to Seoul named Winthrop
G. Brown. The contrast between the two men couldn't have been
more pronounced. Berger was short, dynamic, abrasive. Brown was
tall, white-haired, courtly. He smoked a pipe and resembled no one
quite so much as the archetypal custodian of a Boston bank vault.
Because he suffered from Parkinson's disease, his doctors had ordered
him to play golf and tennis. He had, from all reports, developed a
wicked backhand.

Joseph A. Yager, the vice-chairman of the department's policy
planning council, replaced the ailing Ed Doherty. Ben Fleck, the
"country director" for South Korea, was set to take a year's sabbatical
at the National War College; a specialist named James F. Leonard from
the Bureau of I&R prepared to fill his post.

At Panmunjom, Admiral Smith was nearing the end of his six-
month tour. He would go on to a comfy command in San Diego and
receive that coveted third star. To succeed him Rusk and Brown selected an extraordinarily competent Army major general named Gilbert
H. Woodward. A stocky, beetle-browed armor commander who still

retained the diphthong ("aoot" for "out," "knee-u" for "knew") of his native tidewater Virginia, Woodward had taught political science at West Point and assisted John McCloy in sensitive NATO negotiations. In late April he flew to South Korea.

"Admiral Smith was always worried about what Pak was going to say," remembers Colonel John P. Lucas, the secretary of the Military Armistice Commission. "He was afraid the North Koreans would do something he hadn't planned for, and he kinda let it get under his skin. Woodward was very calm and straightforward. He said it didn't matter what Pak said or did. He wasn't going to take guff from anyone."

On April 22, in response to Pak's request for a summary of the United States' position, Admiral Smith had handed him a paper which said that if, in the course of her voyage, *Pueblo* had intruded into waters claimed by North Korea, the United States would take "appropriate" action. The United States would also promise to keep its ships outside the 12-mile line in the future. In other words, verification of what the United States had already offered orally. Pak scoffed at this. So Smith, in turn, asked him to put his demands in writing.

And on May 8, at the sixteenth private meeting between the two countries, Pak complied. He gave General Woodward a document which, in substance, wouldn't change over the next several months. It cited the "Three A's" as the only basis for a settlement and went on to denounce the United States for a whole host of "crimes." "It was fantastic, completely unacceptable," Woodward says. "You couldn't even get started with that thing." He relayed it to Washington.

"Our reaction was one of horror," the State Department's James Leonard recalls. "It was a bitter pill. But no one could exclude the possibility that we might have to swallow it." There was no point in trying to edit the paper. If the United States did that, it would become, in effect, an *American* document. Besides, the North Koreans would probably disapprove even the slightest changes.

So the question came down to what to do with the May 8 proposal. "My feeling was that we ought to sign it and sign it quickly," says Assistant Secretary of Defense Paul Warnke. "I thought it was so outrageous that you *could* sign it. I felt we were taking a worse beating by keeping those men over there than we ever would by signing something right away, undergoing some momentary pain and getting them back."

Some State Department officials, Katzenbach, for example, agreed with him. Others maintained that signing a document like that would not only cause an uproar at home but also damage United States credibility around the world—particularly in Seoul. "The ROK's were enraged at us anyway," Joseph Yager says. "If we had signed that thing, they would have blown their stacks."

"If you sign the document," General Pak had said at one point, "then we can *talk* about the release of the crew." Another time he had seemed more conciliatory: Once the United States met his conditions, there would be "no obstacle" to prompt repatriation. But there was still no clear commitment that even if General Woodward affixed his signature, the North Koreans would produce the crew. The May 8 paper might be a trap. Rusk opposed signing it. So did Rostow. The President settled the argument. "I don't want that," he said.

"We had no instructions from LBJ to indicate any willingness to apologize," says State Department attorney George Aldrich. "So we were in somewhat of a bind. We had to keep the negotiations going without really advancing anything substantive." Several years before, in securing the release of those two Army helicopter pilots who had strayed across the DMZ, the State Department had used a technique called the "overwrite." The North Koreans had submitted their list of accusations. The senior United States negotiator at the time—Air Force Major General Cecil E. Combs—wrote on the bottom of that paper, "I hereby acknowledge receipt of. . . ." Both countries seemed satisfied. The North Koreans claimed that Combs' signature constituted an admission of guilt. The United States insisted that he had merely signed a "receipt" on a paper whose contents were "meaningless." For the past few months the State Department had thought of this device as a contingency plan: If Pak, for example, had suddenly produced the crew at Panmunjom and demanded something in return, Admiral Smith would have been authorized to sign a similar receipt. Now this device became a positive offer.

On May 28 the two sides met again at Panmunjom. Woodward tendered his offer. Pak was noncommittal. The talks dragged on into June without result. The two negotiators would enter the small hut and take their places at the table without acknowledging each other's presence. Occasionally, Woodward would nod. "He'd nod back," the general recalls, "but he didn't like it." Woodward began receiving large boxes full of Biblical treatises from a woman in California who wanted him to try to convert Pak to Christianity. "I didn't know what the hell to do with them," he remembers. He kept pressing: Could crew members receive mail from their families? Was the crew in good health?

"Pak never answered me directly," the general says. "He'd ask, 'Why are you concerned about the condition of the men? The crew is normal.' He had certain things he was allowed to say, and beyond that, he wasn't forthcoming at all. I tried to discuss this up one side and down the other so the people in Washington could get the full flavor of our talks."

As they reviewed the transcripts, State Department officials kept harking back to a disturbing possibility. "We thought that if we were as devious as the North Koreans, we would pull a nasty trick," remembers George Aldrich, "and the nastiest trick we could think of would be to release the men in driblets." Quickly, they pored over contingency plans. If Pak offered to return only the officers and the two civilian oceanographers, the United States would refuse. If he volunteered to free the enlisted men and keep the others, the United States would accept—under protest. But what if he proposed turning loose half the crew, say forty-one men?

"We were wringing our hands on that one," James Leonard says. "The men who stayed behind would be hostages for North Korea's lies, and we knew we couldn't bottle up the truth forever. It was a nightmare."

★   ★   ★

The shock and worry Rose Bucher had felt at the news of her husband's capture had hardly been cushioned by the mimeographed form which she'd received from the Navy. "The USS *Pueblo*, to which your husband is assigned," it began, "has been boarded by military forces of North Korea while the ship was operating in international waters. The Department of Defense has announced that *Pueblo* is a Navy Intelligence Collection Auxiliary Ship. That is all that should be said about the mission of the ship or your husband's duties. You may be assured that every effort is being made to effect the release of all persons on *Pueblo*. Your anxiety in this situation is understood and when further information is available, you will be promptly notified. . . ."

There it was—one sheet of paper: cold, impersonal. But she'd received scores of comforting telephone calls from officers and men who'd served with Pete on one boat or another. Chuck Clark, for example, had phoned from Japan. The CNO himself, Admiral Thomas H. Moorer, had called from the Pentagon. Idaho Senator Frank Church had pledged his support. Her attorney, E. Miles Harvey, offered advice on dealing with the press. Lieutenant Commander Allen P. Hemphill had been enormously helpful; so had his wife, Jean, and for the first several weeks Rose had assumed that someone in Washington, someone much wiser than she, would develop a formula to bring the men home soon.

"The service always takes care of its own"—as long as Pete had served in the Navy, she had accepted this aphorism as an article of faith. Now she began to wonder. No one had said anything harsh to her directly, yet she couldn't help sensing that the admirals in Washington had passed judgment on her husband and found him guilty. She couldn't help feeling that she was receiving an official cold shoulder.

The tip-off came when she tried to send Easter cards to the wives and families of the crew. As the commanding officer's wife, this was her unwritten obligation. Besides, she wanted to boost their morale. But the Navy wouldn't supply their addresses. "We have found that it is difficult and not entirely useful," explained a captain named James G. Andrews, "to correspond with individuals who are not in sympathy with the Administration or who are looking for a target on whom to vent their frustration. You might inadvertently encourage that type of correspondence. . . ."

Late in March she and the boys moved out of the Bahia Motor Hotel and settled in a ranch-type house in the San Diego suburb of Pacific Beach. She had received one letter from Pete filled with propaganda clichés. Father Wegner at Boys Town received one, too, and called her about it immediately. Then an envelope arrived addressed to Michael and Mark. "As you know, sons," it began, "I am a naval officer and was captain of the USS *Pueblo*. Well, *Pueblo* was a spy ship. . . ." She decided not to show them that.

She telephoned a Navy captain named James O. Mayo, then serving as a liaison officer at the State Department, and pressed him for information. A highly respected aviator—now skipper of the aircraft carrier *Franklin D. Roosevelt*—Mayo allegedly became incensed at these interruptions and, according to her copyrighted article in *McCall's* magazine, once brushed her off by saying, "If you were my wife, I'd like you to get yourself into a nice rocking chair by a quiet lake and stop asking questions."

Most people who knew Rose Bucher prior to the incident assumed she'd do just that. She seemed the typical Navy wife: solid, unspectacular, not a complainer at all. "Her greatest worry in those days was whether or not her son got to pitch in the Little League game," says one commander's wife, a friend from the years in Japan. "But the Navy didn't give her the right time of day when she needed it. She really got her dander up about that. Her whole personality seemed to change."

Few couples encouraged or influenced her more than Allen and Jean Hemphill. Allen, a pudgy, curly-haired officer, had first met Bucher while serving aboard *Ronquil*. They shared an interest in conservative politics and the Gospel according to William F. Buckley, Jr., Jean Hemphill, a plump, bespectacled woman, had long been associated with Republican women's groups. "Jean is a right-wing reactionary extremist," her husband says, grinning; "well to the left of me."

"The three of us became a very close unit," Jean recalls. "Rose was getting mail from everywhere inviting her to make personal appearances. She was so totally shy at first that I started speaking for her myself. I don't think she made a move that wasn't discussed or completely thought out in advance." Suddenly, the reticent housewife became a celebrity. She appeared on network television and talk shows in Southern California. She flew to Chicago and conferred with W. Carleton Voltz, one of the helicopter pilots who had been imprisoned in North Korea. She sent out letters emblazoned with slogans: "Remember the *Pueblo*" and "Let's Rescue the *Pueblo* Crew —Write Your Congressman—Demand Their Release!" She began to make speeches herself, criticizing the administration.

One afternoon in April, after a meeting at her home, some friends decided to form a Remember the *Pueblo* Committee. They ordered thousands of bumper stickers and in May sponsored a fund-raising luncheon. The head of that committee, a La Jolla woman named Barbara Norris, asked ten housewives if they'd each agree to answer ten letters. One hundred letters grew to one thousand and then to ten thousand, and many came back with money inside.

The flood of activity drew some criticism. Mrs. Norris was unperturbed. "There was a left-wing vilification campaign against Rose," she remembers. "Little Communist cells going into operation."

The San Diego newspapers reminded readers every day of the time which had elapsed since the ship's capture. A Chamber of Commerce official, Richard Brady, helped form something called the Release the *Pueblo* Committee. ("They worked with billboards mostly and only got out five thousand bumper stickers," Mrs. Norris explains; "We got out one hundred thousand."). A fourteen-year-old high school girl named Marcee Rethwish organized a prayer meeting at the Balboa Organ Pavilion; one thousand five hundred people attended. She spent her baby-sitting money on *Pueblo* buttons and planned further prayer meetings. "I thought the men of the *Pueblo* needed God and country," she says, "and they didn't seem to have either one."

What they did have, of course, was more committees—hundreds

of them across the country, all competing with each other for attention. And no one seemed to pause long enough to say, "How very odd: this massive display of drum-beating, flag-waving support for an officer who surrendered his ship without even firing a single shot; for eighty-two men whose confessions castigated their country." The winner in this battle of the press releases had no connection with Rose Bucher, Jean Hemphill, Barbara Norris, or any of her clubwomen friends in San Diego County. This was the *National* Remember the *Pueblo* Committee of Prospect Heights, Illinois, and within a few months after its formation in May, it would claim between eight hundred and nine hundred chapters in forty-one states and several foreign countries.

Its founder and chairman was the Reverend Paul D. Lindstrom, a twenty-nine-year-old graduate of the University of Illinois who seemed to have an uncanny flair for publicity. Several years earlier he had established the Church of Christian Liberty, and the endeavor proved so successful that he promptly set up two more churches, as well as something called the Christian Liberty Forum. According to the Chicago *Sun-Times,* six of the church's trustees were —or are—members of the John Birch Society. Lindstrom's press kit says only that the church is dedicated to "combating socialism, Godless communism and all forms of collectivist tyranny." Included in that kit is a small brochure entitled, "Why not start your own religion?"

Although Lindstrom claimed that there was "no official connection between the church and the *Pueblo* committee," he identified himself as a clergyman when he discussed the ship and thereby received more attention than he might normally have gleaned. "We had a Biblical responsibility," he says, "to do something more than just pray."

The "liberals" in the Johnson administration have thwarted all attempts to free the ship and her crew, he declared. The State Department was following "a policy of appeasement." "Talk has been fruitless. The big stick is necessary. We will only get the olive branches of peace by using the sword of power." At a June press conference in Chicago's Sheraton-Blackstone Hotel, Lindstrom said the United States should rescue the crew immediately. "Even if this means war, we should do it; even if we have to take over all of North Korea."

33

For almost two hours every night and most of the day on Sunday, Bucher and Schumacher played chess. The captain favored "cut and slash" tactics which, on occasion, were devastatingly successful. "I remember thinking how it fit his personality beautifully," Schumacher says. "He was the man of action. There was none of this 'sit-back-and think-it-out' business. I beat him bad one Sunday morning, really clobbered his ass. What I had done was set up a special cut and slash defense. He never saw it. It took him six games to figure it out."

Toward the end of May, Super-C allowed all six officers to get together for cards. Bucher and Schumacher challenged Steve Harris and Murphy at bridge. The stakes would be low—one-tenth of a cent a point. Harris objected. So did Murphy, more vehemently.

"What the hell," Bucher said. "You're gonna get hazardous duty pay. And it's tax-free. You can afford it."

Murphy said the money didn't matter. He didn't believe in gambling.

Bucher shook his head. Murphy was such an old lady about some things. And such a child about others. He'd sit at his table during the day and fly paper airplanes around the room. Take Steve Harris. Bucher could understand him. Steve would talk about one of the duty officers and say, "Well, the next time that guy comes into my room, I'm gonna kick him in the shins, punch him in the nose." After a while it got to be sort of a joke. But the important thing was that Steve realized this and went along with it.

What irked Bucher, and Schumacher, too, was Murphy's attitude of moral superiority. He didn't smoke; he didn't drink; he didn't gamble. He never came right out and flaunted these virtues in your face, but you couldn't help feeling that he was forever aware of them, forever measuring you against his standards, finding you wanting and drawing comfort from that. Perhaps this was unfair; perhaps he wasn't thinking these things at all. You couldn't tell. Murphy was so private, so mysterious.

Early one evening Schumacher stepped into Murphy's room and saw a copy of a book entitled *Korea—1964*. Unlike the propaganda which he'd been given to read himself, this was filled with facts and figures. Furthermore, it contained a detailed map of the country, an essential tool for planning escape. Schumacher wanted to pass it on to Chicca and asked if he could borrow it. "I'm not quite finished with it yet," Murphy said. Schumacher didn't get the book for another ten days.

Steve Harris still thought an escape attempt might not be necessary, that the United States would succeed in its efforts at Panmunjom. And when that happened, when the crew finally came home, Congress would begin a probe of the whole affair. The others disagreed. They said the Navy would investigate but doubted that Congress would get involved. The conversation turned to all the things that had gone wrong prior to the incident. How would they handle them in their testimony?

Harris began to criticize Murphy for not cracking down on Armando Canales, for not making sure that the yeoman sent out his reports on time, for not doing *something* about the ship's office. And Murphy kept saying that no, this wasn't his fault, and no, that wasn't his fault, either. Harris leaned across the table. "None of this would have happened," he said, "if you'd had any backbone."

Murphy was too stunned to reply. Bucher and Schumacher stared at Harris in amazement. A few days later, Bucher congratulated him. "I guess Pete thought that he'd found an ally," Harris remembers. "I felt kinda funny being congratulated for belittling someone else."

On May 29 Super-C called another meeting in the Club. He entered the room with his customary flourish and seemed to be in a jocular mood. The men would have to prove their "sincerity," he said, by volunteering for work details. But what kind of work could they do?

Bucher pointed out that he was a professional sea captain. "I'd like to take some of the fishing boats and . . ."

"Under no circumstances," Super-C said.

Friar Tuck said that he had spent six years as an Army officer; he was qualified to drive a tank. Someone else volunteered to fly a plane. Tim Harris said he could become a carpenter. And Stu Russell, the psychology major from USC, declared, "I'm a draftsman, an architect. I can design things."

"What things?"

"Anything," Russell said.

"Well, you could design a new barracks for yourself, and Ensign Harris could build it."

"I'm sure I could design anything that Mr. Harris was capable of building," Russell replied. Laughter.

A few weeks earlier, right after Palm Sunday, Bucher had prepared a list of eighty-odd "traditional American holidays" and asked Super-C to consider granting them to the crew. Included among them were Sadie Hawkins Day, Alf Landon Concession Day, and Max Goulis Day—in honor of the first garbage collector in Omaha, Nebraska.

Super-C had ignored his request. Now Bucher sensed an opportunity to capitalize on the colonel's obvious good humor. He rose to offer a "point of information." Tomorrow, he said, was Memorial Day, one of the most important and traditional holidays of the year.

A scowl furrowed Super-C's brow. He banged his lighter on the desk and began screaming invectives. Silverlips, his interpreter, began screaming, too. "You mean you expect we would give you time to honor the imperialist aggressor forces who killed our women and children in war?"

Bucher tried to explain. But the damage had already been done. Super-C stormed out of the Club. For the rest of their detention, the men would not receive another holiday.

But now there was a change in the daily routine. The men got up at five o'clock in the morning and ate their meals at seven, noon, and seven at night. The food still consisted of turnips and rice and "greens." Harry Lewis the cook from Long Island, estimated the daily intake at no more than 500 calories. The men continued to lose weight. They developed new sores and boils and rashes over their bodies.

June was hot and dry. Rats scampered through the building. In Room 2 on the second floor, Peter Langenberg was trying to fend off the cockroaches. He squashed them under copies of Kim Il Sung's works and the English-language Pyongyang *Times*. The guards passed out "fly-flappers." In Room 6 on the third floor, Bob Chicca and Rodney Duke killed seventy-five flies in one hour. Norman Spear decided that the housefly was "the national bird of Korea."

From time to time, the men pulled up weeds and cut the grass around the building with their tiny penknives. They jogged on the track, played basketball, and converted a volleyball into a football. Injuries multiplied. Rizalino Aluague, the Filipino steward, fractured his kneecap on the basketball court. Schumacher ran into Sterling one day and broke his nose. Hayes and Russell argued constantly over sharing their one pair of glasses. Hammond, Chicca, Strano, and Duke quarreled about religion and started a water fight. Ayling wouldn't stop talking about rapid transit systems. Blansett, the chunky engineman, became so exasperated by this that he lunged at Ayling one day and grabbed him by the throat.

The North Koreans had expressed great concern for the potted plants which they'd set in every room. Tim Harris urinated in his plant every day. So did Gene Lacy. Schumacher tried a different method. "I managed to kill three of these plants by tying knots in their vines," he remembers. "So one day they brought me a new one. It was two or three feet tall with long, rubbery leaves, and it was full of bugs and flies. They said, 'Put water on it; put water on it,' so I really drowned it. Then I went after the bugs and flies with a towel and knocked off all the leaves. I killed it; I chopped it apart."

In Room 6 on the third floor, Angelo Strano was trying to complete the radio. He still hadn't been able to magnetize a nail for the voice coil in the speaker. One attempt had succeeded only in causing the compound's lights to flicker and sending the guards scurrying every which way to find the faulty fuse. Strano wasn't discouraged. A few more weeks and he'd have all the parts. Maybe he could steal a battery; that would improve reception 100 percent.

Chicca was running every day and by this time had regained full use of his leg. He studied the map of North Korea which Schumacher had sent him. This camp was 80 miles north of the DMZ, 30 miles from the west coast, and 130 miles from the east coast. The DMZ was mountainous and patrolled frequently. The west coast was heavily fortified. The route the Koreans would least suspect had to be to the east coast. The duty officers kept dropping hints of progress at Panmunjom. But maybe they were saying this just to keep the crew in line. He would wait a few more weeks—until the start of the monsoon. He realized that his captors considered him a troublemaker; if his attempt was to stand a chance of success, he'd have to appear "sincere" and not provoke them in any way. As hard as he tried, however, he couldn't rid himself of the paralyzing notion that they already knew what he was planning. He had no proof of this. But how else could he explain those sharp accusations against him for "crimes" he hadn't committed or that totally unwarranted beating which Cheeks had just given him? Perhaps he was just nervous, on edge. Of course the Koreans didn't know. How could they?

But then, at a meeting in the Club on June 27, an incident occurred which compounded his fears. Super-C began by requesting the crew's "impressions" of the propaganda movies, then asking, "How is your life these days?" He went on to discuss the number of calories a man needed to stay alive. The Americans, he said, were receiving 800 grams of rice a day, and this was more than the average Korean ever got. Suddenly, he turned to Chicca. "What do you think of that?"

The young Marine suppressed a grin. "I'm very grateful," he said. "I think it's fine."

Silverlips didn't translate the first part of his answer. Super-C apparently thought Chicca was insulting him.

"You are insincere," he shouted, banging his lighter on the desk. "You do not appreciate humanitarian treatment. You will be punished." The duty officers in the Club were screaming hysterically, too, and Chicca felt his knees begin to quaver.

"What do you mean by such behavior?" Super-C was waving his arms, pointing to other members of the crew, ordering them to explain why Chicca was so ungrateful.

Steve Harris stood up in Chicca's defense. He had noticed on the ship that Chicca was always smiling, he said. This was just his way. He wasn't being insincere. Hammond agreed. Super-C shouted them down. Finally, the men began to understand what he wanted. "Chicca's a bad man," a voice in the back of the Club called out. "He's insincere," someone else said.

Gradually, the colonel's anger subsided. He had, he said, some very important news for the crew. He pulled some papers from a black leather briefcase and adjusted his glasses. Negotiations at Panmunjom, he read, had been stalled by the refusal of the U.S. government to accept North Korea's "just demands." Some prominent Americans had realized this, however, and formed committees to oppose the State Department's policies. A Reverend Lindstrom was active in the Chicago area, while in California, Mrs. Bucher—he called her "Madam Rose"—was busy making speeches against the administration.

Bucher's head slumped against his chest. He began to sob, quietly at first, then openly, unashamedly. In all these months of captivity, this was the first news he'd received about his family. He had thought about them so often, trying to imagine the problems, the stresses they must be going through at home; trying finally, reluctantly, to force those worries out of his mind before they enveloped him in a web of despair. And now to hear something like this. It was overwhelming. The room was still. He got to his feet and blinked and tried to speak. The words came slowly, painfully. "I want . . . to apologize to you . . ."—he turned and faced the crew—". . . to all of you . . . for losing . . . control. . . ."

Bucher's health was deteriorating. He had lost nearly 80 pounds. The nerves in his legs were giving him trouble, and dysentery clutched at his innards. McClintock saw him collapse one day in the head and dragged him, unconscious, back to his room. He would not eat. He would not speak to anyone. He marched out to calisthenics with his head down, his arms at his sides, and his fists clenched. The officers always formed a small circle for their exercises. And he always led. But now he stood mute. Tim Harris and Lacy tried to comfort him. So did Schumacher.

"His first reaction to the news about Rose and her activities was illogical," Schumacher says, "just this great outpouring of emotion. Then he started to think about it, you know. 'Christ, there goes my career. I'm wiped out. It's the wrong thing to do.' Finally, he thought, 'Well, she's my wife. I've got to back her up, got to stand beside her.' He kinda snapped out of it."

The speed of his recovery, both mentally and physically, startled everyone. It was as if he had suddenly come to terms with himself and decided his hope of survival was to harass the North Koreans. A guard told him one day to slide his bucket under the bunk. He pretended he didn't understand. He grabbed his sheets and soaked them in the pail. Another guard ordered him to kill the flies in his room. Waving a newspaper, he advanced toward the door and slammed it in the guard's face. Another time, he took off his jacket without requesting permission. A guard told him to put it back on.

"But I'm gonna sweat," he said.

The guard insisted. Bucher obeyed, waited until the guard left the room, then poured a bucket of water over his head. The guard returned a few minutes later and stared at him in astonishment. "I told you it was gonna make me sweat," he said.

He ridiculed the Korean language in front of the duty officers. He extended the middle finger of his right hand in Super-C's presence and said this gesture was the "Hawaiian good luck symbol." The men followed his example. "I figured that if the Koreans caught us, they'd literally beat the hell out of us," Charles Law remembers. "I mentioned this to the captain. He said that if this happened, well, we'd lose the battle. But we'd win the war."

An aura of terror still shrouded the compound. Bucher was kicked to the bottom of the stairs one day "by a guard whose foot met me in the chest." Another guard disapproved of the way that LaMantia was cleaning a windowsill; he pummeled him unmercifully. Before they went to the latrine, the men were supposed to ask permission. Early one morning in July, Charles Ayling felt a desperate need to relieve himself. There were at least three guards between his room on the third floor and the toilet below. He knew he'd have to stop and explain his mission to each of them. It wasn't worth the risk of a beating. He urinated in the water bucket.

Suddenly a guard threw open the door. He caught Ayling in midstream, so to speak, and started hollering. This was an outrage, an "atrocity" against the Korean people. A junior colonel nicknamed Skeezix gathered the crew in the foyer on the second floor. Ayling and his roommates would lose all their privileges, he said. No cards, no cigarettes, no exercise periods outside. For the next few weeks they'd have to clean the latrine four or five times a day. Skeezix said he realized that Hammond had been asleep in another room at the time of the incident. But Hammond was in charge of the men on the third floor; he was responsible for their crimes. And now, because he had failed so miserably, he would have to be replaced. "We thought this was the beginning of the end," McClintock recalls, "that they were going to use this as an excuse to start the mass beatings all over again."

To everyone's surprise, however, conditions began to improve. The men received more rice with their meals and underwent a physical examination. In mid-July Super-C called another meeting. The United States, he said, had finally granted permission for the men to receive mail from home. Peter Langenberg read the first of the one hundred and forty letters he would get during his detention. James Kell heard from his wife in Honolulu. Fetch, the duty officer, asked what the letter said.

"It's all about the pretty girls on the beach at Waikiki," Kell replied mischievously. "In their bikinis."

Fetch nodded. "Bikinis, bikinis," he said. Then he began to giggle.

Gene Lacy studied the letter from his wife, Mary Ellen. She had majored in English at Washington State. She loved to read and was a whiz at solving crossword puzzles. Yet she had misspelled nearly half the words in this letter. Lacy thought that was odd. Then it dawned on him: This was simply her way of sending him a signal, of letting him know that all of his messages, indeed, all of the crew's messages, were coming through loud and clear at home. It was the best news he'd heard in a long time.

July 23 was the six-month anniversary of the ship's capture. Michael Barrett said there was a clause in the armistice agreement which prevented the North Koreans from keeping prisoners any longer than one year. He had heard this "on good authority." Barrett was always spreading rumors. His chair sat next to the window in Room 1 on the second floor. Anytime he saw a new guard or vehicle below, he'd say excitedly, "Something's up." He'd pass the word to his roommates, who, in turn, would circulate it among the crew. And finally, when the rumor came back to him, Barrett would say, "See, this just verifies what I've heard. Other guys have heard it, too. It must be right." His roommates called him "Motormouth." But they liked him and tried to believe his stories.

One of those roommates, John Mitchell, was still cleaning Bucher's room every day. The captain, he remembers, was very skeptical about this armistice agreement "clause." "He told me the only way we were ever going to get out of there was if the U.S. apologized," Mitchell adds. "He said this would never happen. No way. There was nothing to apologize for. We shouldn't expect our country to sacrifice its principles just to get us back. He said he thought we'd stay there for awhile."

34

"Mr. Secretary," a reporter began, "there have been some charges that the administration has been lax in pushing negotiations to free the prisoners of the *Pueblo*—and also some calls that force should be used. . . . Would you comment on that?"

"Well," the Secretary of State replied, "we have tried very hard to get these men back through the normal processes. . . . I think it is rather unlikely that you could get them back alive by military action. . . . I would just say very simply that if anyone wants to form a Remember the *Pueblo* committee, then I am a charter member of that committee. . . ."

The Reverend Paul D. Lindstrom needed no further encouragement. He placed the name "Hon. Dean Rusk, Washington, D.C." on the upper left-hand corner of his stationery and continued his "crusade." The National Remember the *Pueblo* Committee was growing so fast that he couldn't keep up with it. Now there was even a music division. A barber in Canton, Illinois, had written a song entitled "The Ballad of the *Pueblo*," and a group called The Patriots had recorded it.

Lindstrom wrote hundreds of letters requesting funds and signed them "For Christ and America." He peddled thousands of bumper stickers. He addressed the Daughters of the American Revolution and, in Washington, presided over a ceremony at the statue of John Paul Jones. He picketed the State Department wearing a placard which said "Retake the *Pueblo*." He met with Assistant Secretary Winthrop G. Brown and, in a news release, described what happened next:

It seemed strange to us, having heard so much about the tight security precautions at the State Department, that we were free to wander about from office to office. We decided to use this freedom to distribute Remember the Pueblo flyers highly critical of [the administration's] policies. As our roaming about was during the lunch hour, it was possible for us to enter into offices and place flyers on desks and in file cabinets and mail pouches. Our time was limited; therefore, we had to cancel plans for distribution of flyers on the 7th as well as the 1st through 4th floors . . .

In mid-July Lindstrom returned to Washington—this time for a meeting with Secretary Rusk. Rose Bucher's sister, Angela Smedegard, accompanied him. Lindstrom demanded that the United States issue an ultimatum to North Korea. Then he delivered his spiel about "appeasement of Communism." At that, he remembers, "the Secretary became very incensed, chiding me as a clergyman for saying such things while shaking his index finger at my nose. I quickly opened my briefcase and gave him a Remember the *Pueblo* bumper sticker . . ." "The State Department is guilty of unchristian conduct," Lindstrom told reporters a few minutes later, adding, "I would personally go to war."

To his astonishment and dismay, Rusk discovered that his name was being cited as a charter member of a committee which was busy decrying the "dealings in duplicity of our government's leaders." He demanded that Lindstrom remove his name from the committee's stationery. Lindstrom promised to comply—but only if the Secretary accepted certain "conditions." Unconscionable behavior for a clergyman? Most people would say so. But the Illinois House of Representatives took note of Lindstrom's "courage and perseverance," observed that he had conducted himself "with dignity and determination," and passed a resolution expressing its gratitude.

Although her sister, Angela, seemed convinced of Lindstrom's sincerity, Rose Bucher disapproved of some of his tactics. Picketing, she thought, was counterproductive. Her own campaign continued on a less flamboyant scale. With her attorney, E. Miles Harvey, she visited Rusk in Washington. She talked to members of Congress. She helped young Marcee Rethwish organize a second prayer meeting in San Diego. She told reporters that she felt "disillusioned, bewildered and frustrated." The Johnson administration, she said, addressing the annual convention of the American Legion in New Orleans, "has apparently abandoned the crew of the *Pueblo* and allowed our nation's honor to be questioned as never before."

Such declarations only widened the breach between her and the Navy. Some old friends responded to her request for support by saying they didn't want to "get involved." Others shunned her completely.

"I remember, towards the end of the summer it was, inviting Rose to lunch at the sub facility," says a commander's wife. "I was horrified to find out that no one had even asked her before. I introduced her to as many people as I could, and she seemed to enjoy it. But even among that group of wives, there was a certain reserve, a chilliness."

35

Late in July the North Koreans passed out new uniforms. They wouldn't be doing this, Bucher felt, if there was any hope of an early release. And now he had an even more pressing concern. The worst periods of the detention—the times when the beatings increased and the food deteriorated—had occurred at sixty-five- to seventy-day intervals: the end of January, the beginning of April, the first week in June. He could expect another "purge" in August.

All the signs pointed that way. Super-C had confronted Schumacher with his "DPRK EATS IT" poem and threatened to have him shot. The duty officers were interrogating Chicca at length—did they suspect he was planning to escape? And the North Koreans had picked up press reports of a speech that Ohio Senator Stephen Young had delivered in Washington. The peppery septugenarian had stated flatly—and irresponsibly—the the *Pueblo* incident was "another CIA blunder." Super-C interpreted this as proof that the men had been lying when they denied association with the CIA. They would have to be punished.

But first they would have to send out a second batch of letters, addressing them not only to wives and families but also to "important political figures." Lacy wrote to a friend who worked for the Seattle Sewer District, reasoning that "he'd know what to do with it." Schumacher composed a letter to Oral Roberts—"one of the swell moralists of our time"—and showed it to the captain. Bucher rewrote it.

The colonel still wasn't satisfied. "You must think of something else," he said, "that you can do to save yourselves." Tuck suggested convening a court at Panmunjom and telephoning the verdict to President Johnson. Super-C dismissed that idea. He rejected all of Bucher's proposals, as well, and called him "insincere." Finally, Bucher realized what the colonel was seeking.

"Why don't we have a press conference," he said, "with some of the enlisted men?"

Super-C feigned surprise. Then he smiled, exposing his huge front teeth. "That," he said, "is a marvelous idea."

The North Koreans rehearsed the men in their "spontaneous" replies. The accent was on "sincerity." And schmaltz. "You are too serious," a duty officer told Larry Mack one day. "When you answer the question about how you miss your family, you must break down and cry."

On August 13, while the rest of the crew huddled by TV sets in the lecture rooms, Bucher led his officers, oceanographer Tuck, and eighteen enlisted men to a two-story building across the compound from the main barracks. Senior Major Robot nodded to the assembled reporters, then turned to Silverlips. "Now," he said, "let's have a frank talk."

Bucher expressed his gratitude for the "generous humanitarian treatment" which the crew had received thus far. He said it was his "ardent desire" to be repatriated soon and urged the U.S. government to "apologize and admit our guilt." Mack managed to shed a tear. Chicca waited until the TV camera focused directly on him. Slowly, he extended his finger.

Chicca still thought his escape plan was sound. "If I'd said, 'Go,' I think everyone would have gone," he says. "And there were times in my mind when I came close—forty-eight hours away. But I never said a definite, 'Yes, let's do it.'" One reason was the weather. The rain hadn't come. It was still hot and dry. Bucher had told him the other day that he thought any attempt would be suicidal. There were simply too many guards; the whole country was an armed camp. Schumacher agreed. He had been ready to go himself a few months earlier, he said, but now he felt the scheme was too risky. Furthermore, the prospects for a settlement seemed brighter than ever. The North Koreans had the second batch of letters. They had the second press conference. These were bound to achieve results. Reluctantly, Chicca decided to wait and see what happened.

Florence Nightingale had replaced Little Iodine as the chief nurse. There were some other changes in the camp's administrative personnel, and on September 1 a new platoon of guards marched into the compound. Their uniforms were tailored, their shoes were shined, and they wore broader belts. Michael Barrett watched them from his window. "Something's up," he said.

The North Koreans ordered the men to write new letters to newspapers and magazines. Earl Kisler refused. "I'd taken all the crap I could take," he remembers. "I figured it was time to draw the line. So Robot, this senior major, came by with his interpreter and took me to another room. He said, 'Have you changed your mind?' and I said no. He had a stick about three or four feet long and he started beating me about the head and shoulders. Then he took off a rubber-soled shoe and hit me across the face.

"I'd fall out of the chair, and he'd order me back, and this went on until I couldn't find the chair. I was up against the bulkhead, and he was kicking me in the ribs and back. I passed out several times, and when I came to, the interpreter put me in the chair again. He said, 'Sign this letter,' and I said no. My eyes began to close up; I could feel blood all over my face. I thought he was going to beat me to death. The interpreter kept saying it would be very wise for me to reconsider. Finally, I did reconsider. If he had asked me to say my name was Abe Lincoln or Donald Duck, I would have done it."

"Kisler's head was twice its normal size," Rushel Blansett remembers. "It looked like a piece of hamburger."

A guard saw Goldman whispering to Bucher in the latrine one day; he marched him outside and ordered him to repeat the conversation. Goldman shook his head; the guard bloodied his nose and gave him a black eye. Another guard pummeled Aluague for the "crime" of adjusting the cast on his knee. A third, the Bear, clubbed Berens below the right eye, inflicting a permanant scar.

As he had—and as he would for the rest of his detention—Berens volunteered to accept beatings for his ailing shipmates. So did Hammond and Law and Interior Communications Technician Second Class Victor Escamilla. On one occasion some paper which the Koreans had placed over a window in the latrine fell to the floor. The guards told Law to find out who had committed this "crime." No one knew anything about it, so he said he'd done it himself. They didn't believe him. "Keep checking the rooms," they insisted, "until you find the 'criminal.'" Finally Escamilla volunteered to say that he was responsible. The guards beat him for loosening the paper—and Law for "lying" about it.

In his dreams Law imagined that Senior Major Possum was punishing him for some minor infraction. He threw a bucket of bleach into Possum's face. He grabbed a fire ax and hacked at the North Korean's body, chopping off his head and limbs and cutting his torso into small pieces. Then he woke up in a sweat.

For the past few weeks, ever since early August, he had known he was going blind. He thought of the times back on the ship when he and Bucher had competed to spot the evening's first star. His vision had been extraordinary then—20–14 in one eye and 20–13 in the other. But now he had trouble focusing; everything seemed blurred. He couldn't read the figures on the charts in front of him.

The North Koreans had just decided to raise the number of *Pueblo*'s "intrusions" into their territorial waters from six to seventeen. And they had told him, as a member of the navigational team, to assist Murphy and Leach in compiling "evidence." He wanted to "cooperate," to pock those charts with so many errors that they would seem ridiculous. He tried; it was no use. He asked Hammond to take his place and went to see the camp doctor.

The doctor stuck pins behind his ears "to let the evil spirits out." Then he called in a specialist from Pyongyang. The specialist said that Law had an inflammation of the optic nerves. He pulled out a huge needle and gave him the first of thirteen injections in both eyeballs. The shots hurt so much that he cried out. Florence Nightingale couldn't stand it; she had to turn away.

Dale Rigby was still having trouble with the open sores on his body. The North Koreans hadn't been able to treat them successfully. Communications Technician Third Class Paul D. Brusnahan developed a cyst on his spine. Wracked by nausea, he lay on his bed unable to move. Lee Hayes began to turn yellow. Cigarettes made him sick; he couldn't eat, and he had to urinate fifteen times a day. Florence Nightingale gave him some aspirin. Hayes had hepatitis. The North Koreans called it "Botkin's disease." They placed him in a private room on the second floor.

Bucher worried incessantly about the health of his crew. He had to convince Super-C that the constant beatings and substandard diet were taking an awful toll, that the North Koreans had gone too far. Rational discourse would be futile; he'd need to use a subtler method. He decided to pretend that he was losing his mind.

He sat in silence, his eyes downcast, while Super-C suggested new ways for the men to help themselves. Another press conference, the colonel thought, might convince the United States to accept Pyongyang's demands. The officers agreed. Then Bucher jumped up. "Yeah," he said. "I think we ought to write *letters*. That's a fine idea." Super-C seemed puzzled.

"The captain decided he was going to get sick," Schumacher recalls. "He quavered. He said he had lockjaw, and he refused to come to meals. The duty officer didn't believe him, so at one point he actually got himself to throw up. It was a great routine."

Super-C was obviously concerned. Late one evening he summoned Bucher to Room 6 on the second floor. He turned to Silverlips. "You realize," he began, "there are some things I have to do which I don't want to do, which are only part of my job. . . ."

Bucher listened carefully. In all his sessions with Super-C stretching back over nearly eight months, this was the first time he had heard the colonel give even the slightest *hint* that he was not in total accord with his government's policy. And now, as if aware of this himself, Super-C reverted to form. "My superiors have agreed to allow you to have the press conference which you requested," he continued, drumming his bony fingers on the top of the desk. "It may be a way out for you from your situation. . . ."

The colonel droned on for several hours. Bucher got the distinct impression that his tactic had succeeded. The forthcoming press conference would be a test. If he and his men followed the script, conditions would improve. He was sure he could seem "sincere" while at the same time discrediting the whole performance. The prospect pleased him enormously. He noticed the potted cactus plants on the window sills behind the colonel's desk. Their leaves reminded him of Mickey Mouse ears.

The duty officers brought new Olympia typewriters into the Club, and every night for the next week Bucher and the nineteen others who would participate in the conference wrote out their questions and answers. Finally it was time for the dress rehearsal.

"Now it has been more than two years," Ralph McClintock said, in a low, mortician's voice, "since I have seen my family, my widowed, grief-stricken mother . . ."

Laughter rippled through the Club. Bucher turned around to look at him. So did Tim Harris. Colonel Specs, the moderator, banged on the desk. "What's so damned funny?" he asked.

"No, Mac," Bucher said. "I don't think you ought to say *two* years. It's only been one year."

Tears rolled down McClintock's cheeks.

"That's okay, Mac," Tim Harris said. "You're too emotional. Why don't you go on to your next answer?"

"It's worse," McClintock said.

Fortunately, he didn't have to read it. The North Koreans professed themselves satisfied with the rehearsal. The crew was ready to meet the press.

The conference began on the morning of September 12. There were reporters from the Soviet Union, Poland, East Germany, Hungary, France, Italy, Egypt, Japan, India, and several small African states. There was also one American, a sharp-featured man named

Lionel Martin who wore a red plaid jacket, smoked a pipe, and said he represented "The New York *Guardian.*"

The session dragged on for nearly five hours. There was no air conditioning, the fans didn't work, and everyone began to sweat. The reporter from India kept bobbing up in the back of the room to complain, "It is not audible, it is not audible."

Bucher spoke of his desire to return to "our motherland." Mack said he longed for the "bosom of the fatherland." Once again McClintock stole the show. "Oh, how I long to walk down the quiet, shaded streets of my hometown," he began, "to swim again in the rolling surf of old Cape Cod Bay and to indulge in the sumptuous feast of one of Mom's famous apple pies. . . . I swear that I will never again commit such a naughty crime as espionage. . . ."

"Let's get this suck-ass bullshit over with," the East German reporter groaned. The Japanese fidgeted in their chairs. The Russians stifled yawns. The only reporter who kept a straight face, who seemed to believe every word, was Lionel Martin, and now, as the conference ended, he rushed to a microphone. "I still have some questions which . . ."

"Come on," the Indian said, "you can get your answers from studying the record. . . ."

Senior Major Robot rapped for order. Too late; the other reporters had left their seats and were milling about. Everyone seemed to be shouting at once. Martin, the American, still clutched the microphone. "I am convinced that the *Pueblo* crew has been treated humanely," he began. "It is quite evident that they were violating Korean territorial waters. The proof is . . . irrefutable. . . ."

Bucher jumped up on his chair. His men were very young, he said. They had not had "an opportunity to taste either the bitters or the sweets of this life." Some crew members laughed; others extended their fingers. "I don't think it's unreasonable for me to ask," Bucher went on, "that we be *home by Christmas.*" His men began to cheer.

Later that night, in their "wardroom," the officers agreed that the press conference had been an unruly disaster. Surely, they thought, the North Koreans would be furious. They waited for another "purge." But Super-C didn't appear. And Oddjob, his deputy, was all smiles. He seemed to think the conference had been a great success, that it would pressure the United States to apologize, that the men would be going home soon. Schumacher doubted this. But why, he wondered, had Super-C suddenly disappeared? Had there been some sort of breakthrough at Panmunjom?

36

On a table in the office of Nicholas deB. Katzenbach stood a framed letter which a child had written him several years earlier. "To the attorney," it began; "my sister is writing you a letter. She says you are important. Who are you and why are you important?"

First as Attorney General of the United States and then as Under Secretary of State, the tall, bald, former Rhodes scholar from New Jersey had evidenced a unique ability to probe to the core of a complex problem and unravel the string which led to a solution. A direct descendant of Lieutenant James Lawrence ("Don't give up the ship"), Katzenbach tended to agree with the admirals who fumed about Bucher's handling of the *Pueblo* incident. Yet he had once been a prisoner of war himself; he empathized with the suffering of the crew and wracked his brain to think of a way to secure their release.

Throughout the summer there had been no progress at all at Panmunjom. The North Koreans held fast to their May 8 formula. "If you truly want to solve the problem," General Pak maintained, "you will sign our document." And the United States had tried to find out in a variety of ways whether or not a signature would result in the crew's repatriation. But Woodward had never put his question to Pak directly, fearing that such a blunt approach might entangle the United States in a premature commitment. Now Katzenbach thought he saw a way to break the deadlock. Suppose the United States were to phrase its question differently, to ask, for example, "If I acknowledge receipt of the crew on a document satisfactory to you as well as to us, would you then be prepared to release all of the crew?"

On the surface it didn't appear to be very different from what the United States had asked before. But "acknowledge receipt of" wasn't the same as "sign"; "*a* document" didn't necessarily mean the May 8 proposal and "satisfactory to you *as well as to us*"—there were scores of possible interpretations for that. The beauty of it was that the North Koreans would now be under pressure to respond. Katzenbach conferred with Assistant Secretary Winthrop G. Brown and Korea "country director" James F. Leonard. Then he sent a cable to Woodward.

On August 29 Woodward conferred with Pak for nearly two hours at Panmunjom. He repeated Katzenbach's question and stressed the importance of a simultaneous release.

"Well, we have already told you what you must sign," Pak replied.

The State Department interpreted this as encouraging. The North Korean hadn't *rejected* the simultaneity aspect; he simply hadn't addressed it directly. On September 17 Woodward tried again.

"If you will sign our document," Pak began, "something might be worked out. . . ." The barriers were beginning to crumble.

The State Department's chief press officer, Robert J. McCloskey, had spent an eventful summer scotching rumors about *Pueblo* and her crew. According to one account, Bucher had committed suicide. (Hearing this, one high-ranking officer in the Pentagon smiled and said, "Good, the sonovabitch should have done it a long time ago.") According to another, the North Koreans had tried the men, found them guilty, and sentenced them to death. McCloskey denied these reports. Now he was asked about an imminent break in the negotiations. A Seoul newspaper, *Dong-a Ilbo*, said that the United States had made "a flexible proposal on how to apologize." Was there any truth to that? How about stories to the effect that a hospital ward at a U.S. base in South Korea had just been cleared out in order to accommodate the *Pueblo* crew, that buses and ambulances were racing to Panmunjom right now, that the men were waiting for their freedom at the town of Kaesong, just across the DMZ?

"There is nothing new to report about negotiations at Panmunjom," McCloskey declared at his noon briefing on September 13. "Every appropriate diplomatic means to get their release is being pursued. We have an obligation to keep these exchanges private." Three days later he added, misleadingly, "We expect there will be a meeting at Panmunjom, but none is scheduled." And on September 18, "Nothing is scheduled on the *Pueblo*. There has been no breakthrough."

Even as McCloskey spoke, Pentagon officials were distributing copies of a 100-page Navy plan to handle the return of the crew anywhere in the world: Panmunjom, Cambodia, Czechoslovakia, Hong Kong, even Berlin. The plan was inadequate. So highly classified were the negotiations that the men who wrote it didn't know any more than what they read in the newspapers. Even the Secretary of the Navy,

Paul Ignatius, was left in the dark. "The State Department," he says, "didn't cut us in on anything."

On September 30 Woodward and Pak met again at Panmunjom. "If you will sign the document," Pak said, "we will at the same time turn over the men." So that much had been settled: The North Koreans had agreed to simultaneity. One final order of business remained: the nature of the document that Woodward was to sign and how he was to sign it.

"Our position is quite clear," Woodward said. "We do not feel it is just to sign a paper saying we have done something which we haven't done. However, in the interest of reuniting the crew with their families, we might consider. . . ." And on he went to press for acceptance of the "overwrite" proposal. He would, he said, "acknowledge receipt" of the crew on a North Korean paper.

Pak seemed interested. Almost *too* interested. Perhaps the North Korean was equating the words "acknowledge receipt" with the word "sign"; perhaps he assumed, mistakenly, that the United States was ready to accept the May 8 paper; perhaps he simply didn't understand the "overwrite" device. Woodward returned to Seoul and telephoned Korea "country director" James F. Leonard at the State Department. He said he thought Pak was confused. "You better straighten him out," Leonard replied. "Show him at the next meeting exactly how you plan to do it."

"Well, I saw Super-C today," Bucher told Schumacher in the "wardroom" one night, "and you'll never believe what he's got on his collar. The sonovabitch is a general."

And so he was. Gone were the four tiny stars on each shoulder board, and in their place was a large silver star. The men called him GG—for "Glorious General"; he strutted about the camp obviously pleased with himself. He didn't say where he had been, but it was clear that he had received new orders on how to deal with the crew.

The beatings ceased. The men received bread and butter, fresh fish, canned ham, and apples at their meals. Guards marched them one by one across the compound to the "Gypsy Tea Room" on the second floor of the building where they'd held their recent press conferences. Women brought them plates of candy and cookies, offered them bottles of beer and glasses of Ginseng liquor. Officers in civilian clothes greeted them effusively ("How ya doin', Mac?" one asked a startled McClintock) and requested their "impressions" of life in

North Korea. Would they like to return as tourists someday? Would they tell the "truth" at home about this socialist paradise? Would they accept as "friends" any North Koreans who contacted them in the United States? And, finally, would they promise never to reveal the substance of their conversations in this room? Would they sign an oath to that effect?

Some of the men agreed to everything in an effort to seem "sincere." A few deliberately—and bravely—insulted their interrogators. Tuck said the only way he wanted to see North Korea again was through a bombsight. The officers dismissed him. Bailey declared that he would be happy to tell "the truth" about North Korea. His inflection gave him away; his interview lasted only three minutes. Crandell listened as the officers spoke of their plans to "liberate" the entire peninsula. "If your army is so powerful," he said, "why don't you just go ahead and try it?"

The North Koreans herded the men into buses and drove them to Pyongyang to see a stage play entitled, predictably, *How Glorious Is Our Fatherland*. They took them to a circus a few nights later and then to a concert by the People's Army Band. "If you are sincere," a duty officer explained, "you will be going home—perhaps by the end of October." One final excursion remained—to the "Museum of Horrors" in the town of Sinchon.

The fourteen rooms of the museum were stocked with "evidence" that U.S. troops had committed atrocities during the Korean War. A glass case, for example, contained a railroad spike. This spike, the interpreter said, had been used by the imperialist aggressor forces to split open the head of a pregnant woman. A bomb shelter was said to have been employed by the Americans as a gas chamber; there were "fingernail scratches" on its walls. A piece of rope in another display case allegedly belonged to a Lieutenant j.g. Harrison, a CIA agent, who had used it to drag thirty innocent women and children to their screaming deaths. The guide paused before a photograph of American troops.

"Which one is Lieutenant j.g. Harrison?" someone asked.

She pointed to an Army enlisted man, a corporal.

Before the men could go home, the North Koreans announced, they would have to submit a petition to the DPRK requesting leniency and expressing gratitude for their humanitarian treatment. Bucher appointed a committee with himself as chairman, and on October 8 its members began writing. "We were fully authorized to penetrate [Korean] waters," the petition declared, "whenever there was a chance of adding goodies to our spy bag. . . . We are spies that lurk in dark corners. . . . Superspies. . . . We greatly criticize the manipulators of the drawstrings which led us to this unfortunate fate.

". . . We, as conscientious human beings, who were cast upon the rocks and shoals of immorality by the tidal wave of Washington's naughty policies, know that neither the frequency nor the distance of the transgressions [into Korean waters] matter because, in the final analysis, penetration, however slight, is sufficient to complete the act. . . ."

In Washington, Secretary of Defense Clark Clifford recognized that final clause—the legal definition of rape—and burst into peals of laughter.

Glorious General seemed pleased. The men were obviously "sincere." He had one further request: He needed a new set of individual confessions. These statements, he explained, would be kept in Pyongyang as "insurance" and broadcast only if the men "lied" on their return to the United States.

Bucher's new confession covered fifty-six pages and differed in several respects from his prior admissions. Rear Admiral Frank L. Johnson, he wrote, had first contacted him about his espionage assignment in Sasebo, Japan. They had left the ship together and pedaled up the hill on a velocipede "for a short time." They met Buz Sawyer in a candlelit restaurant. They encountered Saul Loxfinger, the CIA agent, who was also there "for a short time." He had a pockmarked face and a severe case of halitosis. Bucher sailed from Sasebo armed with "trinoculars" to help him observe satellites. He also brought along cans of Mrs. Butterworth's beans and a thirty-day supply of long-lasting bagels. These would supply the energy he needed to win the "Spy of the Month" award in the northern Pacific.

Steven Harris admitted that he had been trained at the SPCA— the Special Projects Coordinating Administration. His tutor there was Maxwell Smart. McClintock said that he had run afoul of the "Bowery Street entrepreneurs." A duty officer stepped into Room 1 on the third floor and asked for Baldridge's confession. He read it and seemed puzzled. "I don't understand," he said. "You say that you will leave the army of foreign aggressors when you return to the United States. Does this mean that Navy people are also Army people?"

"Yeah," Russell said. "The army is just a slang term that describes all the armed forces."

The duty officer nodded and turned to leave. Suddenly one man jumped up—the same man whom Hayes had thought was about to break several months before.

"No, they've made a mistake," he said. "They're not the same. The

Navy is separate. The Army is the land forces; the Navy is the naval forces. . . ."

Baldridge, Russell, and Hayes stared at their roommate. How could he have said such a thing? Then the guards entered their room. To administer punishment.

37

At his home in Tacoma, Washington, a forty-nine-year-old businessman named Earl W. Hopkins read the letter he had just received from his nephew, Charles Law, in North Korea. Then he looked closely at the picture which accompanied it. Charlie had lost some more hair; he had also lost weight. But what caught Hopkins' eye was the fact that five of the eight men in the picture had positioned their fingers in a most unusual way. Were they trying to send him a signal?

He read the letter again, but it contained no explanation. Puzzled, he took the photograph to the office of the Tacoma *News-Tribune*. The *News-Tribune* published it on October 10. The Associated Press picked it up, slugged it *"Pueblo* prisoners," and serviced it throughout the country. The New York *Times* carried it on page one; so did the Washington *Post*. Neither paper attempted to explain the prisoners' gestures. But in its issue of October 18, *Time* magazine left no doubt about the signal's meaning. "Last week," its story read, "Pyongyang's flacks tried again—and lost to the U.S. Navy. . . ."

At the State Department, Katzenbach was furious. So was Leonard. "If the Koreans ever see this," he thought, "it'll be curtains for the crew."

The twenty-third private meeting on the *Pueblo* affair took place at Panmunjom on October 10. Woodward and Pak reviewed details of the release. The crew would walk across the Bridge of No Return. Reporters from both sides would be allowed in the Joint Security Area. Neither country would announce that an agreement had been reached until just prior to the transfer.

Was there an agreement? Pak seemed to think so. Now Woodward proceeded to show him precisely how he planned to execute his part of the bargain. He stood at the table, ran his finger diagonally across a piece of paper, and said, "I will write here that I hereby acknowledge receipt of eighty-two men and one corpse. . . ."

Pak seemed startled. He wasn't expecting that at all. As Woodward had feared, the North Korean had obviously come to equate the words "acknowledge receipt" with the word "sign." He glared across the table at Woodward.

"You are reneging on our agreement," he said. "You are employing sophistries and petty strategems to escape responsibility for the crimes which your side has committed. If you really want to get the crew back and reduce tensions, as you say you do, you will sign the document we presented with the exact language. . . ."

On October 23 the two sides met again for three hours and seventeen minutes. Woodward continued to press for acceptance of the "overwrite" device. Pak was even more vitriolic in his attacks on "petty stratagems."

The State Department's hopes for some sort of compromise crumbled completely eight days later, on October 31. That meeting lasted only twenty minutes. Both sides restated their positions. Then Pak stood up. "There is nothing more to be discussed," he said. He turned and left the room.

In the morning Woodward would complete his scheduled six-month tour as senior U.S. negotiator at Panmunjom. His family expected him home. He decided to stay on. "After coming this far, I was sort of enmeshed in the thing," he recalls. "I figured it was a shame to have to bring in somebody else. I said, 'I'll see it through, no matter how long it takes.' "

The North Koreans were due to call the next meeting. Woodward waited. One week passed. Two. Three. There was no word from General Pak.

★   ★   ★

The guard named Fly kept sneaking into Room 5 on the third floor to steal apples and cigarettes. Sterling, Kisler, and Alexander decided to retaliate. They polished an apple to a high sheen, then poked tiny holes in it with a pin. They poured urine into these holes and left the apple to marinate. Several hours later they repeated the process. Sterling polished the apple again and left it on a bookshelf.

Then he and his roommates stepped outside. Fly entered the room. He saw the apple and ate it. He didn't report to work for the next three days.

The winter's first snow fell over the compound on November 9. Schumacher felt depressed. The North Koreans had seemed so sure that the crew was going home. Now everything seemed to have stopped. The duty officers eliminated the exercise periods outside. There were no new "feature fil-ums" or documentaries in the Club. The senior majors, Robot and Possum, devoted their infrequent lectures to "the anti-Japanese patriotic guerrilla struggle" of thirty years ago. What, Schumacher wondered, was the point in that?

Charles Law and his roommates decided that if they were still in this building by the time Richard M. Nixon entered the White House, they'd attempt to escape. "We didn't think Nixon would ever get us out with his policies," Law says, "and we told the Koreans this."

From his window one afternoon Michael Barrett saw a blue Toyota truck enter the compound. Guards began to unload dozens of cases of film. "Something's up," Barrett declared.

Turnips reappeared on the menu. With "greens." Earl Phares figured he'd lost at least 50 pounds. "Tiny" Higgins thought he had lost 100. Ramon Rosales contracted a soaring fever. He lay on his bunk unable to move. Bucher pleaded with Glorious General for medical assistance. The North Korean laughed at him.

Bucher's nightly sessions with GG had ceased a week or two before. He wondered why. "The crew was convinced we'd gone too far," he remembers. "I thought perhaps our efforts had given the U.S. the ammunition it needed to negotiate an honorable return. I passed word that I was intensely proud of each man." One evening late in November GG summoned Bucher to Room 6 on the second floor. He crossed the brown carpet and once again noticed the potted plants in the window sills with their Mickey Mouse ears.

"I wonder why the United States has suddenly reversed its position at Panmunjom," GG began.

Bucher glanced at the general's desk. There was a huge stack of black-and-white photographs. Next to it was an article from *Time* magazine. He recognized the picture of Law and his roommates; he winced as he read the story: ". . . and lost to the U.S. Navy. . . . Three of the crewmen have managed to use the medium for a message, furtively getting off the U.S. hand signal of derisiveness and contempt."

GG was pounding his fist on the desk, screaming at him now. He and his men had insulted the entire Korean people by using this *obscene gesture. . . .* They had spoiled their own chances for repatriation. . . .

"I knew we had accomplished our mission," Bucher remembers, "but I thought this might result in the death of some of the crew. As soon as that meeting was over, I cornered Law in the latrine and told him to pass the word: 'The Hawaiian good luck symbol is no longer an adequate explanation for the finger gesture. Think of something else. If you are beaten, you may tell the Koreans what you have done yourself, but not what others have done.' "

What Bucher would later describe as "the most concentrated form of terror that I've ever seen or dreamed is possible," what his crew would refer to simply, mournfully, as "Hell Week," began a few days later. The guards and duty officers rescinded all "privileges." They grouped the men twelve and sixteen to a room to provide more space for interrogations. They kept the lights on constantly and told the men to sit with their heads bowed down to their waists. Then they set out to punish the men who had used the finger gesture.

The Bear split open Goldman's lip and beat him until blood flowed from his ear. They interrogated Iredale for thirty-six hours, punching and kicking him until, as one roommate remembers, "his head looked like a pumpkin." They forced him to admit that he had sailed on *Banner*. Then they concentrated on Law.

"They wanted me to say that I was a CIA agent," he says, "communicating by secret crossword puzzles. Well, I wasn't a CIA agent, so I didn't see any sense in owning up to that. They asked me about the finger gesture: 'Do you know why the CIA uses it?' " His interrogation lasted thirty-nine hours. In that time he had no sleep and, except for a little soup, no food. "They used a two-by-two on my shoulders and back. It broke in half. They used the halves until there were four pieces. I guess I received between two hundred fifty and three hundred blows. I had quite a bit of trouble walking. I couldn't straighten up. . . ."

Silverlips and Oddjob marched into the captain's room. "Without a word, I was flattened out," Bucher remembers; "a good blow to the kisser that loosened all my front teeth. They beat me into semiconsciousness. They had me on my knees with my nose on the floor. They brought Law in to see me. . . ."

Murphy sat in a corner of his room, staring up at a duty officer. "You're trying to kill me," he mumbled, "you're trying to kill me." The duty officer took him away. Hours later, Murphy returned.

"He told us what he had told the Koreans," Schumacher says. "It sounded to me as if he had really cracked, spilled the whole thing.

He said he thought they already had the information, almost with a conviction that 'well, we shouldn't have been doing this anyway.' I was pretty upset, sort of stupefied that they'd found out all this stuff. The captain was really peeved."

Shouts and screams and the cracks of doors slamming echoed through the building. The men had to write new confessions detailing all their crimes. The barber shop on the second floor—wasn't that where the men hatched plots? And wasn't the barber, Pepe Garcia, a prime instigator? Tim Harris admitted this was true and then apologized to Garcia. So did Layton. Garcia honestly didn't know what this was all about. But the North Koreans didn't believe him.

Senior Major Robot removed his studded belt and placed it in front of McClintock. "What," he demanded, "were your escape plans?"

McClintock said he'd once thought of holding a knife to GG's throat and forcing him to lead the crew away from the compound. It was only an idea. Robot beat him severely for that.

"How about communications?" the North Korean asked. "Who was the link between the officers and the men?"

McClintock shook his head. He said he didn't know.

Robot belted him. And belted him again.

Finally McClintock said that Mitchell had carried messages, "but only about our pay and Navy benefits."

Next morning the guards dragged Mitchell away for interrogation. McClintock felt terrible.

Robot stormed into Room 1 on the third floor. The Bear accompanied him. "You were senior man in this room," Robot screamed at Baldridge. "Why didn't you stop these men from using the obscene gesture?"

"They're all grown men," Baldridge replied. "They can make up their own minds what they want to do."

Hayes was standing next to Baldridge. He saw the Bear rub his right fist against the palm of his left hand. The Bear was looking directly at the one man in the room who always cringed in his presence, the man whom Hayes had been afraid would break down completely.

Now this man jumped up from his chair. "I criticized these men for doing this," he said, shaking violently. "I tried to stop them."

The Bear chopped Hayes in the side of the throat; he kicked him in the knees; he broke his jaw with one punch.

"A few days later they came back for me again," Hayes remembers. "They told me they knew everything, not only about the escape plans but also about the radio. They said I was building a transmitter to spy on them. I wasn't sincere, so I'd be shot. I broke down myself. I told them I was tired of being a prisoner. I said, 'Go ahead and kill me.' They looked at me real funny and said, 'Go back and think about it.'

"What I was really thinking about was killing this guy in our room who was so scared, throwing him out the window and saying that he'd committed suicide. Russell and I talked about it and decided to give him a warning instead. If he did or said anything else, that was going to be it. We didn't want to push him to the point where he'd think his only safety lay with the North Koreans."

The guards had beaten Chicca brutally for his role in plotting escape. They had pummeled Strano for working on the radio. Hammond knew that they would be after him next. "I figured one of the last things they wanted was to have one of us dead," he recalls. "I thought, 'If I can convince them that I'm ready to do away with myself, they might slack off. At least, it'll shake them up.'"

He broke the mirror above his night stand into little pieces and took them to bed with him. He tried to cut his wrists. The glass was dull. He made one incision, but it didn't bleed fast enough. He closed his eyes, took one piece, and thrust it directly into his stomach. Blood spurted from the gash. He lay back on the bed. Suddenly it dawned on him that he might have done too good a job. He thought about getting up and calling for the guards. He didn't have the energy. The blood felt warm on his body. Comfortable. Then he fell asleep.

38

Although he was forty-eight, James F. Leonard appeared to be much younger. A consequence, perhaps, of his trim sideburns or, more probably, the rigorous exercise schedule which kept him slim and physically fit. Leonard had no legal training. At Princeton (class of '42) he had majored in engineering. Nonetheless, he possessed an attorney's grasp of and affection for semantic challenges. And since relieving Ben Fleck as the State Department's "country director" for Korea in July, he had encountered his share of them.

These *Pueblo* negotiations were so incredibly complex. One had to worry not only about the language one used, but also about the *signal* which that language conveyed. And not just to the North Koreans. Any seeming "concessions" to Pyongyang would infuriate the ROK's and likely cause problems at home, as well. The Reverend Lindstrom and his followers would be sure to voice their opinions. The United States was fortunate, Leonard thought, in having such men as Katzenbach and Brown planning its strategy—equally fortunate in having General Woodward in South Korea. Most generals were rather bull-headed; they thought in terms of cannons, not clauses. Woodward was a godsend—a tough, patient man who appreciated the situation's subtleties.

Leonard worried about the silence from Panmunjom. The last meeting had taken place there on October 31, and that was several weeks ago. It was the North Koreans' turn to request another session, but they had shown no interest in doing so. What was it that General Pak had said—"There is nothing more to discuss"? Leonard reminded himself that the North Koreans had not completely rejected the "overwrite" proposal. They had raised so many objections to it, however, that it no longer seemed a promising device. There had to be another way. The obvious alternative was to swallow one's pride, sign the May 8 paper, and then repudiate it as soon as the last man crossed the bridge. The President, Leonard knew, wanted desperately to get the men home in these closing weeks of his administration. He might even accept such a scheme.

But Leonard had qualms about this. No matter what the rationale, the United States would still be putting its *imprimatur* on a false document, adopting what the philosophers call an "instrumental" attitude about truth. And repudiating this document after the fact—well, that constituted a "trick." A great nation shouldn't have to stoop to such levels. Throughout the fall he had written a number of "scenarios"; "Suppose we say such and such. . . . That gives them the following three choices. . . . Then we reply to that by saying. . . ." He sought some way to take the sting out of the act which the United States would probably have to commit. But the answer always eluded him. Then, one Sunday late in November, at his home on Haddington Place in Bethesda, Maryland, he mentioned the dilemma to his wife.

"If you really make it clear beforehand," Eleanor Leonard said, "that your signature is on a false document, well, then you remove the deception." Have Woodward tell Pak—and the world—in advance, she went on, that the paper he was about to sign contained statements which were untrue. If the North Koreans accepted this prior refutation, the United States could proceed with a clear conscience. Furthermore, General Pak wouldn't be able to accuse anyone of "tricking" him.

Leonard returned to his typewriter and composed another scenario, ignoring as best he could the noise that the kids were making upstairs. His wife's idea would give the North Koreans the signed piece of paper that they had been seeking. But it would make fools of them at the same time. It was a little like asking a man who has kidnapped your child to accept an admittedly hot check as ransom. He didn't see how the North Koreans could ever agree to a prior public repudiation, and in his scenario he wrote that they wouldn't. Still, the idea was worth proposing, if only "because it would put us in a better position for the next step." At this point he couldn't imagine what that next step might be.

Next morning he huddled with Katzenbach and Brown. They felt his wife's idea had no more than a 20 percent chance of success but agreed it was worth a try. They discussed it in turn with Rusk, Rostow, and President Johnson and on December 9 sent a cable to Woodward. Request a meeting at Panmunjon, it read in effect. Suggest both the "overwrite" and the "prior refutation" schemes. Point out—this clause was added at Katzenbach's insistence—that the United States was losing patience with Pyongyang. Unless General Pak responded positively to one of these proposals, the United States would withdraw them. The United States would have to conclude that Pak did not intend to negotiate an agreement. There would be no further meetings. The North Koreans would have to deal with the Nixon administration.

What soon became known as the "Leonard proposal" appealed to Woodward immediately. "I said right then and there, 'They'll buy it,'" he remembers. "I figured our chances were better than ninety percent. It satisfied their one condition, a signature on a piece of paper. Never mind the oral repudiation. In the Orient, you know, nothing is more important than the written word. Besides, the North Korean people would never hear about that repudiation. Their propaganda boys would take care of that. And as for the rest of the world, well, they just didn't care."

On December 10 Woodward sent word that the United States was ready to submit new proposals. Would Pak call a meeting? Pak didn't reply. On December 15 Woodward said, in effect, "I will be at Panmunjom tomorrow morning. I expect to see you there." His tactic worked. The sixteenth, Pak responded, was impossible. But the seventeenth, a Tuesday, would be satisfactory.

At eleven o'clock that morning Woodward met Pak for the first time in forty-seven days. He explained both the "overwrite" and the "Leonard proposal." Christmas was approaching. This was a traditional and significant holiday for Americans. President Johnson wanted the men to be home with their families. Then he added Katzenbach's ultimatum. Unless Pak accepted one or the other of these offers, there would be no point in. . . .

For the first time since the talks began nearly a year before, Pak suggested a recess. Fifty minutes later, presumably after telephoning Pyongyang for instructions, he returned to the table. "I note that you will sign my document," he said. "We have reached agreement."

At the State Department, newsmen asked the chief press officer, Robert J. McCloskey, about reports from South Korea that the release was imminent. Such reports, McCloskey replied, "have a history of being regrettably untrue and based on speculation." Well, was he confirming or denying that an agreement had been reached? McCloskey said only that "further meetings are expected." Significantly, he omitted the phrase he'd always used before in referring to the talks. He did not say, "There has been no breakthrough."

Ambassador William Porter, in Washington for consultations, rushed back to Seoul. At the Pentagon a Deputy Assistant Secretary of Defense named Richard Fryklund told the Navy to prepare to implement its Breeches Buoy plan. Then he and Charles W. Havens III, the Pentagon's specialist for POW affairs, flew to South Korea.

★   ★   ★

Woodward sat down with Pak on December 19 and again on December 22. Throughout these negotiations, they had confronted each other across a rectangular table. Pak insisted that the table for their final meeting had to be round. Woodward agreed. The men should be released in inverse order of rank, the North Korean maintained. Bucher would be the last man to cross the bridge. Woodward suspected a trap. No, he said. The captain would have to identify his men as they crossed to the UN side. He should be first. Pak agreed. Woodward brought up the question of announcing their agreement. If either side broke the news prematurely, the other side would be free to say whatever it wanted. Pak agreed. In order to comply with his country's law, Pak continued, there would have to be a two-hour interval between the signing and the actual release of the crew. Furthermore, the signing would have to take place at nine o'clock in the morning. But *which* morning? He didn't say. The twenty-third, Woodward replied, was the last acceptable date.

The haggling over details continued. How many buses would approach the bridge, and where on the road would they park? How many reporters and photographers would cover the ceremony? Where on the document would Woodward sign his name? On the right or the left? Above or below the signature block? As he flew back to Seoul in an Army helicopter, Woodward felt enormously relieved. He didn't look forward to signing that odious document, but he could swallow his pride. There were more important things to consider than that. He wondered about that North Korean photographer who'd snapped so many pictures of him during this last session. Were his adversaries planning to doctor the pictures somehow and spring a propaganda surprise? He'd have to remember to wear a different uniform at the final meeting.

39

"Jesus Christ, what have you done?"

Chicca was standing by Hammond's bunk, staring at the crimsoned sheets, pulling at his friend's shoulder, trying to waken him. Suddenly a duty officer nicknamed King Kong stomped into the room. He looked at Chicca, then down at the bed.

The young Marine's stomach and hands were smeared with blood. He raised himself on one elbow and stared at the North Korean. "Come and get me," he said.

King Kong didn't move.

"Come on," Hammond said. "Why don't you kill me? You chicken?"

"Hammondo, Hammondo," the North Korean cried beseechingly. "Why? Why?"

And Hammond proceeded to tell him. "I couldn't hack it anymore," he said. "I couldn't hack it anymore." King Kong blinked and called for the guards. Would Hammond like to see the doctor? Hammond washed the blood from his wounds, which, luckily, were more superficial than they seemed. No, he said. He wanted to stay with his roommates.

How could anyone describe the terror of the last few days? Tim Harris had tried to commit suicide. And Bucher had seriously thought of jumping out of a third-floor window. But suddenly, without explanation, Hell Week ended. The duty officers restored all "privileges." They told the men they could raise their heads. They scurried to and fro, treating bruises and black eyes with heated eggs and paraffin paks.

"Something's up," Barrett said.

"The United States," GG announced on December 21, "has finally confessed to its serious crimes and is willing to pay for them. You are going home."

The guards and duty officers called the men to the barber shop on the second floor. They searched and stripped them. They provided quilted blue coats, khaki trousers, caps and socks, and black sneakers with white soles. The Bear seemed bitter that Hell Week had ended so abruptly; so did Robot. But Fetch, the duty officer, seemed sorry to see the Americans leave. He stepped into McClintock's room and stuck out his hand. "I can see you in Hawaii," he said, "when it is socialist. We have good time with bikinis." He giggled. McClintock grasped the hand but couldn't bring himself to shake it. "Don't hold your breath," he said.

As a final indication of their "sincerity," GG had said, some members of the crew would have to participate in a last press conference. No one flashed the finger gesture; only a few sought to use double entendres. "We are grateful to the benevolent Korean protective society," Bucher began. "We shall continue to regret our acts against the Korean people. . . ."

The North Koreans herded the men into three buses and, on the night of December 22, drove them toward the train station at Pyongyang. Steve Harris remembered the portrait of Kim Il Sung up on the steeple which he'd seen eleven months before. It was still there. Nothing, he thought, had changed in this strange and depressing land. Then he stepped aboard the train.

★   ★   ★

Ambassador Porter in Seoul was on the phone to Under Secretary Katzenbach in Washington. He waved for General Woodward to pick up the receiver. "General," Katzenbach said, "do you think that if we announce the release here twenty-four hours ahead of time that the North Koreans will object and not return the crew? I want to hear your opinion."

Woodward suspected that Pak would be absolutely furious. Still, he thought, the North Korean could not afford to lose face. He would *have* to go through with the deal.

"Go ahead," he replied. "You can make the announcement. They'll turn 'em loose. They won't dare back up now."

★   ★   ★

At her home in Melrose, Massachusetts, Steve Harris' mother heard the news at three o'clock on Sunday morning, December 22. She had just gone to sleep after hosting a Christmas party for the parents and children of her fourth-grade elementary school class. "I walked right downstairs to the party table and helped myself to everything," she told The New York *Times.* "And for the first time in eleven months, the food tasted good." Then she began to wonder what clothes she should pack for the trip to California. In Clayton, Missouri, Jean Langenberg reacted with disbelief, then joy to the word that her son, Peter, was coming home. For the past few weeks she had been quietly passing out books of matches emblazoned with the slogan "Remember the *Pueblo.*" She started making arrangements for a flight to the West Coast. A special delivery package arrived at her door: It contained thirty-six additional boxes of matches. They seemed awfully irrelevant now. In San Diego, Rose Bucher reached for the telephone. Her attorney, E. Miles Harvey, was calling to report that he had just talked to someone at the Pentagon. "Baby," he was saying now, "this time it looks awfully good."

At eight o'clock that morning State Department Press Officer Robert J. McCloskey stepped before a brace of microphones. "There has been a breakthrough in the *Pueblo* talks," he began.

The train slowed to a stop at Kaesong. The guards and duty officers transferred the men to three yellow and green buses which ferried them the rest of the way to Panmunjom. The buses stopped just north of Korean People's Army checkpoint number four on the west side of the bridge. The duty officers repeated their instructions: The men would cross the bridge in single file. They must not look around. They must not make any signals. They must not run.

At nine o'clock on the morning of December 23, General Woodward took his seat at the round table. He nodded to Pak and, in a clear, strong voice, began reading the statement suggested by a Maryland housewife:

"The position of the United States Government with regard to the *Pueblo* . . . has been that the ship was not engaged in illegal activity, that there is no convincing evidence that the ship at any time intruded into the territorial waters claimed by North Korea, and that we could not apologize for actions which we did not believe took place. The document which I am going to sign was prepared by the North Koreans and is at variance with the above position. My signature will not and cannot alter the facts. I will sign the document to free the crew and only to free the crew."

Pak shuffled some papers. Woodward glanced down at the North Korean document.

The Government of the United States of America, acknowledging the validity of the confessions of the crew of the USS "Pueblo" and of the documents of evidence produced by the representative of the Government of the Democratic People's Republic of Korea to the effect that the ship, which was seized by the self-defense measures of the naval vessels of the Korean People's Army in the territorial waters of the Democratic People's Republic of Korea on January 23, 1968, had illegally intruded into the territorial waters of the Democratic People's Republic of Korea on many occasions and conducted espionage activities of spying out important military and state secrets of the Democratic People's Republic of Korea,

Shoulders full responsibility and solemnly apologizes for the grave acts of espionage committed by the U.S. ship against the Democratic People's Republic of Korea after having intruded into the territorial waters of the Democratic People's Republic of Korea,

And gives firm assurance that no U.S. ships will intrude again in the future into the territorial waters of the Democratic People's Republic of Korea.

Meanwhile, the Government of the United States of America earnestly requests the Government of the Democratic People's Republic of Korea to deal leniently with the former crew members of the USS "Pueblo" confiscated by the Democratic People's Republic of Korea side, taking into consideration the fact that these crew members have confessed honestly to their crimes and petitioned the Government of the Democratic People's Republic for leniency.

Simultaneous with the signing of this document, the undersigned acknowledges receipt of 82 former crew members of the USS "Pueblo" and one corpse.

On behalf of the Government of the United States of America,

Gilbert H. Woodward,
Major General, United States Army
23 Dec., 1968.

He signed his name and handed the paper across the table.

Suddenly, Pak announced that he could not release the crew. The United States had "insulted the entire Korean people" by its premature disclosure of a settlement. Therefore, the return would have to be "renegotiated."

"Do you now repudiate the agreement we made just yesterday? I will repeat that agreement for your benefit." And Woodward did.

"You've twisted my words," Pak replied.

Woodward glared at the North Korean contemptuously. He could not believe that Pak was serious. There had to be some way to test his intention. "I felt like saying, 'What the hell are you trying to prove?'" he remembers. "I decided to give him the needle instead. I said, 'Is there anything I can do to assist you? If you are having administrative delays, if you cannot release the crew at eleven o'clock, then eleven thirty would be acceptable. But I will need a receipt."

Silence. The North Korean saw that his cruel ploy wasn't succeeding. Finally, he reached for the paper and filled in the time of return: eleven-thirty. Then he tossed it across the table.

During the night a light snow had fallen over the rolling hills near Panmunjom. The morning was overcast; the temperature hovered in the mid-twenties. Thin plumes of smoke rose from the chimneys of the "typical workers' homes" on the North Korean side of the bridge. Bucher wondered if anyone lived in those homes or if, more probably, they constituted just another propaganda sham, a Potemkin village. Now a duty officer ordered him to step outside. Ambulance attendants began to remove the wrappings from Hodges' body.

"Is that your man?" the duty officer asked.

Bucher nodded and returned to the bus.

Half an hour later the duty officer came back and told him to stand at attention in front of a small building emblazoned with pictures of doves. General Pak strode up and began to harangue him about his "crimes." The lecture lasted twenty minutes. Pak's interpreter summed it up in thirty seconds.

At the other end of the narrow 250-foot bridge waited Colonel John P. Lucas, the secretary of the Military Armistice Commission. He held a clipboard in his hand and a list of eighty-three names. With him stood a Navy Lieutenant Commander named Paul E. Brooks.

The North Korean loudspeaker was booming out Bucher's recorded confession: ". . . We admit these crimes . . . we apologize for

them . . . sincerely. . . ." An ambulance carried the body of Duane
Hodges across the bridge. And then, just after eleven-thirty—three
hundred thirty-four days, twenty-one hours, and three minutes after
the seizure of his ship—Lloyd Mark Bucher limped toward home. He
clutched a blue cap in his left hand, and as he neared the end of the
bridge, he attempted to smile. Brooks saluted him. So did Lucas. Bucher
returned their salutes and glanced down at the plain wood coffin which
orderlies were transferring from one ambulance to the other. "I have
looked at the body," he said. "It is Hodges." The orderlies draped
an American flag over the coffin and closed the ambulance door.

They came across at thirty-second intervals, the rest of Bucher's
crew, resisting impulses to spit at the guards or flash the finger gesture. Mitchell's feet hurt; his sneakers were three sizes too small. He
stopped and, for a second or two, looked back. He was the only man
who did. Others threw off their North Korean jackets and put on
Army parkas. "It didn't seem real," Law remembers. "I got off the
bus and walked the wrong way for two steps. Halfway across the
bridge I could almost *see* again. I wanted to run like hell. I started
crying."

"How do they look? Are they limping? Do they seem okay?" Inside the radio room at the Joint Duty Officers' building, Pentagon
POW specialist Charles W. Havens was talking on the telephone to an
officer near the bridge at United Nations Command checkpoint three.
Havens relayed the officer's account on an open line to the National
Military Command Center in Washington. Simultaneously, he reached
for a legal pad, began writing short paragraphs in his large, left-handed
scrawl, and passed them across the table to Deputy Assistant Secretary
of Defense Richard Fryklund. And Fryklund started broadcasting live
over the Armed Forces Radio Network.

★   ★   ★

Bucher waited with Brooks and Lucas until the last man crossed
the bridge. Murphy. Then he turned and followed Murphy into the
Army bus.

★   ★   ★

In the Operations Center at the State Department, Katzenbach,
Brown, and Leonard were listening to a relay report from the NMCC
in the Pentagon. Someone secured an open line to the embassy in
Seoul, which in turn had an open line to Panmunjom. Someone else
managed to patch into Fryklund's play-by-play account. Secretaries

passed around dozens of paper cups. And Brown, the seeming Calvinist, produced a bottle of Scotch.

"Apparently the North Koreans believe there is propaganda value even in a worthless document," Rusk declared minutes later. "It is a strange procedure. The North Koreans would have to explain it. I know of no precedent in my nineteen years of public service. . . ."

At Rose Bucher's home in San Diego, attorney E. Miles Harvey, was on the telephone to the CNO flag plot in the Pentagon, which in turn was receiving its "feed" from the NMCC. Harvey nodded, smiled, nodded again. Rose Bucher watched him intently. Harvey hung up the phone, and she ran to embrace him. "It's all over now," Harvey said. "It's all over."

"You're not in a secure area yet," Fryklund was saying. "You have to cool it." The three olive-drab buses passed Korean Peoples' Army checkpoint five, climbed the steep hill, and bounced toward an advance camp outside the DMZ. Bucher and Fryklund sat in the right front seat of the lead bus. "He was extremely tense," Fryklund remembers. "The first thing he said was, 'Do you think we violated North Korean waters?' I told him I didn't, and he said, 'Well, that's right. We doctored that evidence. You look at it carefully and you'll see how we doctored it.' "

The Army cooks at the advance camp had prepared a feast: steak, potatoes, ice cream, and apple pie. But the Navy decided it was wiser to feed the men something bland: chicken noodle soup, for example, ham and bologna sandwiches, saltine crackers, and milk. Bucher was the last man to enter the mess hall. His men stood up and cheered.

Helicopters ferried the crew to the 121st U.S. Army evacuation hospital 10 miles east of Seoul. Bucher remained in the green Quonset hut that served as a mess hall, and at 1:20, less than two hours after crossing the bridge, he appeared at a hastily arranged press conference. "Those guys," he said of his crew, "were simply tremendous. They never once lost their spirit or faith in the United States of America." His face drawn, his eyes reddened with fatigue, he went on to insist that he had followed his orders "to the letter." He maintained that *Pueblo* had "never once" intruded into North Korean waters. "We—I surrendered the ship," he explained, his voice cracking, "because it was nothing but a slaughter out there, and I couldn't see allowing any more people to be slaughtered or killing the entire crew for no reason. . . ."

"Could you tell us if you got rid of the [classified documents and] secret equipment?" a reporter asked.

Bucher paused, groping for words. "We made an attempt to destroy everything," he said, finally. "Well, there, truthfully, we did not complete it."

How about the finger gestures? someone else inquired.

"They were trying to tell you that we'd been had," Bucher said. "We realized that if we were discovered, it was going to be 'Katie, bar the door,' but we felt that it was important that we get that information out. So there would be absolutely no room for doubt in your minds, the American people's minds, that we'd been had."

He talked about his captors' brutality: "I did lose initially an awful lot of weight and got to the point where I was in danger of disappearing. . . . There were many occasions when I didn't think I was going to make it. . . ." He emphasized that he'd signed confessions only "to save people from some fairly serious misfortunes." He referred again to the incident: "And I just couldn't. I couldn't fathom what was happening at the time, and to this day I'm not sure of everything that happened."

Bucher's performance was impressive. To the reporters present, it seemed obvious that he hadn't been "coached" in his replies; there hadn't been any time for that. And if he stammered and contradicted himself in one or two places, well, that just added to his credibility. Bucher limped out of the mess hall to join the rest of his crew at the Army hospital. Watching him, some reporters applauded.

Next morning the officer in charge of the crew's return, Rear Admiral Edwin M. Rosenberg, met the press himself. "I have the utmost admiration for Captain Bucher and his crew," the admiral declared. They are "tremendous representatives of America. . . . As far as the U.S. government and the Navy are concerned, these men at all times acted in an extremely honorable fashion. . . ." Bucher, the admiral went on to say, "is a hero among heroes."

At two o'clock that afternoon, December 24, the *Pueblo* crew honored Duane Hodges in a simple memorial service at Seoul's Kimpo Airport. Wearing a borrowed chaplain's cap, Bucher lowered his head throughout the ceremony. Then, as a band played "Anchors Aweigh" and "California, Here I Come," he turned and followed his crew toward the waiting C-141 StarLifters.

★   ★   ★

In Washington, Rusk summoned Katzenbach, Brown, Leonard—and everyone else who had helped guide the *Pueblo* negotiations over the past eleven months—into his spacious seventh-floor conference room. He thanked them for their efforts, then said, "Now the next thing is, let's get that ship back."

★   ★   ★

The C-141's stopped to refuel at Midway Island. Admiral John J. Hyland, Commander in Chief, Pacific Fleet, had flown there to greet the crew and he, too, referred to them as "heroes." In the tiny snack bar, the men were gulping down quarts of orange juice, eating their first hamburgers in nearly a year, and leafing through copies of their first American newspaper—the Honolulu *Advertiser*. Steve Harris watched Hyland and Bucher conversing in low tones at a corner booth. "I noticed that Pete's expression was grim," he recalls. "I got the impression that it was not going well. Not at all."

Bucher appeared at an impromptu press conference. "Every member of the crew has been subjected to terror of some kind or another," he said. "They [the North Koreans] finally told me they would kill me. And I wasn't particularly upset by this. They put me through one of these drills with an empty gun. . . . I held up pretty well. . . ."

How would he describe his captors?

"Apes," Bucher said. His crew cheered.

★   ★   ★

At Miramar Naval Air Station 12 miles north of San Diego, a Navy band struck up "Seventy-Six Trombones," then drifted into the lilting "This Is My Country." Nervously, Rose Bucher adjusted the white orchid corsage on the left shoulder of her brown suit. "They're coming in," someone shouted, and suddenly everyone in the crowd of *Pueblo* wives and families, newsmen, and Navy officials was straining for a glimpse of the approaching StarLifters, twin black specks growing larger against the afternoon haze.

The first of the giant planes touched down at two o'clock and taxied to within 50 feet of the crowd. Sailors sprang to roll a red carpet over the tarmac. Wearing blue submarine coveralls with "USS Pueblo" stenciled across the back of his jacket, Bucher stepped from the aircraft. He waved hesitantly, and as the band began to play "The Lonely Bull," he limped toward his wife. Tears welled in his eyes. "It's just so great," he said, "you'll never know how great it is." He embraced Rose and turned to comfort Mr. and Mrs. Jesse Hodges. "Your son," he told them, "was a great American."

All around him were tears and cries of joy and then embraces as his crewmen and their families spotted each other in the crowd. Chicca met his ten-month-old son, Jamie. Murphy picked up his nine-month-old daughter, Victoria Lyn. Their expressions combining pride and self-consciousness, Hagenson, Hammond, and Goldman greeted the new additions to their families. One teary-eyed father kept patting his son on the shoulder. "The first thing we've got to do is get some fat on you," he said. Another father could only say, "Well, Merry Christmas, Merry Christmas; it's really good to see you."

Bucher stepped to the microphone. "In the many months that I spent in that land," he began, "my primary thoughts were of the embarrassment we caused the U.S. by losing one of its finest, one of its very finest ships to the . . . uh . . . to the North Koreans. It was during the loss of that ship that several men received . . . wounds. . . ." He paused and struggled to regain his composure. "Our thoughts are of one of our men who fell mortally wounded. His remains accompanied me all the way from Korea. It seems like it was a very short trip. . . ."

Six pallbearers with white helmets and white web belts lifted the casket from the door of the plane and carried it toward a gray hearse. An honor guard fired its volleys. Trumpeters played "The Navy Hymn." Bucher and his crew stood at attention and saluted. Then they turned to enter the buses that would carry them past cheering throngs to Balboa Naval Hospital. It was Christmas Eve. Their odyssey was over.

President Johnson announced that he was "deeply gratified . . . and happy for them." President-elect Richard M. Nixon issued a statement. So did the CNO, Admiral Thomas H. Moorer. The wives of the Apollo 8 astronauts added their congratulations to the flood of messages already pouring into San Diego. "Don't ask about what happened at the time of their capture or during their captivity," Rear Admiral Rosenberg had cautioned reporters. "Theirs and the national interest are involved." In the spirit of the season, most Americans seemed content to postpone judgments and expand their energies on welcoming the prisoners home.

But the questions, of course, remained. In Washington on Christmas Day one old friend and former commanding officer wrote Bucher a long and thoughtful letter. "Very few people in the United States," he warned, "would realize that the worst of it has only begun."

40

The people of San Diego—so still in their conservatism—were absolutely munificent in the warmth and generosity they afforded crew members and their families. The Chamber of Commerce launched a fund drive and soon raised $45,000—more than enough to pay for dependents' hotel bills. A local band gave a benefit performance. Rent-a-car firms donated vehicles; restaurants provided free meals. The American Red Cross set up an office in the lobby of the El Cortez Hotel. One remembers crew members' families wandering through that lobby: a father in a green sweater saying proudly, "My boy told 'em he wouldn't sign nothin' "; another father confiding, "He says the welcome's great, you know; he can't believe this is what people really think of him."

Inside the plain, three-story converted corpsmen's barracks—nicknamed "the pink palace"—on the hospital grounds in Balboa Park, teams of doctors and nurses examined the *Pueblo* crew. "All these men show the effects of malnutrition: loss of weight, instability in balance," declared Rear Admiral Horace D. Warden, the hospital's commander, on December 26. "No doubt there are other disabilities, as well."

Larry Mack had a fractured rib, Lee Hayes a broken jaw. Richard Arnold had lost all feeling in two fingers of his left hand. Elton Wood couldn't move the little finger on his right hand. The damage to Charles Law's optic nerves, the doctors said, was permanent. And what of the other, less overt scars? How long would they afflict these men? "All persons who have undergone [such] an ordeal," Rear Admiral Warden conceded, "are subject to psychological pressures and changes. We must evaluate it."

By four o'clock on the afternoon of the twenty-sixth, doctors had certified that the first thirteen men were ready to undergo a comprehensive intelligence debriefing. On hand to conduct this probe were nearly one-hundred civilian "debriefers" and "technicians" from the National Security Agency, the Naval Intelligence Command, the Naval Security Group, and the Marine Corps' Counter Intelligence Command. The information they gathered, the Navy said, would be restricted to the intelligence community and not be used as "evidence" in any forthcoming judicial proceedings. "We told the men we weren't pursuing culpability," remembers Captain C. Dale Everhart, the lean, dark-haired officer who directed the effort. "Our purpose was only to determine the extent of the intelligence loss."

In length and depth the interviews varied widely. Debriefers required only three sessions with Hayes, the radioman. They needed fifteen with Michael Barrett, twenty-six with another man. Eventually, they collected 270 *miles* of tape. But much of it contained long pauses. "The North Koreans kinda took the wind out of a lot of people," one debriefer was quoted as saying. "Some of these men get faraway looks in their eyes when you talk to them. They switch off like radios."

For a while some crew members fully intended to "put the screws to" the one man whose nervousness in North Korea had caused them so much anxiety. "The captain heard about it and said he didn't want us to," Roy Maggard recalls. "He called a meeting and said, 'Everybody's done things over there they shouldn't have. Just forget it.' He didn't mention no names. He didn't have to. Everybody knew who he was talking about."

By December 28 all except Goldman, Mack, and Bucher himself had been declared physically fit to enter the debriefing stage. Crew members began to receive liberty in downtown San Diego. So very much, it seemed, had happened while they were away. They had amassed nearly $250,000 in back pay; forty-nine of the seventy-four enlisted men had been promoted. The United States had a new President. The Detroit Tigers had won the World Series. Three astronauts had circled the moon. And there were other changes, as well, to which it would be harder to adjust. One man discovered that his wife was four months pregnant. "How does it feel to have your husband home?" a television newsman asked her. "Great," she replied, "but I think we have some problems ahead of us." They would be divorced shortly.

Duane Hodges was buried late in December at a hillside cemetery in Creswell, Oregon. Most of the town's 917 residents crowded into a junior high school auditorium to hear the eulogy. Stu Russell married his fiancée, a vivacious, attractive blonde named Sharon McCartney. Bucher kissed the bride, and the wedding pictures appeared in *Life* magazine. Actor John Wayne appeared at a banquet honoring the crew in the LeBaron Hotel. He handed each man a plaque inscribed, "We will always remember the *Pueblo.*"

One morning early in January, Bucher and nine of his men received Purple Hearts in the courtyard of the hospital's administration building. Rows of metal and plastic chairs under the palm trees had been reserved for friends and relatives. Martial music began blaring over the public address system: incredibly, "This is the Army, Mr. Jones" and "The Caissons Go Rolling Along." Bucher stepped forward to accept his medal and, watching him, one wished that this simple ceremony could proceed with dignity. But it was not to be. A radio reporter started broadcasting live: ". . . Fireman Duane Hodges, the only member of the crew to be killed, he will receive an award later. This award, of course, will be given to his parents. . . ." Bucher said, "Thank you," and saluted. A silver-helmeted color guard trooped away past the fountain. Then a Navy captain stepped to the microphone and announced the winner of the "Sailor of the Month" award. He would receive a $50 gift certificate and two free meals in San Diego.

In the weeks since the crew's return, Murphy had held a press conference and told how he had fooled his captors by doctoring charts of the ship's positions. Hayes and Law had described the beatings they received during Hell Week. But aside from these appearances, there had been a blackout on news about the incident. The Navy told crew members to refuse comment on anything except the weather. Lieutenant Commander Allen Hemphill tried to fill the void. "Pete has two speeds," he said one afternoon, describing his friend; "when he's not all stop, he's full speed ahead. If we ever go to war, I want Pete commanding me. He's the type of guy who gets things done." But how about what happened off Wonsan? "It wasn't a question of fight or no fight," Hemphill said. "It was slaughter or no slaughter. The other guys who say he should have gone down with his ship—they're the old Navy. Pete and I—we're the new Navy."

Perhaps so—but the old Navy was still very much in charge. And it had already announced plans to convene a formal court of inquiry into the *Pueblo* incident. To comprise that court Admiral John J. Hyland, Commander in Chief, Pacific Fleet, appointed five admirals, all Annapolis graduates. His charge to them seemed broad enough:

"The court is directed to inquire into all the facts and circumstances relating to the subject incident, including whether *Pueblo* did at any time during the period of ten January to her seizure procede within twelve miles of North Korea and, if so, whether such action was in accordance with or violation of any order issued to the commanding officer. The court will also inquire into the circumstances surrounding the actual boarding, the details of that boarding, and the events immediately subsequent to the boarding and will also inquire into all the facts and circumstances surrounding the subsequent detention of the ship and its officers and crew. . . . The court will express its opinion as to the line of duty and misconduct status of any . . . personnel and will recommend administrative or disciplinary action as appropriate. . . ."

"This is a matter of accountability," explained Captain William R. Newsome, the balding, olive-skinned, forty-six-year-old New Yorker who would serve as the court's counsel. "The Navy is an institution that demands accountability. When a sophisticated piece of equipment is lost, someone must give an accounting for this loss. People must be held accountable or we'd have no way of control. It's not as if we were operating as a separate entity."

But a court of inquiry, Newsome and his aides hastened to point out, was *not* a trial. It was an investigative proceeding, rather akin to a civilian grand jury. Its duty was to ferret out facts and then make recommendations. It could not determine guilt or innocence; it could not administer punishment. And the Navy, they said, convened such courts all the time. There was the case of the destroyer *Bache*, which ran aground off the Greek coast; there was the matter of the loss of the submarine *Scorpion*.

All of this was true. And yet not since the court-martial of Billy Mitchell in 1925 had any military judicial proceeding seemed so enormously significant or promised such stark drama. There were, on an elementary level, obvious questions to be answered: Who ordered the mission? Why had no help arrived in time? Why had Bucher surrendered without offering any resistance? Why had he and his men signed those confessions?

On another level loomed the more perplexing issues. No American captain had surrendered his ship in peacetime since June, 1807, when Commodore James Barron allowed the British to board USS *Chesapeake* off Cape Henry, Virginia. But even Barron had managed to "fire one gun for the honor of the flag" before capitulating. Navy tradition—and regulation—decreed that no captain *could* surrender his ship so long as he had the means to resist. Navy tradition, however, was composed of ships of the line, *combat* vessels. *Pueblo* was hardly one of them. So did this tradition, this regulation, fairly apply to this ship and this captain in this time of uneasy peace?

How could anyone fault Bucher for placing primary emphasis on saving the lives of his men? Wasn't this precisely what President Johnson had done—albeit on a larger scale—in deciding not to retaliate against North Korea nearly a year before? Hadn't *he* reasoned that to do so might trigger another war or, at the very least, cost many additional lives? Wasn't this respect for human life integral to America's system of values? Was Navy tradition, then, somehow in conflict with these values, and if so, was it *wrong?*

And what could one say about the Code of Conduct, the 247-word executive order which had been issued in 1955 as "a shield against the physical, mental and moral onslaughts of Communism"? It mentioned "the enemy"; it was designed to serve as a guideline in a wartime situation. But was North Korea an *enemy?* Was this a *wartime situation?* Did the code apply to these men? In Article V the code urges prisoners of war to "make no oral or written statements disloyal to [their] country . . . or harmful to [its] cause. . . ." Could Bucher and his crew be blamed for violating that code when the U.S. government had "solemnly apologize[d] for the grave acts of espionage" at Panmunjom?

Perhaps the most pertinent question was simply, How would these five admirals conduct the court? Would they recognize the awesome, overlapping complexity of the issues and try to deal with them meaningfully—or would they simply hew to regulations, ignore the shadings of gray and take the easy way out? Would they whitewash Bucher? Or make him a scapegoat? In time, these admirals would establish themselves as distinct—and rather likable—personalities. But now, in the days before the court convened, one saw them only as five blue suits with sleeves of gold braid. One asked about them and examined their biographies.

The president of the court would be Vice Admiral Harold G. Bowen, Jr., the son of a vice admiral, the son-in-law of another vice admiral. During the Korean War Bowen had remained on the bridge of his flagship, the destroyer *Maddox,* while she engaged in a murderous duel with enemy guns off Wonsan. *Maddox* received a direct hit; shells burst all around her. Cooly, Bowen directed his men to wipe out the shore emplacement. They did, and for that he received the Legion of Merit. Yet there was nothing in his record to suggest a cocky, swashbuckling hero. He held a Master of Science degree in Metallurgical Engineering; he had once served as director of the Atomic Energy Division, Office of the CNO. And he was an excellent pistol shot. One imagined that he would be very cool, very precise.

To varying degrees, the other members of the court seemed to mirror Bowen's characteristics. All had strong ties to the Navy "establishment." All had been tested by what Joseph Conrad once called "those events of the sea that show the inner worth of a man, the edge of his temper and the fibre of his stuff. . . ." All had distinguished themselves in administrative positions, as well.

Rear Admiral Richard R. Pratt, for example, was the nephew of a CNO and the son-in-law of a commodore. He had won the Bronze Star "for heroic service," the Silver Star "for conspicious gallantry," the Navy Cross "for extraordinary heroism," and a Gold Star in lieu of a second Navy Cross—again "for extraordinary heroism." And then he had gone on to serve as chief in Europe of the Defense Communications Agency. Rear Admiral Edward E. Grimm, at fifty-eight, the oldest member of the court, had been wounded during the Second Battle of the Philippine Sea. Days later, ignoring peril to himself, he had guided his ship, the cruiser *Birmingham,* alongside the blazing carrier *Princeton* and tried to put out the fires. He held a master's degree in Business Administration and had served as the Navy Department's Director of Budget Reports.

In 1939 Rear Admiral Allen A. Bergner had captained the Naval Academy football team which beat Army, 10–0. He played tackle that year, a sixty-minute man. His teammates called him "Big Bear." He captained the Navy wrestling team, as well. In World War II, as executive officer and navigator of the submarine *Gar,* he won the Bronze Star, the Navy and Marine Corps Medal, the Navy Commendation Medal. At the moment he commanded the Naval Training Center in San Diego.

The fifth member of the court, Rear Admiral Marshall W. White, was an aviator, the recipient of a Bronze Star "for meritorious service . . . in operations against enemy aggressor forces in Korea." A former skipper of the aircraft carrier *Hornet,* he now directed the Pacific Missile Range at Point Mugu, California.

The formal biographies listed 77 medals and decorations, 184 years of service to and, presumably, unswerving belief in a hard and uncompromising system. One searched these records for hints of possible compassion or bias. Would Admiral Bergner, the youngest member of the court, the submariner, tend to sympathize with Bucher? Would the fact that Admiral Bowen had stood in his crucible off Wonsan make any difference at all? And how about Admiral White, who had directed air strikes against the North Koreans? There were few clues. Bergner, one discovered, made cabinets and refinished furniture in his spare time. Bowen liked to play tennis and squash. And White was reported to be extremely devout.

On January 11 the *Pueblo* crew moved out of the hospital and across the bay from San Diego to a two-story barracks at the Naval

Air Station on North Island. Most of the men were on what the Navy called a "limited duty status"; those whose enlistments had expired during captivity were placed on a ninety-day "medical hold." Several miles away, in a building on Guadalcanal Road at the U.S. Naval Amphibious Base in Coronado, workmen carried chairs into the small amphitheater that would serve as a courtroom. They tacked down a thick carpet, brought in a long maple table and placed it on a stage. They covered it with a thin green cloth.

The court would divide its inquiry into three phases, Captain Newsome told reporters on January 13: the mission and operation of the ship, the seizure, and the detention period. He and his associate, Commander William E. Clemons, were about to screen prospective witnesses. He doubted that all crew members would testify: "We wouldn't want to call ten people to substantiate the same fact." The court would meet six days a week. Some of the sessions would be closed, but not too many. It would be "a typical Navy-type investigation. I'm shooting for something between three weeks and a month."

How about the Code of Conduct? someone asked. Does it apply to these men?

Newsome hesitated. Washington couldn't seem to make up its mind about that. "No," he said, finally, "the Code of Conduct is inapplicable in this situation. We have had an opinion. The crew members of the *Pueblo* were not prisoners of war. They were illegally detained. We are not in a state of hostilities with the North Koreans. Consequently, they are not the enemy. Not being the enemy, we don't have prisoners of war. When we don't have prisoners of war, we don't have the application of the Code of Conduct."

"Captain, if North Korea is not considered the enemy, there is a question of surrender. You can't surrender to a nonenemy, can you?"

"I honestly don't know," Newsome said.

"Captain," someone else asked, "can you comment on whether the five admirals are fully aware of the thirst for knowledge of the people of the United States—beyond the needs of the Navy—about what happened in this episode?"

"The admirals are sensitive to public opinion," Newsome said. "They can appreciate that the public would like to have the facts."

★　　★　　★

Bucher thought it was very strange. Over there, in North Korea, he had worried so much about and tried to plan so carefully for the court of inquiry which he'd known would eventually come. But since his return, he had hardly had time even to think about that. First, there'd been that period of isolation in the hospital. Then the debriefing sessions. He'd had ship's business to conduct, too—he was, after all, still the commanding officer—and there were still so many people he wanted to thank for their efforts on his crew's behalf: Marcee Rethwish, for example, that pretty, fifteen-year-old girl who'd organized those prayer meetings.

What seemed even stranger now was this celebrity business. His picture on the front page of the New York *Times*—who'd ever have imagined that? Not to mention all those TV people. Just the other day, after the Purple Heart ceremony, he'd stepped into a bookstore downtown and purchased $22 worth of reading material: *The Code-breakers* by David Kahn, *The Devil's Dictionary*, a set of Shakespeare's works. The manager had recognized him and insisted he accept the books free. Bucher told Phil Stryker that he felt as if someone had a telephoto lens on him all the time. He couldn't begin to walk to Miles Harvey's office without someone stopping him on the street to congratulate him. It got so bad after a while that he bought a porkpie hat and tried to appear incognito. Harvey, of course, had told him that he'd better get used to it. Hundreds of journalists from all over the world would be on hand to cover the court of inquiry. And he had said no, the San Diego paper might assign someone, there might even be a man from L.A. That would be all.

The fact that Harvey would represent him at the court of inquiry was, he thought, propitious. The slender, dark-haired civilian attorney was already familiar with the case as a result of his work for Rose. He was young and aggressive; furthermore, he was a commander in the Naval Reserve. He knew the ropes. The Navy had also provided him with a military counsel, a crew-cut, rather florid-faced captain named James E. Keys. Bucher didn't know very much about Keys—they'd just talked briefly at Russell's wedding—but the stocky, soft-spoken officer seemed a perfect counterpart to Harvey. For the past four days Keys and Harvey had listened to his story, taking notes and interrupting him every so often to ask questions. In the beginning, of course, they had told him that he had a right to remain silent. But why? He had nothing to hide. As soon as he testified, the admirals would see that he had never violated his orders. The truth would vindicate him. He felt confident of that.

★　　★　　★　　PART FOUR

41

... in the half-light of the big courtroom ... the audience seemed composed of staring shadows. They wanted facts. Facts! They demanded facts from him as if facts could explain anything!
—Joseph Conrad, *Lord Jim*

★   ★   ★

"Attention in the court," shouted a stocky Marine guard standing under a "No Smoking" sign.

Everyone rose. At 8:57 on the morning of January 20, 1969, Admiral Bowen entered the amphitheater and stepped briskly to his seat behind the long table. He walked with a sort of Groucho Marx tilt: a smaller man than one expected from reading his biography, balding, with patrician features and deep-set, laser-beam eyes. Standing at their places were the members of his court: Admiral Bergner, solid and white-haired; he rather resembled a successful high school football coach. And next to him Admiral Grimm, a handsome man with a broad and seemingly sardonic smile. He reminded one of an aging Hollywood matineé idol, and soon he would be nicknamed "Jack the Ripper." On Bowen's right was Admiral White, the slouching, curly-haired aviator, and next to him Admiral Pratt, who had just returned from giving his daughter away at her wedding in the Navy Chapel in Washington, D.C. He wore only two rows of ribbons: a tanned, be-spectacled man whose face betrayed all the emotion of an IBM computer.

"The court will come to order," Bowen said. Floodlights played on the American and Navy flags which flanked the table. Reporters, relatives, and spectators (but *what* spectators: mostly female, mostly plump and middle-aged; titterers; veterans, one surmised, of the Finch-Tregoff trial or dropouts from the *Art Linkletter Show*) took their seats as Captain Newsome cleared away the procedural debris. He read Admiral Hyland's appointing order. Did Bucher understand that, as a party to the inquiry, he could object to the introduction of certain evidence, that he had the right to refuse to incriminate himself? Yes. Did Harvey and Keys wish to challenge any members of the court?

"We have no challenges," Keys said and cleared his throat. It was 9:02. Newsome called Bucher to the stand.

"Captain Newsome," Harvey interrupted, "I wonder if we might inquire whether at this time Commander Bucher is suspected of committing any offense under the Uniform Code of Military Justice?"

Newsome chose his words deliberately. "No," he replied. "At this time Commander Bucher is not suspected of having committed any offense. . . ."

"Commander," Newsome continued, "to the best of your knowledge, what is your present physical and mental condition?"

Bucher had strode into the courtroom with a peculiar jerk-step. He stood now by his small green table and peered at the admirals six feet away through heavy horn-rimmed glasses. His face was pale. His teeth were clenched. He wore his submarine dolphins above the ribbons on his chest; he wore the small circled star which indicated command at sea. His uniform was wrinkled. Had he slept in it? One noticed the silver extension band on his watch and the gold wedding band . . . the wedding ring; where was Rose? On this most important day of her husband's life she was in Washington, D.C., attending the inauguration of President Richard Nixon.

"I believe I have improved physically," Bucher replied in flat, nasal tones, "to the extent that I can fully withstand the anticipated length of time of this court of inquiry. I have gained some eighteen pounds since I have returned to the United States, and mentally, I feel that I am as sharp as I can be . . ."

And quickly he was into the story of his first command, flicking a three-foot-wooden pointer at the schematics of the ship, which rested on an easel, describing the troubles at Bremerton and during the voyage across the Pacific:

"This was simply a different type of ship and only a very few people in the Navy were aware of it. . . . I had a difficult time preparing for the type of operation I was scheduled to conduct. . . . There were many improvements that we were not permitted due to money and time. . . . I did request a destruct system in a classified letter to the CNO . . . the request was turned down . . . the ship's steering was the most troublesome system. . . . I had lost steering as many as sixty times in two weeks. . . . We did have a stability problem . . . one of the things that I recommended . . . funds and time prevented this . . . did not have a watertight door although I had requested one. . . ."

The admirals shifted in their seats, glanced at the round clock over the door to their right, looked at Bucher and down again at the legal pads in front of them.

". . . because the ship was from the Army no such [communications] system was available and I was not provided with. . . . I did feel strongly about this and included it in every one of my progress reports . . . it was not possible to steer the ship from after steering. . . . I had no collision alarm. I had requested it and it was turned down. . . . We left the yard in September without the problem of armament being solved. . . ."

The room was hot. "Commander," Newsome said, "if you care to sit down, certainly do so."

"I feel more comfortable standing," Bucher said.

". . . the .50 caliber machine guns were unfamiliar to my gunner's mate, who had never had any formal training in their use. . . . One of the last things Admiral Johnson said to me was that I should in no way uncover those guns unless it was absolutely necessary, nor was I ever to provoke anyone by the use of those guns. . . . I was not confident in my ability to use [them], and there was no protection of any kind afforded to the man who would be standing there. . . . I was particularly not happy with having to move one gun to the other side of the ship when I wanted to use it. . . . I was in complete *military* command of the ship. . . . CINCPACFLT designated that the operational and management control of the research spaces be under the command and jurisdiction of Lieutenant Harris. . . .

"We went to sea without any destruct device of an explosive nature. . . . I felt that we were being provided with too many nonessential classified publications. . . . I went through and pared that list down . . . we were required to carry the full load. . . . I was convinced that we were going on an operation that [would] be very unprofitable. . . ."

"Did you ever satisfy yourself," Captain Newsome asked, in a marked Brooklyn accent, "that the precautions for destruction in the research spaces were adequate?"

"I did not," Bucher said.

"As the commanding officer of the ship, there was no reason why you could not have ascertained the volume of the classified material in the research spaces; isn't that correct?"

"To a degree, I could not," Bucher replied, "because I wasn't cleared for some of the materials they carried. . . ."

Could five admirals believe such testimony? Perhaps. Could they accept it as *justification?* That seemed another matter entirely, and now, as the questioning continued, one listened carefully for a counterattack.

"You mentioned several times your stability," Admiral Bergner said, removing the fat, unlit cigar—a Roi Tan Blunt—from his mouth. "Was this a mental hazard to you?"

"Well, yes, sir, it really was. This was my first surface ship in a long time, and I was really concerned about it."

"Did you hold a repel boarders drill?" Admiral Grimm asked.

"Repel boarders we did not hold, sir."

"You say you did not hold this for any particular reason?" Admiral Bowen was staring at Bucher, his voice low and smooth. Like an icepick.

"No, sir . . . well, I just did not feel the necessity for holding them, sir. I didn't appreciate it—as a continuing necessity—to hold that drill."

"Which your philosophy rather supports," Bowen said. He nodded to Admiral White.

"Admiral Johnson told you to keep your guns covered in the hopes that you would not make somebody mad. Whose policy was that?" Admiral White asked. "I'm quite sure it was not Admiral Johnson's. It was *somebody else's* policy. . . ."

"It was the policy of the CNO that put the guns on the ship," Bucher said. ". . . I was under the impression that Admiral Johnson was speaking for himself when he said keep the guns covered."

Admiral Bowen looked up. "I don't think we should go into that," he said. There was a pause. "Commander Bucher," he continued, "we have heard from you a great many references to deficiencies that you strove to have improved, quite rightly. However, the ship's preparation continued, and you arrived in WESTPAC, and you sailed off on your mission. Do you feel that on the tenth of January, 1968, you were prepared to carry out the mission?"

"Yes, sir," Bucher said. "There was no question in my mind."

Score one for—for whom? The *prosecution?* One hesitated to use that word; this was, after all, only a court of inquiry. And yet. . . .

On the second morning of the court, the ship's schematics on the easel gave way to a chart of the waters off North Korea. Bucher popped a Sucret in his mouth and continued his narrative. *Pueblo* had proceeded to her assigned operations areas. She had been spotted by the two fishing trawlers. She had experienced communications difficulties. And on the morning of January 23 she had steamed toward Wonsan.

"Who was primarily responsible for the navigation on the ship?" Captain Newsome asked.

"The navigator . . . that was Lieutenant Murphy. . . ."

"And you are *ultimately* responsible, is that right, Commander?"

"I am, as commanding officer, responsible for everything that happens to that ship."

"Commander," Newsome continued, "you have indicated that a good bit of your mission was rather dull and unproductive . . . did you in fact move toward the shoreline at full speed in order to *invite* attention . . . ?"

"Not at all, sir. I did just the opposite throughout the patrol. . . ."

"At any time during your patrol did you penetrate or intrude into North Korean waters?"

"At no time," Bucher said.

Now he was into the incident itself. His lips quivered. The lavalier microphone around his neck amplified his heavy breathing. At the counsel's table a crew-cut intelligence officer, Commander Richard W. Bates, had been drawing ball-and-chain doodles. He put down his pen and listened attentively.

". . . I was not concerned to the point that I thought the North Korean ships were going to do anything more than continue their intimidation and try to get me to do something that would be embarrassing for a U.S. naval ship. . . . Mr. Lacy asked me if we could go to GQ, and I told him I did not wish to go to GQ as I did not wish to give these people an excuse for considering that our ship was in their vicinity and conducting hostile operations. . . .

". . . There was no hope in my outrunning these people. . . . I was completely and hopelessly outgunned. . . . The covers were frozen and could not easily be removed . . . to send a man up to that gun would have meant certain death for him. . . ."

But then the S01 had fired. ". . . the hits that I received in my leg, about five or six pieces, did not bother me. The one that entered my rectum caused considerable pain. Nevertheless, I was able to ignore, completely ignore it and assumed full command of the ship within a matter of five seconds. . . ." The admirals looked down at their legal pads. The court adjourned at 2:32.

Bucher opened his brown attaché case. There were packs of Kools

and Lucky Strikes inside and bottles of pills and pinned to the leather
a small button. "Remember the *Pueblo*," it said. "It's too bad you have
to spend all your time facing the admirals," a reporter began. "There's
a pretty fantastic-looking girl right behind you. The one in the blue
skirt."

Bucher grinned for the first time all day. "You mean lavender
skirt," he said. And he was right.

The court convened again at nine o'clock next morning. Rose
Bucher sat in the front row wearing a blue dress with red and white
stripes. ". . . this shell scattered considerable glass around," her
husband was saying, picking up where he'd ended the day before, "and
it was at this time that Ensign Harris was wounded. . . . Other ex-
plosions were going on all around the ship. Ensign Harris left his chair
and went into the chart room and continued to keep the narrative
there. . . . I considered Ensign Harris' action entirely appropriate. I
wanted a complete narrative kept in the event that help did arrive. I
remember looking at his log once. I thought he was keeping a complete
and excellent narrative of the events as they were proceeding. . . ."

And he went on and on like this in his oddly disengaged way, describing what must have been the most terrifying of moments as if he
were merely reading from the box score of a Little League baseball
game. The mind boggled at the image of this wounded captain looking
over the shoulder of his wounded ensign, reading paragraphs as shells
burst around them. He talked about blood, but one did not see it,
smell it, feel it in that courtroom; the cries of surprise and anguish
were layered over, suffocated by thick blankets of irrelevant detail.
". . . the mattress cover itself is some six feet by three feet in width
and length and of course designed to be slipped over a naval mattress and they are used in the Navy on enlisted bunks. . . .

". . . I ordered the ship ahead one-third and I put the rudder
over to about five degrees . . . in order to follow him. I had decided
at this time that I would offer no further resistance. . . . The incinerator just would not hold all the classified pubs that we had and
the water depth did not permit their jettisoning over the side. . . . I
was thinking about the destruction as it was going on; also I was somewhat angry at what was happening. . . ."

At the noon recess Rose Bucher changed her dress. She came back
into court wearing a trim blue suit and sunglasses. At 1:33 Admiral
Bergner leaned forward over the table. "Commander," he asked, "were
small arms broken out when you went to modified general quarters?"

"No, sir, they were not."

"What information did you receive from your two damage control units relative to the condition of the ship prior to your making your decision to stop for the first time?"

". . . we had no fire, no flooding, and no material casualties. . . ."

Bergner frowned. "For clarification, what significant event occured just prior to your making the decision to stop? What *prompted* you to make this decision?"

"No particular action took place. My feeling was we would be hopelessly riddled and perhaps sustain an inordinate number of casualties, which would interfere with the destruction of the classified matter. . . ."

"After you had stopped and turned to follow the S01 back into port, was there any attempt on the part of you and your crew to set fire to the ship or to attempt to scuttle it?"

"No sir," Bucher replied, "there was not."

"Had you ever rehearsed the modified GQ?" Admiral Pratt asked. "No sir, I had not."

Now it was Admiral White's turn. "Didn't you think that this [earlier] attempt to board you was sufficient reason to cause you to start destructing immediately?"

"No, sir. . . . I didn't know what their intentions were at that time. . . . I did not consider that I had enough positive information as to what was going to happen eventually."

"Your ringing up all stop," Admiral Bowen asked. "This was to do what?"

"Was to comply with his orders to heave to, and to hope that the firing would stop."

"Did you ever consider that you might have been attacked, and if so, what would you do?"

"It never occurred to me. I had read nothing . . . nor had I received any briefings at any station along the way . . . that would indicate there was any danger of my ever coming under attack."

"When you did come upon the situation where you were surrounded, what did you believe was your most important task?"

Bucher faltered. One sensed that he *wanted to say,* "To save the lives of my men." But instead, ". . . My first task was to inform my superiors and my commanding officers and all the people that would need to know what was going on . . . secondly, to destroy the classified matter on the ship."

Admiral Bowen nodded to Captain Newsome, who began reading questions from a sheet of yellow paper, "Did the ship suffer any casualties below the water line?"

"None to my knowledge," Bucher said.

"When you made your decision to surrender—was that your personal decision without the counsel of your other officers?"

"That was my decision."

"Commander, one of the—certainly one of the most classified elements on this ship were the personnel, was that right?"

"Yes, sir."

"So that in making the decision to surrender your ship . . . you also made the calculated decision that you would also surrender this additional classified element of your ship, the personnel?"

"Yes, sir, that is correct."

There was a short recess. At 2:47 on this third afternoon of the court of inquiry, Captain Newsome returned to the counsel table. His expression was grim. "Commander Bucher," he began, "it is my duty to apprise you that the facts revealed . . . render you to be a suspect of a violation of the United States Naval regulations, article 0730, which reads, 'The commanding officer shall not submit his command to be searched by any persons representing a foreign state; will not permit any of the personnel under his command to be removed . . . by such persons so long as he has the power to resist.' You are further advised that having been so informed of that offense, you do not have to make any statements with respect to it. And any statement that you make . . . thereafter [can] be used as evidence against you in a subsequent trial."

Subsequent trial! Rose Bucher slipped on her sunglasses and began chewing gum. Her husband blinked, clasped his hands together, and looked down at the table. Then he sipped from a glass of water. Two wire service reporters left their seats and stepped quickly to the door.

"We obviously anticipated [this] situation," Miles Harvey was saying now; "in view of your warning, Commander Bucher persists in his desire to fully and completely tell this court of inquiry the details of the twenty-third of January and the events subsequent thereto." Harvey turned to his client: ". . . one question and one question only. Commander Bucher, at the time the North Koreans set foot on your ship, did you any longer have the power to resist?"

"No, I did not," Bucher said.

And so it had come to this. Never mind the extenuating circumstances. Sweep away all the irrelevant kindling. What mattered only was that 152-minute period on that freezing afternoon in the Sea of Japan; his dilemma was summed up in the clause ". . . so long as he has the power to resist." But how did one measure "power to resist"?

In horsepower? In bullets? In will? Suppose he had sent one gunner to cross the icy deck and the man had been shot down. Would he then have been expected to keep sending replacements? Where did one draw the line? At five bodies? At fifteen? Was courage quantitative? Would it have made any difference if he had fired one shot himself? A symbolic gesture, of course, but precisely what Commodore Barron had done in 1807. Six years later Lieutenant James Lawrence had uttered his famous command: "Don't give up the ship." The scaffolding of Naval tradition. Did anyone remember that—as he lay dying—Lawrence had done just that?

"I think you can continue with your testimony," Captain Newsome was saying. "You were at a point when the North Korean forces were on board the ship, and I believe that they had entered the radio spaces."

Beads of sweat formed on Bucher's brow. He blinked again and coughed nervously. "That's correct," he said. ". . . my concern was the possibility of aircraft showing up, in which case I was going to grab the mike of the 1MC and announce as quickly as I could for my men to attempt to resume control of the ship. . . . the American ensign was still flying, although upon arrival in port, just before we tied up, they sent one of their enlisted men to the bridge and hauled [it] down . . . the crew was led off the ship and I continued to insist. . . ."

Thursday morning, January 23rd: one year to the day since *Pueblo*'s capture. Rainstorms had swept the state for nearly a week, causing mudslides in Los Angeles and San Franciso. As she entered the courtroom, Rose Bucher carried a copy of the Los Angeles *Times*. "Emergency in California," the headline read.

"Just prior to the time that the boarding party came aboard," Captain Newsome began, "you authorized Lieutenant Harris to send a message indicating that the destruction of classified material would be incomplete?"

"Yes, sir, I did."

"Did you know that you would not have time to complete destruction when you authorized the boarding party to come aboard the *Pueblo?*"

"Yes, sir, I did."

"When the boarding party came aboard, did it occur to you that they had a plan to seize the ship?"

". . . I still did not know what they intended to do. I considered it a strong probability that they were intending to capture the ship, but I was not completely convinced of that."

Admiral Bowen stared at him. So did Admiral White.

"You indicated that the publications in the mattress covers were not thrown over the side," Admiral White said. "Were they too big or did you just not have time to get to them?"

"No, sir. I do not know why they were not thrown over the side."

"Commander Bucher," Harvey said, "was there any portion of the *ship's* allowance of classified material [as opposed to the research detachment's allowance] or any classified material for which the *ship* was responsible that had not been destroyed?"

"To the best of my knowledge," Bucher replied, "all the classified material belonging to the *ship,* that *I* had signed for, had been destroyed."

"I have a point to make," Admiral Bowen said, very cooly, very precisely, as if he were spearing a butterfly. ". . . the commanding officer was ultimately responsible that *all* classified material on the ship was disposed of. Is that correct, Commander Bucher?"

"That is correct, Admiral. I was responsible for the entire ship. However, I did not know, nor was I privy to, the amount of material. . . ."

There was a short recess. Tim Harris darted into the courtroom and dropped a note on Bucher's table. "Dear Captain," it began, "we've made it this far together and we'll finish it together—Bucher's Bastards." Bucher read it and looked up. But Harris was already gone.

"You can continue your testimony if you will," Captain Newsome was saying.

A hush fell over the courtroom as he began describing those first few hours in the Barn: ". . . that I would be given two minutes to sign the document or I would be shot. I was told to kneel down on the floor and I knelt down right here"—his fingers clutched the wooden pointer—"facing the wall. I knew that through human torture . . . it occurred to me that being shot . . . would be a blessing. So I knelt there on the floor and during the entire two minutes. . . ." He paused. Tears welled in his eyes.

Captain Newsome approached the long green table and whispered to Admiral Bowen, who nodded. "Would the commander like a recess at this time?" Captain Newsome asked.

Bucher gulped a glass of water. "Sir, I would rather get this over with right now if I may. I . . . I am sure I can do it. . . ." He wiped his forehead. "Sir, during the entire two minutes that I was laying there on the floor, I . . ." Another glass of water. A deep breath. ". . . I repeated over and over the phrase, 'I love you, Rose,' and thereby kept my mind off what was going to . . ."

Rose Bucher slumped in her seat. She cupped her left hand over her sunglasses.

Bucher was trembling visibly now. A Navy doctor, Captain Ransom J. Arthur, rushed to his side. The admirals turned away.

". . . happen . . . the colonel then said, 'Kill the sonovabitch' . . . the gun was clicked . . . and the interpreter said, 'Well, it was a misfire' . . . and I knew damn well that it had been a game that they were playing with me . . . and he said, 'We will now begin to shoot your crew' . . . and I was not prepared to see my crew shot. . . . I was convinced that they were animals and I told them at that time, I said, 'I will sign the confession.' . . ."

And finally, mercifully, a ninety-minute recess. Captain Newsome put his hand on Bucher's shoulder. Harvey unhooked the microphone around his neck and led him out of the courtroom. Into a light rain.

"Commander, I have one question," Admiral Bergner said when the afternoon session began. "What was your objective in not eating?"

"Did you have a door in your room?" Admiral Grimm inquired.

"Was there any real reason why you did not use your bed to get some rest?" Admiral White asked.

An aura of unreality pervaded the courtroom that afternoon. Listening to such questions, one felt, at first, a surge of anger and then, surprisingly, deep compassion for these five honorable, lonely men who had entered the shadows of Bucher's despair and had not known what to say.

42

"The Navy is searching for facts, not scapegoats," Admiral Thomas H. Moorer declared on January 25. "A court of inquiry must begin with a blank record. Newspaper accounts, rumors, secondhand reports or prejudgments cannot be considered. I am deeply troubled—the Navy is deeply troubled—that what was a routine and totally correct legal procedure has been widely misinterpreted."

Captain Newsome's "warning"—which really was "routine" and tendered only to inform Bucher of his rights—had created a public relations nightmare. Admiral Bowen received scores of letters and telegrams. One was addressed to "Bowen and his pimps." A second declared, "I resent your prostitution [sic] of Bucher and his fine men"; a third said simply, "One Jesus Christ crucified is sufficient." Admiral Bergner's telephone rang at all hours of the night. ("I kept telling these people, 'We can't court-martial anybody,' he remembers, 'We don't have the authority.' ") Admiral Grimm was told by one irate Californian that "If you will stop persecuting Commander Bucher, my four brothers and I will go and get the *Pueblo* back for you."

"Commander Bucher feels that an overreaction has set in concerning the warning," attorney Harvey said on January 27. "In his and our opinion, the hearing has been completely fair." If Captain Newsome had not delivered the warning, "he would have been derelict in his duty." All of this was true. Yet some reporters refused to stand when "those punks"—the admirals—entered the court. Public opinion seemed convinced that Bucher was being "framed."

In fact, however, the admirals reserved their sharpest thrusts for the "experts" from Washington, the operations and intelligence officers from CINCPACFLT and COMNAVFORJAPAN. They summoned Captain John L. Marocchi from Hawaii and Captain E. B.

(Pete) Gladding from his home in Texas; they questioned Lieutenant Ed Brookes, Lieutenant Commander Duane Heisinger, and Captains William H. Everett, Thomas L. Dwyer, and Forrest A. Pease from Yokosuka. They heard from Rear Admiral Frank L. Johnson (Annapolis, '30) in closed session. Then they asked him to testify publicly.

The pudgy, pear-shaped admiral tapped his black shoes on the gold carpet. He rubbed his hands together and twiddled his thumbs. He fixed his sleeve for the seventeenth time and brushed at the silvery locks atop his soft, Kiwanis Club face. He talked about the *"Pu-ay-blo."* "I would like to assure the court, Commander Bucher, and the *Pu-ay-blo* crew," he began, lamely, "that had I conceived in any way that there was a jeopardy to . . . the ship, I never would have sent [her] out on that mission without requesting—and getting—proper protection."

There was an uneasy silence.

"Admiral," Captain Newsome said, "were you particularly concerned about the amount of classified material that *Pueblo* carried?"

"Well, not specifically. . . ."

"When you visited the *Pueblo,* did you discuss armament . . . ?"

"At no time," Admiral Johnson replied, "was it my intention to restrict the use of these weapons to the commanding officer when he decided he should use them . . . this is the responsibility inherent in command. . . ."

"You testified that there was in existence some contingency plan to protect . . . *Pueblo,*" Admiral White said. "In this case, were there any forces really available?"

"As I mentioned, I had this on-call arrangement with the Fifth Air Force and Commander, Seventh Fleet. . . ."

Admiral White shook his head. "So when we add it up, then, we really had a contingency plan to use forces which do not exist?"

"There were no forces available to me."

"Wouldn't it be feasible to assume that if a hostile nation would attack [across the DMZ], they might also be willing to come across a line of water and attack an unarmed ship?"

"In my decision-making process," Admiral Johnson replied, shifting uneasily in his chair, "I again go back to the fact that this had not been done to a [U.S. ship] in over one hundred fifty years. . . . If you were a betting man . . . a bookkeeper would give you such fantastic odds . . . that maybe even somebody as rich as Howard Hughes could not pay off on it. . . ."

"You have referred frequently to this on-call concept," Admiral

Bowen said icily, "which I believe is somewhat misleading, since nothing was on call. Is that standard phraseology?"

"This on-call concept is like any other on-call situation, that depending on the situation, depending on the availability of forces, you take whatever action is possible—considering those two factors. . . ."

"Well," Admiral Bowen snapped, "it certainly didn't take care of the situation we had. Therefore, I think it is suspect in its validity."

"Thanks so much for being honest, Admiral," Bucher said, when it was over. Obviously shaken, Admiral Johnson nodded and patted Bucher on the back. His lips moved, but no words came out.

Rear Admiral George L. Cassell, the former assistant chief of staff for operations at CINCPACFLT headquarters in Hawaii, followed Admiral Johnson to the stand.

"I must conclude," Admiral Bowen said, "that the whole operation of the *Pueblo* was planned without any external means for her protection, that international law was her only protection. When this basic assumption was violated, did you expect that ship to protect itself?"

"Yes, we did," Admiral Cassell said.

Bucher stared straight ahead, not looking at him.

"Did you think that *Pueblo* could defend herself adequately with two .50 caliber machine guns?"

"Yes, I did."

Admiral White seemed troubled. "The ship received a hazardous duty allowance for classified publications," he said, "yet the risk of this mission was estimated to be minimal." He looked up. "How does hazardous jibe with minimal?"

"This is outside my field," Admiral Cassell replied. "I'm not able to explain that rationale."

A lanky, crew-cut captain named John H. D. Williams flew in from Washington to testify about the proper way to destroy classified documents and equipment. "Emergency destruction," he began, "is one facet of physical security, which is one of the three recognized major divisions of . . ." The admirals glared at him. Reporters groaned. It was going to be that kind of morning.

"I cannot conceive of any ship having to conduct emergency destruction more than one time," Captain Williams observed. ". . . crypto equipment is permitted to sink with the ship in waters over one hundred fathoms, in accordance with NWP-50-A. . . ." Here was the archetypal bureaucrat, rolling his tongue over his lips, quoting "certain pertinent references from documents" in sonorously slow tones, explaining now that according to regulation number such-and-such, cryptographic material "could be shredded and streamed over the fantail at dusk, providing that there are no other ships present, providing at least six bags of material are streamed at once, and providing that the crypto and other material are intermixed in the process. . . ."

Admiral Grimm flashed a sardonic smile. "That makes life a little difficult if it's not dusk, doesn't it?"

But Captain Williams didn't see the humor. He went on to insist that Bucher and his crew should have destroyed all their classified documents—he estimated they weighed one ton—in an hour or less. Even under gunfire.

"Captain," Harvey asked, "in your opinion, which would be more important, the destruction of classified material that might fall into the hands of unfriendly nations or the protection of human life?"

"That's a judgment matter, and I've already read into the record the definition of 'top secret.'" He proceeded to read it again. Lights played on his plastic nametag.

"So destruction of classified material is absolutely paramount?"

"Based on the authority in this manual, yes," Captain Williams said.

"Captain, in this one-hour estimate, what contributing factors do you take into account for the wounding or death of a man?"

"I cannot predict what the results would be, other than to reduce the personnel available to perform the vital function of destroying the documents."

"Have you any familiarity with the use of TNT? Have you any familiarity with submarines?"

Captain Williams reached for the carafe and started to pour a glass of water—his fifth in less than an hour. His hand shook. The water spilled onto his uniform. "Now I do," he said. Laughter.

Admiral Bowen was tiring of this performance. "It seems to me," he said, leaning forward over the table, "that in a highly technological Navy, in the area of destruction of classified material and equipment we haven't moved very far since the Stone Age."

Captain Williams reddened. Later, stepping out of the courtroom, he brushed quickly past a group of reporters. "I *abhor* publicity," he said.

During the recess Bucher stood alone by the easel, staring at the schematics of his ship. The various compartments had been designated so impersonally: "G" for the forward crew's berthing; "H" for the engine room; "N" for the captain's stateroom. Admiral White stepped up and placed his arm around Bucher's shoulder. For a moment neither man spoke.

"How come your husband looks so much healthier than Pete?" the Washington *Post*'s George C. Wilson asked Carol Murphy one morning in February.

"Well," she said, "I think he stayed on top of it over there."

The tall, prematurely gray navigator was the first of the ship's officers to follow the captain to the stand. Bucher peered at him through sunglasses. Rose Bucher, wearing a white sweater and brown skirt, was chewing gum. On her lap was a large brown purse, and she began stroking it, as if she were petting a cat.

"What kind of working relationship did you have with the skipper?" Admiral Bergner asked.

"We had a very close relationship, sir. The entire wardroom was small. . . . It was a very close wardroom, sir."

Rose Bucher placed her purse on another seat.

"Was it your interpretation," Admiral Pratt asked, "that you wouldn't use the .50 caliber machine guns in self-defense in any manner?"

"No, sir," Murphy said. "I could see that there was latitude to use the weapons, yes, sir." He paused. "We were trying to not look like a warship . . . trying to use international diplomacy."

"If the commanding officer's intentions to surrender had been known to you any earlier," Admiral Grimm said, "would you have taken any other action?"

"Sir, . . . I don't think there would have been any other decision possible. . . . We had the short end of the stick all the way around. . . . We, of course, had eighty-three personnel . . . who could have gone up there, but . . . they had eighty-three or more bullets. . . ."

"In your opinion," Harvey asked, "at the time the North Koreans boarded the *Pueblo*, did Commander Bucher any longer have the power to resist?"

"I can say the decisions that I was aware of . . . would have been essentially identical. . . . I can see no difference in the end result, sir."

One by one, the other officers and senior enlisted men agreed. No, they said, Bucher had not had the power to resist. Yes, they said, he had made the only decision possible under the circumstances. Yes, they considered him to be an outstanding leader; they would "follow him anywhere." The admirals listened, scribbled notes, and asked their gently probing questions. One could almost count on Admiral Bergner to inquire about "relationships"; on Admiral Pratt to say something about the ship's "set and drift"; on Admiral Grimm to ask how many bags of classified documents had been thrown over the side. Only on a few occasions did the admirals betray their frustrations.

In closed session one afternoon Steve Harris recounted how the two Marine interpreters, Chicca and Hammond, had come aboard just prior to *Pueblo*'s departure from Japan; how no one had realized until too late that they really weren't fluent in Korean.

Admiral Bowen glared at him. "But didn't *you* give them a test?"

"We have heard considerable testimony concerning how weak the ship was in regard to watertight integrity," Admiral White told Lacy; "ramming would almost sink it immediately and so forth. . . . I don't believe this. . . . I get the impression that the ship had pretty good watertight integrity. Do you agree?"

"Yes, sir," Lacy said, and then, a few minutes later, "There was no way to [jettison classified documents over the side] without exposing yourself to the torpedo boats. They had all the accesses pretty well covered. . . ."

"But you could have opened the doors quickly, thrown it out, and ducked back inside," Admiral White said. Silence.

Norbert Klepac, the tall, craggy-faced boatswain's mate, described how he had taken the line from the North Korean P-4 and placed it over the bit.

"But didn't you have an urge to throw it back?" asked Admiral White beseechingly.

"I didn't want to receive the line, let's put it that way, sir."

Rodney Duke told the court that all the portholes had been shut the moment that Lacy ordered Condition Zebra.

Admiral White leaned forward. "Do you think you could have put a Thompson submachine gun out the porthole and mowed down the boarding party?"

"I know I couldn't have," Duke replied. "It would have taken a pretty tall man."

"Well," said Admiral White, his cheeks flushed, "I think I could have tippy-toed up and peeked out of there with that gun and mowed them down."

Bucher sat with Harvey and Keys at their small table, taking notes and rising to shake hands with his men as they left the stand. He swallowed pills frequently and used a magnifying glass to read the documents before him. The microphone picked up the sounds of his hoarse breathing. His shoulders seemed squinched; the expression on his face was that of a desperate, "cornered" man. He drank ice water constantly. He trembled. Occasionally, he wept.

Life magazine carried his picture on its front cover; so did *News-*

week. "The picture was okay," Rose Bucher told *Newsweek's* Karl Fleming, "but the story sorta stunk." She had not, she insisted, dabbed tears from her eyes during her husband's testimony. A few days later Fleming presented the Buchers with the framed cover picture. Bucher was delighted. Rose was not. "Naaah," she said. A San Francisco newspaper published a rumor that the Buchers were planning a divorce. At their request, Captain Vincent C. Thomas, the chief public affairs officer at the court of inquiry, branded the story untrue. Harvey and Keys advised them to enter and leave the courtroom holding hands, and for the next few days they did.

Bucher spent his noon recesses autographing photographs. In the hallway outside the court, he mingled with reporters. ("You're from Washington? I remember, I was at Boys Town, we played Gonzaga at Griffith Stadium. Thirty thousand people. We beat 'em; really played over our heads that day." He paused. "It was a long time ago.") He turned and noticed that two of his men, Hayes and Baldridge, were waiting to testify. "The thing to remember," he said, "is just to relax." And then, when Baldridge had finished and been excused, he approached Admiral Bowen. The family of one of his crew members, he said, still did not know the extent of their son's injuries. Baldridge had described them in some detail. Would Admiral Bowen ask reporters not to publicize this? He would and did.

"I can't say that I would have done anything significantly different had the incident occurred today," Bucher told newsmen one afternoon.

How did he feel about the court?

"I'm not discouraged," he said. "I just don't know."

Did he blame Steve Harris for not destroying all the classified documents?

"That's a totally unfair question," Harvey said, grabbing Bucher's arm. "Come on, Pete, we gotta go; we gotta go." Reluctantly, it seemed, Bucher broke off his interview with the TV reporters and stepped into a brown, four-door Oldsmobile sedan. "Nixon's the One," its bumper stickers proclaimed, and "Remember the *Pueblo.*"

Away from that low-slung, cream-colored building on Guadalcanal Road, Bucher seemed a different man entirely. His face became animated; he laughed easily. His shoulders no longer squinched together. One remembers him standing on the sidelines during a touch football game, wearing a straw boater with a red sash and lustily exhorting his men to score. Or stepping into The Mexican Village—"the body exchange"—at night to sip martinis with Schumacher, Lacy, or Tim Harris and tap his feet to "that shitkickin' music." Or gathering his officers at a wetting-down party on February 8 and leading them in a throaty chorus: "Here's to *Pueblo*—she's a fine ship; Here's to *Pueblo*—she's a peach; Boomyackle, boomyackle, boomyackle, boom. . . ." Then one would see him hours later inside the courtroom, still a gaunt and tortured man. "He was literally reliving every minute," Captain Keys remembers. "I was surprised he didn't break down more often."

On February 13 Bucher returned to the witness stand to answer further questions. There was a testiness in his manner now, a *desperation*, as if he sensed the admirals didn't believe what he was trying to tell them.

"You testified that you could steer using the engines only from the engine room?" Admiral White began.

"Oh, no, sir. That's not true. I didn't say that. . . . So when I say we didn't have emergency steering, I mean it. We didn't have it, Admiral."

Admiral Pratt asked about the sequence in which flags had been hoisted on the day of the incident. There seemed to be some inconsistencies between what Bucher and his signalman had said.

"Leach is confused about it," Bucher replied. "I am *positive* about it. . . . And there was one other discrepancy in Leach's testimony. . . ."

"What was your relationship with Mr. Murphy, your working relationship?" Admiral Bergner asked.

Bucher hesitated. He had decided some time ago that any public airing of his problems with Murphy would only demean the inquiry; it wouldn't serve a useful purpose. "Well, sir," he said now, "that relationship was always tempered by the fact that Mr. Murphy had a limited amount of sea experience. . . . I was required to give him, I thought, much more detailed instructions as to just how I wanted things done. . . . I expected, perhaps, too much of Mr. Murphy . . ."

"Was there any personality clash between you and him?"

"Well, sir, that's a little bit too harsh. He had a definite way that he was used to doing things. . . . I was coming from a different branch of the service. There were differences of opinion, but nothing that wasn't resolved by my just making a decision."

Up to this point in the proceedings most observers had assumed that any "conflict" on the ship had involved Bucher and Steve Harris. It was hard to imagine two officers with more diverse backgrounds and personalities. The party-going extrovert from Nebraska versus the shy, nonathletic Harvard graduate. Was Harris Iago to Bucher's Othello? The testimony about the research detachment's autonomy, the "ship within the ship," reinforced this view. Furthermore, Bucher was said to be extremely unhappy about Harris' performance during the incident. Hadn't he neglected to shake hands with Harris in court? Didn't this prove something? Bucher's remarks about Murphy seemed to indicate that the equation was more complex.

Yes, Murphy said over the telephone, he and his wife would be delighted to come to dinner. And so, on a rainy evening late in February, they appeared at Mr. A's, a fashionable restaurant in San Diego. Would they like cocktails? No, of course not. Would Murphy mind if his host had one? "One," he said. Murphy could not discuss the incident in any detail until the end of the court. But he would be happy to chat about his background and offer general comments.

It was impossible, he said, to be a nice guy and a good officer at the same time. To be effective, you had to keep your distance. Had Bucher kept *his* distance? "I'm glad to see the crew line up and back the captain," Murphy said, sidestepping neatly. "It means I really did a good job as XO." One pressed him and put the question another way. Wasn't it remarkable that Bucher had such an obvious rapport with his junior officers, Schumacher and Tim Harris? Murphy paused; there was only a trace of bitterness in his reply. "Skip and Tim are awfully young," he said. "They're more impressionable."

Murphy testified again next morning. Questioning him was Captain Newsome's associate, Commander William E. Clemons, a red-haired Mississippian with a tattoo on his left forearm. On December 7, 1941, Clemons had stood on the burning deck of the battleship *Nevada* and, in his rage and frustration, thrown *potatoes* at Japanese planes attacking Pearl Harbor. "Lieutenant Murphy," he drawled, "at any time during your detention did you depart from the tenets of the Code of Conduct?"

"Yes, sir, I did . . . I could hear that the other two officers in the passageway were going to admit to the intrusions and to the spying. . . . My resistance was not in any way going to help the national security of the United States. . . ."

"It was your personal feeling and judgment that it was useless to resist?" There was an edge to Clemons' words now.

"Yes, sir," Murphy replied, "because I felt they would get what they wanted in the end by one means or another. . . . I said, 'Why should I as an individual fight the war singlehandedly when others . . . seemed to have fallen . . . ?' "

At his press conference on January 13 Captain Newsome had said that the Code of Conduct was "inapplicable" to the *Pueblo* crew. Now, on February 20, he declared, "It's become obvious that the code *is* applicable in this situation. . . . One of the tasks of the court is to examine the code to see whether or not it meets our present needs, to see whether or not it's adequate under all circumstances, to see whether we can propose any revisions to it. We have an excellent vehicle for doing that right now."

Why was the Navy reversing its position? "We have had long and learned dissertations from other sources," Captain Newsome replied. Which sources? No comment. What had happened, in fact, was that the Navy had simply decided to protect its flank. The original plan to call fifteen or twenty witnesses during the court's final phase clearly wouldn't suffice. Someone might complain later that he had not been given a chance to testify openly. So the decision had been made: Every member of the crew would have his day in court. And if this additional testimony shed any new light on the Code of Conduct, well, that would be all to the good.

Admiral Bowen turned to Schumacher: "Did you believe in the Code of Conduct when you were captured?"

"Yes, sir."

"Do you still?"

At dinner the night before, Schumacher had said he was worried about his forthcoming testimony: "It isn't that dramatic a story. I was only kicked in the ribs and back. I wasn't . . . they didn't do to me what they did to some of the other guys." One suspected he felt *guilty* about that.

"I'm just not sure," he said to Admiral Bowen now. "I think we were in a unique situation. They had our service records, documents from the ship; they had the ship itself."

"Are you telling me that you believe in the Code of Conduct but you would interpret it to fit the situation in which you found yourself?"

"Yes, sir," Schumacher said. "It was a guideline, and we deviated from it knowingly. . . . None of us wanted to do what we had to do over there. It became a question of what we could do in the form of resistance. The commanding officer was the one who first hit upon all the subtleties and doubletalk . . . a lesser man, it would probably have driven him out of his mind. The commanding officer had enough sense to know that what had happened was done and the most important thing was to keep the crew alive. . . ."

The admirals stared at him. Schumacher's hand gripped the water glass. "It's very difficult," he said, "to take an eleven-month period and try to compress it in a couple of hours' testimony and have it come out the way it was. I . . . I regret I haven't the capability to convey fully what it was like."

The questions seldom varied. Were you familiar with the Code of Conduct? Did you deviate from it knowingly? Why?

"Fear was the main thing, not being really educated," Earl Phares said.

"To exist, I guess," John Mitchell said.

"I wasn't afraid to die," James Kell said. "But I wasn't prepared to accept any torture."

Admiral Grimm removed his glasses and looked at the crew-cut yeoman, Armando Canales. "Are you a passive individual?" he asked.

"I'm just mild-mannered. I don't go into anger," Canales said.

Throughout all of the testimony, there was this odd detachment, this almost lifeless quality, this stoicism. An emotional shield which crew members used to blunt the probing questions. But at which point would that shield crack and splinter apart? It was impossible to predict in advance. One remembers Tim Harris, the feisty ensign, responding to a question from Admiral Bergner about his "mental attitude" during captivity.

"I had extreme hatred for the North Koreans," he began; "the only thing I wished . . ." Suddenly he lowered his head. He tapped his feet on the carpet. He covered his face with his hands. ". . . wished more than anything was that I could . . ." He cried, and his whole body shook.

"Could I rephrase my question?" Admiral Bergner said. "After the initial phase, did you get stronger?"

"Well, yes sir. . . ."

"Let's wait a minute here," Admiral Bowen said.

Harvey put his arm around Harris and gave him a handkerchief.

"Let me withdraw the question," Admiral Bergner said.

But Harris didn't seem to hear him. "What I wanted to do," he said, tapping his pencil on the table, "was to take . . . my life. . . . I couldn't do it. . . . I was hoping eventually I'd hear some bombers. . . ."

The admirals looked down at their legal pads.

One morning a sailor assigned to the amphibious base entered the courtroom on a routine errand. Moments before, Bucher had seemed calm and relaxed. Now he stared at this sailor, an expression of absolute terror on his face. Why? Did this man remind him of Duane Hodges? One would never know. There was another morning like that—toward the end of the court. Ramon Rosales, the slender storekeeper, was at the witness table, and Admiral Pratt was asking what had sustained him during the detention period.

"My faith in God and my country," Rosales replied, "and the decisions of my CO."

Bucher placed his head in his hands and wept quietly.

But the drama of the court's first days was altogether lacking now, replaced by an ennui, a sense of weariness. The stories of North Korean brutality no longer elicited gasps from those marvelous spectators, most of whom, it seemed, had already gone back to daytime television. Rose Bucher took notes; occasionally she played with a rubber band. At the counsel table Commander Bates drew rectangular doodles and passed them to the officer on his right. "And what," Commander Clemons would ask a witness in his abrasive, bulldog manner, "did you do next, if anything?" Admiral Grimm would rub his hand over his face. Admiral Bowen would glare at Clemons, then look at his watch impatiently.

"Let's not continue to go over ground which we have firmly in the record," he would say.

For awhile the admirals had thought of feeding the testimony into a computer. They discarded that idea as impractical. On a blackboard in Room 175, just down the hall from the court, they kept a running score of the bags of classified material lost to the North Koreans. At night they read and reread the transcripts from the day before. All of them were still responsible for running their own commands; all had abandoned their social life "for the duration," and outside the court one saw them only occasionally: Admiral Bowen one Sunday afternoon on the tennis court at the Del Coronado Hotel —a fierce competitor with a strong second serve; Admiral White having lunch at the Amphibious Base Officers' Club with his son, a Navy lieutenant, and his daughter-in-law, the admiral saying in his Missouri twang, "When you're a dive bomber pilot and you commit yourself to a dive, you don't pull out because you're being fired at. . . ."

On March 10 Bucher returned to the witness stand. He mentioned his efforts to discredit his captors' propaganda. He called the North Koreans "cruel and brutal savages. . . . I requested better treatment for the crew," he said. "I could hear . . . their screams of pain, but . . ." Tears clouded his eyes. He blinked repeatedly and struggled to continue. "My overall personal evaluation [of the crew]," he said finally, "was that they represented the United States of America, the United States Navy, and their families in an outstanding manner." He went on to cite forty-one of his men for their "cunningness and ability to fool the North Koreans" as well as for their "marked courage." He included all of his officers except Lieutenant Murphy.

Next morning he appeared again to answer questions from the

court. The black horn-rimmed spectacles he had worn through so many previous sessions were absent now. He clasped his hands calmly on the table before him, and yet there was in his manner an almost desperate intensity. "I was acting in faithful response to my orders," he declared. "My orders were specific as to my not to start a war out there. . . . I never surrendered the ship. I never struck the colors. The Koreans pulled the colors down. I've used the word 'surrender,' but I just don't feel it's as accurate a term as 'seizure.' . . . I was overwhelmed by tremendous odds that did not give me hope for survival. . . ."

"Did you ever consider using your Thompsons?" Admiral White asked.

"No, sir."

"Did you ever consider conning the ship from the engine room?" He gulped. "No, sir, I did not."

"If a situation requires 'repel boarders,' " Admiral Bowen began, "is that a matter of survival?"

"Not necessarily, no, sir."

Admiral Bowen rolled his pencil on the green-felt table cloth and in an icy voice repeated the question: "Is that a matter of survival?"

"It's a matter of the loss of the ship, the salvation of the ship," Bucher said, "yes, sir."

"Was the classified material destroyed as effectively as it could have been?"

"No, sir."

"Why not?"

"We did not use all the means that would have been available. We could have taken the bulk of the printed material, thrown it into the head, poured diesel oil on it, and made a fairly complete destruction. I didn't think of it. I hold myself responsible. . . ."

"Your resources available were not used?"

"Yes, sir."

Captain Newsome closed his folder.

On Thursday morning, March 13, the court convened for the last time. "Mr. President," Captain Newsome said, "we have no further evidence to present."

Bucher stood by the small table, adjusted the microphone to nose level, and gripped the sides of the black lectern. "Having made the decision many years ago to become a naval officer of the line," he began huskily, "I eagerly sought command at sea. My first command was the USS *Pueblo*. . . . Many of my suggestions and requests were not approved. . . . I do consider that my ship was inadequately provided with proper destruct systems. . . . I hereby state unequivocally that, at the time of that seizure, we did not have the power to resist."

During the course of the hearings Miles Harvey had called only two witnesses for the "defense." (He had, on the spur of the moment, invited a third. But former President Johnson declined to appear.) One, Vice Admiral John V. Smith, the former U.S. negotiator at Panmunjom, had testified, predictably, that the North Koreans were "mad dogs . . . Communists . . . only one step above animals." And although he had shaken hands with Harvey, he had ignored Bucher altogether. The second witness, Commander Peter Block, the former skipper of the submarine *Ronquil,* had been asked if he thought Bucher was *"abnormally* concerned" for his crew. No, he had replied, but the damaging word remained in the record and, presumably, in the minds of the admirals. All in all, very few points for the "defense."

"A court of inquiry is, by its very nature, a cruel business," Harvey said now, in his final statement. "It cannot bring back Duane Hodges, cause the return of the USS *Pueblo,* completely heal the scars that many of the crew will carry for the rest of their lives. . . . Probing into disasters at sea may seem merciless because almost everywhere else we, as a nation, have abandoned the requirement of accountability. However, on the sea, there is a tradition older than the traditions of our nation and wiser in its trust than our new morality. It is the tradition that with authority goes responsibility and with both goes accountability. During these last eight weeks Commander Bucher and his crew have rendered their account. . . .

"The fact that [Bucher's] immediate superior should chastise him in a fitness report for attempting to obtain those things which are now minimum standard items on AGER's is one of the tragic footnotes to the story this court has heard. . . . Destruct gear now installed has been described by the experts with great pride. Commander Bucher would have settled for three cans of TNT. We have seen a demonstration of water-soluble paper. Commander Bucher would have settled for a reduced publications allowance. Detachments are now departments. Commander Bucher was promised this almost two years ago. The .50 caliber guns have been removed. Commander Bucher thought they were inappropriate when put aboard. . . .

"Commander Bucher had been told that harassment could and should be expected. He was warned that he was not to be provocative or aggressive. This was emphasized by the statement, 'Commander, you are not out there to start a war.' . . . The skipper followed his orders precisely . . . [he] did everything in accordance with his previous instructions. . . ."

Harvey spoke for twenty-one minutes. At 9:55 Admiral Bowen reached for his gavel. "This court," he said, "is closed."

Bucher stepped outside into the rain to face the TV reporters. His wife, wearing red shoes and a blue coat, stood beside him and held his hand. "I will wait [for the verdict] with considerable apprehension," he began. "I love the Navy. I want to stay in, if they'll let me. It's my life."

43

Since January 20 the court had met for more than two hundred hours to hear one hundred and four witnesses (eighty-one in open session) provide 3,392 single-spaced, legal-sized pages of testimony. The admirals had flown to Norfolk, Virginia, to inspect *Pueblo*'s sister ship, *Palm Beach*. To be sure, they had *not* dug into *"all* the facts and circumstances" surrounding the incident. They had not summoned shipyard officials from Bremerton or the Commander, Service Force, Pacific Fleet, Rear Admiral Edwin B. Hooper, from Hawaii, or even the former Commander-in-Chief, Pacific, Admiral U. S. Grant Sharp, who was living in retirement in San Diego. Nor had they solicited testimony from anyone at the Naval Ships Systems Command, or the National Security Agency, or the Defense Intelligence Agency, or the Office of the Joint Chiefs of Staff. "These agencies were simply beyond my cognizance," Admiral Bowen remembers. "I didn't have the horsepower to take on the entire U.S. Government." He and his colleagues had assumed from the beginning—correctly, as it turned out— that Congress would probe into the "why" of the *Pueblo* affair, that their job was simply to determine what happened.

So now they began the arduous task of adding it all together: the facts, opinions and recommendations which they would have to submit to the convening authority, Admiral John J. Hyland, in Honolulu. There had been conflicts in the testimony, of course: the number of bags of documents jettisoned over the side; the actual state of the sea at the time of the seizure; the various estimates as to how long it would have taken to remove the tarps from the machine guns and open fire. What seemed surprising, though—given the capriciousness of human nature and the fact that all of this had happened more than a year before—was there were so very few *significant* discrepancies.

None of the admirals suspected that outright perjury had been committed. But all sensed that they had not heard the *whole* truth. Perhaps it had been a mistake, they thought, to keep the crew together in the same barracks at North Island. Crew members pretty well knew in advance which questions were going to be asked. They read about it in the papers. They had to be influenced, too, by the fact that Bucher maintained control over their destinies. After all, he wrote their final fitness reports. The admirals suspected that Bucher and Murphy hated each other's guts. They couldn't find anyone willing to talk about that. They had, in closed session, heard about the one man whose nervousness in North Korea had caused so much anxiety. And later, on several occasions in open court, Captain Newsome had asked, "Do you know if there were any members of the crew who were *mistrusted?*" But no one talked about that either.

"Their allegiance to each other was remarkable," one admiral says. "It outweighed any other considerations." The man in question had not actually *collaborated.* And his name had not yet been revealed publicly. Perhaps, the admirals thought, it was best to leave it that way.

Over the next ten days, working closely with Newsome and Clemons, they developed a list of 543 basic facts. There was little disagreement on any of them. Nor were their any real arguments over the 135 separate opinions. In many respects, they agreed, the "system" had let Bucher down. That business of divided command—the squabble over detachment versus department status for the ship's CT's—had been unfortunate, to say the least. And the zeal which so many different organizations and agencies had evidenced in funneling classified documents onto that ship—with no coordination at all—was worrisome indeed. The Soviets had installed destruct devices on their AGI's years before. So the Navy had been foolish to deny *Pueblo* similar mechanisms. Then, too, there was that estimate of "minimal" risk and the warning that Admiral Johnson had issued about using the guns. Clearly, these had conditioned Bucher not to expect any real hazards on this first mission.

Everything that Bucher had said about the ship's stability, her age, her steering problems, her lack of communications was, regrettably, true. But had any of these factors made any difference on the afternoon of January 23? The admirals thought not. It seemed obvious from the testimony that Bucher had relied for advice on Schumacher, Lacy, and Law—and hardly at all on Murphy. His lack of rapport with the XO was another handicap. At the same time it also seemed clear that Bucher had not—for one reason or another—drilled his officers and men to prepare for every contingency.

What it all boiled down to, of course, was whether or not he had had the power to resist. The admirals quickly—and unanimously—agreed that he had. He could have used his small arms, they said, to mow down the boarding party. Or continued steaming out to sea and, through adroit maneuvering, thwarted or at least delayed any seizure attempt. He could have dismantled his engines, they pointed out, and tried to scuttle the ship. Bucher and Lacy had said this would have taken too long. But hadn't that expert from Washington, Captain Albert S. Giorgis, testified that a well-trained crew could have done it in an hour? At the very least, the admirals concluded, Bucher could —and should—have resisted until he had made sure that all of his classified documents and equipment had been destroyed.

"That man could have been the greatest hero in the history of the U.S. Navy," Admiral Bowen would say several months later in Honolulu. "But he let government property get away. When the captain fails, the system fails. It opens up seams all the way to the top. For a commanding officer to do anything other than guard his ship with his life is indefensible. I'll admit it takes guts; that's what you gotta have. The thought of saving his crew is interesting, humane, but it had nothing at all to do with the job he was assigned to do. Tradition? Yes. The reason it's tradition is that most people have done it."

"If he had only fired one shot," Admiral White would sigh at his parents' home in rural Missouri, "it would have made all the difference. Just one little bitty squirt of machine-gun fire, and that whole thing might have been over. They might not have had that boarding party in the first place."

"I may die in the process," Admiral Bergner would explain at the Naval Training Center in San Diego one morning, "but I know that when I put on a blue uniform, I'm expected to stand in harm's way. So is every officer." The admiral would go on to describe how he was applying "human factors" principles to military management: "Our product here is people; we have to keep ourselves oriented to people. . . ." And a visitor would remember that just at that moment the NTC band marched past his window playing—yes—"Yankee Doodle Dandy."

But now—inside that low-slung building at the Amphibious Base in Coronado—the admirals moved on to other opinions. Steve Harris' performance, they felt, both prior to and during the incident, had been sorely disappointing. So had Murphy's on the day of the seizure. Bucher's behavior in North Korea had been exemplary. And there were other crew members, as well, the admirals agreed, who had distinguished themselves: Schumacher, for example; Law, Kisler, Chicca, Hammond, Rigby, Bailey, Sterling, and Hagenson. What about the Code of Conduct? It was, the admirals decided, basically sound.

With these facts and opinions at hand, they set out to write their recommendations. Five of their proposals concerned the Code of Conduct. Roughly a dozen others pertained to the operation of the AGER program. Finally, they came to the crunch: what, if any, disciplinary action to suggest.

"We must set an example for eight hundred fifty thousand Blue Jackets," Admiral Bowen said, in effect. He took a hard line. Admirals White and Bergner agreed with him. They urged that Bucher "be brought to trial by general courts-martial" for allegedly "permitting his ship to be seized while he had the power to resist, failing to take immediate and aggressive protective measures . . . , complying with the orders of the North Koreans to follow them into port, failing to complete destruction of classified material . . . and permitting such material to fall into the hands of the North Koreans," and finally, for "failing to ensure, before departure for sea, that his officers and crew were properly organized, stationed and trained in preparation for emergency destruction of classified material."

Yet in their *opinions*, these three admirals had agreed that "during his internment, Commander Bucher upheld morale in a superior manner; that he provided leadership . . . and that he contributed to the ability of the crew to hold together and withstand the trials of detention. . . ."

To Admiral Grimm this seemed vaguely hypocritical. "The analogy I used," he remembers, "was, 'We're going to hang this man, then come around and pin a rose on him.' Really, the court was convened to look into the whole twelve months which included a couple of very bad days. I felt strongly about the things Bucher had done wrong, but I didn't think any good would come out of a court-martial, and I said so." Admiral Pratt tended to side with him. The court's members agreed to adjourn for the night "and sleep on it."

Next morning, the split was three to one, with Pratt still undecided. Bowen pressed hard for a court-martial. So did White—who Grimm remembers was "fierce at times." Finally, realizing they had no chance of swaying the majority, Grimm and Pratt said they would go along. They could, of course, file a minority report, but this would serve no useful purpose. Now they discussed what to recommend for the other officers.

Steve Harris, they decided, should "be brought to trial by general courts-martial for three alleged offenses: . . . in that he failed to inform [Bucher] of a certain deficiency in . . . the research detachment; failed to train and drill the research detachment properly . . . and failed to take effective action to complete the emergency destruction. . . ." Murphy should receive "a letter of admonition for alleged dereliction in the performance of his duties as executive officer. . . ."

Grimm still held one trump card. If his colleagues were going to recommend stiff punishment for the ship's officers, he insisted, they could not ignore the performances of, say, Admiral Johnson or Captain Gladding. The suggestion was a painful one for Grimm to make. He had served with Admiral Johnson in Newport, respected him, considered him a friend. But the court had to be consistent.

White knew Johnson well and admired him enormously as "just a wonderful man." Nonetheless, he and the others agreed with Grimm and recommended now that both Johnson and Gladding receive letters of reprimand: Johnson for "derelict[ion] in the performance of duty in negligently failing to plan properly . . . for contingencies such as occurred during . . . *Pueblo*'s mission and negligently failing to verify . . . the feasibility of [the ship's] emergency destruction [procedures];" Gladding for allegedly ". . . failing to ensure the readiness of *Pueblo*'s research detachment" and ". . . [failing] to provide intelligence support to *Pueblo* during the mission."

The admirals wrote and rewrote their findings of fact, opinions, and recommendations half a dozen times in an effort to find phrases which satisfied everyone. The exercise reminded Grimm of the time he'd spent in the Pentagon years before agonizing over complicated JCS papers. Finally, on April 10, Bowen signed the court's report. One inch thick between pink covers, it weighed 2½ pounds and had taken twenty-eight days to prepare. He forwarded it to Admiral Hyland in Hawaii.

To Hyland, Bucher's "failure to put up any resistance at all" was "incredible . . . shocking . . . unforgivable." Still, he worried about the court of inquiry's recommendations. A general court-martial, he realized, would "drag on for months and months" and result in further damage to the Navy's already tarnished image. Far better, he thought, to reduce the charges against Bucher and Harris. "A letter of reprimand was not really suitable punishment for what I considered had taken place," he remembers, "but it was the only available thing." Bucher and Harris, he said, should receive such letters. He agreed with the court's opinions and recommendations in Murphy's case but struck out the first charge against Admiral Johnson and vetoed the letter of reprimand to Captain Gladding altogether. Attaching a six-page endorsement to the report, he sent it to Washington on April 18.

The CNO, Admiral Moorer, concurred with Hyland's recommendations. And he in turn passed the report to John H. Chafee, the Secretary of the Navy.

At 10:30 on the morning of May 6 Chafee appeared at a hastily called Pentagon press conference. "The court of inquiry," he announced in a flat New England accent, "has completed its proceedings. . . . As a result of my review, I have decided that no disciplinary action will be taken against any of the personnel involved in the *Pueblo* incident. . . . I make no judgment regarding the guilt or innocence of any of the officers of the offenses alleged against them. . . . I am convinced, however, that neither . . . the state of discipline or morale in the Navy nor any other interests require further legal proceedings . . . with respect to Commander Bucher, Lieutenant Murphy, and Lieutenant Harris, it is my opinion that . . . they have suffered enough. . . .

"The charges against Rear Admiral Johnson and Captain Gladding relate to the failure to anticipate the emergency that subsequently developed. This basic, general accusation, however, could be leveled in various degrees at responsible superior authorities in the chain of command. . . . The consequences must in fairness be borne by all, rather than by one or two individuals whom circumstances had placed closer to the crucial event. . . ."

"Do you consider the *Pueblo* incident closed?" a reporter asked.

"I do," Chafee replied.

★   ★   ★

At his home in Melrose, Massachusetts, Steve Harris heard the news in a telephone call from Rear Admiral Francis J. Fitzpatrick, the Assistant CNO (Communications and Cryptology). He felt "overjoyed, enormously relieved" and stepped outside to tell reporters that he "would gladly serve with Commander Bucher again anytime, anyplace." Within two months—as a lieutenant commander—he would report for duty to the Naval Security Station in Washington, D.C.

★   ★   ★

At the Naval Air Station, North Island, in Coronado, California, Bucher, Murphy, and Miles Harvey had gathered for an early and rather awkward meeting with the Navy's Deputy Judge Advocate General, Rear Admiral Donald D. Chapman. Bucher wore work khakis open at the collar. Murphy appeared in his blues. At 7:30 A.M. Pacific time the admiral opened his attaché case, fumbled through sheafs of scribbled and typewritten notes—curiously, he was the only man in the room who seemed at all nervous—and declared, "I have something here I want to read to you. . . ."

"I have one other thing to do," Chapman said after reciting Chafee's statement. "All officers are to select their next duty assignments. . . ."

"I'm sorry, Admiral," Bucher began, "this is a trying morning. When do you need my decision?"

"Right now."

Bucher protested. He had been promised that he'd have at least a month to make up his mind. Harvey requested more time.

"I'm going down to the law center," Chapman said. "Can you give me a call in, say, twenty minutes?"

"I think I'd like a school," Bucher said. He mentioned the Industrial College of the Armed Forces and the Armed Forces Staff College. Murphy also asked for a school.

"I'm sorry. I think that's not in the cards." The admiral closed his attaché case, said his good mornings, and strode out the door.

"Well, I'm leaving," Murphy said. He shook hands perfunctorily with Bucher and Harvey and then was gone. In less than ten days he would resign his commission, complaining bitterly that "the results of the court of inquiry in regard to my career leave me no alternative. . . ."

The verdict infuriated Bucher. He turned to Harvey and said he wanted a general court-martial.

"If you do that," Harvey replied, shaking his head, "you can count me out. It's sayonara." There was no guarantee that the Navy would grant such a request. Bucher would only be asking for trouble.

Reluctantly, Bucher agreed. He listed his duty assignment preferences. His first choice was SUBPAC headquarters in Hawaii, his second SUBFLOTONE in San Diego. Harvey called the law center.

"I may have been a bit hasty in what I said about a school," Admiral Chapman began. Within twenty-four hours Bucher would receive orders to the Navy's postgraduate school at Monterey for a one-year course leading to a master's degree in management. Now he called Rose and asked her to bring his dress blues to the Amphibious Base, where he and Harvey would hold a final press conference.

"Commander Bucher is extremely relieved that the proceedings have been completed," Harvey told reporters. "He is definitely satisfied with the outcome and is looking forward to his next duty assignment. . . . As far as we are concerned, Commander Bucher has been cleared. There are no charges standing against him. We feel this is a final resolution. . . ."

★　★　★　EPILOGUE

44

Chafee's compromise decision was politically shrewd. It took the Navy off the hook. It satisfied the old salts who could say that he had not exonerated Bucher's conduct at all; the "don't give up the ship" tradition remained intact. And it pleased, as well, millions of ordinary citizens who didn't want to see Bucher endure any more punishment. "If the Secretary ever runs for office," one caller said, "tell him he's got my vote."

There is, of course, a natural tendency to reduce the *Pueblo* affair to the simplistic proportions of one man's dilemma, one man's decision. Was Bucher right—or wrong? (The debate continues today. Most officers above the rank of commander castigate Bucher harshly. "He's going to wish he'd been more heroic," one vice admiral said. "It's better to be a dead hero than to live to a ripe old age and read nasty things about yourself in the papers." In the lower ranks, however, among the lieutenants and lieutenant commanders, there is widespread sympathy and even admiration for the man. Perhaps it is true, as Allen Hemphill once observed, that there are "two Navies.") By releasing only the recommendations of the court which pertained to disciplinary action—and labeling the others "classified"—Chafee contributed to this tendency. His decision skirted the larger, more important questions.

Are such missions as *Pueblo*'s really necessary? Are they worth the risk? Why was the military establishment unable to see that such a disaster might occur? Unable to prevent it from happening? Unable to react when it did happen? Finally, who was to blame?

Throughout the spring of 1969 a special subcommittee of the House Armed Services Committee endeavored to find the answers. Chaired by New York's able Representative Otis G. Pike, the sub-

committee heard testimony from—among others—Lieutenant General
Joseph F. Carroll, the director of the Defense Intelligence Agency;
Lieutenant General Marshall S. Carter, the director of the National
Security Agency; Lieutenant General Seth J. McKee, the former com-
mander of the Fifth Air Force; Admiral Thomas H. Moorer, the CNO;
Admiral U. S. Grant Sharp, the former Commander-in-Chief, Pacific;
and General Earle G. Wheeler, the chairman of the Joint Chiefs of
Staff.

"Reconnaissance activities of [Pueblo's] type must continue to be
conducted," the subcommittee reported on July 28, "to insure the
availability of information essential to our national security interests.
However [we] are not convinced that the magnitude of this activity is
completely justified nor are [we] persuaded that the many millions of
dollars [expended on it] are fully and properly utilized. . . ."

"There exist serious deficiencies in the organizational and administrative military command structure of both the Department of the
Navy and the Department of Defense . . . ," the subcommittee concluded. "[The] vast and complex military structure [is] capable of acquiring almost infinite amounts of information [but is unable] to relay this information in a timely and comprehensible fashion to those
charged with the responsibility for making decisions. . . . The problem exists and it has frightening implications. . . ."

"What I am trying to make clear," Admiral Moorer testified, referring to the Pueblo mission's approval, "is that no single individual
made the decision. . . ." So the question, "Who is to blame?" remains
unanswered. Congressman Pike maintains that "there's blame enough
for everybody here," and he is probably right. The military establishment has grown too large, too cumbersome, too rigid. The generals
and admirals recognize this, albeit reluctantly, and blame it on the
"overcentralization" which occurred during the McNamara years, the
unwritten dictum that every decision had to be made in Washington.
If the Secretary of Defense, they ask, insists on bypassing the chain of
command and issues orders directly to a destroyer skipper—as happened during the Cuban missile crisis—what initiatives are left to the
field commanders? Aren't they simply errand boys? There is some merit
to this view. Yet it is also true that in this Cold War period, civilian
officials must exercise stringent controls. The consequences of possible
military miscalculations are so far-reaching that to do otherwise would
be foolish indeed. In the case of Pueblo, these controls were obviously
not stringent enough. And the results were disastrous.

How disastrous? Did we—as Georgia's Senator Richard Russell
has charged—"present the Russians with the results of hundreds of

millions of dollars' worth of research"? "The compromise of a great deal of classified information involving naval operations, both tactical and otherwise," the Pike report declared, "represents a very serious intelligence loss."

The *Pueblo* incident demonstrated—perhaps more shockingly and convincingly than any event in recent years—the real limitations of American power. Pentagon planners had long stressed that the United States was capable of engaging in two and one-half "wars of national liberation" simultaneously. What happened on January 23 shattered that assumption. It crumpled other assumptions as well. There was the premise—rooted in one hundred sixty-one years of naval tradition—that no one would every try to hijack a U.S. ship on the high seas. "It's a new ball game now," Admiral Johnson said at Coronado. There was the conviction that U.S. nuclear capability would persuade hostile states not to take precipitous action. The North Koreans called that bluff in January, 1968, and—fifteen months later—called it again by shooting down an unarmed EC-121 reconnaissance plane. There was the belief that U.S. servicemen were somehow "stronger," "tougher," than their Oriental counterparts. Yet Bucher was broken within thirty-six hours.

In its report the Pike subcommittee called for "a complete review of our military-civilian command structure and its capability to cope with emergency situations." This has not yet been done. Still, some noteworthy changes have resulted from the *Pueblo* incident. The Pentagon is perfecting an "optical scanning system" which, it says, should improve its communications enormously. The 303 Committee has been dissolved. During the 1968 campaign, President Nixon vowed to abolish DIA. He hasn't followed through on that promise—and presumably won't. Still, Defense Secretary Melvin R. Laird has ordered a task force to fix—once and for all—the responsibility for the various U.S. intelligence-gathering activities between DIA, NSA, CIA, and the military services.

★   ★   ★

One sunny morning in June, 1969, this reporter stepped aboard *Banner* at her berth in Yokosuka. The "GER-1" on her bow had been painted over ("We don't want to be *too* conspicuous," explained her new skipper, Lieutenant Commander Donald L. Pfister). Twin .20 mm mounts and a grenade launcher had replaced the .50 caliber machine guns, and there was a destruct system on board which could take care of classified materials and documents in short order indeed.

The only trouble was that *Banner* wasn't going anywhere. She had, in fact, completed only one regular mission—code-named "Dolorous"— since *Pueblo*'s seizure eighteen months before, and then she remained at least 70 miles from land. "It's ironic," said Rear Admiral Daniel F. Smith, Jr., the present Commander, Naval Forces, Japan. "Back in 1965 we told *Banner,* 'Get your fanny back up there.' Now we can't even get permission to sail her out of port."

Last September the Navy decided to cancel its AGER program altogether. (Presumably, it will rely on combat ships and aircraft to obtain intelligence data in the future.) *Banner* was decommissioned in November and tossed on a scrap heap in Japan. *Palm Beach* was decommissioned as well. And *Pueblo?* Intelligence sources indicate that she is moored at the North Korean port of Najin, near the Soviet border. The State Department says it has not abandoned efforts to secure her release. There has been no progress on that score; nor—one supposes—is there likely to be. Meanwhile, the last of the AGER's remains on the list of "active commissioned ships of the United States Navy." Under the category of "miscellaneous craft." Although regulations say that every commissioned ship must have a commanding officer, *Pueblo* has none. Her situation, the Navy explains, is "not normal."

45

And what of *Pueblo*'s crew? Of the eighty-two survivors, thirty-six remain in the Navy, and they are scattered about at installations from Maine to California, from Florida to Washington State. Charles Law, a chief petty officer now, teaches "survival" at the Fleet Air Training Unit on Whidby Island, Washington. He married a girl he met in San Diego. Larry Mack is running a photo lab at the Naval Air Station in Pensacola, Florida. Harry Lewis is a "watch captain" at the U.S. Naval Station in Brooklyn, New York. He doesn't cook anymore. Only two of the men are posted overseas—Robert Hill in Londonderry, Northern Ireland, and "Doc" Baldridge in Sasebo, Japan. And only one, signalman Wendell Leach, requested or received sea duty.

Bob Chicca now attends the University of California at San Diego. His buddy Bob Hammond goes to Plymouth State Teachers College in New Hampshire. Peter Langenberg has returned to Princeton to major in Soviet Studies. Alvin Plucker is studying art at McCook Junior College in Nebraska. Ron Berens is a postman in Wichita, Kansas. Skip Schumacher is selling insurance in St. Louis. Norman Spear works for the Cemetery Division, Department of Parks, City of Portland, Maine. He spends his time "digging graves and swapping stories."

Most of the men have suffered some damage to their vision as a result of the diet in North Korea. They bear other scars, as well, both physically and emotionally. One, Bill Scarborough, died under mysterious circumstances. A few are drinking too much. There have been half a dozen divorces or separations. The city fathers of Jay, Maine, honored John Grant in their Memorial Day parade. "Four little kids ran by and called me a traitor," Grant remembers. "That spoiled everything. It's been tough, this readjustment, you know. One day my wife looked at me and said, 'What did they *do* to you over there?' I realized I was looking for a fight, trying to take it out on her. I guess I'm not as easygoing as I once was."

Lee Hayes gives speeches for an organization called TRAIN (To Restore American Independence Now), an affiliate of the John Birch Society. Earl Phares has joined the "Up With People" band. Many of their shipmates have veered far to the right politically. They mutter about "hippies" and make no effort to conceal their bitterness at this country's failure to retaliate against the North Koreans. "Someone in the Pentagon ought to have his ass strung from a tree because of what happened to us," Roy Maggard says. Among the crew it is a popular sentiment.

The men phone each other from time to time to chat about cars and jobs and girls. And about how it was "over there." They also keep in touch through a newsletter called—for no particular reason—"Ah, To, He Say," which Stu and Sharon Russell publish several times a year. They worry about their skipper, wonder how he's getting along, and call him frequently. The bond which links them to him is permanent. "He's the greatest man I've ever known," Larry Strickland says. "The debt we owe him, well, how can we ever repay it? He got us out alive."

★   ★   ★

His men have drifted away from him now, but Bucher is still their skipper, their "father." He wears a turquoise and gold ring which Bob Chicca designed. He sent $100 to "Doc" Baldridge—who was home on leave in Missouri—to help him pay for a speeding ticket. He gave John Grant a 24-piece sterling silver serving set as a wedding present. He flew to Creswell, Oregon, and visited Duane Hodges' grave. It upset him to find out that Captain Newsome would receive a Legion of Merit for his work at the court of inquiry. "None of my guys even got *recommended* for medals," he says bitterly, "and some of them were truly heroic."

During the court of inquiry I had seen him almost every day, and now—one evening after it was over—I stopped by his home in Pacific Beach for cocktails. On one wall, etched in bronze, was a copy of the Declaration of Independence. There were plaques and framed certificates (Admiral in the Nebraska Navy) and color photographs of *Pueblo* and the submarines *Ronquil* and *Besugo*. On an adjacent wall hung watercolors which Bucher had painted himself.

I mentioned my plans to visit Hawaii, Japan, and South Korea to research this book and asked if he had any old friends I should look up along the way. A list of eight or ten names, I said, would certainly suffice. He provided thirty-nine. As it turned out, I was able to see more than half of them. I sent him cards from Yokosuka and Seoul and weeks later, back in San Diego, called to tell him about the trip. Bucher, his wife, and the two boys were visiting relatives in Wisconsin. They were driving West in a few days. Perhaps we could meet at Glacier National Park in Montana.

It had been nearly four months since I'd seen them last, and in that time both Pete and Rose struck me as having changed. Rose was relaxed, cheerful, and thoroughly pleasant, no longer the tough, cool woman she had seemed at the court of inquiry. Pete was still smoking heavily, still having trouble with his eyes; in other respects he seemed fit enough. He'd gained weight, his hair was growing back fast, and the last piece of shrapnel had just forced its way out of his leg. The gaunt, tortured expression had disappeared from his face. He was looking forward with boyish enthusiasm to the boat trip that he and his family were planning down the Middle Fork of the Salmon River in neighboring Idaho. They would shoot the rapids, he said; that would be really invigorating, challenging.

We spent one night at the Glacier Lodge, then drove north past spectacular scenery to the Many Glacier Hotel near the Canadian border. We hiked to Swiftcurrent Lake and Lake Josephine. We stopped while Pete photographed wild roses, bear grass, and black-eyed Susans and then trekked back in time for martinis on the hotel porch. There was a hootenanny that second night, and college students crowded the recreation hall. They recognized Bucher immediately; still, they hesitated to approach him—fearful, presumably, of disturbing his privacy. Finally a tall boy from Pennsylvania walked over to shake Bucher's hand. He was a biology major at Allegheny College, he said; he wanted to go to Officers' Candidate School in Newport after graduation but didn't think his chances for admission were very good. What did Bucher think of OCS? Did he have any advice?

"Great," Bucher said. "I think I can help you." He promised that he would call a friend at the Bureau of Naval Personnel in Washington. His friend would straighten everything out.

A lovely dark-haired girl asked him if he knew Father Schmidt at Boys Town. Yes, he did, Bucher said. He'd gone back to Boys Town in April and seen him there. The girl kept beaming at him and asked him to dance. Rose nodded, as if to say "Go ahead," and soon he was shaking his arms and hips to that fast music, rocking back and forth, grinning widely. The college students stopped and watched him and cheered.

"I guess I'll have to live with this thing for the rest of my life," he said next evening at dinner in Missoula. He had gotten accustomed to "this celebrity business" ("Oh," he would say pleasantly when a student approached him, "where do *you* go to school? Tell me about *yourself*") but he didn't really enjoy it, and he was bothered by the fact that so many of the kids applauded him for the wrong reason. It wasn't a question of "placing people before property" or "violating establishment rules for some higher moral purpose" as the New Left liked to put it. He had followed his orders to the *letter*. "Yeah," he said over a second martini, "if they ever declassify all those op orders, you can see I followed them *exactly*."

We had driven back through the park and south to Missoula that afternoon. The float trip wasn't scheduled to start for another three days, but Bucher said he wanted to be completely *ready*, to get closer to the jumping-off point. He'd already plotted and replotted his course on maps of the river and shown me a guidebook which described the rapids as "tricky, treacherous." He thought he could drive from Missoula to Salmon, Idaho, in five or six hours.

Several weeks before, in a series of articles for the *Christian Science Monitor*, Murphy had written, "The captain didn't have a thorough understanding or appreciation of surface warfare. . . . I certainly expected *Pueblo* to retaliate. But instead, the captain ordered. . . . The captain clambered. I rushed. . . ." Now, at the Red Lion Inn, I asked Bucher if he'd read these pieces. He hadn't, but fifteen men in his crew had called and volunteered to rebut the XO's charges. He had told them to cool it; no sense stirring up that conflict all over again. But at the same time he had wondered why Murphy had written such things, so he had telephoned him in San Diego. Murphy wouldn't speak to him.

The subject obviously depressed him. He ordered another martini. He talked about the men in his crew to whom he felt especially close: Schumacher, Lacy, Tim Harris, Law, and Chief Goldman. The Navy had processed everyone so quickly in San Diego when the court was over that he really hadn't had the chance to tell them good-bye the way he wanted to. He felt bitter about that.

The court of inquiry's verdict still upset him. "I really hate this outfit now," he said. "I'm really disillusioned. So many guys make captain by sliding uphill. I can't even get a confidential clearance anymore. Can't even get a job as a *postmaster* with the federal government." Rose told him to hush, but he kept on, all the rage and frustration fully evident. "I would have given my eyeteeth to have been asked some more questions, to help the Navy back in D.C. But the debrief, you know, that was pretty cursory, and since then, there's been nothing. The same thing's happened to Skip [Schumacher]. The Navy doesn't want to know. They pretend it never happened. It's as though we got leprosy."

He had tried so hard to forget that afternoon in the Sea of Japan, but he still saw the S01 and the P-4's in his mind's eye. He heard the shells whistling overhead and the staccato bursts of fire. He felt the cold pressing against him, the icy helplessness, and there was just no way he could send a man to that .50 caliber gun. He was just as sure of that now as he had ever been. But there were other things about which he wasn't so sure, and they disturbed him immensely. "I had this dream one night," he said, "that on account of some legal technicality the State Department was sending me back to North Korea, back to prison. I was manacled, and when I woke up, I was dripping with sweat and. . . ."

Rose tugged at his sleeve. "Come on, Pete," she said. "Finish up and let's go."

Next evening a pleasant woman named Jo Crosby invited us out for dinner. She had been a baby-sitter for the Buchers years before in San Diego; she was living here in Missoula now with her daughter Nancy, a former WAVE. Bucher didn't feel up to it. He wanted to talk about the float trip; he sensed that Jo and Nancy would only ask him about the incident. Rose persisted, and finally he agreed. The dinner progressed smoothly enough and we returned to the Crosbys' to watch the Sunday night movie on TV: *Dr. Strangelove*. Bucher had seen it three times, loved it, wanted a print. That phrase that Peter Sellers used—"purity of essence"—those were the exact words Steve Harris had put in one of his confessions. Confessions; he began to blink and shake his head. He thought it was time to leave, he said. He couldn't watch TV anymore without experiencing terrible headaches.

But in the morning he seemed cheerful again, almost exuberant. Wearing madras walking shorts and a yellow knit shirt, he hoisted the suitcases into the trunk of his lima-bean-green Ford LTD. With any luck, he said, he would be in Salmon, Idaho, at twilight. He would spend the next six days shooting the rapids, relishing the wilderness.

"Be careful," I said. "It'll be pretty embarrassing if you capsize and the Coast Guard has to fish you out of that river. Or if you get captured by the Indians."

"Yeah," he said, but he didn't laugh. A pained expression flickered across his face, and I wondered if my clumsy joke had touched a nerve. Suddenly I realized—or was it only my imagination—that this was no ordinary float trip. This was a *serious* thing, a challenge he had sought and determined to conquer. And I sensed that he would spend the rest of his life seeking new challenges, new opportunities to prove to *them* "the fibre of his stuff." Rose and the two boys stepped into the car. We said our good-byes and waved, and as the LTD pulled out of the drive I noticed the two decals—American flags—on the rear windowpane. Then he was gone.

CONTRIBUTORS

ANGELOSANTE, Lieutenant Carmen, USS *Palm Beach*
ALDRICH, George H., Department of State
ALEXANDER, Communications Technician First Class Michael W., USS *Pueblo*
ARMSTRONG, Oscar V., Department of State
ARNOLD, Mr. and Mrs. Everett C., Santa Rosa, California
ARNOLD, Lieutenant John P., Naval Security Station, Washington, D.C.
ARNOLD, Fireman Richard E., USS *Pueblo*
AUSLAND, John C., Department of State

BADER, William B., Senate Foreign Relations Committee
BAILEY, Communications Technician First Class Donald E., USS *Pueblo*
BAILEY, Lieutenant Commander James L., *Pueblo* Court of Inquiry
BAKER, Lieutenant j.g. Warren P., USS *Banner*
BALDRIDGE, Hospital Corpsman First Class Herman P., USS *Pueblo*
BALL, George W., New York, N.Y.
BAME, Engineman Second Class Richard I., USS *Pueblo*
BARRETT, Communications Technician First Class Michael T., USS *Pueblo*
BAZZEL, Lieutenant Commander Roderic C., San Diego, California
BEHR, Lieutenant j.g. David, Long Beach, California
BERENS, Boatswain's Mate Second Class Ronald L., USS *Pueblo*
BERGNER, Rear Admiral Allen A., *Pueblo* Court of Inquiry
BERRY, Captain Fred T., San Diego, California
BIESEMEIER, Communications Technician Third Class Patrick J., USS *Banner*
BISHOP, Major Charles E., Kadena, Okinawa
BISHOP, Lieutenant Commander Robert P., Yorktown, Virginia
BLACK, Lieutenant Commander Rudolph R., Washington, D.C.
BLOCK, Commander Peter F., Key West, Florida
BLOUIN, Vice Admiral Francis J., Washington, D.C.
BONESTEEL, General Charles H. III, Washington, D.C.
BOWEN, Vice Admiral Harold G., Jr., *Pueblo* Court of Inquiry
BRINGLE, Vice Admiral William F., Commander, Seventh Fleet
BROOKES, Lieutenant Edward A., Arlington, Virginia
BROWN, James F., The White House
BBOWN, Ambassador Winthrop G., Department of State
BRYANT, Don, University of Nebraska
BUCHER, Commander Lloyd M., USS *Pueblo*
BULL, Communications Technician First Class Brian, USS *Banner*

CAMPBELL, Lieutenant Colonel Robert T., Kadena, Okinawa
CANALES, Yeoman First Class Armando M., USS *Pueblo*
CANNING, Lieutenant John U., CINCPACFLT Intelligence Division
CASE, H. Edward, Omaha, Nebraska
CELEBREZZE, Lieutenant Anthony J., Cleveland, Ohio
CHAFEE, Secretary of the Navy John H., Washington, D.C.
CHICCA, Sergeant Robert J., USS *Pueblo*
CHISM, Lieutenant David M., Naval Supply Depot, Yokosuka, Japan
CLARK, Commander Charles R., USS *Banner*
CLARK, Mrs. Charles R., Pt. Mugu, California
CLEMONS, Commander William E., *Pueblo* Court of Inquiry
CLIFFORD, Clark M., Washington, D.C.
COLWELL, Vice Admiral John B., Washington, D.C.
COOK, Rear Admiral Ralph E., Director, Naval Security Station
CORSON, Lieutenant Colonel William R., USMC (Ret.), Chevy Chase, Maryland
COYNE, Patrick, Secretary, President's Foreign Intelligence Advisory Board
CRANDELL, Radioman Second Class Charles H., Jr., USS *Pueblo*
CROWE, Communications Technician Second Class Bradley R., USS *Pueblo*

CRUTCHFIELD, Dr. James A., University of Washington, Seattle
CULVER, Representative John C., Washington, D.C.

DEES, Lieutenant Colonel Robert W., Fuchu, Japan
DIFILIPPO, Lieutenant Angelo E., Mechanicsburg, Pennsylvania
DENNER, Andrew J., The White House
DORENKAMP, Commander Kurt F., Coronado, California
DOHERTY, Edward, Department of State
DUGAN, Lieutenant Colonel James F., Omaha, Nebraska
DUKE, Communications Technician Second Class Rodney H., USS *Pueblo*
DWYER, Captain Thomas L., Washington, D.C.

EAGLEBERGER, Lawrence S., The White House
EASTON, Lieutenant Commander Ervin R., CINCPACFLT Intelligence Division
EDDY, Major General Dayton W., Office of the Joint Chiefs of Staff
EPES, Rear Admiral Horace H., Jr., Office of the Joint Chiefs of Staff
ERICKSON, Richard A., United States Embassy, Seoul, South Korea
EVERETT, Captain William H., Staff, COMNAVFORJAPAN
EVERHART, Captain C. Dale, Staff, CINCPACFLT

FARMER, Les, Greenville, Texas
FARRIER, John M., Department of State
FERRALL, Rear Admiral William E. (Ret.), Seattle, Washington
FINCH, Richard W., Department of State
FLECK, Benjamin A., Department of State
FRYKLUND, Deputy Assistant Secretary of Defense Richard
FUBINI, Dr. Eugene, Washington, D.C.

GALLERY, Rear Admiral Daniel V . (Ret.), Oakton, Virginia
GARCIA, Storekeeper First Class Policarpo P., USS *Pueblo*
GALINSKY, Lieutenant Commander Jerome J., Fort Meade, Maryland
GINSBURGH, Brigadier General Robert N., The White House
GINTHER, Communications Technician First Class Francis J., USS *Pueblo*
GIORGIS, Captain Albert S., Naval Ships Systems Command
GLADDING, Captain Everett B. (Ret.), Greenville, Texas
GLAESER, Lieutenant Commander Frederick W., Naval Intelligence Command
GLEYSTEEN, William H. R., Department of State
GOIN, Hospital Corpsman First Class Bradley G., USS *Palm Beach*
GRAHAM, Lieutenant John E., Jr., Puget Sound Naval Shipyard, Bremerton, Washington
GRANT, Communications Technician Second Class John W., USS *Pueblo*
GRIMM, Rear Admiral Edward E. (Ret.), *Pueblo* Court of Inquiry
GRONWALL, Hans-Fredrik, Stockholm, Sweden
GROJEAN, Captain Charles D., Office of the Chief of Naval Operations
GUNNELL, Major James E., Wright-Patterson Air Force Base, Ohio

HAGENSON, Electrician's Mate First Class Gerald W., USS *Pueblo*
HALL, Lieutenant j.g. Charles B., Jr., Intelligence Division, CINCPACFLT
HALL, Melvin, The White House
HAMMOND, Sergeant Robert J., USS *Pueblo*
HARDY, Dan, Bethesda, Maryland
HARLFINGER, Rear Admiral Frederick J. II, Naval Intelligence Command
HARRELL, Brigadier General John W., Jr., 314th Air Division, Osan, South Korea
HARRIS, Lieutenant Commander Steven R., USS *Pueblo*
HARRIS, Lieutenant j.g. Timothy L., USS *Pueblo*
HARVEY, E. Miles, San Diego, California
HAVENS, Charles W. III, POW specialist, Department of Defense
HAYES, Commander James C., Staff, CINCPACFLT

HAYES, Radioman Second Class Lee Roy, USS *Pueblo*
HECKMAN, Lieutenant Commander Donald C., Staff, COMNAVFORJAPAN
HEISINGER, Lieutenant Commander Duane L., Staff, COMNAVFORJAPAN
HEMPHILL, Lieutenant Commander Allen P., San Diego, California
HEMPHILL, Mrs. Jean, San Diego, California
HIGGINS, Engineman Third Class John C., Jr., USS *Pueblo*
HILL, Boatswain's Mate Third Class Robert W., Jr., USS *Pueblo*
HODGKINSON, Lieutenant Commander John T., Staff, DIRNAVSECGRUPAC, Hawaii
HOKENSON, Lieutenant Commander Carl L., Jr., Staff, COMNAVFORJAPAN
HOLLOWAY, Rear Admiral L. III, Office of the CNO
HOLMBERG, Lieutenant Commander William C., USMC, Alexandria, Virginia
HOOPER, Vice Admiral Edwin B., COMSERVPAC, Hawaii
HORN, Captain Maury A., SUBFLOTSEVEN, Yokosuka, Japan
HOROWITZ, Commander Norman, Staff, DIRNAVSECGRUPAC, Hawaii
HOWELL, Captain Willard Y. (Ret.) , Office of the DCNO
HYLAND, Admiral John J., CINCPACFLT, Hawaii

IGNATIUS, Paul R., Washington, D.C.
INMAN, Commander Bobby R., Intelligence Division, CINCPACFLT
IREDALE, Harry III, USS *Pueblo*
IRVINE, Rear Admiral Donald G. (Ret.), COMNAVFORKOREA, Seoul, South Korea
ISAMAN, Rear Admiral Roy M., Commander, Carrier Division Seven
ISMAY, Commander Arthur P., Office of the CNO

JENKINS, Alfred LeS., Department of State
JESSUP, Peter, Chevy Chase, Maryland
JOBE, Commander James K., SUBFLOTSEVEN, Yokosuka, Japan
JOHNSON, Commander Clayton F. (Ret.), Office of the Naval Historian
JOHNSTON, Al, Naval Ships Systems Command
JONES, Lieutenant Commander Carroll S., Office of the CNO

KAELIN, James W., Lynchburg, Virginia
KAHN, David, Great Neck, Long Island, New York
KARON, Lieutenant j.g. Eileen, Sasebo, Japan
KATZENBACH, Nicholas deB., Department of State
KAUFHOLD, Lieutenant Francis F., Puget Sound Naval Shipyard, Bremerton, Washington
KEENE, Spurgeon, Jr., Washington, D.C.
KELL, Chief Communications Technician James F., USS *Pueblo*
KELLEY, Captain Edward G., Office of the CNO
KEYS, Captain and Mrs. James E., *Pueblo* Court of Inquiry
KILPATRICK, Richard N., Department of State
KISLER, Communications Technician Second Class Earl M., USS *Pueblo*
KMOCH, Hank, Hartford, Connecticut

LACY, Chief Warrant Officer and Mrs. Gene H., USS *Pueblo*
LAMANTIA, Communications Technician Second Class Anthony A., USS *Pueblo*
LAMBERT, Rear Admiral David (Ret.) , COMTRAPAC, San Diego, California
LANGENBERG, Communications Technician Second Class Peter M., USS *Pueblo*
LANGUEDOC, Commander Arthur J., Bureau of Naval Personnel
LAW, Quartermaster First Class Charles B., Jr., USS *Pueblo*
LEE, Jim, Historian, Military Armistice Commission, Panmunjom, Korea
LEE, Rear Admiral Kent L., USS *Enterprise*
LEONARD, James F., Department of State
LEWIS, Commissaryman First Class Harry, USS *Pueblo*
LEWIS, Robert C., American Red Cross

LINDSTROM, Rev. Paul D., Prospect Heights, Illinois
LITTLE, Lieutenant j.g. Will, Staff, COMNAVFORJAPAN
LOOMIS, Rear Admiral F. Kent (Ret.), Naval Historical Foundation
LOWRANCE, Vice Admiral Vernon L. (Ret.), Defense Intelligence Agency
LUCAS, Colonel John P., Secretary, Military Armistice Commission, Panmunjom, Korea

MACK, Photographer's Mate First Class Lawrence W., USS *Pueblo*
MACKINNON, Lieutenant Commander Richard A., Intelligence Division, CINC-PACFLT
MACONIE, Commander Robert T. (Ret.), Intelligence Division, CINCPACFLT
MAGGARD, Engineman Third Class Roy J., USS *Pueblo*
MAROCCHI, Captain John L., Intelligence Division, CINCPACFLT
MARSHALL, Seaman Larry Joe, USS *Pueblo*
MARTIN, Mr. and Mrs. Fred W., Omaha, Nebraska
MARTIN, Ken, Bremerton, Washington
MATTESON, Jack, Washington, D.C.
MCCAFFERTY, Arthur J., The White House
MCCLENDON, Rear Admiral W. R., Commander, Carrier Division Nine
MCCLINTOCK, Communications Technician Second Class Ralph, USS *Pueblo*
MCCOMISH, Commander Daniel R., Naval Supply Depot, Yokosuka, Japan
MCDEVITT, Rear Admiral Joseph B., Judge Advocate General, Department of the Navy
MCDONALD, Admiral David L. (Ret.), Ponte Vedra, Florida
MCDONALD, Lieutenant Commander Richard R., Fort Meade, Maryland
MCDONALD, Commander Thomas E., (Ret.), Malibu, California
MCGARVEY, Patrick J., Defense Intelligence Agency
MCHUGH, Lieutenant Commander Richard M., Naval Security Group Activity, Kamiseya, Japan
MCKEE, Lieutenant General Seth J., Fifth Air Force headquarters, Fuchu, Japan
MCKENNE, Lieutenant Commander Donald C., Intelligence Division, CINC-PACFLT
MCNAMEE, Chief Quartermaster Eugene R., El Cajon, California
MILLER, Rear Admiral Gerald E., Office of the CNO
MITCHELL, Charles T., Omaha, Nebraska
MITCHELL, Electrician's Mate Third Class John A., USS *Pueblo*
MOKE, Lieutenant Commander Paul David, Intelligence Division, CINCPACFLT
MONROE, Colonel James L. (Ret.), Washington, D.C.
MORRIS, Lieutenant j.g. Albert E., Intelligence Division, CINCPACFLT
MULLANEY, Colonel John F. (Ret.), Defense Intelligence Agency
MURPHY, Carol, San Diego, California
MURPHY, Lieutenant Edward R., Jr., USS *Pueblo*
MYERS, Ronald P., Department of State

NAGACHI, Emiko, Yokosuka, Japan
NEWSOME, Captain William R., *Pueblo* Court of Inquiry
NIESS, Albert E., San Diego, California
NITZE, Paul H., Deputy Secretary of Defense
NOLAND, Bruce, Warrenton, Virginia
NORRIS, Mrs. Barbara, La Jolla, California
NOWOKUNSKI, Major Edward D., Kadena, Okinawa
NYCE, Commander William E., Intelligence Division, CINCPACFLT

O'BRIEN, Rear Admiral Leslie J., Jr., Office of the CNO
ORCUTT, Lieutenant Colonel Robert R., Fifth Air Force Headquarters, Fuchu, Japan
OSETH, Captain John M. (Ret.), Arlington, Virginia

OSTRONIC, Francis J., Potomac, Maryland
OTTEY, Commander William H., Jr. (Ret.), San Diego, California

PADGETT, Commander Harry E., Staff, CHINFO, Los Angeles, California
PAGE, Benjamin, Tallahassee, Florida
PAK, Gun, Office of the Foreign Ministry, Seoul, South Korea
PALRANG, Maurice H. (Skip), Boys Town, Omaha, Nebraska
PEASE, Captain Forrest A., Staff, COMNAVFORJAPAN
PECK, Edward L., Department of State
PETROVIC, Rear Admiral William F., Puget Sound Naval Shipyard, Bremerton, Washington
PFEIFER, George J., Boys Town, Omaha, Nebraska
PFISTER, Lieutenant Commander Donald L., USS *Banner*
PHARES, Storekeeper Third Class Earl R., USS *Pueblo*
PIKE, Representative Otis G., Washington, D.C.
PLUCKER, Quartermaster Second Class Alvin H., USS *Pueblo*
POPE, Commander John W. R., Jr., Fort Meade, Maryland
PORTER, William J., Ambassador to South Korea
POWELL, Commander George W., *Pueblo* Court of Inquiry
PRATT, Rear Admiral Richard R., *Pueblo* Court of Inquiry
PREECS, Daniel, Naval Ships Systems Command
PRIEST, Major Raymond A., Jr., Headquarters, Fifth Air Force, Fuchu, Japan
PROCTOR, Captain Erman O., Staff, CINCPAC, Hawaii
PUGH, Rear Admiral Paul E., Staff, CINCPAC, Hawaii

RAPER, Commander Albert D., USS *Palm Beach*
REDFIELD, Commander and Mrs. John M., Coronado, California
REED, Commissaryman Second Class Ralph E., USS *Pueblo*
RETHWISH, Marcee, El Cajon, California
RIGBY, Storekeeper Third Class Dale E., USS *Pueblo*
RINDSKOPF, Rear Admiral Maurice H., Staff, CINCPAC
RIVERO, Admiral Horacio, Jr., Commander in Chief, Allied Forces, Southern Europe
ROACH, Clyde, Staff, CINCPACFLT
ROBIN, Communications Technician Third Class Steven J., USS *Pueblo*
ROE, Frank W., Seattle, Washington
ROEDER, Vice Admiral Bernard F., San Diego, California
ROSANIA, Captain Hugh J., Staff, CINCPAC, Hawaii
ROSENBERG, Rear Admiral Edwin M., Commander, Amphibious Group Three
ROSTOW, Walt W., Assistant to the President for National Security Affairs
ROWBERG, Brynhilde, Department of State
RUSK, Dean, Washington, D.C.
RUSSELL, Storekeeper Third Class Edward S., USS *Pueblo*

SAMS, Colonel Monroe S., Kadena, Okinawa
SCARBOROUGH, Engineman First Class William D. (deceased), USS *Pueblo*
SCHNEIDER, Rear Admiral Frederick H., Jr., Office of the CNO
SCHULTZ, Rear Admiral Floyd B., Puget Sound Naval Shipyard, Bremerton, Washington
SCHUMACHER, Lieutenant j.g. F. Carl, USS *Pueblo*
SHARP, Admiral U. S. Grant (Ret.), CINCPAC, Hawaii
SHEPPARD, Communications Technician First Class James A., USS *Pueblo*
SHILLING, Communications Technician Second Class John A., USS *Pueblo*
SHULER, James L., Greenville, Texas
SIEVERTS, Frank A., Department of State
SIMON, William, St. Louis, Missouri
SIMS, Commander H. Kelley (Ret.), Office of the Joint Chiefs of Staff

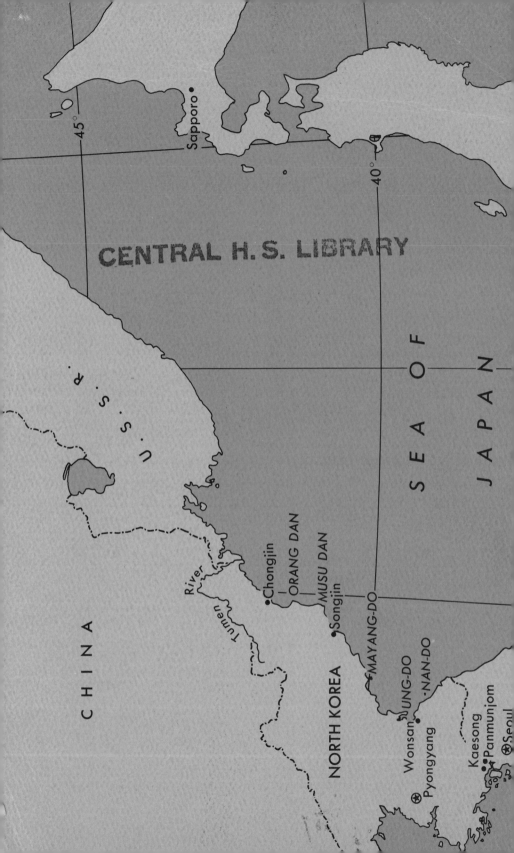